The Yellow Wind

◉ ◉

Colorful regimentation: Communist Chinese propaganda dance teams

⊙ ⊙ ⊙ ⊙ ⊙ ⊙ ⊙ ⊙ ⊙ ⊙ ⊙ ⊙ ⊙ ⊙

The Yellow Wind

*An excursion in and around Red China
with a traveler in the Yellow Wind*

by
William Stevenson

⊙ ⊙

Houghton Mifflin Company Boston
The Riverside Press Cambridge

⊙ ⊙ ⊙ ⊙ ⊙ ⊙ ⊙ ⊙ ⊙ ⊙ ⊙ ⊙ ⊙

COPYRIGHT © 1959 BY WILLIAM STEVENSON

LIBRARY OF CONGRESS CATALOG CARD NUMBER: 59–11830

SECOND PRINTING

The Riverside Press
CAMBRIDGE · MASSACHUSETTS
PRINTED IN THE U.S.A.

To Glenys

China is a country of 500,000,000 slaves ruled by a Single God and nine million Puritans.

> CHANG PO-CHUN, *Minister of Communications in Peking during the 1957 free-speech movement*

CONTENTS

1. The Living Church

2. Shocking the Neighbors

3. Back Through the Looking-Glass

ILLUSTRATIONS

(All photographs by the Author)

Introduction

◉ ◉

"WHAT do you know about Pavlov?"

My inquisitor was Harry Comfort Hindmarsh, a rugged individualist from Missouri who turned the *Toronto Star* and *Star Weekly* into highly successful and enormously wealthy newspaper properties. I was one of his reporters. On a day in the spring of 1952 he called me into his big, bare office and barked his question at me from behind a smoldering cigar.

I shrugged. All I knew about the Russian scientist was that he once kept a laboratory of experimental dogs with "castration, hunger or induced gastric disorders" inflicted on his captive patients. I had a sudden vision of dogs with their brains removed, sagging machines of flesh and blood taught to obey artificial stimuli, their eyes glazed, mouths half open, robots of the canine world.

Hindmarsh saw me shiver. "Suppose," he said, "that Pavlov's theories could be applied to a quarter of humanity? Suppose six hundred million people arrive at the middle of the twentieth century still in a medieval society but anxious to leap into our highly technical age?"

Obviously he meant China. I had just returned from Korea where the war had expired into uneasy peace. The Chinese Communists were a new power in a world which was changing with dizzy speed. While the West was entering the mysterious new age of automation and the atom, Asia was emerging from the shackles of feudalism and an ancient technology that dragged behind our own by a thousand years. The new nations of Asia, no longer wards or colonies of Europe, demanded equal attention with the rest of humanity. Each was attempting to accomplish within decades the technical improvements that in the West came slowly.

Hindmarsh was still talking. "In many ways the Chinese might seem suited to this kind of mental regimentation. They need drastic remedies for their problems and they've had a long history of submission to strong central authority. Their leaders seem to have a new technique of terror followed by persuasion: something they call Indoctrination. It's a kind of substitution of brute reason for brute force. I suppose it could only work among people who haven't any history of democratic growth. Well? . . ."

He stared at me coldly and continued, half to himself: "More than half the world has no acquaintance with our system of free speech and enterprise and few understand how long it took us to find and by what painful routes." He leaned heavily over the desk. "Now," he said, "*if* the Chinese found a way of running a Communist state without brutality, if they could put blinkers on the eyes of intellectuals and teach the illiterate to read Marx and Lenin, don't you think they might have the underdogs of Asia, the Middle East and Africa within their reach?

"Just go back to Korea and take a look at those Chinese prisoners who refuse to be converted to democracy. They've been indoctrinated — that's what we're told. Just find out what the word means . . ."

And it was in this odd fashion that I became a traveler in the fresh winds now blowing out of China. The prisoners in Korea led to other stories and so I was drawn into the glittering lands that once came within the confines of the Chinese world: into the countries of Southeast Asia, the borderlands of inner Asia and the Russian Far East.

My base was Hong Kong, where two and one half million Chinese huddled together with a few thousand Europeans, a tiny relic of the past perched on the broad shoulders of the new China. From here I flew to places that once paid tribute to the Dragon Throne: to Vietnam, Laos, Cambodia, Thailand and Burma; to the Malay Peninsula and the three thousand islands of Indonesia sprinkled at its feet; to Korea and the islands of Japan; to the borders of Tibet, the Himalayan kingdoms and to Turkestan and Mongolia.

Everywhere the tender trap of Chinese Communism seemed to be closing slowly, gently and irresistibly. Sometimes it seemed even to have one paw of the Russian bear firmly yet persuasively incased.

This book emerges mostly from journeys between 1954 and 1957. It is a solitary attempt to examine this tender trap fashioned out of Marx, Lenin and Confucius. You must visualize the author as a lonely wanderer groping through unfamiliar darkness, looking for some familiar shape and hoping that Oscar Wilde could have been wrong when he wrote: "I can stand brute force but brute reason is quite unbearable. It hits below the intellect."

For the secret of all tender traps is that they strike below the intellect.

Hong Kong   W. S.
December 1958

1

The Living Church

◉ ◉

We must use persuasive reasoning. If our reasoning is persuasive and to the point, it will be effective. In reasoning we must begin by administering a shock and shouting at the patient "YOU ARE ILL!" so that he is frightened into a sweat and we tell him gently that he needs treatment.

MAO TSE-TUNG

I can stand brute force but brute reason is quite unbearable. It hits below the intellect.

OSCAR WILDE

CHAPTER ONE

Brains as Well as Faces Must Be Washed

◉ ◉

THE YOUNG MAN blinked helplessly at the television cameras, stumbled and almost fell, then opened his mouth to speak. The voice was not his own. It croaked an imbecile's answers to simple questions. All over Great Britain on that peaceful April evening in 1957, millions must have shuddered. What they saw was a scientist robbed of his senses after only twenty-five hours in a soundproof box. He was a Birmingham psychologist who recovered his judgment within minutes after goggles were taken from his eyes. The show was presented as an experiment in "brainwashing" and it demonstrated that violence was not a necessary weapon in forcing a man's collapse. Nobody had beaten him; nobody fed him drugs; he had no chain marks on his wrists as proof of his ordeal.

Some days later this Reuter report appeared in the newspapers of the Western world:

> A Chinese Communist Party spokesman said today that people needed to wash their brains as well as their faces. The spokesman, Mr. Chou Yang, a Deputy Director of the Party's Propaganda Department, told a foreign press conference that the present rectification campaign in China meant a thorough "brainwashing" for all Party members but it would not be done as demonstrated recently on B.B.C. television.
>
> Mr. Chou added: "Though some people think Ideological Remolding not very pleasant words and Brainwashing worse, in

the changing world situation people need to wash their brains
as well as their faces."

This seemed an improbable bombshell to be dropped by
the Chinese themselves but it was accurately reported by David Chipp, the Reuter man in Peking, and it confirmed the
worst fears of those among his colleagues who, like myself,
were able to circulate inside China. The entire mainland had
been under Communist rule for eight years. In that period
the Chinese asserted themselves as a nation to obtain from
their Soviet allies several concessions in areas which had been
under Russian pressure for many decades. Some friends of
China thought they saw in these concessions and in the re-
affirmation of Chinese traditions a cause for optimism.

Such well-meant optimism was encouraged by the survival
of men like Chang Po-chun, a robust and intelligent State
executive. As Minister of Communications, he helped me on
occasions to speed transmission of cables. He seemed a courteous
old gentleman but in the past he was bourgeois which proved
his undoing. If he was proud of the new China and its bold
leaders, he was himself no Communist. His existence as a minister in Peking was one of many reasons why a Western observer
like myself could honestly believe there were good influences still
at work in what we called Red China.

Minister Chang was essential to the regime. He was the most
experienced specialist in a group of some two dozen who studied communications with Western technicians. Therefore he
was also contaminated. He had the Oriental genius for dissembling his thoughts and because of this, he was a potential
danger to his own rulers.

Until the year 1957, such men could nurse secret doubts and
fears without risk of exposure. However, during the previous
twenty years the leaders of the Chinese Communist Party formulated a technique by which it was possible to control the simple thoughts of simple people and also to implant certain
reflexes in the minds of their officials, who could thereafter engage in Party activities while separated from superior authority.
This system did not betray itself easily to foreigners accus-

tomed to the technical apparatus of dictatorship. The Chinese, having little else to work with, used human beings as their basic means of communication. Of course they employed loud-speakers, radio networks and printing presses too. But a for-mer peasant and self-educated scholar called Mao Tse-tung had long ago recognized in the peasantry a natural device for spreading propaganda. He had written as far back as 1927, regarding a revolutionary movement in his home province of Hunan: "[Our] political slogans are flying about everywhere, entering into the heads of adults, youngsters, old men, children and women in countless villages and coming out of their mouths."

Today you may look for Nazi-like machinery to disseminate ideas in China; you may search for Orwellian gadgets, hidden microphones, built-in TV-eyes and tape recorders. Even if they existed, you could cut all the wires and pull out all the plugs and still have to deal with the main circuit and its twelve million human cells. These twelve million are the Party members. Despite ruthless weeding out, their numbers have soared from three million when Mao and the Party first came to power. Each is expected to use eyes, ears and voice constantly in the service of The People, the Party and the ex-peasant who is known throughout China by the modern euphemism for an Oriental despot, "Chairman" Mao. This mass of people forms a vast brain in which most human impulses now flash down well-worn channels traced originally by Party leaders.

So it was really only a matter of time before Minister Chang would have to grapple with this monstrous mass mind. On June 14, 1957, he capitulated after almost six months of so-called "struggle" with Party zealots.

Once proud as only a Chinese could be, with some forty years of devoted duty to China behind him, the Minister of Communications now made this public statement:

I have committed serious ideological mistakes . . . My stand was not firm, my understanding was confused and I assumed a most flippant liberalist attitude in dealing with state policies so that I came under evil political influences . . . Due to my inade-quate studies, my bourgeois ideology has not been transformed and so my ideological advancement has not kept pace . . . I have failed to live up to the expectations of the Communist Party and Chairman Mao. I am greatly ashamed. I shall strengthen my studies, undergo ideological reform and continue penetratingly to investigate the roots of my mistaken ideology.

How had he been trapped into this confession? The answer could be found in a speech made one year earlier by Mao Tse-tung in which he called upon all intellectuals and technicians to express their innermost thoughts. Mao's free-speech movement was full of delicate little references to the Chinese past and it was labeled "Let all flowers bloom." What it did not make clear was the fact that Mao reserved to himself the right to distinguish between flowers and weeds.

My first encounter with thought control came in the Koje Island prisoner compounds off the south tip of Korea in 1952. Here 170,000 restless prisoners were crammed in unwieldy groups of 5000 to each compound. Technically they were captives but often they seemed like the real rulers. They ran their own cages as miniature "People's Democracies" and they negotiated with their guards as if they represented sovereign nations. The guards fetched and carried food and fuel, and the guards held the guns. Few, however, ventured inside the compounds. The American commanders in time learned there was only one way to deal with these obstinate prisoners, but when they attempted to starve them into submission there was an immediate outcry from Western liberals. Thus for many months the Americans were unable to deal with this festering problem in the only way which seemed practical and likely to cause the least damage: by the use of brute force. They were in danger of being defeated by the brute reason of their own prisoners who were always willing to negotiate, but never willing to yield in their demands. In the end it was trained Chinese from Formosa, skilled in anti-Communist techniques evolved by the Nationalist leader Chiang Kai-shek and his eldest son, the Moscow-educated General Chiang Ching-kuo, who *persuaded* several thousand prisoners to choose the Western side.

Even this use of persuasion caused sour comment from many

Westerners, myself included. The converts were herded into new stockades where they waved friendly flags with the same zeal as their recent comrades yelled defiance. At that time, we missed the true lesson which only the Nationalist Chinese could appreciate: that the prisoners were in a highly suggestible condition of mind.

Later I talked with Western prisoners released from Chinese jails. They told of blinkered days and nights when they lost touch with all reality and became willing to believe an illiterate, hawking guard who picked his nose and smelled of garlic. The guard would insist that black was white, literally, and lo! black was white. Then would follow more intensive interrogations; requests to rewrite one's autobiography and ceaseless but seemingly reasonable discussion, followed by long periods of silence. The slow breakdown in sanity was never allowed to develop too swiftly.

The objective was almost always to reverse whatever the prisoner believed to be true. Often the influence of this indoctrination was so persistent that a newly released Westerner remained under the spell. One American scholar caught in Peking when the Communist regime took charge insisted that he could feel only gratitude to his jailers. "They might have put me in chains," he kept repeating. "But they did not. They might have shot me for spying. But they fed and clothed me."

It was idle to point out to him that none of his confessions revealed any sort of criminal activity. "I was breaking the laws of China," he insisted and shook his head uneasily when told no such laws had been promulgated.

Indignation was more easily aroused by the brutal methods of torture and force employed in Russia and East Europe. But in that part of the Communist bloc, Bolshevik self-criticism was little more than a group activity, a sort of comradely inquest on a bungled job. It was the Chinese who used self-criticism as well as criticism in an utterly ruthless way, applying it to every individual in the land.

Whether you called the Chinese technique "brainwashing" or regarded it as a scientific method of hidden persuasion, it undeniably existed and demanded study. The experiment in

China promised to spread into most of Asia and Latin America because it offered a formula for the organization of collective action among crushing numbers of people who, disillusioned with their old religions and philosophies and blaming their ills on richer and stronger nations, would respond to the discipline of fanatics.

It began to seem that what was human in our race was under threat, since we are distinguished only by our claim to possess souls and it was hard to believe the victims of Chinese indoctrination were much different from Pavlov's brainless dogs.

A speech was made around this time and broadcast by Radio Peking which indicated the path China was about to follow. It reflected the independent nature of the regime, but it was made by a man often identified with Soviet Russia, the Grey Eminence of the new dynasty and its senior political theoretician, Liu Shao-chi, destined to become Mao's successor in 1959.

> Colonies and semi-colonies are reservoirs of world imperialism [he proclaimed]. It is therefore necessary for colonial and semi-colonial people and the working people of imperialist countries to unite to fight against their common enemy — imperialism.
> The path taken by the Chinese people . . . is the path that should be traced by the peoples of various colonial and semi-colonial countries.

There was nothing here about the glorious Soviet example. This was the proud chieftain of a new giant in Asia, issuing instructions to comrades of the yellow races. "Working classes! Unite with *all who are willing to fight imperialism,*" he advised.

But this bellicose attitude changed. Red China found a need for peace, internal stability, capital, and the accumulation of technical knowledge in order to realize her amibitions to become an industrial power. Her energies became directed inward. Nevertheless the diplomatic offensive had to be maintained and it gained new strength as Premier Chou En-lai, an urbane and subtle henchman of Mao Tse-tung, began to seek friends and to influence neutrals among the underdeveloped nations of Asia and the Middle East. He had the great advantage that China had already shocked these countries into an appreciation of Communist Chinese strength. As we shall see, Mao Tse-tung's theory of first shocking the "patient" into a sweat and then prescribing the remedy for his ailment was to be applied both to external and to domestic problems.

If Earl Attlee was right in describing democracy as "government by discussion," then it could be well argued by the time I first entered China in 1954 that China was democratic. The flow of discussion was enormous. The voices droned on, irresistible and inexhaustible, driving toward a conclusion predetermined by the leaders. The man who launched these verbal steam rollers was the Party Chairman, Mao Tse-tung, who proclaimed his desire to see all intellectual flowers bloom, but then set about the task of uprooting the stinkwort and poison ivy which appeared among the sweet red roses fertilized by so-called free discussion. Mao's faith could not permit strong rivals. His Communism must predominate, and challengers had to be struggled against just as an apostle would struggle for the soul of a sinner.

During that first tour of China I found it difficult to believe the Russians were as popular or as influential as the Peking regime proclaimed. Sometimes an official would betray pride in the fact that the Chinese revolution began before the Russian revolution and outlasted it by thirty years. There was extreme caution in discussing Russian aid, much lip service but little genuine enthusiasm.

CHAPTER TWO

The Walrus and the Carpenter Go Walking Hand-in-Hand

◎ ◎

THREE YEARS before World War II began, Mao Tse-tung told biographers that in his youth — "I had somewhat vague passions about nineteenth-century democracy, Utopianism and old-fashioned liberalism and I was definitely anti-militarist and anti-imperialist." He became instead a Marxist although he knew little about events inside China and still less about foreign affairs except whatever he imbibed while reading furiously through the great Chinese classics and a potpourri of Western writings, some of them by crackpots. While absorbed in political theory, he knew little about who governed his own country. The Empress Dowager was dead two years, he confessed, before he discovered the change in rule. When he bewailed the dismemberment of China, he referred to states regarded by the outside world as independent. He turned to Russia for guidance when millions were losing faith in Stalin.

He betrayed a tendency to oversimplify on the basis of piecemeal knowledge. Thus in an eight-hour speech in 1940 he explained why Soviet Russia should become the sole source of strength:

> With all imperialist countries as her enemies, China cannot obtain independence without the aid of one socialist country and the international proletariat. In an era of revolution and war

where capitalism is definitely dying and socialism begins to flourish . . . there are only two ways open to all decent people in colonies and semi-colonies. They must either join the imperialist front or join the anti-imperialist front. They must choose between these two. There is no other way.

Many years later I saw the Walrus and the Carpenter publicly join hands in Peking. A squat pugnacious Russian named Nikita Khrushchev clapped himself onto a platform loaded with Chinese dignitaries. Nobody paid him much heed among my own small group of strangers. Who in September 1954 would have suspected this Ukrainian tippler of having the will or weakness to let Mao Tse-tung achieve equality?

Mao clapped politely back and fifteen thousand people in the Hall of Magnanimity sent up a roar that echoed through the Sea Palaces and bounced down the rows of loudspeakers overhanging the Forbidden City next door. I looked at the flushed faces around me as fat pencils of quivering blue light swept slowly over them. The first block of seats was packed with wooden Chinese features whose excitement was betrayed by flashing eyes of deepest black. Then came the delegates from "fraternal countries": the Bulgars, Rumanians, Czechs, East Germans, Poles, and of course the Russians. Those in front had earphones clamped to their heads. Those behind gripped mimeographed sheets. The blinding arclights shifted across the body of the hall, revealing Tibetans and Mongolians, living Buddhas and their fellow bonzes in saffron robes. There were Kazak shepherds in blankets, Black Miaos in flowing blue robes, Koreans and border tribesmen, men in the black habits of monks and a wildly applauding group identified in the program as the "Capitalists' Association."

Now it was our turn. The pigtailed girls who swung chunky black cinecameras down upon us wasted little time with my glum, perspiring visage.

There were more rewarding subjects: Thais and Indonesians, a sprinkling of delicate little Burmese maidens, a knot of watchful Japanese, and numerous Europeans. Most of the Europeans were labeled "peace fighters." The Europeans constituted a white-faced minority and a divided one at that; for I

could find nothing familiar about many who stood and clapped
this pagan ceremony with mechanical rhythm, until I thought
of hot-gospelers and the hysteria of an evangelical campaign.

Khrushchev brought a message from the Supreme Soviet: . . .

> China has become a powerful factor in the liberation struggle
> of all the oppressed nations against the forces of imperialist
> reaction and colonial enslavement . . .

Since then, the significance of those words has become more
apparent. Stalin was dead. Only one great revolutionary figure remained, a man long ago suspected of heresies, but now
the leader of the world's most populated nation: Mao Tse-
tung. He had no nuclear bombs; no capacity for making
cannon or jets; not even a solitary factory to make a truck.
But he had six hundred million people; as many people perhaps as populated the entire globe two centuries earlier when
the vast empires of Russia and China collided along the
southern marches of Siberia and came to terms.

Now I met Mao for the first time. The scene had shifted
across a tiny artificial lake built for an empress to the Throne
Room of Purple Effulgence. Sandalwood carvings filled the air
with soft perfumes. A gray light filtered through the circular
ceiling. Alert officials moved swiftly and silently over deep
Tientsin rugs. It was some days later and Nehru was there,
Prime Minister of the only nation ever to challenge China's
Far East influence in the days of sail. Now India was again
a competitor with China to hold the interest of a new and
resurgent Asia; an Asia whose people were more numerous
than the yellow grains of sand that make a desert, often just
as exposed to the whims of climate, and waiting to be given
direction and drive by some powerful desert wind.

There was Nehru, brought forward by Mao, followed by
that extraordinary group of Chinese leaders who have stuck
together through all the years to give their Communist allies
the unique lesson of "collective leadership." Mao waved one
hand. The group fell into line. More arclights and the soft
whir of cameras. The lights died. Mao led Nehru away to

meet the Dalai and Panchen Lamas, spiritual and puppet leaders of Tibet respectively, whose territory Mao's armies had just occupied, bringing Chinese power back to India's northern frontiers.

Two years passed before I saw Mao again. Every Communist Party in the world had sent its representatives to Peking to draw what lessons they could from the Eighth Chinese Communist Party Congress. There were unidentified agents too from Latin America, North Africa, the Middle East and those parts of Asia outside Chinese control. All seemed absorbed by the reawakening of a China which to me now looked as if it were once again indulging in its ancient dreams of a Celestial Empire surrounded by barbarians. Not everyone among the Party faithful from abroad cared much for what he saw. "Some friends in fraternal countries do not much approve of our policy," observed Lu Kan-ju, a Chinese People's Congress delegate.

But whatever doubts persisted in the Kremlin, the Soviet President assured his Peking hosts: "By your genius you have enriched the great treasury of Marxist-Leninism." Voroshilov put his finger upon the evidence of genius. China, he said, had been peacefully transformed into a socialist phase of revolution. "We are closely following and are inspired by the magnificent development of particular forms of democracy in the Chinese People's Republic."

He talked of the "democratization" of capitalists and I remembered the Shanghai factory owner who told me about this transformation. He was a little wrinkled old man who explained how he voluntarily liquidated himself. He saw the way things were going: shops and mills sliding into an uncomfortable association known as Joint Private-State Enterprise. He knew this was the first step toward State ownership but he was wearied by the blandishments of comrades. Finally he offered to go into partnership with the State. He was thanked for his progressive ideas but reprimanded for making the offer from ulterior motives. He must go back and think *why* he should liquidate himself as a capitalist. He was a

sinner and the comrades were wrestling for his soul. They
accepted him only when he proved that he himself had won
the inner struggle.

In the Soviet Union such a man either submitted in terror or
was liquidated with a gun. In China the weapon was remorse-
less reason. In the autumn of 1956 this was a lesson to
which many Russian leaders tuned an attentive ear because
brutality had failed to prevent a public and moral defeat at
the hands of unarmed Hungarian rebels.

The ludicrous notion began to take shape that Russia was
becoming increasingly dependent on China to advise on strategy. The Communist world was suffering disillusion about the
Soviet Union, particularly since Khrushchev had revealed the
madman whom millions had revered as the great and all-wise
Stalin. It began to appear that the Russian empire in Eastern
Europe would fall apart unless some new source of inspiration
could be found: and in the crucial years of 1955 and 1956,
that inspiration became identified as Mao Tse-tung. Whether
the Russians liked this or not, it was apparent they had to go
along with the idea for at least long enough to let their
Chinese comrades reassure the restless satellites, whose inherent resentment of Moscow's dictation bubbled up into open
rebellion after the denunciation of Stalin by his successors.

Perhaps it was about this time that the Chinese Communists
became drunk with their own power to manipulate the mighty
Soviet Union. The Chinese had no sense of national boundaries when they talked in political terms: humanity was divided
only into the Good, the Wayward and the Wicked. Mao set
forth the conditions for converting the Wayward and suppressing the Wicked, and he applied his doctrine to neighboring states with the same firmness as he applied it internally.
But he showed infinite patience in dealing with foreigners
because, while remaining a good Communist, he was also
Chinese and understood very well the time-tested techniques of
old China in winning control over most of Asia.

His politic refusal to recognize State boundaries enabled
Mao to examine post-Stalin Russia with a critical eye. For the

worst twenty years in his forty years of Communist struggle, Mao had been hamstrung more than helped by the Soviet Union. By the year 1955, with Stalin dead, Mao began to make bold decisions of his own that affected international communism. He also made less pretense of utter devotion to his Russian Big Brother and there were times when he allowed disputes between them to leak out to the Western world.

Chinese officials began to quote their own history and their own classical writers more often, obviously because they were encouraged to do so by their leaders. Suddenly I found it possible to talk about Confucius with the authorities and not hear him compared disparagingly with Gogol. As for Dr. Sun Yat-sen, founder of the Chinese revolution, his name was now adored and his muddled philosophies (suitably edited) became a part of the officially approved literature of the day.

With the resurrection of Confucius in a comrade's cap came the expulsion of the Marxist-Leninist priests from the Confucian Temple in Peking. The old Hall of Great Perfection was redecorated and the official jargon became increasingly sprinkled with delicate references to the great sage. Many scholars were thrilled. Perhaps it hardly mattered to them that the phraseology of Confucius was undergoing a slight transformation so that older intellectuals might be more subtly impregnated with Mao's modern philosophies.

Six vermilion lacquer tablets were restored to their former condition in the temple. Rather to my surprise, no effort was made to modify the events which they commemorated thus:

Conquest of Western Mongolia. K'ang Hsi, 1704.
Conquest of Eastern Tibet. Yung Cheng, 1726.
Conquest of the Miao Country. Ch'ien Lung, 1750.
Conquest of Sungaria, land of the Kalmuks. Ch'ien Lung, 1760.
Conquest of Eastern Turkestan. Ch'ien Lung, 1760.
Conquest expeditions to Szechuan and Yunnan. Ch'ien Lung, 1777.

This was franker than the word "liberation" and suggested

that perhaps the Chinese were no longer so sure that the
world began with the Russian revolution. There were even
fleeting mentions of celestial matters. To the twenty-three
million children being prepared for confession and the Party,
there was this counsel from their Youth League adviser: "Keep
your head in heaven and your feet on the ground."

Heaven was a word of sure-fire effectiveness, impermissible
until the regime became sure enough of its own faith. By then,
Communist powers of conversion found no difficulty with
such concepts as Heaven, nor indeed with its mandate.

The Mandate of Heaven was the crude means by which
Chinese might show lack of confidence in their rulers, inas-
much as failure to discharge his duties exposed an emperor to
the challenges of his would-be replacements. Once a dynasty
toppled it was dismissed as having lost the mandate. China
has no history of restored monarchies. Nobody was so stupid
as to give loyalty to the defeated. The switch in allegiance
usually began with the scholar-gentry, a class of officials who
really ran the practical affairs of their country (and still do, so
far as I could see). Power and strength were enough to command obedience.

If Mao's regime forced its way to power by rallying the
peasants and initiating them into the new religious order of
Communism, there might seem to millions of Chinese every
reason why Mao should sit on the Dragon Throne. There was
nothing historically wrong, either, in his preference for wearing boiler suits. The acid test, however, would be whether his
new dynasty fulfilled the hopes and ambitions of his people.

A threat to Mao's supremacy, therefore, would be always
posed by President Chiang Kai-shek in Formosa. His money
and military power backed by the United States persuaded
many Overseas Chinese to sit on the political fence. Inside
China, repeated leaflet raids by Chiang's aircraft kept millions
aware of this rival claimant to the Throne.

To an outside observer, therefore, it was fascinating to trace
the rise of these two contestants; to see how they had both
recognized in Marxist-Leninism the means of achieving power;
and to see how both made use of Russia and the United States
to promote their own aims. One was forced to conclude that

Mao earned the Mandate of Heaven with surprisingly little physical help (although considerable obstruction) from Stalin, whereas Chiang permitted his regime to sink into corruption and therefore, by Chinese standards, deserved to lose.

Both men were followers of Dr. Sun Yat-sen. One of them worked humbly in a Peking library and when he had sucked Sun dry of ideas, he turned to the Bolshevik Revolution for new ones; thus Mao Tse-tung evolved the Marxist slogans that were given a Chinese folklore twist. He proved that Asia wanted perhaps much more than a full belly — she wanted a native ideology dressed in modern costume but cut from a traditional cloth.

But Chiang was always protected against physical or mental contamination from the peasants. Through no fault of his own, no doubt, he thought the lesson left by Sun Yat-sen was that money, power and lip service to a Confucian code of behavior were the solution to modern China's difficulties. His followers became weak and decadent as they relied more and more on foreign aid. They demonstrated in yet another way the corrupting influence of Western charity.

In 1924, Chiang Kai-shek was sent to Moscow by Dr. Sun Yat-sen. Chiang was then president of the Whampoa Academy, a military establishment set up near Canton. Cadets were divided into two groups. Some called themselves the Sun Society and resisted efforts by Soviet advisers to take control of the Academy. Others belonged to the Union of Youth and became outstanding figures in the Communist regime of Mao. They included Chou En-lai, Chu Teh and Lin Piao whose names since the Korean War have been only too familiar to opponents, critics and weak neighbors of Communism in the Far East.

As Chiang made his way to Moscow, the last political lectures of Dr. Sun were being prepared. "The Communism which we propose is a Communism of the future, not of the present," he wrote. Another time he talked of "a new discovery and political theory and a fundamental solution of the whole problem . . . distinctions should be made between those who can rule and those who can do things . . ."

His naïve ideas were confusing. But there was no confusion

in the mind of the thirty-two-year-old scholarly man in the
National University Library at Peking. Mao Tse-tung was
way ahead in plans and when Sun died the following year,
Mao began to organize a peasant movement in Hunan. It was
his home province in central China, just south of the Yangtse.
There he perpetrated his first heresy in the Marxist-Leninist
faith: "Leadership by the poor peasant is very essential," he
wrote in a later report. "Without the poor peasants, there will
be no revolution . . . Within a short time hundreds of millions
of peasants will rise with the fury of a hurricane; no power,
however strong, can restrain them. They will break all the
shackles that bind them and rush towards the road of liberation."

This was the first hint that in China had appeared a future
successor to Stalin, a man who was quite prepared to adjust
the Communist dogma to changing or different national conditions. Thirty years later, when Mao's methods were
much more easily identified as "Chinese," the rise of Peking's prestige in the Communist world had reached the point
where Premier Chou En-lai could openly invite senior officials
from other Soviet bloc countries to study the latest innovations.*

But when Mao's first report was published from his 1927
investigations, he was marked down as a potential trouble-
maker. The chief Comintern adviser, Manabendra Nath Roy,
dismissed Mao as an opportunist. This passionate son of peasants had openly contradicted the dictum that peasants were
only pack-horses for a revolution that must be accomplished
by urban workers.

Mao is in many ways a traditional Chinese figure who can
assemble a poetic sampler or plan the grand strategy of a war
and then turn with equal confidence to the direction of vast

---

* Chou En-lai told visiting transport ministers from other Communist
states to study China's campaign to resolve conflicts between The People
and their leaders, reported Radio Peking on 25 May 1957. This campaign ignored the Soviet view that such contradictions were impossible.
It was launched by Mao Tse-tung in two speeches promulgating a new
fundamental extension of Marxist theory.

schemes in water conservancy and the reform of agriculture. What is not traditional is the spread of this man's influence throughout that one third of humanity living in overcrowded and backward lands. Mao is more widely worshiped and yet more elusive, more coldly calculating and yet far earthier than any dictator in this century of despots. He is becoming chief pundit of the Communist world, quoted reverently by his own faction in the Kremlin and by revolutionary leaders among the underdogs far away in Africa and Latin America. In an age crowded with Titans, his slightly effeminate figure looms above the clumsier tyrants. Where Hitler ranted and raved, Mao whispers.

"You are autocratic!" Mao's enemies cried. And the para-doxical dictator answered: "My dear gentlemen, you speak the truth. We are indeed . . . We have been called upon to put into effect the authority of The People's Democracy, which is the dictatorship of People's Democracy, and we shall deprive the reactionary party of the right to speak and only allow that right to The People."

So a single voice claims to speak collectively for the Chinese and only in the dull terminology of economic plans. Daring explorations, vast schemes of colonization, the struggle with huge and violent rivers, all these dramatic and vivid enter-prises are churning away in the minds of a few leaders, while the masses plod doggedly on, imagination bogged in a thick gruel of doctrinaire proclamations.

Mao, his consultants and acolytes, have found a way to po-larize one quarter of humanity's thoughts without rhetoric, television or the usual soporifics. Partly it is done in accord-ance with Confucian morality: "To govern by means of vir-tue may be compared to the North Star which remains stead-fast and unmoving: all the stars are turned respectfully toward it."

And if this were entirely the case, it might seem that China had found a system of peaceful government unique in history. But Western policy has been based on the belief that Mao rules by terror alone. Unless we understand why the Chinese can be shepherded as well as jackbooted into obedience, we shall continue to talk pompously of combating militant Communism as if this were some sort of juggernaut with spikable guns, deflatable tires or penetrable armor. The vision of a Goliath in chainmail has become the excuse for our supporting less subtle dictators and the expenditure of more arms money in Asia than was spent in actually fighting any war. If such precautions are necessary, it should not be forgotten that many Asians feel the Chinese to be inspired by a religious fervor while we purchase our allies with silver. This is valuable ammunition for Mao and for his successors who, groomed like scions of any dynasty, will maintain the drive for peaceful "liberation" of the rest of Africa and Asia.

Mao, who told his ragged partisans to take arms and ammunition from Western arsenals, now insists that words are bullets and with patient arrogance turns our publicity armories against us. It is time to look more closely at this man who has remained steadfast and unmoving so that all turn with varying degrees of respect to face in the one direction.

CHAPTER THREE

Hair-Anoint-East, the Man in the Red Mask

◉   ◉

YOU MIGHT expect Mao Tse-tung to resemble the fierce and in-
flexible mask which for years he displayed to the outside world.
Most people first see him, if they ever see him at all, as a white
moon face under a peaked cap rising on the red horizon of
Peking's Gate of Heavenly Peace. Above him bob giant Chinese lanterns. Below him, acknowledging his languid waves of
one arm, passes what must be the biggest parade of human beings in history. They jog-trot past, eighty or a hundred abreast
and hard upon each other's heels for five unbroken hours,
crying out for ten thousand years of life for Chairman Mao as
they jostle under the streaming banners. In the first years of
the regime, these October 1 eruptions began under crisp blue
skies and the air was filled with the shrill pipings of whistles
tied to the legs of pigeons, the deeper whine of jets and the
synchronized crackle and pop of firecrackers, while later came
ornate rockets whose glowing sticks fell sizzling out of the
suddenly constellated night. Then in 1956 it poured with
rain. All that summer there had been drought in the north
and floods to the south. The parade was almost washed out
and there followed a winter of discontent when China faced
dire economic problems.

In that winter, sitting cozily in the dark and low-beamed
eatinghouse called Three Tables, or huddled round a chestnut
vender's blazing fire which hissed softly whenever a snowflake

spiraled out of the darkness, we debated the mystery of the Forbidden City and its new occupants: "Was Mao a mandarin in
Marxist robes?" Of course the comrades denied it. There were
strangers from East Europe and even Russia who seemed less
sure. They noted a certain glumness among Chinese leaders as
if the capricious weather were causing twinges of memory,
taking them back to times when natural calamity was a sign
from Heaven that its mandate was being withdrawn from the
undeserving incumbent enthroned behind vermilion walls.

An Oriental inscrutability hid Mao from public view. Once
I asked if he was ever quoted, except from Party-approved
speeches. We were sitting in another narrow restaurant called
for the sake of variety Three Stars where the kitchen staff
played poker while the manager wiped cutlery stamped with
U.S. Navy imprints. The question was passed around and
someone volunteered an anecdote. In Peking, he said, were
many Mongolian-style eating places which catered to Moslems
and therefore could cook only mutton. There had been a
shortage of meat, however, and the grumbling of the Moslems
was said to have reached Mao's ears.

"If socialism is bad for mutton, it's good for nothing," Mao
was alleged to have said, thereupon ordering special rations
for the restaurants concerned.

There were other stories of a similar kind. Peking's citizens
are not renowned for any particular sense of reverence and
there were lusty jokes about the Twenty Imperial Censors of
the Politburo and the Eunuchs of the Standing Committees.
Often at receptions you would find among the hierarchy a
small bald-headed man with a knee-length beard. He was extremely solemn and, if fitted out with a fishing rod and curling
boots, might have passed for a garden ornament. I asked who
he was and after the third toast was told: "We've got three of
those we switch around. They make impressive decorations."

Nevertheless it was difficult to pin anyone down on specific
points such as where Mao lived and worked, what his daily routine might be and whether he still did a great deal of walking.
The Chinese were close-mouthed about such details and you
picked up what snippets you could from foreign Communists

or by hard experience. I first glimpsed his daily routine, for instance, from an exhausting encounter with Premier Chou En-lai's staff which began at three o'clock in the morning and continued until dawn with short intervals.

Some of us had complained that it was useless to cover news in Peking when priority was given to the Soviet Tass Agency and Radio Moscow. A week later the few foreign pressmen in our hotel were hauled from bed in the middle of the night and made to proceed to the Foreign Office, which is tucked away within a warren of narrow lanes with high walls known as *hu'tungs*. Tea was served, candies and cigarettes were handed round and after the formal preliminaries were completed, a spokesman entered with interpreters.

"The information department of the Ministry of Foreign Affairs of the People's Republic of China welcomes you," said the spokesman in Chinese. His words were repeated in Russian, Japanese and English. "A meeting has been taking place between representatives of China on the one hand and representatives of the Soviet Union on the other hand. A bulletin will be issued."

The urgency of the summons, the long journey in pitch-darkness and the solemnity of the occasion had suggested that a declaration of war was the least we could expect. We decided to return to bed and wait for the bulletin there. It took an hour to get home, plunging into the wrong *hu'tungs*, falling into ditches and tripping over the winter stockpiles of coal-dust. I was just asleep when the door was flung open and a gaunt messenger announced in messianic tones the advent of Part One of the Bulletin. I grunted rudely and when he left snuggled back under the blankets. At once the door crashed open again, on went the light and my scornful courier stood like a sentinel until I got up with all resistance gone.

This pantomime was repeated three times while the bulletin emerged paragraph by paragraph with all the verbiage and legal prolixity that seems necessary when one Communist fraternal and everlasting ally puts through a deal with another fraternal and everlasting ally. At the time it seemed like a revenge upon us for our complaints, because it never happened

again and the only permanent change was that henceforth
the New China News Agency took precedence over everyone,
Tass and all (something no Soviet satellite succeeded in achieving for its native-born agencies).

Out of this incident arose some pointed inquiries about
Mao's working schedule. This particular communiqué had been
handled personally by the Chinese leader because it dealt
with a considerable withdrawal of Russian military influence.
Mao conformed a good deal in this period to imperial tradition and rose in the first half of the Hour of the Tiger (3 A.M.).
His day normally ended at the second half of the Hour of the
Pig (10 P.M.) On important occasions he worked beyond
twenty hours and it was claimed that only Chou En-lai could
stick to the same grueling pace. Sometimes Mao went out for
dinner and for one bewildering week I found myself almost
daily within *gam-bai** range (although not on quite those
terms) with the reverend Chairman himself. This happened
while Nehru was in town. The Indian premier was known to
believe in fraternization with the press. Mao on stage plodded
steadily through his food, preferring a spoon when chopsticks
were impolite to a foreign guest, and often at the same time
smoking a cigarette cut in half. ("Because he must reduce
his smoking," whispered his cancer-conscious interpreter.)

His reputation for flexibility seemed confirmed when he
walked up to David Chipp at a state reception and was greeted
with a stream of Chinese. David was learning Mandarin and
bravely decided to try it out on Mao. "*Wa-sher-ying-kwo-
jen,*" said David, prodding himself in the chest. "I am an

---

* *Gam-bai* is a toast frequently offered to a dining companion. If the
recipient responds, he must drain his glass. It is a reliable rule of thumb that
if a Chinese is willing to get drunk with you in this manner, he will prove
a very hard drinker indeed and you would be better advised to reply in
self-defence *sui-biyen* which seems to mean "as you like it" and permits
you to retire from the fray somewhat more gracefully than by sliding
gently under the table. The Chinese take a dim view of drunks and it
once took me some considerable time to recover the prestige I lost by
tripping and falling into a fountain placed (for reasons best known to the
inscrutable Japanese who built it) bang in the middle of a shabby restaurant
in Manchuria.

Englishman." It was a fact of which Mao was doubtless aware but he seemed lost in admiration before he passed on to weightier matters. Later Chou En-lai announced that "the Chairman is learning English."

There was a time when Mao deeply resented the use of English. As a boy he scraped enough money together for private schooling and then found tuition was given exclusively in that language. Later he made his men speak only Chinese on all formal occasions, taking the view that his people had been humiliated long enough by the imposition of foreign tongues.

His early days obviously must have influenced his later political decisions. It seems worthwhile recounting briefly his own development, if only to demonstrate how inextricably it has been entangled with China's past. Observers who sometimes tried to show that Mao thought first of all as a Chinese and then as a Communist have been accused of attempting to soften world opinion toward the Peking regime. This accusation seems a curious attempt to ignore facts. And if it is true that Mao has successfully combined the salient characteristics of traditional Chinese society with Marxist-Leninist notions, surely this does not necessarily mean that the final product is less formidable? On the contrary, as I think we shall see, the result is infinitely more subtle than Slavic Communism and, therefore, appeals widely to those already disillusioned with Russia.

Foreign influences were already shaping Mao's destiny when he was born of yeoman stock in a part of China which has the same isolationist instincts as the American Midwest. His father had lived in the family village of Shao San during a period when Western traders sowed the seeds of great change. The village "Behind the Mountain" is sixty miles from Changsha, then an ancient literary and educational center on the Siang Kiang River at the very heart of China's most profitable rice bowl. When I went there, a number of old people were available who had trained themselves to recall Mao's childhood living conditions. But — and I remember thinking this oddly revealing — none could offer anecdotes that were not enshrined already in popular legend. It was like meeting George

Washington's schoolmates after the American Revolution only to hear how he chopped down a cherry tree.

Mao Tse-tung, whose name can be rendered rather meaninglessly as Hair-Anoint-East, was born in 1893. His people, the Hunanese, take a proud and precise view of life. Prussian in their manners, perhaps, they have been called the Germans of China by Mao's oldest fighting comrade, Chu Teh, who learned some of the military arts in Berlin.

Their ancestors came on the wings of the Yellow Wind that flies out of Central Asia, and this same wind breathed life into their civilization which began so long before Christ's birth and survived the millenniums. They followed first in the mainstream of dry air blowing across the Gobi Desert and the northwest steppes where a fine yellow loam dust is snatched up, and for tens of thousands of years has been showered upon northern China, piling up slowly and grain by grain, burying natural resources but creating a vast loess territory of spongelike soil where man can grow food. Here the prototype Chinese settled.

Another element entered their lives. The Yellow River boiled over the upper loesslands and burst into the great plain of Northeast China with still more of the yellow loam. Here, unconfined for four hundred miles to the sea, the river pregnant with disaster could swell and deposit the silt wherever it chose. Time and again, silt filled the river's own bed and millions died in floods. The Yellow River valley might have remained empty forever, making its annual transformation from desert to marsh and back again, but for the remarkable energy and resource of the newcomers. Slowly they built up a system of dikes, canals and irrigation channels to cheat the eccentric waters. To control these public works, priestly kings were needed. The centuries revolved, the kingdoms amalgamated until there was already a Chinese civilization when many of our western ancestors were still in woad.

While ancient Greece discussed democratic government, the Chinese only disagreed about systems of authoritarian rule. The elements shaped their harsh society, and to conquer these climatic enemies they submitted to the leadership of men who could conquer flood and famine. Only a ruler of heavenly grace could possibly survive because any natural calamity was taken as a reflection on the emperor's ability and probity. In the West, many complicated forms of government might take shape and men become martyrs in a struggle for individual freedom and some often vague concept of human rights. In China the Mandate of Heaven spread a protective mantle over the Yellow River people and beyond, so that before the Holy Roman Empire claimed celestial patronage there was a Chinese Empire that encompassed most of Asia. For the men at its heart there was no great philosophical or political inspiration except a mounting collection of moral precepts and what has been called the Chinese Constitution of the Right to Rebel. A rebellion in this context was likely to occur when a king manifestly lost his mandate.

Mao's ancestors settled the Yangtse Valley, a rich green region which was soon crisscrossed by canals and waterways. This became the province of Hunan which paid the biggest imperial taxes, yielded the best rice and tea and concealed beneath its hills of pine and bamboo certain precious metals. Its peasants spoke with thick, slurred accents that were unintelligible to anyone from Peking. Luckily, their officials wrote in ancient ideographs that were universally understood. This script, the world's oldest written language still in use, preserved ideas in the most graceful and intricate strokes. Without these ideographs, China would have fallen into utter disunity since millions by now spoke utterly different dialects.

These millions were governed by the classic language of ideographs and the people who could afford to learn it. No matter what changes took place at the very top, this educated class still went on managing people and affairs. Their history of rule went back through all the upheavals of empire to Confucius who launched a great moral and ethical code about 500 B.C. Confucianism became one of the world's greatest ideological systems, but China's decay began when the system itself started to rot. (Chinese Communists scent trouble whenever they see their own faith beginning to deteriorate into a modern version of neo-Confucianism in which lipservice counts more than deeds and there is worship of outstanding individuals.) For eight hundred years, the Confucian cult was a mixture of superstition and time-serving. Great figures were worshipped in temples where youngsters were taught to mumble their way through Confucian and other philosophical tracts.

By the time young Mao Tse-tung, at the turn of the twentieth century, ended his first period of schooling at the age of thirteen, there were cracks in the encrustations of form and ritual that lay thick upon his generation. The ruinous reign of the concubine Green Jade, the Empress Tz'u Hsi, was ending. She traced her lineage to a great Manchu leader said to have been born to a virgin. Prophecy said the clan's supremacy would end forever with a woman bearing the mark of a fox. Such was Green Jade, born amidst portents at the Hour of the Tiger, and destined to die while her successor still worked barefoot in the Hunanese rice paddies.

What linked this wayward empress to the boy who would one day hang his own massive portrait on the Dynastic Gate guarding the southerly entrance to the Imperial City of Peking?

Mao's poverty, though later blamed like other afflictions on Western "exploitation," was largely the result of decay within the dynasty. There would have been no opium trade without corrupt officials to encourage it, for instance, and there would have been fewer national calamities if public waterworks were less neglected. The gap between Mao's people and the alien Manchu rule widened. The bureaucrats who should have upheld Confucian law were incapable of stopping the rot and the heavenly wrath was expressed in floods and disasters so that poverty and despair spread over the land.

When the Empress Dowager, and almost simultaneously her son the Emperor, died, Mao had just resumed his education. He had spent two years in middleschool and at the age of eighteen in the year 1911 he was swept into his first revolution. Conspirators working for Dr. Sun Yat-sen's alliance of secret societies were packing gunpowder into bombs in the back of a small house in Wuhan, the big metropolis about two hundred miles from Mao's home. Accounts differ, but there was an explosion and when the dust settled, the Chinese revolution had begun.

Mao must have been a distinctly odd character at this time. He joined one of the small revolutionary armies without really understanding what had caused all the fuss that eventually would lead to his own enthronement. He was engrossed in his own reactions: the bitterness of being the poorest boy in school; the later triumph of writing letters home for illiterate army comrades; and the stupid fact of being married since the age of fourteen to an older girl selected by his parents and with whom he never slept. It was not a self-centered anger, however, that seems to have driven him into long solitary marches through the countryside. His own experiences slowly merged into a sympathy and understanding for his people so that in time his personal sentiments were projected into a battle for their welfare. Eventually, of course, this became a dangerous form of egocentricity in which many kinds of brutality were performed from love of The People. As Mao rejected one earthly pleasure after another until he was almost inhumanly austere, his great passion for The People allowed him to obey his own emotions with clear conscience. These included resentments left over from childhood. Whereas the Colonel McCormicks of our own world could use weapons like the *Chicago Tribune* to take revenge on British public-school mates, Mao was to employ the world's greatest force of peasants to overthrow the causes of his own early tribulations.

Mao conducted his self-education program sitting in the provincial library all day and fortified by a noon meal of two rice cakes. He read widely and his half-formed ideas were stimulated by materialists and sociologists like Benjamin Kidd, whose words stuck in his mind: "There must be sacrifice of the individual for society, of the present for the future."

His mind ranged over the knowledge he was imbibing piecemeal while he stalked around the countryside, exposing his body to hardship. He managed another six years of college before going to Peking National University library as an inconspicuous librarian. There he lived as a most unusual bookworm in an age of revolt against formal education. A new

republic had been set up by Dr. Sun Yat-sen. His organization of secret societies, the T'ung-meng-hui, introduced the
first experiment in parliamentary procedure ever attempted in
China, and later became the Kuomintang.

Sun had little faith in parliaments. He resigned from the
presidency in favor of the former viceroy Yüan Shih-kai. Yüan
died in 1916 and China was allowed to slip back into chaos.

During this period, young China was breaking with the past.
We read of intellectual ferment. It is emphasized today that
the leaders of Red China spent all their formative years in this
era of discontent. Western influence had shattered the old
arrogant conviction that China was the center of the universe,
surrounded by barbarians. Writers were dimly aware that
their nation had been frozen into the immobility of a 2000-
year-old Chinese ideograph. They rebelled against the Confucian belief that this society had been at its most perfect all
those years ago. Confucians wanted to march solemnly backwards into that golden age recorded on the oracle bones and
parchments of 1500 B.C. But the rebels blamed most of their
national woes on the fact that you could still read those oracle
bones. China, they argued, had become just as immutable as
that ancient script and they were prepared to throw away a
written language which symbolized their lack of progress.

By the time young Mao was rustling among the dried papers
behind Peking's library walls, there was popular irritation with
this classical language and resentment against an examination
system which barred poor people from official posts. Dissatis-
faction mounted until on May 4, 1919, the students of Peking
rioted.

This incident began as a protest against a further Chinese surrender to Japanese demands which were becoming increasingly
arrogant. It was basically a revolution against orthodoxy and
it was the first occasion when there was an open expression of
Chinese public opinion. Students all over the country joined
the demand for a new language. Their desires were summed
up by one of the leaders: "They want a literature written in
the living tongue of a living people and capable of expressing

the real feelings, thoughts, inspirations and aspirations of a growing nation . . . in the new world and its new civilization."

Where was Mao during this ferment? Tucked in dusty archives or manning the ramparts? Nobody quite knows except that his ideas had already hardened. By 1920 he called himself a Marxist. From that time on, his views were colored by Communist doctrine. The man who fought alone against orthodoxy was to join those who found pat solutions in orthodox Marxist theory. Mao made a youthful vow that China should stand proudly above her restored empire, but now he moved toward Russian tutelage. This self-made scholar rejected examinations which had to be written in the Confucian "eight-legged style" where form was more important than content: and yet now he prepared for the Communist recitative. His companions were Comintern agents whose dogma was more tyrannical than any he had abandoned.

It would have been difficult then, and it is still difficult now, to suppose this ardent nationalist would stumble blindly in Stalin's footsteps or those of any other foreign arch-priest. But Mao had no personal experience of Western society. His knowledge was limited, and based on observation of the selfish lives led by wealthy traders living in China's foreign enclaves. His glib concepts of Anglo-American motives in Asia came from the polluted sources of Moscow's information services. His emotional rejection of Western interference in Chinese affairs sprang from deeper roots of nationalism.

His association with the Comintern began in times of upheaval. He was, by his own evidence, resentful that China had lost her vassals. His education was so erratic that he knew little about the great changes in the British Empire after the turn of the century and could not believe an imperialist nation might voluntarily assist its own colonies to independence. His mind was fixed upon internal troubles. Warlords ruled. Thousands of peasants were dying in small battles or from the pestilence and flood which was widespread. In Treaty Ports where foreign governments maneuvered their favorite warlords in a bigger game of power politics, resentment

mounted against the West. Small indignities, pinpricks of foreign prejudice against the Chinese were to become a flimsy
foundation on which both Nationalist and Communist leaders
were to build a new chauvinism.

The men who were to canalize this antagonism and utilize
its energy in "Hate America" and similar campaigns met secretly in the French quarter of Shanghai in July 1921. It was
the first session of the Chinese Communist Party.

While Mao conspired, Sun Yat-sen perspired in Canton
where his Kuomintang hung on by fingertips to Southwest
China. Odd improvisations on Western democracy were being
circulated by Sun. His idea of true equality was that men should
take the official appointments to which they were equal. He
criticized the West for failing to practice this equality and he
seems to have believed some men to be more equal than others,
so that it was the most equal ones who should take supreme
command of the nation. To clarify this point, he divided society into three groups: "discoverers, promoters and practical men." He thought China should be ruled by "discoverers"
who had vision and foresight to guide the "promoters" or
managers who would direct operations among "practical men."
What he proposed was almost a combination of Communist
and Confucian ideas.

So it seems that even Sun, who was not handicapped like Mao
by the pressure of Comintern influence, still could find little
virtue in Western social systems. He was an intelligent Chinese of the period, free to roam the world looking for answers
to China's problems. He was not tied to sinister foreign advisers. In the end, with all these advantages, what he left was
the *Three Principles of the People* when he died in 1925.
It was a curious legacy of authoritarian concepts purporting
to represent a "New Discovery" in political theory.

This is not an attempt to trace China's history in this century
but only to show some of the conditions from which Mao drew
inspiration. Sun's discoverers have become the Chinese Politburo, and his promoters in Peking today are efficient and capable men who need not be Party members if they know their
jobs. More and more in recent years we find Mao experiment-

ing within this Communist framework. For instance, in 1954, a sweeping proposal to collectivize the land was submitted by the agricultural expert, Teng Tzu-hui, whose ideas seemed much too ambitious. Mao had them investigated nevertheless, and one year later suddenly reversed agricultural policy to set in motion a colossal program which ultimately swept millions into People's communes within three years. Teng, who was a veteran Party member, was proved right. But it was also decided he had been right for the wrong reasons and he was quietly sentenced to a period of ideological reform.

This diversion indicates Mao's readiness to experiment today as much as when he first challenged Soviet doctrine. From the start he looked upon the peasantry as the mainstay of revolution. He urged the Party to exploit peasant discontent and create a rural army to seize power. The Comintern said the urban proletariat must make the revolution and that the "centers of power" were in the cities. In 1923 Mao was publicly reprimanded for deviationism. In 1927 he reported on uprisings among his Hunanese peasants and this made his deviation worse. He organized the uprisings himself but he also praised the ingenuity and high moral purpose of peasants who led the revolt, and asked: "Are we to get in front of them and lead them or criticize them behind their backs?"

Stalin had already influenced the Kuomintang (K.M.T.) under Chiang Kai-shek and he must have regarded this upstart Mao with a good deal of suspicion. The Russian dictator was badly advised. He hoped to make the Communist Party the dominant factor in the Kuomintang whose armies had been marching steadily north. He sent a fatal telegram to the Indian Comintern chief, Manabendra Nath Roy, urging measures that would result in a purge of the K.M.T. and expansion of Communist influence. Roy showed this to K.M.T. collaborators, expecting these orders to be executed. Both he and Stalin had been misled. The collaborators told Chiang, who thereupon killed every Communist he could catch.

Stalin and his sharpest agent in China were fooled for the same reason foreigners are often misled by Chinese. The K.M.T. leaders could recite Marxist scriptures just as faith-

fully as they could repeat *The Mencius Analects* or the Four
Books and Five Classics before examiners. This did not mean
they were Marxists any more than they were practitioners of
Confucian ethics of government. As a result of Stalin's mis-
judgment four hundred Communists were executed by Chiang
in Shanghai. Mao's first wife was shot. Chou En-lai, lately back
from studies in Paris, barely escaped. None of this was allowed to embitter relations with those primarily responsible
and Chou, the future Prime Minister and foreign expert,
made five subsequent journeys to Moscow.

Meanwhile Mao was organizing his peasants in what was
called the Autumn Crop Uprising. For this he was expelled
from the Politburo. He rallied a ragged army of men and hid
in the bordering Chingkan mountains. Chiang Kai-shek, having openly split with the Russians, was getting eager support
from bankers and foreigners who were belatedly worried about
Stalin's interest in China. The Kuomintang was soon established throughout South China and Mao's contemptible little
band was encircled.

Another victim of the Kremlin's miscalculations joined Mao.
He was Chu Teh, former mercenary of warlords, hugely fond
of wine and opium and one-time owner of four concubines.
This giant voluptuary gave up singing bawdy songs in favor of
the "Internationale." He saw the light in Berlin, joined the
Party, assumed command of a peasant army back in China and
was promptly defeated. The trouble, he soon discovered, was
his obedience to Russian advisers who advocated the seizure
of cities first.

Chu Teh joined Mao, the renegade champion of seizing the
countryside and letting the cities wither. They are said to have
talked all night on their first meeting in 1928 and their subsequent alliance gave Mao the physical power eventually to
take full command of events. One of their early military bulletins was frank and realistic: "The masses completely failed to
understand what the Red Army was . . . We marched across
snow-covered and icy mountains closely pursued by the enemy.
We sometimes covered thirty miles a day. Our sufferings increased." Later, reporting the defeat that led to the Long March,

Mao displayed that ruthless self-criticism which carried him far beyond Stalin's lackadaisical example: "We panicked and we fought stupidly."

The Long March followed a period in which Mao ran his own Chinese Soviet Republic. It was then he is first recorded as pronouncing a significant Chinese Communist precept: "Soviet democracy has progressed far but not far enough . . . Persuasion should replace dictatorialism vis-à-vis the masses."

Mao and his military chief were joined by Chou En-lai who had finally seen the folly of blind obedience to Russian advice. These three victims of Stalin's earlier pigheadedness were forced into the grueling Long March by yet another Kremlin dictum. They were told to ignore an offer of alliance from a "People's Government," set up in coastal Fukien by rebels, which Moscow did not recognize. Thus Mao was denied an outlet to the sea and in 1934 he had to break out of Kuomintang encirclement.

Some instinct made him lead the survivors back by way of many detours to the loesslands, back to the sources of the Yellow Wind whose breath gave their ancestors birth.

The Long March took more than a year, covered six thousand miles of rugged terrain, including eighteen high mountain ranges, and it cost Mao the lives of his second wife and seventy thousand men out of the original ninety thousand who escaped. It was an epic of which the Chinese were justifiably proud. They went first to the southwest and then northward along the Tibetan borderlands, finally setting up headquarters at Yenan in Shansi province. Mao's enemies found it hard to intercept him because he never betrayed his objective and was prepared to sacrifice a great deal rather than panic into hasty actions. The dogged, slow and determined progress of his Long March with all its diversions was a pattern followed many times in handling domestic and foreign problems.

Echoes of the Long March are often heard now in public speeches. There was, for instance, the ordeal of the Great Snow Mountain and the poisonous grasslands. Starving columns of Red Army troops marched across a foggy plain of

yellow grass and their legs swelled with strange red blisters.
It was deathly cold at night. Yet Chu Teh risked these horrors to make three crossings in search of lost columns of men.
For such veterans Mao Tse-tung spoke a special language when
in 1957 he told his followers not to fear "poisonous grass."
He was urging reluctant Red Army leaders to accept a relaxation of control over intellectuals. He meant them to go forward firm in the Party faith, to wrestle with alien thoughts
turned up in a new national self-analysis campaign.

There is a picture of Mao in the Yenan days sitting in a yellow cave, smoking his home-grown tobacco, reading a dog-
eared copy of the Chinese classics and clothed in tattered blue
tunic. He seems to be in hibernation, a sample of his species,
preserved in the yellow dust from which his people sprang
and waiting to be called forth as China's father figure.

"Since 1935, the Chinese Communists have received no assistance or advice from the Comintern," declared Mao in 1943.
If this was the case, Party documents of the period reveal
an astonishing capacity for not only questioning Soviet
Russian techniques but for expanding boldly upon some. Leaders
repeatedly affirmed the inevitability of Communist society and
they called insistently for a subordination of all human traits, individual impulses and personal idiosyncrasies to a gigantic mass
will.

There was every reason to emphasize their independence
though. A popular novel then, as indeed it is now, *Mr.
Decadent: Notes on a Journey,* gives an insight into the Chinese prejudice against foreign ideas. It is an allegorical tale
in which a boat is threatened with total destruction. Mr.
Decadent could cure boils for an almost incurable character,
Huang. When Mr. Decadent ventured to sea he came across
a boat in danger of being wrecked and offered help. He had
with him a compass and measuring instruments. Suddenly the
sailors cried: "He must be a foreign devil to possess foreign
instruments. Kill him before he takes over our boat." Passengers and crew were worked up into a frenzy against Mr.
Decadent and threw him overboard, shouting "Kill him! Kill
him!"

The boat was a symbol of China, endangered by the refusal of her people to understand or utilize foreign methods. The character Huang was the Yellow River which erupted so often that it was almost impossible to patch it up.

Mao used such tales to good effect. He wrote in colorful contrast to men like Chen Yun who talked in sepulchral tones of a Party formed in the image of "a living church incarnating the historic will." Around him the theoreticians analyzed conditions which might lead to a unanimous and energetic society. Mao drew *his* inspiration from earlier guerrilla campaigns and classic Chinese tales.

He was more of a personal hero to his men. "Mao Tse-tung's revolutionary theories, derived from reality, are tested against and developed under the impact of reality," wrote a major theorist, Chang Ju-hsin. He lectured on "Mao Tse-tung's Scientific Foresight" and "Mao Tse-tung's View on the Integration of Theory and Reality."

Mao was in a fair way to inherit the Mandate of Heaven. Not even Japan's attack at the Marco Polo Bridge in 1937 disturbed his sense of destiny. Any Russian who read his *New Democracy* of that time must have wondered at his simplifications which, to a Chinese scholar, were full of allegory. Any Russian would have wondered even more about his advice on the absorption of foreign influence which he compared to food "first chewed, introduced into the stomach, digested and separated into essence and residue so the essence becomes our nourishment and the residue be rejected."

Even as Mao disclaimed Comintern aid, Stalin sent along a faithful watchdog to become secretary of the Consultative Committee secretariat of the Chinese Communist Party and vice-chairman of the Military Council.

He was another Hunanese, the cold and humorless theoretician, Liu Shao-chi, who had been under direct Russian influence since 1920. A dedicated man of immense self-discipline, he was left behind by the Long Marchers on Comintern advice to organize underground groups. Liu is said to have criticized Russia for not understanding China, although rumored to be leader of the Russian clique. Some consider that he maneuvered Mao in accordance with Kremlin wishes but, until Stalin's death, he seems to have been used more as a channel of communication to Mao than as the string that pulled a puppet. When he joined Mao in Yenan he had been twice already to study in Moscow.

His ally was a secret-police expert, Kang Sheng. For five crucial years before Japan's undeclared war began, Kang was studying security methods in Moscow. He took over Party Intelligence work and possibly counterespionage on reaching Mao's headquarters. He has always been a mysterious and unknown factor on the Politburo.

It would be tedious to trace Mao's World War II history. As late as 1945, Stalin was saying with every appearance of sincerity (according to Harry Hopkins in his diary): "We do not regard the Chinese Communist Party as a serious factor. We recognize only Chiang Kai-shek."

Stalin's biggest mistake, perhaps, was to let the Chinese discover that when neglected and alone they could triumph over seemingly impossible odds. From this they deduced that their Party could add considerably to Marxist-Leninist theory. This is sometimes called Mao-ism by outsiders, but the chances are that in the innermost corner of the Party mind it is regarded as Chinese-ism. Mao was simply the instrument by which the wisdom of four thousand years was used to enrich the foreign philosophy called Communism.

Given time, one wonders if Chinese Communism will become so heavily freighted with old national sayings, bits of folklore and the wisdom of ancient sages that the Russians may be persuaded that it is they who have enriched a foreign ideology called Confucianism.

Certainly it is the Chinese technique for making revolutions in underdeveloped countries which prevails today. The peasantry, they insisted, were like a mighty ocean: "And we are the fish who, so long as we can swim in that sea, shall survive."

Mao called his ragged Red Army "a furnace in which all prisoners are melted down and transformed." He made some fascinating adaptations from old Chinese military stratagems and his mind dwelled on methods for overcoming both internal and external enemies. He listed five types of conspirator: the local informer, the inside agent, the "reversible" spy, the unconscious carrier of information and the daring and imaginative lone wolf. His advice on spying was taken from Sun-tzu's tactics twenty-five hundred years earlier during the Spring and Autumn Dynasties. So too was a masterly condensation by Mao of guerrilla philosophy:

> Enemy advances: we retreat.
> Enemy escapes: we harass.
> Enemy retreats: we pursue.
> Enemy tires: we attack.

Thus Mao used much of his time extracting what he considered most adaptable from the history of China's feudal empires which he said "created such brilliant cultures in ancient times." He wrote poetry too, but although this is often quoted to prove his sensibility, the plain fact is that Chinese poetry can be put together rather as you assemble a jigsaw puzzle or knit a scarf. It can be compared to Winston Churchill writing in the style and idiom of Chaucer and has little to do with creative art.

Far more important was the acquisition during this period of formidable skill in applied psychology. The Yenan rebels found they could get predetermined reactions to slogans and phrases beyond anything known to Russia. They cross-indexed the minds of peasants until they had what amounted to an ideograph for all the commoner thoughts and impulses. They used an old harvest song, the *yang-k'o,* to plant ideas among the masses.

Mao's use of the dance was brilliant. In it, you took two steps forward and one back. Progress was slow but inevitable. It became the pattern of Mao's war against the Kuomintang, against tribes that obstructed his Long March and against internal and external enemies of the Republic. You advanced one step too far and then retreated if faced with any opposition. Miraculously and to everyone's bewilderment, you were still one step ahead.

CHAPTER FOUR

Bloodless Victors on the Red Burma Road

◉   ◉

The truly great General will serve his Emperor best by mastering the art of conquering hostile territory without bloodshed, of capturing cities without entering them and of vanquishing the enemy without giving battle.

Sun-tzu, often quoted by Mao Tse-tung as greatest of Chinese military strategists, writing 2500 years ago in *Ping Fa, The Art of War.*

On the morning of December 14, 1956, a curious company assembled above the narrow gorges of the Mekong where it plunges down through Southwest China after a brief flirtation with three other mighty Asian rivers. Northward rose the mountains of Tibet whose melting snows also fed the Brahmaputra, the Salween and the Yangtse-kiang. Only the last of these seemed to win approval from leaders of our party, for they were Chinese Communists whose armies were using sandbags now instead of rifles as they wrestled with the Yangtse as if it might be the last enemy. True, by virtue of their grip on Tibet, they controlled the headwaters of the other rivers. Yet one felt they resented the escape of the Brahmaputra down to the Bay of Bengal where its power was allowed to dissipate by the shiftless rulers of India and Pakistan. As for the Salween, there were plans for its use once the Burmese people allowed themselves to be saved from Western imperialism.

The Mekong? Well, today it divided Thailand and Indo-china but I had seen what arrangements were being made by Chinese evangelists to liberate and unite the peoples of those poor, benighted lands.

Beside me loomed Chen Hui, a burly young zealot from the Peking Foreign Office whose mind worked like a calculating machine when the drinking was heaviest. He was reading a book and sometimes he recited passages to Michael Tomagat-ski, a deceptively cherubic Russian with steely blue eyes be-hind rimless spectacles. The only home Tomagatski had known was a Ukrainian orphanage: his tutor was the Soviet State. Now, at thirty-two, he had a wife and three children and a comfortably important post as *Pravda's* correspondent in China. He liked to sit up until dawn writing notes by candle-light.

We were traveling down the Burma Road in a convoy of worn American cars. The border was still nearly two hundred miles away but already the signs of activity were prodigious. From the hillsides poured straggling lines of coolies with loads on their backs. Each carried five to a dozen baskets and each long, narrow wicker basket held about eighteen pounds of provisions. Hungarian diesel trucks flew past with fuel drums bulging their canvas sides. Bandsmen of the Thirteenth and Fourteenth Armies of the Chinese People's Liberation Fourth Army jumped from two Molotov trucks parking beside us.

The troops in flat caps and chin straps were young and painfully smart. They carried starched white gloves in their tunic belts and disappeared soundlessly into a wayside inn.

We followed. The wooden hostelry leaned on three sides of a courtyard. From the kitchens on one side ran dungareed, pigtailed girls with bowls of rice for our drivers, who were rubbing the dust and grime from their antiquated but efficient Chevrolets. There was steamed Kunming chicken for the Army elite. They squatted on the cool earthen floor of what had once been a restaurant for wartime drivers hauling supplies from Burma.

For us, the disused stables. The floor was thickly carpeted in pine needles brought by wrinkled old women. Along the road

ahead moved more of these human carriers, like hobgoblins
under their burdens of pine branches. Sometimes the bushes
and trees that lurched along the horizon concealed soldiers in
sand-gray overalls, the fifth man in each group bulging with a
bandolier of rice.

More people joined our round table. There was Martin
Doering, limping heavily from injuries in a World War I air
crash. He had been cook in a Nazi concentration camp for
six years, chief economic adviser (he explained) to the Communist East German regime, and now he prowled about China
with a journalistic notebook stuffed full of curiously unjour-
nalistic statistics.

With him came Lushiya Duheroff from East German Radio,
hating the presence of a Western stranger. She sat as far from
me as possible, beating the dust from her trousers and plant-
ing her booted feet firm and square among the pine needles.
Our relations had been unfortunate from the start. There
were tense moments during interviews when she tried to frustrate my questions, perhaps too pointed for her taste, but
seldom an embarrassment to the Chinese who brushed aside
her objections and answered with aplomb and what seemed
to be accuracy.

The slender, courteous figure of Li Phu-how moved into
place beside me. He alone was close to home. French-educated,
sick from malaria contracted in the jungle swamps of North
Indochina, he had retreated with the Communist Vietminh
guerrillas and seen them gather strength across the border from
China before advancing in triumph to capture his town of
Hanoi. Now the French were gone forever from Indochina
and Hanoi was capital of the Communist north. Li's reward
was faithfully to transmit official communiqués from Peking to
his Government's news-agency. He had been separated from
his wife for years at a stretch during the fighting. Today they
had a child and a small dormitory-home in Peking. Why, then,
did he seem disillusioned and unhappy when he talked softly
with me in English and French, sometimes switching to mandarin for the benefit of a Chinese comrade?

We dipped our lacquered chopsticks (chewed at the ends

like schoolboys' pencils) into a bowl of *chieh-tsai,* a sort of cabbage unknown in the West. There was a clay pot of fish heads, fried rice and pork in thick sirup. Only Dinu Hervian of the Rumanian News Agency abstained. He suffered from ulcers and a general reluctance about living in China.

"My domestic life is confined to a glorified dormitory," he told me once. "My boy is already ten years old. He cannot make friends in a hotel. He does not speak any language understood by other boys. My wife teaches him. It is a lonely life." He sighed.

The last of our party resembled in almost all particulars a Chicago gangster of the mid-twenties. His square jaw and hard eyes were just visible beneath a broad-brimmed fedora. His fists were jammed deep in the pockets of an ankle-length overcoat and occasionally he withdrew one hand to flash a camera that seemed most frequently to be pointing at me. He was Chiang Shiang-wsi, former North Korean Army colonel who now packed a Soviet Kiev 35-mm. instead of a pistol. Unlike Comrade Hervian, he was delighted with the vagaries of life in Peking.

"Many times I go to Peking opera," said this Korean caricature of Al Capone. "I like it very much. But in all theaters there are toilets for Chinese men, toilets for Chinese women and toilets for 'Foreign friends.' The comrade on duty always pushes me from 'Foreign friends' to the Chinese men. He insists I am just another Chinese." He slapped his thigh and roared with laughter.

Such were my companions on this brilliant December day in Yunnan. There were two others. One, a Russian-speaking interpreter, would have preferred a theatrical career and used breaks in our journey to demonstrate the extraordinarily complicated movements by which the Monkey God stole peaches from the King of Heaven in the acrobatic opera currently playing near the Peking Thieves' Market.

Also outside, but with his head buried in a book of poetry, was Choirboy Ma. His ambition was to become Ambassador to Washington for the People's Republic of China. Young, gifted, he was a curious blend of Old World Chinese courtesy

and lively inquisitiveness. He was just back from Tibet and
thought it would be indeed the ideal launching site for the
first space ships.

Inside the stable was a mixed aroma of forest smells, cow
dung and sickly-sweet Yunnanese brandy made (so it said on
the bottle) from rose petals. Our conversation with Chen
snagged on a thorny issue uppermost in the minds of con-
scientious cadres. As he expounded the problem of "subjectivism and objectivism" his voice for once had lost its usual
detachment.

I said: "Wasn't it Mao Tse-tung who wrote: 'Cow dung is
more useful than dogma — it can be used for fertilizer'?"

Chen hesitated but was not to be diverted from his theme.
His face assumed the kindly mask of a divinity student.

"And so you see," he said, "subjective analysis of a political
situation and subjective guidance of work inevitably result in
either opportunism or adventurism. Let us take a case in point.
A certain leading cadre in a fisheries collective ordered a production team to build him a big net to stretch right across the
river. He was guilty of subjectivism. He thought he could
catch all the fish in the river at one time. Had he understood
the correct policy of objectivism he would have known the net
could not be built. Of course other cadres were at fault in not
exposing bureaucratic elements guilty of commandism . . ."

"Well, wait a minute," I interrupted. "Why couldn't the net
be built?"

"Because it would have weighed five hundred tons," said
Chen, momentarily down to earth.

"Then why do you employ jargon to conceal plain common
sense?"

Madame Duheroff shifted her boots and spoke sharply in
German to Doering who lifted the rose-petal brandy and
asked with ill-received levity: "When is a bottle not a bottle?
That is dialectical materialism too."

Choirboy Ma came in singing some lines from *Carmen*.
Chen's face softened as he stood up and rested a paternal hand
on his junior's shoulder.

"Then shall we go?" he said, and there was no one who
mistook his command for a question.

The road was churned into red mud in the lower valleys. As we climbed each mountain range, it looped first through pine forests and then swerved into dense bush that gradually decayed until there was nothing but stony highway flanked by boulders and barren moor. Sometimes we crawled along snow-flecked ridges and talked about fishing in the jade-green rivers far below. Then down we plunged, feeling the air grow warmer until we were back again among the papayas and mud-walled villages with tropical cacti sprouting from their glazed-tile roofs.

Choirboy Ma was jammed between the Germans, who kept up an incessant jabber into a wire recorder. The car slithered and swung like a big-dipper. Doering noted the neat little survey teams posting their red flags along a projected railroad from Kunming to Rangoon and duly barked details into his microphone. Ma kept his eyes glued to the cheap booklet dancing between his hands.

"It's a poem about a princess who lived here centuries ago," he explained.

"She fell in love with a common woodsman. The king intervened and she ran away with her love into these mountains. The king employed a priest of magic who killed the woodsman. The princess died of grief. Her body turned into a cloud and you can see it sometimes floating above the peaks in search of her lost mate."

Chen's book was twenty-five hundred years old. It was called *Ping Fa, The Art of War by Sun-tzu,* so greatly admired by Mao Tse-tung, no mean expert at the game himself.

I was puzzled, as much by Chen as by Mao and the Chinese folklore on which the ruler of China draws so heavily. You read Sun-tzu and think you are listening to Mao: "If there is dissension in the enemy camp, profit by it to rally the discontented to your cause . . . Treat your prisoners well . . . Supply and arm yourself at the expense of the enemy."

Mao Tse-tung says: "Rely on the war industries of the imperialist countries and of our enemy at home. We have a claim on the arsenals of London as well as on our own."

Mao, I reflected, showed unmistakable reverence for dead Chinese heroes and philosophers. He was twenty-six when he began to travel the hard revolutionary road that led to power in Peking and the mock-modest role of overalled emperor of the largest nation on earth. As librarian in Peking National University in 1919 he met Chen Tu-hsiu, then unacknowledged leader of Chinese Communists. Chen was professor of literature, Mao a clever young peasant from South China. Eight years later it was Mao, steeped in Chinese classics and determined to preserve his peasant outlook, who proclaimed: "Several hundred million peasants will rise like a tornado of tempest, a force so extraordinarily swift and violent that no power, however great, will be able to suppress it."

Mao was dismissed from the Politburo and repudiated by the Communist Party Front Committee for such heresy. A decade later, when Mao was in control as Party Chairman, Stalin was obliged to confess: "The special feature of the Chinese revolution is the revolt of the armed masses against the armed reactionaries."

It was a small prize, perhaps, for Mao's careful policy of offering Stalin no offense. It is, however, odd that, until Stalin made this concession, he was almost totally ignored by Chinese Communist propaganda. Instead, Mao adapted Marx and Lenin to China, set the revolution against the immense pageantry of Chinese history and sprinkled his works with earthy Chinese proverbs, quoting from popular legends and lecturing on the need to invent slogans whose graceful characters would not only sound but *look* good.

It was odd to think that China's claim to being a great power depended utterly on Russia to provide the guns, tanks, planes, gasoline and industrial ability. Yet it seemed also true that the Soviet Union found itself unable to proceed without the close co-operation of China. Even now, Premier Chou En-lai was sent to Moscow and East Europe to reassure the satellites after the Hungarian uprising. And that revolt, together with a climactic disturbance in Poland, followed the historic 1956 Eighth Party Congress of the Chinese Communist Party at which a well-known European Communist had told me: "What's happening here is going to put Europe on its ear."

Was China, then, an enormous tail to wag the Russian dog? And was the Communist cant and jargon only a formula by which Chinese executives in Peking might pursue their own objectives?

These were weighty thoughts and I dozed. Suddenly the car screeched down to bottom gear. Two stocky riflemen stood guard on a swaying suspension bridge. Grenades swung from their hips and red stars flashed in the sunlight that came shafting down into the narrow gorges. We rattled over the boiling river and gathered speed again.

Only by eliminating landlords can we reform! declared the Chinese script dancing across a slab of rock.

To work is glorious . . . The words materialized out of the swirling dust . . . *To exploit is* — there was a break while we swung round another bend and the final whitewashed character appeared in solitary defiance — *wicked!*

On the roadside were ragged peasants squatting with stone and hammer over a pile of rocks. Some were children. Some were old men sucking on long-stemmed pipes. Boys split the bigger rocks with hefty chisels suspended from bow springs lashed horizontally across bamboo tripods. Each section of the Burma Road for more than five hundred and fifty miles from the Yunnanese capital of Kunming is covered by such work gangs. Each gang of "volunteers" has been drawn from the neighboring countryside and is held responsible for one hundred yards of unpaved highway.

Today the gangs were out in force, their tiny red and gold "socialist emulation" flags fluttering at each section. Again it seemed that Mao's special kind of Communism must fit China like a glove, for were these competition flags so very different from the traditional Chinese banners awarded to outstanding workers in lieu of bonuses?

Mules blocked the road ahead. The traffic was thickening. Everyone who was going anywhere was moving our way. We pulled into the ancient walled township of Paoshan as dusk concealed the muleteers whose hoarse cries continued late into the night.

There was no doubt of it. The men who ruled China were

presenting a new aspect to outsiders like myself. I strolled through the darkened streets of Paoshan. Gone were the ghoulish white effigies of Mao, gone the portraits in every shop. Two years ago I might have been followed. Now the authorities relied upon an alert citizenry to report any suspicious move. A few traders sold mandarin oranges beside smoky flares stuck in the cobblestones. Slavic music echoed through the drowsing township from loudspeakers in the army barracks on the hillside above. Somewhere a man banged angrily at his bolted door, shouting for admittance. Sewing machines whirred behind a shop's closed shutters.

There was a teahouse beside the soaring arch of the south gate. The enclosing walls, first built two thousand years ago to guard against invaders, were fifteen feet thick; under the curving roofs that rose in three tiers above the gate were the new guardians against subversive thought — sinister gray little loudspeakers.

They were silent. Instead a blind storyteller recited rhymes to the dry click of bamboo castanets. His repertoire was much the same as that of Yunnan's minstrels down through the centuries, except that it had been pruned here and there and a few items of uplift interjected. He had done a three-month course in the abandoned temple near Peking which became the State School for Minstrels. Now he stood on a table in the teahouse, singing the old tales and then, in that same ancient staccato rhythm, warning against the four evils that plague the countryside.

"Kill flies, mosquitoes, rats and sparrows," he chanted to the monotonous clack of the castanets.

Shuffling of feet and the muffled snort of mules echoed through the arch from the medieval court beyond. Women and children were assembled in disciplined ranks facing an old temple. On the steps stood a man in blue pants, fiber cape thrown over his back, holding a slate up to the light of a flaming torch.

Tiny clouds of mist issued from the distended nostrils of mules already weighted with panniers of rice bowls. Round slabs of salt lay about the yard like broken columns in a ruined

colosseum. The man with the slate gave brief, muted orders
and the lines of human carriers shambled forward to pick up
their loads.

Three days later I understood why we had hurtled so far
and so fast. Premier Chou En-lai was conducting a demonstration of brotherly love for the neighbors next door in Burma.

The marching columns of coolies and mules, trickling like
human streams down fractures in the mountains, had con-
verged into a mighty flood across the valley of Mangshih.
Where before I had seen a radio diffusion loudspeaker in
every village of more than twenty households, there were now
dozens of the little gray trumpets lashed to bamboo poles. But
the multitude gathered, split into groups, dispersed and melted
magically into the outskirts of the small, new town in complete
obedience to short blasts on the whistles of their leaders.

Chen became a changed man. We had been mildly sloshed
together on the raw grain spirit called *mao tai*. Now he assembled our party and addressed us through Choirboy Ma,
who interpreted. A few hours earlier we were shouting at
each other in English, Chen's accent betraying his American
education as the argument got hotter. Now he stared blankly
through me and waited for Ma to translate my questions.

Chou En-lai was coming up from Rangoon with the Burmese
Prime Minister, U Ba Swe. There was to be a festival of
friendship to show the wicked imperialist powers they could
not break traditional bonds between their countries.

(Five months earlier Burmese officials let it be known that
Red Chinese troops had entered Burmese territory. There
were three possible areas of Chinese penetration along the
1500-mile frontier. Later Peking admitted that troops had
trespassed there.)

Chen announced now that these troops had just completed
their withdrawal. I asked for details: where were the troops,
what units and when could we see them?

Madame Duheroff clucked angrily. "It is not necessary to
know these things."

I said the Burmese might very well like to know but the

gathering broke up hastily. Chen dropped his official pose, took me aside and promised to try to get details. But there the matter ended.

Tomagatski telephoned Moscow, no mean feat from a subtropical valley buried almost one thousand kilometers from the nearest city. His "story" was dictated, presumably to some eager cub reporter in the *Pravda* newsroom. It was identical to that sent out to Rumania, East Germany, North Korea, North Vietnam and Peking, which is to say that it was precisely as handed out by Chen. At least the communications seemed good.

I banged angrily at my own typewriter. To my astonishment, the sour phrases were faithfully transmitted by the improvised cable office set up in a Red Army truck. Since censorship is so strictly imposed in Russia and the satellites, it seems worth recording here part of the story which went out untouched by the Chinese:

> What China seeks [I cabled in part] is agreement on disputed territory occupied by her troops this summer.
>
> Burma is asked to give up part of this invaded area in return for withdrawal of 4500 Chinese troops from the wild and unwanted Wa states. This leaves China with three important villages, about 21,000 peasants and a vital pass.
>
> To many Burmese this seems a classic case of heads-I-win, tails-you-lose.
>
> But the tough-minded men who lead China today have convinced their own people this is both reasonable and fair. The new Peking policy is to settle all such problems under a mist of platitudes, by patient and unswerving discussion until everyone finally perceives the correctness of Chinese arguments . . .

In later dispatches, also untouched by any censor, the point was emphasized that there had been heavy infiltration across the Chinese border, that indoctrinated youths from Communist schools admitted they believed most territory north of Rangoon belonged to China, and that the present demonstration bore out the claim that Mao was using persuasive techniques in place of force.

That afternoon the two Premiers crossed into Red China. U Ba Swe, who later resumed his post of Burmese Defense

Minister, looked mildly startled as Chinese troops goose-stepped past him. He had temporarily replaced U Nu whom he regarded as "a good Premier for foreigners: he can translate Shakespeare into Burmese." It was U Ba Swe who organized his own Socialist Party down to primary school level in the hope of fighting the Burmese Communist Party's spreading influence among university students. He led guerrillas against Japanese forces and now believed a Buddhist revival might help Burma retain her independence.

With him was Chou En-lai, beetle-browed but also baggy-eyed after stumping around Southeast Asia and with the prospect ahead of touring East Europe to calm the satellite peoples. Behind came Madame Kung P'eng, a woman of great charm and sensibility, ingenuously listed in the Peking directory as chief of Foreign Office Intelligence.

"I read in the Cambodian newspapers that you brought your wife to Peking," she said to me in greeting. Then she turned to Chen to begin an animated discussion about their families back in Peking. They were interrupted by Chou En-lai, clutching flowers he obviously preferred to discard.

The Chinese Premier made a speech. He blamed "colonialist powers" for misunderstandings that had arisen along the border. He added: "We apologize for these poor arrangements. Please forgive us as you would forgive your brothers."

The poor arrangements were those I had seen in preparation along the only good line of communication — the Burma Road. They were also evident in the six new guest houses, three triple-story "hotels," ten dormitories and a theater. All this brick and concrete was spanking new, enough to accommodate several thousands in a forested vale of normally a few hundred folk. There were also an outdoor theater, floodlights, an industrial and trade exhibition, electric power and a sea of red banners and paper flags.

Seventeen thousand people drawn from the sparsely populated countryside slept in units under new thatched roofs on bamboo poles. On the border itself (still undefined) there were four empty oil drums to mark the Burmese post. The Chinese had built a bridge, two concrete pillboxes, a rest house, two double-story customs posts and a triumphal archway.

"Free discussion" was announced between tribal leaders from the area in dispute. The Chinese produced 130 cadres who sat down with 210 tongue-tied tribesmen from the south. The cadres talked, their guests munched Yunnanese pears.

"What were they discussing?" I asked Chen.

"How can I say? It was a private, free discussion. However, it may be noted that a broad measure of agreement was reached."

All this time the vast gathering of peasants smoothly changed gear to keep pace with events. There would be uncanny silence until a signal was given, then uproar. Early each morning they were led into the great amphitheater where they waited, subdued. Then as if seized by some irresistible, common emotion they would shout, sing, beat drums and leap in the air with joy at the entry of Chou.

Or if it was U Ba Swe to whom attention was focused by some unseen master of ceremonies, cries of friendship for Burma reverberated through the banyan trees and sent parakeets screeching into the distant rain forest.

Once I watched twenty extremely pretty girls waiting with the folk dancers, singers and actresses. The girls wore costumes of their own tribes: Tibetans in rainbow-striped aprons, Flowered Miaos sheathed in robes, willowy T'ais and stocky Chin-Paos. Their faces lacked animation until without warning they screeched with excitement, eyes flashing, and ran pell-mell across the ground to pelt flowers at a wooden platform.

The platform, however, was empty. The girls were rehearsing their enthusiasm. They retrieved the flowers and walked back to their places, watched by their director with a whistle in his hand.

Sometimes the whistles blew. Sometimes the loudspeakers blared. There were no armed, uniformed police. One child in a group of ten seemed able to command utter obedience. It was very nearly like a mass demonstration of telepathy.

Yet this was not some blunt monster of uncounted heads. These were peasants drawn from a wide area, only ten years ago so backward that each community kept to itself while bandits preyed on all. These were people of whom it was still being said by the old China hands: "Communism can't touch 'em, they're too individualistic. China will absorb Communism as it absorbs everything."

Whatever it was these people *had* absorbed, they were also now a part of it. For every ten bovine faces, there was one leader to drive them on. I watched these lean, dynamic leaders urging their legions into a final frenzy when the last dawn broke and U Ba Swe and his thoughtful aides started home down that part of the Burma Road which is still Burmese. All night there had been the crash of drums, impassive faces passing under the glare of red lanterns to the high-pitched chants of children.

Ahead for the Burmese Premier were a hundred and twenty miles of hard driving through empty countryside. It was easy to envy the tranquillity of his small nation, to reckon his eighteen million people untouchable. One was tempted to ridicule events in the valley: the expenditure of time, energy and money on the paper paraphernalia. Here, to promote the impression of prosperity, Chinese stalls had been erected and freighted with small consumer goods but behind the façade was harsh self-discipline and common hardship.

By any normal reasoning my companions at least should have found cause for cynicism. Instead they were shopping. Tomagatski with a novel by Bret Harte under his arm was buying a rusting can of imitation English tobacco, salvaged like much else from World War II stocks. Li had a tin of Australian powdered milk for his baby daughter. Herweyen wondered if he could get a Japanese camera. Chiang had some old American razor blades.

Only Chen,* perhaps because he alone was Chinese, bought a cigarette lighter made in Shanghai. "They're not very good," he said apologetically. "But at least we did make them ourselves."

---

* Chen "volunteered" less than one year later to work on a collective farm. It was a time of mass migrations to bleak areas of China requiring colonization: a time of large-scale transfers to rural work of young government officials whose dialectic fervor had been softened by privilege. A mutual acquaintance saw Chen on the day of his departure and commiserated with him. Chen drew himself up: "I welcome this opportunity," he said, "of improving my experience and rectifying my work style."

CHAPTER FIVE

A New Cult in the Wilderness

◉ ◉

Less than five per cent of the people in China occupy more than half our territory. They are National Minorities, tribesmen once regarded as not part of the Chinese race. We must convert them and convince them they are Chinese.

MAO TSE-TUNG ADDRESSING A SECRET SESSION OF THE SUPREME STATE COUNCIL IN 1957, QUOTED BY POLISH COMMUNISTS.

FROM THE EDGE of the wilderness a frontier crisis was visible, laid out like a surgeon's chart and misleadingly simple. We were on a mountain chain that stretched from East Tibet to Malaya and Java. Behind were the high mountains, in front were the peaks and hills sinking to a distant ocean. Around us lived a tangle of humanity, head-hunters and Mongoloid tribes and the princely Shans, over whose bodies the emperors of China and the kings of Burma had fought for a thousand years.

The kings and emperors were gone and where I stood was a whitewashed hut that looked like a public lavatory, but was in fact Culture Station Number 7 of the Chinese People's Republic. Far below us were massive stone gates raised six hundred years ago to guard China's trade routes, and near them trickled a tributary of the Irrawaddy. Burrowing under the green matting of jungle, then swiftly crossing the open end of a valley, the dusty brown track known for centuries as "Ambassador's

Road" was a solitary reminder that royal envoys had scurried back and forth bearing gifts, slaves, concubines and protestations of everlasting friendship while armies prepared their invasions.

The culture station was, in its way, a little white monument to a new dynasty where reason reigned. It marked a new Chinese approach to the question of who owned these surrounding mountains and sometimes sinister valleys: the Land of the Coffin Tree.

At some future date, I was by now assured, the Chinese would actively assert that these 77,000 square miles of rugged territory forming a triangle between India, Tibet and China belonged to The People: that is, to the Ka Was, the feudalistic Shans and the soldierly Kachins. The Chinese would be so determined upon this point that they would bravely risk armed resistance by Burmese "imperialist lackeys" to answer any appeal from The People.

The culture station, in a grove below the thatched village of San Tai Shan, was arousing these tribes to the need for "liberation." In any other language, it would be called a center of subversive activity. But the men with me believed with utter faith that they were spearheads of a glorious crusade to enlighten their brothers in Burma. They were wrestling with the enemies of sin, poverty, illiteracy and political ignorance among the thousands of migratory peoples who had squeezed into the formidable nooks and crannies of this high country.

The sun glittered on the wire-rimmed spectacles of Si La San, former Christian missionary in Burma, member of a leading Kachin family. Comrade Si's task, he explained to me without embarrassment, was to unite and "liberate" his people — 300,000 Kachins in Northern Burma and 74,000 Chingpos (the Chinese name for the same people) in China.

My Communist companions cross-examined him in the usual inhibited way. Choirboy Ma made sure I missed nothing. I left the trickier questions to Tomagatski, the Russian who scribbled his cyrillics at splendid speed into a red notebook decorated with yellow stars. Yet there were times when my Communist companions, from a sense of delicacy, did not press

their inquiries quite as far as a blunt and insensitive representative of the capitalist press would like. Then, to the credit
of the Chinese, my crude and clumsy curiosity was received
with courtesy and polite, if not always relevant replies.

Comrade Si had been a Sunday School teacher for American
Baptist missionaries at Bhamo, a small town associated by the
Burmese with several defeats inflicted upon invading Chinese
armies. Bhamo is the southern end of "Ambassador's Road"
which winds up to Tengyueh in Yunnan and the Chinese
associate it with an embarrassing incident following one of
these military repulsions. A Burmese king demanded a daughter of the Emperor of China for his harem.

The way the Chinese tell the story, a local prostitute was
accordingly camouflaged as an imperial princess and the ignorant savage, King Hsinbyushin, was delighted by the painted
and powdered impostor. This twist to history saved Chinese
face by demonstrating their superior cleverness, but quite evidently it did not impress Comrade Si.

"I went to Bhamo as a boy," he said. "I always thought it
was a part of China. I joined this missionary church when I
was twelve but everything it taught was meant to serve American purposes. By the time I was twenty-four, I had become
leader of the League for Unity and Liberty of the Kachins. I
was asked to go back into what was called China at that time,
in 1947, to help organize our people and to teach them."

"You could cross the border freely?" I asked.

Devoutly, Madame Duheroff said: "Nobody knows where
the border has ever been. *That* is what we dispute." There was
a brief silence.

Comrade Si, with shining salvationist honesty, resumed:
"Yes, we could cross the border quite freely. But it was an
arbitrary border drawn by the British without regard to the
distribution of our tribes."

"Premier Chou En-lai just described to us how the British
spread such discord and disorder along this border that it had
to be closed!" I exploded.

"That is so," replied Comrade Si without a blush.

He peered shortsightedly at his notes again. "Ah, hmmm.
Yes, I was a mountain official, a member of one of the five fami-

lies who became leaders of the five major tribes of Kachins. Our people were Mongolian and we had a written language when our great southward treks began, long ago. But everything was written on hides and sheepskins and these we burned as we climbed over the high mountain passes. Thus we destroyed our historical documents all those centuries ago."

His people had been a turbulent, energetic race. Their villages still clustered in groups of twenty to one hundred around a *duwa* who, like a medieval English manorial lord, might ask for their services in harvesting or housebuilding. Kachins controlled the jade mines, trafficked in slaves from Assam and levied road tolls from caravans. Like the Lahu and Wa tribes, they kept to the high land while the Shans (or T'ais) lived in the valleys. The Shans have been divided for centuries into baronial estates into which the Kachins infiltrated.

"The Chinese — that is, the Han peoples, for of course we are all *Chinese* — the Hans oppressed the Shans and in turn the Shans oppressed us," said Comrade Si. "We were called *yeh-jen*, the savages, by Hans and we in turn used that name against other tribes.

"Our backwardness in recent years was the result of colonial oppression. The British kept us in poverty and made our young men fight in their armies. My movement for freedom and unity will help put an end to colonial evil everywhere."

I asked: "Are you still chairman of the League?"

Comrade Si nodded and Madame Duheroff said, with a significant look in my direction: "But only in China."

"Is that a statement or a question?" I asked her.

She tossed her head. "I meant that naturally the League would only operate in China since what goes on in Burma is Burma's own responsibility."

I said: "If your movement exists only in China now, its purpose must be to put an end to Chinese colonial oppression?"

There was much sucking of teeth at this one. Then Comrade Si explained: "We are still in process of transformation to Communism. All people in China will go over to Communism and my movement assists in the process of direct transition for my people."

"Are your Kachins in Burma transforming to Communism?"

Choirboy Ma interrupted with a charming but fleeting smile: "That is a matter for the Burmese Government to decide."

"Yes, but *are* they?" I persisted.

Comrade Si ignored the warning looks. "I believe they desire to go over to Communism."

"On what do you base this belief?"

"I heard this from some of the Kachin representatives who came here from Burma," he replied. "They confessed they admired our progress here in China. In fact, the Kachins in Burma have had better living conditions than ours here. But the speed of progress in China is higher."

"Who were these Kachin visitors?"

"Old friends, relatives, and former schoolmates," said Comrade Si. "The former Kachin State Minister in the Union of Burma, Duwa Zau Lawn, was once my headmaster. Then the present State Minister, U Zanhta Sin, went to school with me. The financial and state secretaries of Kachin State are old friends and also in the party were brothers. Some of them continued farther into China, to Peking and Shanghai, and they reported a very good impression of what they have seen."

I asked after the famous Kachin mutineer, Naw Seng. There was an appalled silence. Then and later, I tried in vain to get even an acknowledgment of his existence. "General" Naw Seng has the distinction of having been a rifleman and a lieutenant in the service of King George VI, a captain in the Burmese Army and a colonel of the Chinese People's Liberation Army.

Naw Seng is one of several Asian figures who are accused of being Communists because they were associated with uprisings against established authority and later fled to China. It might be more accurate to say they became converted to Chinese ideas *after* their escapes to Peking. Among them is Pridi Phanom-yong, the Thai rebel, who has been living in Canton at Chinese expense and of course there is Dr. K. I. Singh whose revolt in the Himalayan kingdom of Nepal was defeated with Indian help. Dr. Singh has been admitted back into Nepal where he is again politically active after a lengthy exile in Peking. There he enjoyed Chinese hospitality for which one presumes there will be repayment some day.

These are names to catch the eye. But there are thousands

of obscure young men and women from Thailand, Burma, Nepal and other neighbors of China, whose sojourns in Communist training schools are worthy of closer interest. Culture Station Number 7 is only one of hundreds along the 1500-mile Sino-Burmese border. Its purpose is threefold: to indoctrinate the youngsters of surrounding tribes or villages and slowly incorporate their territory into doctrinaire schemes to increase food production; to select tribal leaders whose authority can be gently undermined and at the same time send to district "National Minority Institutes" those youngsters capable of conversion into Communist cadres; and finally, to spread the news of China's superior system throughout adjoining territories.

This is *my* interpretation of what I saw and heard. The Chinese who explained these things would be horrified to hear themselves accused. They were dedicated to tasks they were persuaded to regard as conceived by themselves. Their leaders took the precaution of explaining to each that his job was a glorious duty to The People, innocent of any sinister motive.

"Feel your way and when you come against anything hard, draw back," were the instructions given to the British Commissioner to Burma in 1887, Sir Charles Crosthwaite.

Precisely the same method is practiced by the Chinese on Burma's borders in the middle of the twentieth century. The words, in fact, serve as a guide to Peking's policy toward all difficult minorities, including Tibetans who at one peak in *their* expansionist period had also ruled in this same Sino-Burmese region.

Thus although Chinese Red Army troops were reported in Upper Burma in August, 1956, amid loud Western accusations that an invasion was under way, these troops had been quietly operating on what is technically Burmese soil for three years. Once discovered, they withdrew quietly. They had a sound historical precedent: in the Ming Dynasty many Shan princes were subdued and Chinese military posts were established, the soldiery being instructed to marry local women to complete the Sinification of the region.

There is not much strategic value to the Land of the Coffin Tree. The Chinese for centuries have preferred to use the straight-grained, durable and sweet-scented wood that grows

here in the manufacture of their heavy, lacquered coffins. The
planks often weigh 100 pounds and are carried over 7000-
foot passes to this day by coolies whose movements in and out
of Red China are scarcely controlled. But the new Chinese regime pursues the old pretensions of former dynasties and is
not after Upper Burma for its coffin wood. By one of those
queer tricks of history, the coffin tree is called *taiwania* because
it was first found in Taiwan or what the West calls Formosa,
another object of keen interest to the comrades.

Perhaps few places better illustrate that China's rulers are
concerned with people, not boundaries. There is no "frontier" in the usual sense. There are minority communities. They
have been committed neither to Burma nor to China. They were
victims of a great human migration which started thousands
of years ago when the Chinese, the Sons of Han, pushed down
from central Asia. Even today, the migration continues in
small ways. Nobody knows for sure, but Burmese officials guess
that in the first decade of Communist rule at least one million
people drifted out of China into their own tiny land.

One million migrants, in a nation of eighteen million. How
many hate the Chinese? How many are carriers of the gospel
from Peking? The Burmese are an easygoing people. You
cannot easily visualize them toiling with the single-minded
purpose of the Chinese. Yet in the north the Chinese have
trained (among many strange peoples) the Ka Was who practice human sacrifice. You cannot easily imagine a Ka Wa warrior chanting tribute to Peking's leaders.

Nevertheless a Ka Wa did stand before me to sing: "In the
olden times the Ka Was were like the grass under a big stone
. . . Chairman Mao is the hero who smashed that stone."

Both the Ka Was and Naga tribesmen have a bloody history
of feuds, sacrificial executions and lusty superstition. The Chinese claimed to be converting them. I asked, not very hope-
fully, to see how they went about taming wild aborigines who
had defied earlier British armies. The reply was an invitation
to more "culture stations" and I became the first foreigner
(except for a mobile group of Russian linguists) to watch this
curious struggle between the self-appointed messiahs and their
hapless customers.

It might be useful, before we join the head-hunters in the next chapter, to outline the wider problems of Peking in handling 35,000,000 non-Chinese within its gates.

These are descended from the aborigines who survived the waves of Chinese migration. In Yunnan there are 5,700,000 of them in a total population of less than 18,000,000. This powerful minority group includes Tibetans, opium-smoking T'ais, and serfs like the Yis who are sold in bondage to feudal barons, or the Ah Chungs who owned big orange-growing estates and large tracts of land, thus acquiring great merit with their masters, the Chinese. The problem of their potentialities as a Fifth Column could be solved by simply eliminating them. Stalin's technique was fully covered by Khrushchev's secret speech* at the Twentieth Party Congress.

Mao Tse-tung found other ways admirably suited to Chinese patience. When Yis attacked Red Army Scouts during the 1934 Long March, the order went forward from Mao: "Proceed without bloodshed. Make them understand we are friends, not enemies. Explain."

The explanations have continued ever since, particularly among the recalcitrants of the Northwest: the Uzbeks and Manchus, the Uigurs and Tatars of Sinkiang province. The concessions to outward show, the renovations to Buddhist temples and the subsidies for Moslem muezzins are not merely to impress the religiously minded of China. If the alien faith of Christianity is destined to die from an abundance of State

* "A decision was taken and executed concerning deportation of all Karachai from the lands on which they lived," according to the text of Khrushchev's speech made available outside the U.S.S.R. "In this period, at the end of December 1943, the same lot befell the whole population of the Autonomous Kalmyk Republic. In March 1944, all the Chechen and Ingush people were deported and the Chechen Ingush Autonomous Republic was liquidated.

"In April 1944, all Balkas were deported to far-away places from the territory of the Kabardino-Balkar Autonomous Republic and the Republic itself was renamed the Autonomous Kabardin Republic. The Ukrainians avoided meeting this fate only because there were too many of them and there was no place to which to deport them. Otherwise, he [Stalin] would have deported them also." (Laughter and animation in the hall.) Khrushchev did not mention the Crimean Tatars, Volga Germans and Balts, who were likewise deported and "un-nationed."

sponsorship, it will be a lingering death. Priests and pastors attend the seminaries of Party choice and the church bells ring out, timid but convincing. The visitors go home suitably impressed; home to Europe or Australia, or if they are Buddhists to the gentle familiar landscapes, perhaps, of Burma.

"The theory of Pan-Hanism must be corrected," declared Mao at the Sixth Congress of the Chinese Communist Party at Yenan in 1938. "In their relations with the national minorities the Hans [Chinese] must learn to look upon them as equals and must strengthen their bonds of friendship with them. The Hans must be forbidden to insult the national minorities and to display their contempt for them, either in actions or words."

Or, to bring the matter up to date: "We are here as brothers," said Premier Chou En-lai as he greeted the reinstalled Burmese Prime Minister, U Nu, at Kunming early in 1957.

"Yes," agreed U Nu. "We are visiting our relatives."

The brotherly embrace of the Sons of Han may look to some Burmese like the smother-love of an Asian lord protector. The Praise-God Barebones who works among tribes in Upper Burma really does believe he has been called as soldiers in a great crusade. In calmer times, his government's claims might be worthy of our consideration. For the sad truth is that Britain, far from being the machiavellian schemer Chou En-lai professes to believe, preferred to interfere very little in the affairs of the frontier peoples. When Burma became independent of British rule (an imperialist action about which Mao Tse-tung was said to be frankly incredulous until Stalin imputed some perfidious motive) the Burmese Constitution of 1947 gave semi-autonomous roles to the Kachin, Shan and Kayah states.

This solution was a poor compromise but it was the result of earlier neglect.* When the Mongols conquered China in the

---

* Until 1956 there were bands of K.M.T. soldiers, remnants of Chiang Kai-shek's forces, roaming these hills in search of opium or counterfeiting currency in their jungle retreats. This opium traffic is frequently blamed on Communist China. Not unnaturally, the Peking regime has tried to end this threat to prestige as well as to the security of the southeastern borders, and at one time accused U.S. aircraft of dropping supplies to

thirteenth century, they steam-rollered southward into what is now Yunnan. The Shans then had a kingdom extending over most of modern Yunnan with the capital at Dali, today a transport center for a wild region of Southwest China. They retreated and until the middle of the fifteenth century their feudal states covered most of Middle and Upper Burma. The baronial chiefs called themselves Lords of the Sky, the *Saohpa*, known to most Burmese as *Sawbwa*. During successive generations, they became subservient at times to Imperial China, at other times to Burmese kings and sometimes they succeeded in ruling themselves. During their vassalage to Burma, the sawbwas sent their daughters as brides to the royal harems and their sons became pages at court. Like knights of medieval England, the amount of tribute they paid depended on their accessibility. The more remote sawbwas sent haphazard offerings of gold and silver flowers and were the first to permit eighteenth-century Chinese Imperial power to convert them into Chinese prefectures.

Today it is estimated that two million Shans live in Upper Burma against more than ten million of the same racial family in China. They have a common written language, Tai, in which "educational" books are printed by Peking for distribution among all Shan settlements. These included an estimated six million in Laos and seven million in Thailand.

"We have divided the Shans and neighboring communities according to their progress in civilization," I was told by one of the earnest Culture Station Number 7 cadres. "There is, of

these guerrilla bands. As to who is responsible for the neglect, part of the blame lies with Britain. China claimed Bhamo and territory north to the Irrawaddy after British troops occupied Upper Burma in 1885. A vital link between Shan and Kachin states, the Namwan Assigned Tract, was leased in perpetuity on payment of about £75 annually to China, but frontier wranglings went on until after World War II, with 200 miles of border adjoining the wild Wa country remaining undefined. British occupation did little to alter affairs in the area except that Shan royalty was reduced and scientifically defined as seventeen sawbwas, eleven hereditary governors and four "superintendents of the Silver Revenues." Many of these are said keenly to oppose incorporation into the Union of Burma and may be persuaded by Peking's cautious policies that their future lies with China.

course, much cross-breeding. We have eliminated insulting nicknames — for instance, the Yis were once called by us 'tottering weaklings.' This is not in accordance with Chairman Mao's correct approach to Pan-Hanism."

So the border dispute has taken a bewildering turn. Instead of Chinese warlords who moved the frontier posts by force or guile, there are young men in blue caps who calmly fit the borderland peoples into Registration Tables.

Their two main targets are the Shans and Kachins. I questioned a Shan vice-chairman of the Dehung Autonomous *Chou* which caters for both racial groups. An autonomous *chou* is part of a national minority region; it is an administrative unit in which one or two minority groups preserve their religions, customs and languages in accordance with the doctrinal basis of Communist Chinese policy. This asserts the equality of nationalities in Articles 50–53 of the Common Program of the Chinese People's Political Consultative Conference.

It is the equality of animals in a zoo. Each group is neatly caged, lives on a traditional diet and is taught to perform tricks. The clever performers are elected to represent the other animals in Peking; the voting is conducted among inmates of the same cage, whose keepers have taught them the trick of selecting a marked card.

Is this a cruel and cynical version of Chinese endeavors? My friend the Dehung vice-chairman should be allowed to speak for himself.

"Now here we have," he said with a generous wave of his hand in the direction of Burma, "feudal Shans, head-hunting Was and the primitive Kachins who are practicing a form of communism already. Others are in a state of slavery. Here in China we deal with each in accordance with the category in which they fall.

"We do not, for instance, struggle against feudal landlords, tribal chiefs and Shan princes. Instead we guarantee them their political status, a fixed income, education for their children, the opportunity of themselves going to school and retention of their titles.

"When you guarantee them these things, why of course they raise their hands and ask to have their power abolished."

CHAPTER SIX

"It's a Little More Expensive to Convince the Upper Classes"

◉ ◉

I ASKED what schools handled such strange students and was taken to Kunming National Minorities Institute. Pupils lent a touch of insanity to my arrival. They wore their tribal costumes like art students at a fancy dress ball. Some banged drums, others walloped gongs and chanted folk songs.

"Here we cater to all superstitions," said Wang Y-tsung, director of the Institute. "Here is a classroom for Christians. Here is a Buddhist class and the Moslems are over there."

The faint perfume of opium curled up the stairs. "Ah, the class for opium smokers," said Wang. "In time we hope to cure them all."

There was a living Buddha from the Tibetan foot hills, a jungle prince and a reformed witch doctor. The building was large, modern and new. It rose square, flat-roofed and solid out of the wilderness and was just as unexpected as a Victorian school matron sitting indomitably and uncompromisingly on the edge of Paradise.

For Yunnan *is* a kind of Eden and the hill people were represented here by youngsters who seemed at first glance to have stepped out of a pastoral dream.

I was interrupting a rural frolic. A T'ai dancer in bright greens and yellows, head wrapped in a chartreuse turban, skipped to the beat of an elephant's-foot drum, spreading an eight-foot-long artificial peacock's tail behind him and rustling it at the bare feet of posturing, pretty damsels. A bunch of Tibetan girls twirled in their holiday aprons of colored stripes. Three young men puffed and panted under a great jointed, paper and bamboo dragon. There were stocky little Penlung women stamping their feet to make the silver bracelets on their ankles tinkle and spin. A boy played softly on his flute.

This was an overwhelming and determined demonstration of the freedom granted to minority groups in China. A Christian tribesman knelt at his devotions before an open-air altar and the Hwei Moslems lined up for their special mutton rations.

"And now let us talk," said Director Wang. He waved a hand and the entire scene dissolved as if he had shouted: Cut! The human peacock gathered up his tresses; the dragon staggered away behind the departing maidens and the Christian brought his prayers to an abrupt close.

"We have sixteen hundred students," said Wang briskly. "About eleven hundred of them were already Government cadres and the others were 'active elements.' They graduate from here to jobs as heads, section heads, vice-*chou* and county heads.

"This school is divided according to social development and not just into first, second and third grades. What we have is the Feudal Department, the Department for People Not Yet in Class Society (*they* have no class consciousness) and a Department for People from the Interior.

"We will now talk about Policy Research for Upper Classes. For purposes of identification, grouped into the Upper Class bracket are living Buddhas, monks, priests, princes and such officials in tribal areas as prime ministers."

I swallowed hard and hastily looked out through his office window. The costume ball was now rearranging itself. A Ti-buried in a book. Three Flowered Miaos in striped robes sat in a decorous circle on the lawn. The drummers and flutists betan in British Army Gurkha hat leaned against a tree, nose stood by their instruments, notebooks in their hands.

Director Wang was a slender, intense sort of man whose mind worked like a well-oiled calculating machine. He caught my glance and smiled. *He* knew there was little risk of my catching him out, or of his prompters missing a cue.

"The Upper Classes come here to study: first, the Great Motherland; secondly, current Government policy; and thirdly to hold free discussion. The free discussion is so that the Upper Class student may express himself freely and discuss any incorrect thoughts with the presiding official who will then explain the correct policy of the Great Motherland."

I enquired politely if occasions might arise when the Upper Class student had the right idea and the presiding official was wrong.

Wang looked puzzled. "Well," he laughed, "do you suppose, for instance, that an opium smoker could be right?"

"He might think Mao Tse-tung is a fool," I said recklessly.

There was a pained expression on Wang's face. "You mean, he might criticize our Chairman?"

I nodded.

"But how could he possibly criticize Chairman Mao?" asked Wang. "What could he criticize him *about?*"

Madame Duheroff whispered to Herr Doering who bent close to interpreter Chen.

"What are you thinking about?" asked Chen.

I shot him a startled look.

"*I* know," he said with a waggish smile.

He leaned confidingly across to me. "You are wondering about the opium."

I denied this hotly. He smiled: "No, do not apologize. Of course in China officially we do not smoke opium any more, nor do we grow it. But in the remote districts, many tribal people still smoke opium and they also grow their own. It will take time to educate them. But I knew you would be wondering about where their opium came from."

"Well, how *do* you cure an opium addict?" I asked.

Wang beamed. "We do not cut them off at once," he said. "That would be incorrect and would only turn the smoker into an enemy. We have to work gradually. We allow them a ration and in the free discussion periods we ask them to explain why they smoke. Then we reason with them, and show how their thoughts on opium-smoking have misled them. We explain how wasteful it is to spend money on opium that might be spent on building a road for The People.

"We keep talking even though we give them their opium. The less they smoke, the more we talk. After a certain point, the less they smoke the less talking *we* do until their own self-study brings them to redemption."

Everybody looked relieved. I asked about other vices.

"Yes," said Wang, squaring up to it bravely, "we do have sex problems among Upper Classes like prime ministers who come from environments where their relations with women were — er — chaotic. Our policy is: 'not in Kunming.' They can do almost anything else but they must not break our social order here by stealing women.

"They are not punished for misbehaving with women. They are merely *persuaded* that their outlook is unhealthy and unfair to The People."

He saw that I was prepared to question him further and said hastily: "We must carry out our long-term policy of achieving unity with tribal leaders and we must avoid any direct clash with these leaders and so of course it would be foolish to get worried and act precipitately when this question of cheating among women arises . . ." He mopped his brow. "And so we must not be in a hurry to re-educate them toward a correct outlook on the matter of women."

"You mean, some of them have several wives? Or do you mean they have concubines?"

There was a general scuffling of feet and Madame Duheroff announced that she wished to take photographs *at once*. Dinu Hervian, the Rumanian, caught my eye and hurriedly concealed a smile. Comrade Chen, who by this time knew very well how my mind worked, shrugged and translated the questions.

"Not in Kunming," repeated Wang. "They must keep the social order here."

"But suppose they bring their women with them?"

"We seek to educate them and by persuasion to cure them of unhealthy habits," said Wang.

"How do you convert people from such practices?"

"You mean, how do we help them find redemption," Wang

corrected me. "We use the system of peaceful consultation. Also we guarantee their income which in the case of certain tribal chiefs may be very high indeed."

"Is bribery enough?" I asked.

"Not bribery," Wang insisted. "Good deeds. We show them the right way by practicing good deeds."

He began to enumerate the good deeds; and then came one of those startling little revelations which make it so much more worth-while to talk with the Chinese than with their opposite numbers in Russia.

"Upper Class students eat the equivalent of a county head," said Wang.

This was almost too good to be true.

"You mean, everybody is graded as to what he eats?"

"Well, of course," said Wang. "If you work in a factory or go to school, you have to eat in a canteen and of course you're entitled to a certain grade. The salt miners in Yunnan, if they are very good workers, are rewarded with permission to eat in the nutritious canteen; that is where they get nutritious food like soya-bean milk.

"Here, prime ministers and bonzes alike get pocket money of ten yuan monthly, irrespective of their guaranteed incomes, and they eat on the level of county heads.

"All students who do not hold official tribal jobs are fed and clothed by the State and *they* get fed on the Yunnan University standard."

There was now a definite movement among the European comrades to terminate this discussion. I followed unwillingly. We paced through the corridors where the opium smokers puffed away between interminable lectures, where Buddhists recited their prayers and the Christians could play with their Christmas Trees.

"We decorate their temples, we give special treatment and we go slow on land reform," Wang was saying. "We do nothing to create small conflicts that might grow into major disputes. We work through the people of the regions where we wish to spread our message."

He rubbed his hands. "And we expect to convert *all* our national minorities to Communism within five years."

CHAPTER SEVEN

Recipe for an Execution

◉ ◉

THE SPADELIKE OBJECTS hanging in a row on the bamboo wall were shoulder blades.

"Cannibalism," said Fang Lien, "is bad for production.

He followed my anxious glance. "This is the house of a witch doctor. He keeps the left shoulder of every beast he sacrifices."

Fang's melon face split into a grin. He was a fat, jovial man. I suppose you would call him a Chinese commissar. He had a high-pitched giggle and kept his cap on the back of his shaven head. He walked feet foremost and looked as if he would bob right up again if you pushed him over, not only because he wore bell-bottomed trousers of Russian cut. His center-of-gravity really did appear to be somewhere near his ankles and hidden under his plain gray tunic was a quaint funny bone. He was chief executive on the Yunnan National Minorities Commission and confessed that his job among jungle tribes was a severe test for any emissary of Mao.

"Take this business of human blood as fertilizer," he said. "What a waste. But it is all part of Ka Wa superstition and we have to be careful."

We were on the edge of Ka Wa territory, on a high ridge above the Shweli Valley. Fang sucked mandarin oranges bought by the driver of his Molotov truck and we sat in a long-hut on stilts. Women of the local Peng Lung tribes

rustled behind screens of woven banana leaves and chickens
scratched under the loose bamboo floor.

"The sacrifice of a man among the Ka Was is the result of
good motives," Fang continued. "Only the method is wrong.
The good intention is to pacify the gods and so increase food
production."

"You mentioned cannibalism — ?"

Madame Duheroff pressed forward eagerly. "Ja!" Her face
was suffused with excitement. "We should know more about
the sacrifices. It is necessary to understand how the comrades
are dealing with such problems."

The commissar tittered. "If a warrior cheats with the wife of
another, the husband may kill. Then the body is cut up and
certain parts — "

The German peered up from her notebook. "May we know
what parts?"

Fang explained.

". . . And the husband may force the wife to eat the cooked
pieces. Otherwise the problem is really one of head-hunting.

"We have practiced three kinds of compromise when the
problem of human sacrifice comes up. Sometimes we can persuade several tribes to share one man. The victim is beheaded
and each village borrows the head in turn. Secondly, if we
can trick them into accepting a fresh corpse, we dig up a body
and let them perform the rites on *that*. Thirdly, we may buy
an old man."

He sipped jasmine tea from a flask supplied by his pigtailed
companion who carried refreshment in her army haversack.
He seemed to relish our astonishment.

"Yes, we find some very old, very poor man and we offer the
money to his family. Old men are a burden to others, they are
not productive and usually the family is glad to improve its
prosperity a little."

"But what about the old man? What does he get out of
it?"

Fang offered me an orange, cocked his head on one side and
said: "We persuade him."

Madame Duheroff began to mutter, throwing me suspicious

looks. Tomagatski pushed his rimless spectacles farther back
on his snub nose and went on writing. The Korean was asleep
under his broad-brimmed hat. Herr Doering and the Rumanian exchanged puzzled looks. Little Li's narrow, Vietnamese
face tightened and his long fingers began to play nervously
around the edges of his notebook.

Finally I asked above guttural protestations: "How do you
persuade an old man it's in his interests to lose his head for a
sum of money paid to his family?"

"*Persuasion*," said Fang smoothly. "Persuasion is essential
of course. Force is forbidden. We convince an old man. We
make him understand how necessary it is for the progress of
society and the welfare of The People that he should — er —
take part. Usually this process of explanation is sufficient."

He warmed to his subject. "You see, the Ka Was are a numerous and difficult people. There are about half a million
equally distributed on either side of the border between Burma
and our Fatherland. We want to stop this practice of be-
heading, which is worse in the month of sowing. Essentially
our compromises still involve killing people but we *are* making progress. We are working on the witch doctors and the
warriors. However, we cannot watch all the villages all of the
time. There are raids, and bitter feuds persist after many
generations.

"The prestige and glory of the warrior class is being replaced
under our persuasion. We point out that it's a disgrace, not
a brave deed, to go out and behead someone in the next village.

"We try to pay the witch doctors to find alternative victims
of sacrifice. If the witch doctor has a strong influence, he can
get the village to accept the body of an animal. Some have
even substituted mice for men."

It would be odd, I thought, to be challenged here with the
question: Are you a mouse or man? Once in these same hills
a Japanese battalion was massacred for giving the wrong answer.

"Do you lose many men? — that is . . ." I hesitated, then
drew a finger across my throat.

"Oh yes." He paused. "Yes, we have had some comrades
unfortunately — as it were, eliminated."

He bowed his head. "They died, of course, in a glorious cause."

I nodded and told Fang about the luckless Japanese, without adding that they, too, probably considered their cause quite glorious. It happened in late 1941. The stocky warriors advanced up the Salween valley from Burma, anxious to subjugate settlements of Lisu tribes. The Lisus were cannibals converted to Christianity. So they turned the other cheek and offered the invaders food and barrels of rice beer. The troops ate and drank and with these appetites satisfied they looked around for other sport. Quarrels arose. Challenges were issued. Who among the Imperial Samurai would acquit himself best with the village maidens?

The local chief was outraged. He assigned a few diseased women to the Japs and while they dallied, the Lisus plotted. Next day the conquerors pushed farther into the interior and at noon, trapped by the irritated Lisus in a narrow gorge, they were crushed by rocks hurled from dizzy heights. A few survivors later claimed their attackers fell upon the corpses to satisfy more exotic appetites.

Fang listened to this gruesome tale with a respectful smile. "They were not properly converted," he said gravely. "Christian conversion only meets imperialist requirements. It is not part of The People. As for the Japanese, we harbor no resentment. We understand it was not the Japanese people who committed such atrocities. They were victims of imperialist ambition."

I walked off alone to reflect upon this curious answer. There was such an unreality about this day that I fell into a dream. When a large hair-crested drongo flew out of a bush and somersaulted in pursuit of flies, I jumped as if an elephant had sprung from a movie screen.

The metallic blue bird swooped up into a thorny *tage* tree which splashes its fiery red blossoms on these hillsides. Fang and the rest of the party droned away in the distance, intent on an uplifting interview with the village headman.

I stretched between the roots of a banyan, the valley at my feet, and tried to get Fang and all his works into perspective. Scattered through the wild country for three hundred miles

north were five thousand cadres whose job was to evangelize
among the tribes. Once, in the year 1910, a Chinese official
was dispatched through the same territory to encourage tribal
chiefs to appeal for Chinese protection. When a British column of troops went to investigate these activities, it vanished.
The wildmen could not be trifled with. They were in the
same category as the primitive hill people of the adjoining
Himalayas. They lived in a political no man's land, protected
for centuries by precipitous hills and deep gorges, a fierce
and untamed branch of the human race.

The same beliefs ran through these valleys. There was a
Land of the Dead and there were gods who examined the soul
on its way from earth. The warriors who killed many enemies gained great merit in the Hereafter. The man with many
slaves and a dozen wives was allowed to inherit a divine paradise but the poor bachelor passed on to an equally humble estate in heaven. For a man who abided by the rules of earthly
good behavior, the future was grim when he came to face the
inquisitive guardians of the Land of the Dead.

Could the Chinese change this where others failed? Nehru,
using different tactics, was in trouble with Naga hill tribes in
nearby Assam. Nagas were head-hunters previously left alone by
the British. Under the same influences and sharing the same kind
of territory, the Nagas and Ka Was were equally difficult
people to force into any stranger's mold. For them an earthly
life of peace and universal brotherhood meant laying up trouble in paradise. They were in consequence the fiercest up-
holders of jungle law.

I squinted through the papayas to where I imagined that
other wartime supply route, the Stilwell Road, must join our
own. Two hundred miles west lay the Naga country. The
contrast between Indian and Chinese methods of handling tribal
problems was a striking one. Here the Chinese were absolutely sure of the rightness of their cause. They had an
impregnable mental shield provided by daily indoctrination.
In handling tribesmen they employed the old French adage:
"We may persuade others by our arguments but we can only
convince them by theirs."

The Indians however were morally uncertain. I remembered standing on the road above Imphal with an Indian Army major, less than eight months previously. "Sorry old chap," he apologized. "Must stop you here. Native trouble again, y'know."

I recalled how he plucked his mustache, a worried expression in his eyes. "Frightful mess, really. Come and have a peg. Tell you all about it."

It had soon become clear why three hundred thousand Nagas were resisting Indian good-fellowship. The problem facing India was precisely the same as that facing China: how to control border tribes and ensure they would not provide passage for invaders.

But the men sent by Nehru to Imphal, on the Indian side of the border, were bureaucrats and soldiers. The bureaucrats were condescending and considered the Nagas barbaric. They doled out roads, medical clinics, schools and farming utensils as if they were the Lady Bountifuls they openly reviled but secretly admired under the British Raj.

The soldiers were British trained and their approach to a troublesome tribesman was forthright: "Kick 'im around a bit."

Their common problem was a partly crippled Naga leader, Zapu Phizo. He wanted an independent Naga State and claimed this was promised him by the Indian Government after the British handover.

My major friend thought he could see where things had gone wrong. He blamed the British for neglecting the border problem but also admitted India treated the Nagas shabbily by repudiating the earlier promise of freedom. Zapu Phizo, who fought with the Japanese in World War II, was far more widely supported than Delhi cared to admit. The trouble now was that these hills were vital to the Indian frontier with China and Tibet.

"We have to defend ourselves against Communist infiltration," said the major. "But of course you will never get Nehru to admit that."

Political officers in the area believed the Chinese had already got to Phizo, which was hardly surprising. His Naga National

Council boycotted the local elections, refused to pay taxes and sabotaged the Indian administration. Four years earlier friends of Nehru described to me in glowing terms the enlightened Indian policy toward the Nagas and laughed at warnings that Phizo was not a man to accept patronage.

Still full of good intentions the Indians had, in fact, treated him as professors who coach a promising pupil. When a column of Assam Rifles disappeared amid ugly rumors that the Nagas were taking heads again, Nehru flew north to Kohima to lecture tribal leaders and demonstrate his policy of determined goodwill. By 1956, such was the force of his pacific arguments, Kohima was the center of a battleground in which Naga guerrillas ambushed convoys, burned police posts and even attacked the town.

Little is known about this savage private war. The area has been sealed off and only hand-picked observers enter. The Indian press maintains a curious silence in sharp contrast to its lamentations over mistakes in Western foreign policy. There are few better illustrations of the bankruptcy of Western ideas in Asia than this spectacle of a great nation, lately freed from colonial rule, failing to practice its own preachings and, therefore, unable to win friendship and co-operation from the Nagas. For what India does today in this region is a pale reflection of recent British policy and attitudes plus a confusion of military force and Fabian myopia.

Such, anyway, were my dolorous reflections astride another hilltop east of Imphal waiting for the confident comrades. They were innocently droll, it was true. Who else but fanatics could talk seriously of persuading old men to the execution block? They were also men of purpose, so thoroughly steeped in Maoist lore that they submitted to the harshest disciplines. Each of a dozen Chinese cadres with whom I spoke in this region was married; more than half had been schoolteachers and had enjoyed a prestige that in former days would have entitled them to comfort and privilege. None expected to see his wife and children more than once or possibly twice in a year. They lived in primitive conditions in an alien and often exasperating world. For these and other hardships they were paid about $4 extra monthly. If they got to a big city, it was to attend a mass conference of cadres in Kunming or (very occasionally for a chosen few) to travel to Peking and participate in some collective orgy of self-examination. Their strength was to be found in their utter dedication, which meant frequently confessing their faults and errors.

The Indian Army major was human, likable and Blimpish. He had nothing in common with the Nagas. He said: "You've got to knock sense into these chaps — no use just talking."

And the Indian Political Officer was inclined to say: "Nonsense. We must put some trust in the Nagas' word. Give them a feeling of pride and provide them with social welfare so they will see the advantages of co-operating with us."

But the Chinese displayed no such divisions of opinion. They checked their behavior and actions constantly against standards laid down by Mao Tse-tung: "Explain . . . The Hans must be forbidden to insult the national minorities . . . look upon them as equals."

All over China, at this very time, the message was being hammered home. Pan-Hanism, a sort of Chinese superiority complex, was condemned in editorials and instructions to cadres. Throughout December, there was a rash of self-condemnation and Communist officials were urged to proceed slowly in introducing social reforms. On the very day I sat looking across tribal country toward the Tibetan foothills, there appeared in the *Lhasa Jih Pao* this typical admonition:

Cadres with Pan-Hanist ideas do not trust Tibetan cadres or else think they are stupid . . . Characteristic of the contempt for Tibetan cadres is the way, for instance, some Han cadres, accustomed to sitting in chairs, pay no heed at all to the custom of Tibetan cadres who sit on cushions. Tibetan cadres enjoy drinking buttered tea and Han stewards made no effort to provide it . . . Some Hans regard with contempt the Tibetan liking for dances . . . To overcome these faults, intensify theoretical study and educate in patriotism and internationalism. Intensify political studies.*

* *Lhasa Jih Pao*, December 19, 1957: This daily newspaper, established after Chinese occupation of Tibet, reflects official Peking policy.

The reason for all this self-analysis, as we shall see later, was the uprising of Tibetans earlier in the year. What made it unusually interesting was the final paragraph:

> Most important of all, if we can overcome Pan-Hanism, the nationalism in certain areas will also be subsequently overcome with comparative ease.

My conclusions were gloomy after the day's session with a Chinese commissar who spoke confidently of converting head-hunters and coaxing old men to the sacrifice. But the next encounter was to reveal a very different side of the story: a sort of Marxist version (with unique Chinese touches) of the *Teahouse of the August Moon.*

CHAPTER EIGHT

Witch Hunt in a Marxist Jungle

◉ ◉

EACH TIME he opened the drill book, the commissar of the culture station was on familiar ground. He was a cautious, foxy man and shivered from a slight fever, first breath of another malarial attack. His home for the past two years had been wooden planks, laid horizontally across one corner of a Chinese hut, hidden by jungle creepers. His neighbors were illiterate tribesmen.

One of them could be seen far below in a pocket of land. A road scoured its way through the red earth, a solitary link with the outside world. There were five terraced rice paddies folded into the loops and twists of the road. In one of the paddies, a man with blue cotton pants rolled above the knee squelched through mud behind his wooden swing plow. His fiber rain cloak hung over his bent back like the carapace of a black beetle. If he stretched his arms on either side, he could almost touch both banks. The paddy was no more than ten paces long. Between the man and the capital of China were many wide rivers, tier upon tier of mountain barriers and the flimsiest of paths and dirt roads.

Only a lonely figure sloshing through a crescent of wet paddy. But in Peking's Domesday Book he had a name and number, a family history, a prescribed position in the new social order, and he had a purpose.

It was the cultural commissar's job to define that purpose,

to make the solitary plowman a useful cog in China's agricultural machine. The commissar might have been a good staff sergeant, perhaps, or an efficient tax collector. Instead he was official shepherd to 371 households scattered over two mountains.

Sergeants are good at transmitting orders. He got them day by day: leaflets and posters, special instructions to cadres and just recently three hundred copies of *A Short History of the Communist Party of China*. Daily his reports moved back, squiggled lines on thin rice paper rolled into thick envelopes on which he daubed bold Chinese characters with a brush dipped in *sumi* ink. The signature was always the same: Comrade Miao.

Miao Fa-yung, forty-two, former schoolteacher, Party activist, veteran soldier of the Chinese Red Army, was a political commando sent to preach Peking's gospel among twenty-five hundred tribesmen.

And, he now confessed to me, he had almost failed in his task.

"These people came to me," he said, "and complained: 'We were all equal before you brought Communism here. Now you make us unequal.' For a time, as a result of my wrong policies, everything here was utter chaos!"

This was not whispered to me in a clandestine rendezvous. Miao was a man who had made mistakes, and I was directed to him by Tau Ching-pan, a gentleman with two wives and the post of chairman for this tribal region. A big, genial T'ai, he gave me the vital statistics almost in one breath: "We have committed many errors. Although I have two wives, we are educating the people to give up polygamy. Yes, I earn 240 yuan monthly." (About $92.)

Then he sent me along to Cultural Commissar Miao, one of two hundred "responsible cadres" in his area.

Miao arrived full of bustling efficiency late in 1954 to organize mutual-aid teams in the border regions. Among his several previous occupations he had worked in a tobacco factory and he brought with him a supply of Yunnanese cigars which were an immediate success among the villagers.

He was also a researcher on the Communist Party's "history committee" in Yunnan and was inclined to become professorial and recondite when explaining his actions to the natives, and this was less successful. He built the culture station opposite a tribal leader's long-hut. One morning he found a rude suggestion painted on his door and on the neighbor's long-hut the words: *This is my property.*

Miao, while reciting these events, took me to the long-hut and sure enough, there were the Chinese ideographs fading but still defiant. A pole was stuck in the packed earth of the tribal leader's compound, and from it there hung a bow with a white crescent and star suspended at either end. "To denote that he watches over the tribe by day and night," grunted Miao and we walked back to his culture station in silence.

At first Miao had asserted his authority: "Wrong," he told me, "because of course I *had* no authority. I was guilty of Pan-Hanism. But I told the tribal leader to erase the signs. He was the only man capable of having written them. Later, when I understood better the correct policy of Chairman Mao, I made him paint them back on. Now he must not remove the sign until *he* can persuade *us* to let him, and for correct reasons."

I glanced at him quickly but there was no suspicion of drollery on his solemn face.

His charges were a mixed group. There were 164 Peng Lung families, about 120 Kachin and 78 Han families. There were also nine Li Su households who practiced a corrupt sort of Christianity.

"All were in what we call early or primitive Communism," the cultural commissar said. "They were supposed to make the direct transition to socialism. Their land was commonly owned; what they grew belonged to the community."

Herr Doering had limped away to take photographs but he hastily rejoined us.

He seemed full of alarm. "Then we cannot consider these people to be exploited?"

"Oh they were exploited all right," said Miao. "Their primitive communism taught them to share their troubles — but some were too poor to help others, and some were too rich to care. Exploitation also exists in the form of religion and superstition. They believe in devils." His voice dropped. "They sacrifice animals to cure illness. They chop down trees to direct evil forces at someone they dislike."

To humor the priests and soothsayers, he took part in sacrificial rites. Kachins gathered round an altar where the chief witch doctor slit the throat of a chicken, tore away one wing and then cut open the belly to examine the fresh liver for omens. Fortunately, the divine prediction was that Communist Chinese interference in tribal affairs would prove beneficial all around. A prior promise that Peking would guarantee the witch doctor's income was not, of course, publicly proclaimed.

"But at that time, I was trying to get people to join four co-operatives," said Miao, "I tried to — er — apply our universal experience without consideration to local conditions." He was going by the book. Then late in 1955, certain directives hurtled out of Peking couched in the familiar language of Mao Tse-tung. "We were told to attract by example; to use persuasion; to explain and discuss instead of applying — er — *forceful* argument."

Miao called his fellow cadres together. There were twenty-four appointed from the local tribes whose knowledge of Marxist theory was shaky, to put it mildly. The cultural commissar and his two assistants from Kunming directed operations but took great care to give their colleagues a sense of active participation.

"We had to organize labor and stop waste. Many features of Kachin life were wasteful to production. Bad habits among the young, for instance." He leafed through his notebook dolefully. "In one village there were thirty girls sleeping indiscriminately with the men. Sometimes they would lie together until three in the morning. The men were always tired. This is still something we have a lot of trouble with, this staying up until all hours having unhealthy relationships. It is bad for production. If a man at the age of thirty has passed an average of one entire night a week in this fashion, we estimate a total wastage of labor amounting to one thousand working days in his lifetime.

"Other men were wasting too much time walking to market. If a man is fifty now, he must have spent thirty of his years just walking to market."

Madame Duheroff wanted to hear more about tribal sex life. Miao gave a disapproving cough. "I will finish explaining about our errors first," he said stiffly.

"We tried to introduce a division of labor. Actually, they already had a working knowledge of this, practiced in accordance with old customs. Men plowed, did heavy labor; the women cooked, gathered firewood and so on.

"We organized labor on more efficient lines. But leaders of our Production Teams complained that some men were dodging work. Before, these men would have been punished. Now we had to follow the correct Party line of going to the masses and of asking what was wrong. We found these men were ashamed because in our new division of labor we give them tasks which put their manhood in doubt — such as gathering firewood.

"Chaotic conditions still exist because of this. We are still explaining and persuading men to do what was formerly women's work. Yet still, the team leaders arrive at the work site and cannot find their men. It takes a lot of patience . . .

"All the awkward questions came from the Kachins. For instance, we agreed to award ten work points for every laborer who did one morning's work (we paid no money: the value of a work point varied with changes in the local economy). After a month of this system, the number of adult workers decreased, production went down and there was much grumbling. We asked the menfolk what was wrong. They said the biggest and strongest men also had the most children. Since everybody got the same award, men with big families just stayed at home and sent all their children into the fields. The family with the most children got the biggest income.

"Well, we devised a method of grading the workers. The able-bodied peasants were very pleased with this. But the young ones said: 'You Communists are making us unequal.'

"It took us *six months* of discussion to work this one out. The strong men wanted to keep the system; the weak ones said it was unfair to penalize them."

Poor Miao scratched his head. "In the end, I concluded that you simply could not translate into their languages any normal explanation. You could not put into their words such phrases as *work norm* and *socialist emulation drive*."

Until then, I had listened to Miao with a good deal of sympathy. It seemed that he was using flexibility and intelligence to handle his problems. When he found that the drill book did not contain all the answers, he improvised his own. Or so I thought.

Then I said: "If your aim was to help these people grow better crops, enjoy better living conditions and abandon evil customs, you surely were not obliged to talk about *work norms* and *socialist emulation* drives to them?"

He looked startled. "In the end, we did not try to *teach* them these things — no, of course not. We just made them do it."

"Do what?"

"Work in accordance with correct Party practice. You cannot go on talking when they are incapable of understanding. So you make them follow the correct system and wait for their conscience and understanding to accept the concept of equality in this light."

So much for the campaign against Pan-Hanism, the new policy of persuasion and Mao Tse-tung's admonition to act in accordance with local conditions. You talked, argued, pleaded and when all this failed, you waved a big stick. You were careful not to outrage local customs, you asserted the equality of the tribes-people, but nevertheless it was your objective to eliminate the customs and initiate the people into the superior wisdoms of China.

I said: "In other words, this new policy of free discussion is all one-sided. You keep on discussing until everyone agrees with the Party view?"

The cultural commissar showed astonishment that I should even ask the question. One of the Peking officials said quietly: "Flowers from a greenhouse can be pretty but delicate. That is why Chairman Mao has the policy: 'Let diverse schools of thought contend.' Free discussion is between those with correct views and those with wrong views; between the true Marxist-Leninist and those who do not understand or have strayed. Of course, in dealing with backward" — he hesitated and corrected himself — "in dealing with a national minority with no written language, denied the opportunity to study thoroughly Marxist-Leninism, we must try to explain but also at times make the people learn by practice."

Miao nodded his head eagerly. "We had no trouble with these people in setting up co-operatives. We just talked to them for three nights. There was trouble however with people who thought the co-operative was a magical thing. Perhaps we *did* emphasize too much the improvements in production that would result.

"But what else *could* we do? These people had such strange ideas. They thought in a co-operative that all the women would be shared under a big blanket. They liked this idea but it was a misconception. On the other hand, they also thought in a co-operative that all private property would become commonly owned and they opposed this; whereas, of course, it was one of our objectives.

"The sense of private ownership was *very* strong, even though the land was commonly owned. So we had to compromise. For instance, today a *mithan* cow belongs partly to the co-op and partly to the former owner. Slowly we shall detach the half that is privately owned."

I asked which half. Nobody smiled. A semi-naked Peng Lung warrior, propelled from the rear, stumbled through the door. He carried a bow which projected pellets instead of arrows. Behind him were half a dozen women in striped woven skirts, their teeth stained black from chewing betel nuts. A Kachin tribesman leaned against one wall, picking his nose, his free hand resting on the usual long-knife stuck in a waist sash.

"Disease is bad for production too," Miao was saying. "Unfortunately, these people have wasteful ways of dealing with sickness. So there is double waste — the waste of an ill worker and the waste of curing him by witchcraft."

There were several ways of driving out sickness. Among the Kachins, a witch doctor was called in for consultations. Usually he prescribed a feast for which a draft animal was often killed. Every part had to be consumed at a sitting by the patient's family and neighbors, except for one whole shoulder of the slaughtered beast.

I asked to meet a witch doctor. "We have promoted most of them around here," said the cultural commissar.

The authority of witch doctors, it seemed, was best undermined by raising their incomes and elevating their rank. Some had been persuaded to study simple medical laws. Wherever a witch doctor's influence was powerful, though, he was left alone. In some parts, good use had been made of the local wizards in settling feuds. The example was quoted of the bitter fighting which had continued through several generations between the sprawling families of Wan and Li. At its climax, Li's grandmother was brutally murdered.

This should have entailed a retaliatory raid and the public execution of a Wan. The Chinese, intent on pacifying the region, persuaded the angry Lis to accept compensation. Negotiations took place on neutral ground between their respective villages, in a clearing reached through groves of wild lemon. Priests acted as go-betweens. The action took place before a mixed and restless audience, among them tall strangers in coarse skirts woven with red and black wool in the Tibetan fashion. Here Tibetan influence was noticeable; traders from the snowy ranges came within a few days' march of the region. Their trinkets played an important part in the haggling over the Lis' dead grandmother.

She was killed with a Kachin knife. The Li family demanded compensation for each part of her body. The Wan witch doctor, playing the role of an advocate, shook out a pile of ornaments. He offered a silver amulet, heavily studded with turquoise, coral and jade in exchange for the old lady's head. There was a pair of red and blue Tibetan boots for her legs, a curved knife for her knees and a copper prayer wheel for her eyes. The old lady's ribs were reckoned to be worth a flint pouch and there were many lengths of coarsely woven cloth for her skin. Finally, the Wans offered the ritual slaughter of a sheep.

"Whose idea was this?" I asked in some admiration.

"It is one of the forms of compromise," said Miao. "The method had been used before, but we adapted it in the hope of reducing the feuds and achieving unity among the peoples. Of course, it encourages a sense of personal ownership, but you see we accept the fact that in their transformation to socialism all these villages must go through the stage of class society where such things exist."

It was a pity that a good story had to be spoiled by such a patter. I have extracted bigotry from the tale because in essence this was a practical effort to end hostilities and crime in the region. Perhaps the Chinese will go on justifying their policies in these wild places until a sane and expedient administration has been established; one that a Westerner would call a sound and healthy form of government even though Peking continues to reconcile it with Marxist-Leninsim. It is hard to be dogmatic about Marxist deviations; and a Chinese doctrinaire can find support for contradictory assertions and policies in Holy Writ. Only time will show whether, underneath all the blather, they have evolved a worthier system.

In the case of the family feud, both the Wans and Lis were said to be living harmoniously together following the settlement. Grandmother Li's bones had bought peace. But tranquility was restored also by the patience of the cultural commissar and I thought he deserved credit for it.

While we were talking, the crowd around Miao had grown. He selected four of the younger women and gently propelled them into the center of our circle.

"Sex life is chaotic," he admitted. "However, we are making progress."

In at least one village, the nonsense between the sexes had been curbed. No more romping behind the rice stacks. No more cuddling under the coconuts. How had this wasteful custom been curtailed?

For the first time, a look of triumph illuminated the cultural commissar's face. "Perhaps we cannot translate into their simple language the full purpose of labor heroes and model workers," he said. "But we can always teach by example. So we are working on certain young people to set this example."

He cast an approving eye over the girls. "Now here," he announced in a declamatory voice, "are four who do not hold hands with boys at night but have a happy and healthy outlook . . ."

CHAPTER NINE

Echoes of War in a Valley of Tombs

⊙ ⊙

Two DAYS of hard travel along the Burma Road brought us to a great bowl in the mountains. We branched westward and climbed down into the Valley of Tombs. The vast and placid Lake of Erh touched the foot of the encircling peaks. Thousands of family vaults covered the lower slopes, circular stone mounds that looked like doorways into a honeycomb. Sometimes the early sun stabbed through that clear and glittering air, touching the whiteness of these extraordinary catacombs until they resembled overlapping rows of teeth in a shark's jaw, while far in the distance gleamed the snowy highlands of Tibet.

Our journey now had assumed some of the aspects of a royal progress. We stayed in rest houses provided as in previous centuries for passing warlords or senior administrators. At each stop, local officials came and reported to us on the projects under way. I was struck by the evident reversion to methods favored by strong imperial regimes; and also by the fact that those officials I met were inspired by great devotion to the cause of their people. The gods were overthrown and the masses had become God. These calm little officials, reciting their statistics by the yellow light of oil lamps, were impressive in their dedicated zeal.

Along the lakeshore, hemmed in by tombstones, was the ancient walled city of Tali. It was a peaceful place. We became

easier to live with under its magic influence. The solitary
drifter from Western decadence felt himself less isolated. We
sang snatches of opera to one another, held a bottle party in
the marble baths where hot sulphurous waters bubbled up
from below ground, and went fishing on the lake, six thousand
feet above and five hundred miles from the Gulf of Tonkin.

Such benign influences made me regret taking unfair advantages of our mentor, nicknamed by this time Chairman
Chen. He did indeed resemble Mao and sometimes, possibly
carried away by this similarity of pose, he would bark an
order at me. This was out of character, since the modern
Chinese official will go to infinite lengths to induce in you some
action that meets his approval without his actually suggesting
it. But I was a trial and a tribulation and though he tried
hard to be convivial, Chairman Chen could not conceal his
dislike of myself and all that I stood for; it was a contempt
he bore for all dissolute and selfish people. I honored him
for it. He wore his Communism like a suit of armor and was
for ever crusading against lust, greed and inequality.

He barked once too often, however, and I thought grimly
that he should remember he was no longer interrogating Allied
prisoners in North Korea. Later at lunch we sat round a table
groaning with delicacies: Kunming steamed chicken, a clay pot
of fish-head soup, sliced beef with hot peppers, boiled turnips
dipped in treacle and then plunged into cold water, and a sort
of shortbread.

Tomagatski asked me: "What are you writing in your notebook."

Someone else said jokingly: "The banquet — he is describing how we gorge ourselves."

I said: "No, I was just noting that throughout this journey
we have never once shared a meal with the drivers. Where do
they eat? In the kitchen?"

Chen's eyes widened for a second, the only clue often to
Chinese emotions. I felt instantly sorry for hitting him in his
one vulnerable spot. As the son of a rich Shanghai banker,
with youthful memories of physical luxury in the United States,
he tried earnestly to reject all material comforts in his new

life. He did live, as I knew, in the most humble circumstances. But for him, this austerity required an intellectual effort all of the time. The drivers did not eat with us simply because of an oversight.

He was an honest man and I do not think he ever consciously lied in answering my questions, although we traveled together over most of China. I imagined him as a junior Cromwell. He could be shaken out of his cold detachment by any discussion of Mao's philosophy or the greatness of China. He had a curious, inverted pride of race. "We Chinese know that we are poor and backward," he would tell me. "We make no claims to superiority in anything."

Or, bitterly: "You really think I'm a privileged person, don't you? You think I'm out of touch with the peasants because I need an interpreter through whom to talk. But each of us must do his job the best he can. And I work hard at mine."

And so he did. Chairman Chen was a glutton for work. He was also highly intelligent, with a remarkable memory and a great curiosity about many things. We debated a wide range of topics. How to tickle trout; the decline and fall of the airship, which we agreed deserved a more useful fate; the American automobile industry for which he expressed great admiration. Once he argued with conviction that a tree could suffer; that it was possible to hear its heartbeats.

Heaven knows what miseries of spirit he underwent at his American college or what insults, real or fancied, he suffered for being Chinese. But he professed to be a fierce friend of Russia and he never really concealed his contempt for the West. Our political arguments were, by common agreement, an utter waste of time. "I know I'll never convert you!" he said resignedly although in truth he never tried.

Perhaps I dwell on Chen too long. But he seemed to me (having known him for two years) a man who epitomized the regime. If you could understand his complexes, you might perceive the motives of his leaders. He knew about his puritanical reputation and tried to dispute it. Yet it would have been impossible to make him enjoy an evening's fun in New York,

London or Paris. He would not see the sumptuous dishes but only the wretched dishwashers. He would not admire the chorus line but only shed tears for poor girls driven to prostitution. If, however, you reminded him that his own regime had driven millions to insanity, suicide and exile, he would declare in a voice cold with anger that these victims had opposed The People's will.

There was a story about this time, circulating among more outspoken Poles in China, that Mao Tse-tung reprimanded the President of Communist Poland for allowing youngsters there to be infected by decadent American rock 'n' roll. Poor old Josef Cyrankeiwicz, a burly bullet-headed zealot, was caught off base and stuttered something about "different behavior patterns along the different paths to socialism." Mao was not amused.

An innocent action might be transmuted into a deed fraught with political significance. I would no more give coins to a ragged urchin than paste up a poster proclaiming *Hurrah for Capitalist Exploiters!* It was easy enough to encourage the hotel waiter to keep money you slipped into the palm of his hand. But the action could cause offense. Waiters and other public servants took an obvious pleasure in feeling independent of charity. I hated to find a price for their pride.

Tali had been the capital of the Shan kingdom of Nan-chao until the Mongols driving south in the thirteenth century overran it. Foreigners like myself had not been seen there in a long time.

Small children were not easily put off. They followed me through the narrow cobbled lanes, under arched gates and into the shadow of three white pagodas. After the Kingdom of Tali underwent Chinese conversion and the local Burmese Shans became subjects of Peking, there were floods and calamities. Almost two thousand years ago, the Chinese rather astutely put the blame on a dragon in the lake. The pagodas were built to keep down the monster and the ancient ideographs were still decipherable: *Conquer the floods!*

My youthful followers had swollen into an army. They

tugged at my sleeve, grinned into my camera and wanted to be photographed individually, then in groups, standing on their heads or perched on the high stones placed at the entrance of their homes to trip devils. No Pied Piper ever enjoyed greater success.

Then the East Germans discovered me. Perhaps Madame Duheroff expected me to play "Rule, Britannia!" on my little flute and lure the children of Tali away through the mountains into some capitalist perdition. Juvenile enthusiasm did not somehow transfer itself to the two dour intruders. Martin Doering limped over. I was trapped in a swarm of leaping, cheering youngsters and with difficulty forced an exit.

"See how our Chinese comrades love their Russian friends," said Doering. He was rewarded with a simper from Madame. "Yes," he added, noting my surprise. "They were all shouting 'Soviet friend' to you."

A young Chinese official who joined us looked embarrassed. At the first opportunity he said: "These children used the phrase 'Soviet friend' in the same way they would use the word 'foreigner.' They don't know the difference between an Englishman and a Russian."

The incident ended our brief honeymoon. Most of the Satellites (as I now began to think of the other Asians and East Europeans in our party) snapped and barked away, sometimes at me and sometimes at the Chinese, while Tomagatski and I held our peace.

Only one man who should remain anonymous began suddenly to confide in me. "I've had enough of China," he said. "At home, you can at least buy wine and go and enjoy yourself."

I glanced at him in astonishment. "These people scare me," he finally admitted. "It's like living in a convent, with confessions twice a day. I'm almost ashamed to get into bed with my wife."

Tomagatski never betrayed his feelings. I admired the bespectacled little Russian's modest and capable way of working. So many Russians in China, you were told, were clumsy louts. Tomagatski was not one of them. He spoke fluent mandarin

Chinese. He was the same age as myself, thirty-one, and shared the same hopes and misgivings about the future of his children, just as any other young parents in an atomic age.

There were other Russians in the area. A story was told that two Chinese discussed a new arrival from Vladivostok.

"He has feet like temple steps," said one, "hands so big they encircle the Altar of Heaven. His chest is like the Great Wall and his back is broad enough to carry the Monkey God and all his generals."

"But what about up here?" asked his companion, tapping the side of the head.

The first man shrugged, rolling his eyes and dropping his jaw like an imbecile. "After all," he said, "he's Russian."

There was another story.

"This Russian has hair on his chest, thick like the fibers in a rain cloak."

"Never mind, comrade. At the end of *our* second Five Year Plan we too shall have hair on our chests."

Simple and rather silly which, even if they did circulate widely, might not be truly indicative of Chinese sentiment. Yet it was evident that in Yunnan, the sojourn of Russians was brief. The impression grew that here, anyway, the Chinese were not anxious for Moscow's political advice. Technical guidance was another matter. There were Russian linguists among the backward tribes; Russian engineers on short, supervisory trips to small factories; but the main problem, the political status of the minority, one third of the local population, was one the Chinese preferred to handle in their own way.

It seemed significant that an official had joined us from the Yunnan Foreign Office. I asked him why there should be a special provincial department of foreign affairs. "We always have had one," he replied.

The desire for an independent Yunnan state was always known to exist among leaders who regarded the Chinese as intruders. I was tempted to goad Chen with rumors of a Free Yunnan Movement. After all, if the Chinese were digging into history to find British scapegoats, they might as well dig deeper and blame the Mongols who drove the Burmese Shans out of this territory and turned it into a part of China. As recently as World War II, the feeling of separation from China was strong. The Governor of Yunnan had even suggested a distinctive Yunnan assistance program to U.S. officials at Kunming, along the lines of Marshall Aid to China.

Yet, and here was the paradox, there were few other places where the feeling of returning to a medieval period in the reign of some great Chinese emperor was so strong. There were few portraits of Mao Tse-tung, but the Peking imprint was strong. There was little claptrap about "glorious Russian leadership" but a good deal of old-fashioned Chinese nationalism among officials carefully selected and indoctrinated.

Here I heard again the story that Stalin had once sent Mao a textbook on Russian guerrilla warfare in World War II. Mao passed it on to his greatest expert on partisan tactics, General Lin Piao, whose Fourth Field Army was first into the Korean war. He reported back: "If we had used these lessons, we should have been annihilated ten years ago!"

Similarly, if the tough Stalinist tactics with national minorities were applied in Yunnan, there would have been an uprising. As it was, I felt sure that most of the Satellites were a trifle uneasy about what we were being shown. The East Germans, with characteristic devotion to doctrine, plainly felt that the Chinese were not practicing Marxist-Leninism. Tomagatski, on the other hand, kept on scribbling his notes with the air of an earnest student.

I have said that, so far as it was possible to check, nobody seemed to answer questions with deliberate lies. On the other hand, there were many evasions. Most of these were concerned with living standards.

There were severe shortages of pork, edible oils and even rice in regions beyond the vicinity of the Burma Road. There was unemployment. There was lack of money to finance the bigger and more ambitious projects originally planned.

Corvée labor was widely used, just as in the past. Peasants were assigned to specific tasks: water control, road repairs, supply distribution and cultivation of virgin land. These public works required a skilled management to plan, recruit, organize and feed the labor forces. This management formed a powerful bureaucracy.

"Same as it always was," I commented to an official. "You're still a ruling bureaucracy."

We were walking through a marble works. It had become part of a giant collective. The craftsmen chipped away at the blocks of marble, fashioning the same inkstands, the same paperweights and ornamental plates the same age-old ovals of veined stone that fit into the backs of ancestral rosewood chairs. There had been a time, not long ago, when they were turning out busts of Mao. Times had changed. There were not even slogans on the walls or emulation banners.

"We are fighting bureaucratism all the time," replied Comrade Chieh Min. His own title, ironically enough, stretched forth in the full panoply of beadledom: Director of Affairs-in-General for the Autonomous *Chou* of Tali.

He took me to see the Cormorant Fishing Production Team of the collective.

"There is a norm for each cormorant," he explained. "A certain number of fish should be caught monthly by the birds."

The cormorants were tightly ringed about the neck. There were a dozen birds for one flat-bottomed punt which the fisherman poled slowly over the lake. The birds dived, partly swallowed the fish and then disgorged them into the boat.

I said: "Who counts the number of fish caught by each cormorant?"

Comrade Chieh indicated a blue-tunicked figure under the village banyan.

"Does he spend all his time counting fish?"

The Director looked uncomfortable. "Yes," he admitted.

"He's a young man," I said. "He could be productive instead of just standing there adding up figures. You see, you've got bureaucrats everywhere the moment you try to organize on such a big scale."

"Our Chairman says we must fight bureaucratism," repeated the Director obstinately.

This was perfectly true. Mao was always launching campaigns against bureaucrats. Undoubtedly he knew that here was the one weak spot in Marxist-Leninism. His massive society was erected on theories by Karl Marx based on observed facts in Europe. But Marx had carefully ignored Asian society where the ruling class did not own the means of production. The ruling class was made up of bureaucrats. And while kings might come and kings might go, the happy civil servant went on forever in real control.

The bureaucrats proliferate in China today and every effort to make them "close to the people" leads to more ludicrous campaigns. There was even a drive to stop the bureaucratic discussions on how to curb bureaucracy. Peasants complained of too many political meetings; then senior officials complained of too many Party gatherings to study how to reduce the number of meetings.

"Our government is like the banyan," said the Director as we admired this giant fig tree. It was a king among banyans, its ancient roots thrusting up new trunks, the branches interlacing, and the dusty leaves harboring a multitude of odd creatures. There it stood, guarding the queer little township of Yu Nun where cormorants had to meet norms and where statisticians counted the cormorants, and Party members kept an eye on the statisticians.

The banyan was a gathering place for coolies. Small boys moved in single file with yokes on their necks, heavy rice bags balanced on the yokes. Old women shuffled forward to have loaded panniers hung upon the ends of their carrying poles.

A former Chinese Red Army colonel stood in the cobbled square, shouting out numbers and peering up as another coolie moved into place. An old woman's bundle began to slide sideways. It overbalanced with a crash, scattering firewood everywhere.

The ex-colonel was beside her in an instant, on his knees, helping gather the wood.

His reaction seemed instinctive but it must have been the result of intensive propaganda, for the Chinese (as they would be first to admit) are not a publicly courteous people. Of course it was easy to point out the huge army barracks built beside each of the towns through which we passed, and to suggest this military burden was one cause of the manifest poverty around us. But the troops could be seen working on building sites or helping in the fields. It was common to see a soldier helping a peasant with his burdens.

Mao, nevertheless, was trying to change human nature. That the task was impossible seemed clear from the frequency of antibureaucratic movements. Inevitably the army drifted away from its earthier contacts. From time to time, there was the rare spectacle of a mayor or a minister shoveling coal or digging ditches. No doubt this was good for the health and it might induce a temporary sense of humility. It led to good habits but there was an uneasy feeling all the time that Mao was a stern headmaster whose pupils needed touching up on occasions with a stout cane.

Again and again, as China pursued the path of nonviolent conquest, the army got fat and comfortable. Edicts had to be issued: officers' wives were growing fond of luxury; too many young lieutenants thought they were superior to the troops; there was too little attention paid to political study and the role of a *peasant* army.

This emphasis on the importance of peasants was familiar in another context. I discussed it one night as we walked through hushed streets to the local bathhouse.

Wooden shutters covered the shop fronts and a full moon lit our way. The North Gate was a gigantic old arch in three tiers. A mule train moved softly over the stones, ghostly with its strange undulating shapes.

I said: "People who understand Marxist-Leninism claim that China has never really applied its principles."

This challenging statement failed to evoke a response. I went on talking anyway, glad to impose some views on the comrades instead of having to note their own dreary recitations.

"Fifty years ago," I continued, "China had more than a million members of the scholar-gentry. Today you've twelve million Communist Party members. Where's the difference?" (Short pause. No reply.)

"There isn't any. The scholar-gentry were people who passed

an elaborate examination and they provided Government officials and also helped run the country. They were the ruling class."

A voice in the darkness, provoked but not unfriendly, said: "You are full of theories. You are always full of theories."

"No, I'm only repeating what I've read. But look at the functions of the scholar-gentry compared with Party members. In the old days, Peking made the decisions on armed forces, official appointments, taxation, justice . . . But there was no body of law except the Penal Code. So the gentry handled civil disputes. They did welfare work, maintained temples and made sure that the high moral principles of Confucius were understood. They conducted village meetings and lectures to expound Confucian doctrine. And that, I reckon, is the way it works today. Only now you call it Communism."

Another voice said: "We are applying Communist principles to the specific problems of China."

"But when you think you're being very good Communists," I insisted, "you're really showing traditional devotion to your leader and at the same time practicing some very sound Confucian teachings."

Unfortunately this led to a wrangle about Confucius. Yet it was a fact that the Party and the old scholar-gentry were in much the same tradition. It was the gentry in the past who listed peasants as the most important among commoners; putting them ahead of artisans and merchants although they were much the poorest class.

Of course the comparison ends there. Mao Tse-tung, extolling the peasantry, had urged that "the army be merged as one with the masses." But he added: "It will then be invincible in the world."

Still there was a touch of the past in the admonition to good behavior, the constant reminders of Communist (formerly Confucian) disciplines. For instance the Chinese Red Army had been undergoing a purge. In the awful jargon of the new age, officers were told: "Some comrades develop the bad habit of sitting in offices without proceeding to the midst of their men. They are falling into serious bureaucratism and documentarianism, conceit and self-complacency, *the nondevelop-*

ment of criticism and self-criticism and even the suppression of criticism and retaliation against the critics."

What sort of madness was this? Documentarianism, indeed. The nondevelopment of criticism! Yet there *was* a Confucian ring to it.

We were inside the bathhouse now. Candles were brought. A long, skinny old man uncoiled himself from a wooden bench and flip-flopped across the creaking floor. Another pulled the great copper kettle from an open fire. Steaming vapors began to rise from the row of marble pits. We plunged in.

The comrades began to ·chatter. Their voices rose above the roaring waters. I eavesdropped, being unable to do much else.

"We went two years without washing water in the jungle," shouted Li, the emaciated Vietnamese. "It gets like a Turkish bath in the north. We were supposed to be fighting French imperialists. I spent most of the time fighting mosquitoes . . ."

"I remember — you evacuated a lot of civilians into the Tai mountains," said another voice. "We heard about it. After four years, they were on hands and knees begging for salt. They were all night-blind. From lack of salt. After sunset they were totally blind."

Li yelled: "Exactly! We were stupid that way. We had insufficient water so we washed in our own sweat. We burned huge fires when the day was hottest and danced round them until the perspiration poured like a waterfall. Then we washed in it. But you know what? The salt was washed out of our bodies. Soon we were covered with sores. They would never heal. We got sick and weak only from lack of salt."

There were more war stories. Chiang, the Korean with a Chicago hat, was recounting an incident. "Those Americans," he said. "They put down a barrage to knock the top off our observation post. It was on the highest point of a small hill. They used dive bombers, artillery, mortars . . . On the fourth day our hill was reduced by six feet. Next morning we put up a sign. It was in very good English. I think the Americans thought it was funny. It said *Please — small-arms fire only . . .*"

Chen, always a faithful interpreter on these occasions, filled out the details. But most of the conversation was in English

with occasional snatches of Chinese. Never Russian. And I
thought how odd it was to hear these former enemies using the
common language of those they professed to hate.

Later, with grave courtesy, they apologized for inflicting
these memories upon me. But they needed little encouragement to continue. I began to place Li in the scheme of things.
An old Indochina communiqué came back to mind:

> Black-clad Vietminh Communists crept into French military
> airport early today planting plastic bombs on bombers and com-
> munications planes. It was second raid in three days. At Hai-
> phong transports and bombers were blown up on tarmac. Red
> leader escaped after ten-minute gun battle in middle of runway.
> Concerted attack on French air power like this could threaten
> slender supply line to vital places like Dienbienphu.

I regarded Li with new respect.

Not for the first time, though, one was forced to contemplate the odd clumsiness of Peking's propaganda. There must
be scores of extraordinary and true adventure stories arising
from the Chinese Red Army's remarkable history, from its
Long March into retreat as a force of disciplined peasant rebels
to the major conflict of Korea. But these stories, to mean anything, had to be told the way I heard them recounted in Tali's
bathhouse. Instead they were so clothed in political claptrap
that they became unintelligible. The Korean War ones were
particularly odious: the hero invariably made a last self-criticism to his group leader before diving into the jaws of death
crying: "For Chairman Mao and the Party! . . ."

If the Chinese should ever introduce a really sophisticated
note into their propaganda, then indeed some startling changes
would be afoot. After all, propaganda is a means of propagat-
ing a faith. It gives a clue, therefore, to the true character of
its originators, even if we think of it today as entirely false
and misleading.

Sometimes the Chinese have reached a high point of urban-
ity and even humor. But not often. An attempt was made by
the last man you would expect it from, the Minister of Public
Security, Lo Jui-ching, who has a sinister reputation. He was

talking to a Peking conference about (oddly enough) the army. He warned the public to be more vigilant against rogues, spies and anti-Communists. Then he quoted the case of Sergeant Li Wan-ming who promoted himself to be chief of staff of the Chinese Twelfth Field Army.

Minister Lo heaped scorn upon the many people duped by Sergeant Li during his rise to power. Li was a top sergeant in Chiang Kai-shek's 208th Division. He was captured by the Red Army at Nanking, escaped, and forged credentials that got him into the Military and Political Academy of the Second Red Field Army. From there he faked more appointments: to a job in municipal administration; thence to a ministerial post, and so on. By forging telegrams and letters, Li joined ten different government bureaus in ten different cities and built up such an outstanding (but totally untrue) record that he was inadvertently given a real job as chief of the administrative department in the Ministry of Forestry.

Horrified at the prospect of honest labor and a little aghast at the dizzy heights he had attained, Li hastily forged himself a telegram. It requested most urgently that he go at once to the Twelfth Field Army as a senior military adviser and commander of its 35th Division. The Minister of Forestry was deeply upset that his new protégé should be taken away so swiftly. But, being a realistic man and accustomed to disappointments, he tried to help all he could.

"The Forestry comrades were so obliging," reported Public Security Minister Lo with heavy sarcasm, "they even gave him, without hesitation, an air ticket to his new post."

Then, throwing his hands up in despair, Minister Lo cried: "Oh that we should have a Gogol in China to relate this story to us all so that we might 'lie on fagots and taste gall.'"

We had been on the road two weeks and covered some twelve hundred miles before I appreciated with just how much fascinated horror some of my non-Chinese companions were regarding the social experiments displayed to view. As good orthodox Communists from Europe and Russia, they seemed appalled by the cavalier Chinese dismissal of entire groups of people as "undergoing ideological reform."

Their reasons for being shocked were entirely different from mine. They felt the Chinese ran a grave risk of becoming contaminated by class enemies, since they preferred to argue with them rather than merely liquidate them. Of course the weapons of force were always there, ready for instant use, but the Chinese view was that opposition could be uprooted only by "struggle." This meant mentally wrestling with your political opponents. And to get them involved in such combat, you had to persuade them first to reveal their innermost thoughts.

My Chinese consorts made it clear they tackled all potential enemies in terms of political classification so that whether it was a tribe of hillmen or the merchant class of Chinese, the problem was to invade their mental citadels.

As we drew back from the Burmese border, we plunged more deeply into rural matters. The Chinese discussed methods of overcoming resistance among farmers and peasants as they previously talked about converting the miniature "nations" of tribes along the border. The word they employed was "transform" and I had the odd feeling that they regarded the magical transformation of capitalists into comrades as requiring much the same patient effort as the transformation of, say, India into a Communist society.

"The task is the same whether we wish to transform Tibetans or intellectuals still tainted by bourgeois ideology," said one official.

I replied that this did not conform with Soviet practice. Stalin would not have lumped people everywhere into such broad classifications without reference to national boundaries.

He gave me a cold look. "Stalin was not always right," he said. "He even had to admit he was wrong about us."

(This was certainly true if the Yugoslav Communist leader Tito and his Foreign Minister, Kardelj, were to be believed. They reported these words from Stalin at a meeting in 1948:

After the war we invited the Chinese comrades to Moscow and we discussed the situation in China. We told them bluntly that we considered the development of the uprising in China had no prospects, that the Chinese comrades should seek a *modus vivendi* with Chiang Kai-shek, and that they should join the

Chiang Government and dissolve their army. The Chinese comrades agreed here in Moscow but went back to China and acted quite otherwise. They mustered their forces, organized their armies and now, as we see, they are beating Chiang Kai-shek's army. Now in the case of China we admit we were wrong.) *

It seemed to me the Chinese were still showing this same contempt for Russian advice. But officials were swift to stunt any budding notions I might have about Titoism.

I said to Chen that it looked as if collective farms were being organized on the same competitive basis as in Yugoslavia. "Yes," he agreed. "We have adopted a similar system." Then he added swiftly and emphatically: "However, we are not using such a system in building up our industry. In Yugoslavia there is Tito's method of competition between factories. But not here."

Industrial plans were to a large extent dependent on crops. By 1957, the Chinese Communists seemed in all their published economic schemes to be anxious to reduce their reliance on Soviet help. But natural calamities struck the countryside with depressing regularity and since most new factories, loosely speaking, were financed by surplus farm crops, the outlook was grim. So I asked to see as much of the peasants' new society as possible. I wanted to estimate China's chances of pursuing industrial ambitions which had been scaled down heavily already. I also wanted to see the same technique for transforming a Ka Wa head-hunter applied to a Wicked Landlord.

* *Tito Speaks*, official biography by Vladimir Dedijer.

CHAPTER TEN

Redemption for a Wicked Landlord

"LANDLORDS are the most wicked members of society," said Chen as we ducked behind walls of sorghum and mud. "But we provide a way out. That is the genius of Chairman Mao. We always give an exit.

"Great Chinese generals whom the Chairman much admires always preached this strategy. If you do not provide an escape route, then your enemies will stand and fight. This is true in war and agriculture. To eliminate certain people, surround them but leave a narrow path of retreat. So let us find a landlord who has met salvation."

Four Willows Village was surrounded with high walls that crumbled with neglect. Bandits were a nightmare of the past and chickens roosted in the old defense works. An iron broadsword weighing at least two hundred pounds leaned against wooden doors into the temple courtyard which had become, incredibly, The Peasants' Recreation Hall.

I was faced with four giggly girls. They were the Committee for Reading of Newspapers and I won fleeting fame by identifying myself as an Honorable Scribe for Publication of Enlightenment . . . Our flirtation was brief. I asked them for news. They said a wicked imperialist plot by Anglo-French gangsters to steal Suez from Egypt had been stopped by Russian threats of atomic retaliation. I therefore proposed to tell

them about a diabolical Russian attack on Hungarian patriots
in a place called Budapest.

They replied tartly that they already knew about Hungary.
The Soviet Union had selflessly rushed troops there to defend
The People whose popular government appealed for aid
against plotting Imperialist-Fascist spies.

Prettily tossing their silky pigtails, they returned to their
solemn duties. Soon each sat in a corner with her attentive
little audience of illiterate old peasants, their chirps transforming the world into two teams of Goodies and Baddies.

"I was angry at being classified a landlord," said Yang
Chang when he was finally discovered wiping his streaming
nose between finger and thumb. "My redemption came last
autumn when I clearly saw my mistakes. I was a muleteer. I
built up my business with my own brain and muscle. But gradually the People made me see how I had exploited them. Two
landlords were executed, one brigand was killed and ten or
twenty landlords went to jail."

Yang dangled one of his numerous children on a bared knee.
The courtyard was a cloud of dust from the rice threshers.
Smoke curled up from under thick-tiled roofs of a village that
was already old in Julius Caesar's time. I tried to imagine the
revolution that had swept through this pastoral scene only seven
years before.

The Meetings of Accusation had been most terrifying of
all. In some parts of China, landowners were fleshed, flayed,
dragged behind plows, hanged and lynched.

"We had to arouse the peasants," said Ho Hung-kwang, director of these operations. He was a quiet sort of man, with a
face like the surface of a very deep and tranquil pool. He
read from a thick sheaf of papers. One hundred years ago he
would have been head of a *pao-chia*, the ancient police system
based on collective responsibility among rustics. In those days,
families were controlled in units of ten or one hundred. Now
they were controlled in similar units, with supreme command
in the hands of Ho.

Yang the Wicked Landlord waited for Ho to finish. Ten or
twelve men gathered round. This was a familiar ritual. They

were ready to squat and talk tirelessly until dawn struggling, as it were, for my enlightenment.

On the barn door opposite were new and attractive posters. An old man bending to retrieve an ear of corn behind a hay-cart said: *Every grain is the precious result of man's labor.* An impressionist painting of a security trooper prodding his rifle at a ragged wretch was more militant: *Crush counter-revolutionaries!*

He rocked on his heels and said: "We had to shock the peasants out of their submission to tyranny. People blamed the gods for flood and famine. We showed them that the real enemies were a handful of exploiters."

New legends had to be invented and humans substituted for devils. Each village had to find sixteen Exploiters. At Four Willows, in 1950, they were lined up in Pig Market.

"We must admit it was hard to find any big landlords," murmured Ho. "The largest hereabouts had only four acres."

Mass accusations brought all the bitterness and hate of the past to a boil. Agitators among the peasants began by hurling abuse at the victims. Stones were thrown. Slowly the crowds were worked up to a pitch of hysteria difficult to imagine.

I looked at Ho and then at Yang. So far as I could see they were the same kind of men. Their faces were prematurely old, their clothes were patched and patched again until nothing was left of the original material. They had suffered the same misfortunes, prayed to the same gods, shared their rice and sweet potatoes when times were bad, and possibly they had got drunk together and quarreled amiably over the same women. Yet the time had come when Ho became an accuser and Yang his victim. Why had this been done? Or perhaps of greater importance — how?

First came the Land Reform Corps of dedicated youngsters from the provincial capital. Their first task was to Get Close to the Peasants by means of the Five Goods: *thinking, learning, work, work style and physical labor.* There were twenty of them who billeted themselves around the village with another magic phrase on their lips: *Let Us Share Three Things: food, living quarters and labor.*

This visitation took place after Red Army troops had been in the area long enough to reassure the peasants. Army political officers had already talked endlessly about the new era in which all the causes of distress would be removed. Now the Land Reform Workers began what was called importantly Popular Investigation: *hu-k'ou tiao ch'a*. Not unwillingly, the local people talked about their grievances and slowly a list was drawn of the worst Exploiters.

To win local confidence and to build up a dossier on the Exploiters, the Land Reformers conducted a program called *fang-ping wen-k'u* or Visiting-Poor and Asking-About-Pains. Old people were encouraged to recite over and over again their unhappy memories and this was known as Disgorging-Bitter-Rice. The entire campaign was a Thought Mobilization in preparation for the trials to follow. During this time, a number of peasants were given nicknames. Ho was identified as Go-Ahead Ho but his neighbor who was less co-operative became Slow-Witted Yang.

Mao Tse-tung had said: "To put it bluntly, a brief reign of terror was necessary." And so the more obvious Exploiters whose presence was not required at the public trails were swiftly assembled. It was not clear whether they were dealt with by the army or by peasants already worked up by the Land Reformers. At any rate, an unknown number of the bigger landlords were tied to wooden plows and dragged around the fields in a new sport named for the occasion *chian-ti-kuang-tze* or Grinding-the-Earth-Roller. Of course they died and were soon buried.

There must have been by this time a smell of blood around the place. Chairman Mao had decreed that justice for the time being could be safely entrusted to the peasants. "Their eyes are perfectly discerning," he said. "As to who is bad and who is not, who is the most ruthless and who is less so, and who is to be severely punished and who is to be dealt with lightly, the peasants keep perfectly clear accounts and very seldom has there been any discrepancy between punishment and crime."

A few haggard wretches were now wandering around with placards on their backs: *Feudal Landlord*. There was at the same time a Distribution of Floating Riches, the land itself having been already parceled out. The labeled landlords were urged to find redemption by disgorging their hidden treasures: Dig-for-Bottom-Wealth. If they failed to do so, either because they were frightened out of their wits to disclose further possessions or because they simply had no further wealth, they were liable to the accusation: Saboteur-of-Land-Reform. This same charge could be directed against anyone who did not wholeheartedly join in the national witch hunt.

The accusation meetings were a sort of grand finale to the macabre carnival of hate. If a sister or cousin showed signs of personal sentiment toward an Object of Struggle (the defendant) there were cries of "False Humanitarianism!" from leaders of the mob. A friend or neighbor who was suddenly smitten with pity or some similar weakness might be accused of Personal Relationism. Consequently the man on trial looked in vain for support from family or friends. Usually they cheered and booed the loudest.

All this had come to pass after years of submission to fate. Already, it seemed to me, it was gone and done with. "You must allow us to make mistakes," said one of my Peking companions. But was revolutionary justice still dispensed in this same rough-and-ready manner?

I asked Ho this question. He hedged. I realized he could not possibly have any concept of what I meant by the word justice. For him there was only crime and punishment. The only law had been that exercised by the Exploiters over the Oppressed. Some had power to define the crime and the others took the punishment. He thought in those simple terms because for him it had been quite as simple as that. If there was any improvement now in the system of trials, well, it must be counted a gain. Still I kept prodding, though I felt it was like asking an Ancient Briton to explain *habeas corpus*. He said that now Four Willows was part of a collective, there were several committees to deal with social problems and settle family disputes. There was no crime.

"No crime?"

"No crime," replied Ho firmly.

"What about this Law and Order Committee you mention?"

"It posts guards in the fields to protect crops."

"Guards against what?"

"Counter revolutionaries," said Ho. "It also supervises landlords."

Yang looked up and fidgeted with silver coins hanging from his son's wrist. "I was lucky and got through the Land Reform net first time. I was an Exploiter who never got caught."

There were appreciative chuckles.

I asked Ho: "How do you figure he exploited people? He built up his own business out of nothing and contributed to the general good."

"He lived on the work of others," said Ho. "But there is a way of redemption for such men. In 1953 we put out the net again. This time he was caught and classified."

Yang lost all privileges. He became, in his way, a prisoner. But in China there are other ways of keeping a man captive besides putting him behind bars. This is why honest travelers seldom report the spectacle of labor gangs under armed guard. Prisoner Yang was put into one of twenty-three Production Teams known euphoniously as The Brick-and-Tile Committee. Other teams in this collective made a curious list. They included The Rice-Huskers, a group called Fishers and Hunters, The Horse-and-Cart Team and another simply entitled Caravan. The last one was made up of sixty bent little old women who scuttled home that evening with staggering loads of firewood.

Stripped of all his rights, fearful of further punishments, Yang was subjected to intensive self-analysis. He wrote his autobiography again and again. Discrepancies were discussed to a point of exhaustion. Then in the spring of 1956 it was agreed to put landlords on the road back to full citizenship. Yang was reported on by his workmates, "because those who work with you know you best." All the old ground was covered again. Comrades talked to him late into the night, probing for some lingering trace of his earlier individuality.

"Are you saved, brother?" was obviously their theme although Yang put it differently. "I was declassified as a Wicked

Landlord two months ago," he said. "I am grateful to the Party and to Chairman Mao for their correct leadership in helping me to see the truth."

Yang was out under license but one thing was made abundantly clear. He would never quite shake off the past. He had been an Exploiter. Should another brief reign of terror become necessary, he might easily find himself back among the Bricks-and-Tiles.

Chinese have developed their end of the Burma Road which here crosses into Burma. Banners proclaim eternal friendship between Chinese and Burmese.

Burmese bowman is attending the Chinese "culture station" on the other side of the border. He will spread Mao's gospel among the tribes of Upper Burma, preaching subversion, and recruiting Communist agents.

A multitude gathered in a hidden valley, conjured out of the remote hills by a wave of Peking's magic wand. Barracks and a tent city were built in seven weeks to hold 17,000 peasants.

Red Chinese troops relax while awaiting their Premier on a visit to a rural area.

Young Pioneers await
the order from cadres
in background to laugh
and sing.

These girls, drawn from different tribes of China, are trained to perform their local dances and songs while spreading the new gospel of Mao and Marx.

The cormorants were tightly ringed about the neck. There was a "norm" for each, and one official counted the number of fish they were forced to disgorge. They belonged to a "Fishers and Hunters Team" of the embryo People's Commune.

Gossip session at a jungle subversion center known as a "culture station."

"Here," said the Commissar, "is a young woman of clean habits and healthy outlook."

Wicked Landlord Yang
had found redemption.

School for the coolie was sometimes a black-board on the roadside.

Fiddles and drums of
the storytellers were
still drawing the crowds
despite the competition
of a lecture on dialectics
next door.

CHAPTER ELEVEN

Requiem for an Industrial Plan

◉ ◉

WHEREVER we paused, I was struck by the new attitude of rural officialdom. There was little talk about mechanization. All the emphasis was upon human labor and the need to scale down local industrialization plans. It became perfectly obvious that China was not going to be the huge and lucrative market for tractors and other farming machinery contemplated by Western businessmen.

The reason seemed to be a widespread poverty and the ill-concealed evidence of food shortages. Problems of food distribution had not yet been solved and while there was a glut of sweet little mandarin oranges in Yunnan, the same fruit was rare around Shanghai. Instead, you could buy for the equivalent of $11.25 in Shanghai a rare kind of Tartary melon. The price represented almost one third of a tram driver's monthly salary and it covered the cost of flying the melon from Sinkiang in the northwest.

Yet there was tranquillity and an air of organization about the countryside that seemed very much like a calm after the storm. Armed police were rarely seen and then, often as not, riding on haycarts with broad grins on their faces. You had to remind yourself of what seemed an impossible fact: that this was the scene of the greatest revolution in history. During the year just past, about one in every four peasants in the world had been herded into co-operative or collective farming by

Peking's zealots. (Within two years they occupied 26,000 People's Communes.)

This collective miracle turned out to be fairly easy to explain when closely examined. But you had to know the full story. You had to understand the technique of tension and then persuasion. Perhaps, too, it was not entirely accidental that the peasant since the dawn of Chinese history ranked higher in the social order than anywhere else in the world. By the time Mao Tse-tung mounted the Dragon Throne, China's peasants were badly in need of some co-operative type of farming which would enable them to share knowledge, implements and the tasks of irrigation.

Terror had scorched those who opposed Communist plans. Fear and incessant propaganda from Mao's chatterboxes weakened resistance. But once again the old problem nagged the regime: the problem of bureaucracy. Officials grew slack, threw their weight around, abused their powers and obeyed orders without using imagination or understanding.

Mao galvanized them all with a speech in the summer of 1955: "The mass movement is ahead of the leadership and the leadership is not catching up," he pronounced.

He then issued orders that seemed utterly fantastic. Only a few days earlier, local Communists had been reporting the disbanding of farming co-operatives which, it was said, were created hastily and now operated at a loss to the State and the peasants themselves. Now Mao castigated his officials and reversed gears. At the time his speech became public, there were less than 17,000,000 families in co-operative farms and less than 55,000 families in collectives. That is: 14 per cent of the whole peasant labor force were on the path to becoming salaried State workers. Eighteen months later, about 90 per cent of the country worked in mild or severe forms of collective.

Grain has always been vital to China's economy and the decision to break completely with traditional farming methods did expose the new regime to great dangers. What precipitated Mao's action? How had he executed his plans without apparent bloodshed? He was in the position of the monarchs who considered agriculture to be so important that they performed a ceremonial plowing each spring.

Each emperor, unlike Mao in his boiler suit, would dress in the costume worn by the Sons of Heaven for such occasions. On his purple and yellow surcoat and gown were embroidered the Twelve Ornaments including sun, moon, stars, pheasant, dragon and rice grains. He wore a mortarboard with pendants, and a leather girdle studded with precious gems, high boots with white soles, and in his hand he held a yellow rod.

The emperor thus accoutred would throw back his long sleeves and advance into the fields around the Altar of Agriculture. All was yellow around him: yellow oxen, yellow plows and yellow costumes to conceal the haggard faces of his minister of finance and the viceroy of the metropolitan province. They were haggard because of the earliness of the hour, because of the awful consequences should some mistake in the ceremony bring down heavenly wrath and also because the high boots had exceptionally thick soles which made walking difficult in the yellow mud. The emperor's task was to make eight furrows from east to west, the minister to his right and the viceroy to his left, while princes and other officials plowed another eighteen furrows into which were scattered rice and millet.

Today rice and millet are China's wealth. But there is something else, as Mao recognized when he issued his edict without festooning it with idle ceremony.

China's real wealth is her people. Again and again I was reminded of this by officialdom. Said one agricultural official: "We have to use more manpower, more animals. Mechanization cannot come yet. Labor is less costly."

Such interviews were sufficient authority for writing that China, perhaps sensibly, was not going blindly to follow Russian mechanization of the land.

(Six months later Premier Chou En-lai said: "Our main task is to increase production per acre by better use of manpower and animal power. Cost of production on mechanized farms might well prove to be higher than the cost on nonmechanized farms. Labor is still much cheaper than machines in China. Our big, State-owned mechanized farms, when set up even with gift tractors, are not unmixed blessings.")

Later a diplomat asked me why I thought this was going to happen. "Officials told me," I replied. He looked skeptical and I thought once again that brain-washing was not exclusively Chinese. In the West, honest men advising the U.S. Secretary of State had convinced themselves and Mr. Dulles that American newspapermen should be prevented from entering China because they would only act as carriers of "enemy" propaganda. The astonishing assertion was made that newspaper reporters were too simple-minded to make useful evaluations. It all added up to an admission that some U.S. leaders did not trust their own people's strength of character. "What could you find out that isn't already in their propaganda?" demanded one anti-Communist crusader with crushing scorn. I told him. This confirmed his view that anyone who got too close to the evil mainland was in danger of contamination.

Of course he had some excuse. Violent anti-American propaganda was appearing in Communist papers even while some Chinese, through the Indian Government, seemed to be scouting on the prospects of American aid of the sort given to Poland and Yugoslavia. These cautious overtures from Peking were rebuffed during Nehru's 1957 visit to the U.S.A. and this inflamed Chinese propagandists. "Hate the American Killer" was one headline . . . "Americans think nothing of killing people among their 'allies' and raping women at will."

It is in a way comforting that propagandists on either side of the world usually fashion a boomerang against themselves. Peking's propaganda chief, Lu Ting-I, probably hardened Western opinion *against* his regime more effectively than any other single human being. Stooping, shrivel-faced, mouth puckered into a bitter little grimace, middle-aged Lu is a product of an early American education and later training by Moscow. He is in many ways a Kremlin gremlin in China who has used every deceit to poison his own country's relations outside the Communist bloc, thus binding her more strongly to his latter-day Russian tutors.

Beyond Lu's barrage of hate, however, you found Chinese officials who were obviously glad to meet a visitor from the barbaric West. I was getting more license than the phrase "conducted tour" implies. China was clearly in bad economic shape and local officials were quite ready to discuss this. Experienced reporters like Jacques Loquin of the French News Agency predicted accurately that big and significant adjustments were being made to economic plans. Whereas one year earlier it had been possible to say China aimed to build a strong industrialized country modeled on the Soviet Union, it was now clear that many ambitious schemes were being shelved.

Heavy industry was still a cornerstone of China's plans. But it seemed apparent that earlier optimism was yielding to a more sober appraisal of facts. Chou En-lai had already revealed how desperately short they were of technicians and he presented his own twelve-year plan (worked out, of course, by the invisible and anonymous Collective Leaders) to raise the number of "ordinary intellectuals" from less than four million to ten million.

This was a curious echo of the prescription left by Dr. Sun Yat-sen for dividing a newly emancipated China into categories of people, like an efficient and intelligent colony of ants. The plan for producing intellectuals explained that they fell into three classes. Upper-class intellectuals were doctors, teachers, engineers, writers and artists *and they totaled one hundred thousand only.*

Ordinary intellectuals were laboratory workers and skilled factory hands. Third-class intellectuals were really workers with some ability to read and write and obey instructions.

Almost ten per cent of the very small group of upper-class intellectuals were said to be in need still of ideological reform "as a doctor would cure his patients." Their thoughts needed remolding "as naturally as you wash your face each day."

Production targets for this unique plan were: one million upper-class intellectuals by 1968, and an increase from 3,800,000 lower-class intellectuals to a bumper ten million. There was also a target for 1963: this was the date set by the Chinese Premier for "the transformation of the majority of intelligentsia into progressive thinkers who accept Marxist-Leninist viewpoints."

In this way, provided China could buy time with her "peaceful coexistence" policy abroad, it was hoped to return to the bigger schemes later. Meanwhile, with this meager force of technicians of whom many were politically unsafe, a slower program was agreed upon for development of the fuel and power resources, the iron and steel, chemicals and machinery without which China could never stand as an equal among the world's economic leaders.

How could several hundred million people be persuaded, however, that it was now in their interests to develop an agricultural and light industrial economy when it was previously vital they should sacrifice all comfort to build heavy industry?

The answer was that Mao and his Persuasion Brigades could persuade the peasants on almost any subject, *provided they took their time and studied every thought and action of the peasants.*

When it was time for war in Korea, the experts knew how to arouse the pride and fighting spirit of the country. When Peace was expedient, the whole countryside roared Peace. Birth control was bad: birth control was good. Flippant drama was counterrevolutionary: comedy helped socialism. State steel plows were vital to farms: State steel plows were useless. This dockyard must be built: it must not be built. I had seen enough of these reversals to believe Mao had a genius for practicing his own advice on how to spread ideas among the masses "until the masses regard them as their own."

But he could do much better than that, proving the reversibility even of words until Black not only proved to be White, but could be transformed back again. Thus Mao instructed his millions of human mouthpieces in 1957: "Democracy is relative to centralism: freedom is relative to discipline. They are two conflicting aspects of a single entity, contradictory as well as united, and we should not one-sidedly emphasize one to the denial of the other. We cannot do without freedom nor can we do without discipline; we cannot do without democracy nor can we do without centralism. Our democratic centralism means the unity of democracy and centralism and the unity of freedom and discipline. Under this system the people enjoy a wide measure of democracy and freedom but at the same time they have to keep within the bounds of socialist discipline."

Freedom, it was clear to at least one reader, meant Slavery. For there was no clear definition of where the disciplinary boundaries lay. In fact, as Mao himself confirmed, this dangerous but invisible margin could be shifted according to circumstances by the authors of these extraordinary inversions.

The biggest reversal of all had been the overnight switch in land reform. Turning his full fury on agricultural officials, Mao had accused them in the bad crop year of 1955 of "stumbling like old women with bound feet." His method of galvanizing them out of a stumbling gait in one direction into a brisk canter in the opposite direction seems worthy of further study.

CHAPTER TWELVE

"Let Us Now Admit It. China Is Poor and Backward"

◉ ◉

WHEN a Chinese wrote the word for the place he loved best, he drew a pig under a roof. This was the ideograph for "home." Even in the Forbidden City where all the talk may be about atomic research or a new steel town, it is this modest little sign which is still used after the brushes are dipped into sticky Chinese ink and new State documents are written. If you search the trays of leaden ideographs in a Chinese typewriter (clumsy, like a crude computer) you will find the sign for "male" is still a combination of two 2,000-year-old characters for "field" and "strength."

The ruler who forgets these humble origins of China is apt to have his poor memory sharply and permanently cured by the peasants. All through the millenniums, China's emperors have wisely placed the fieldworkers in second place in the social order. Today Mao Tse-tung sits secure because he has gone one better. He insists that the peasant comes first, and although an outsider might question whether this is really the case, Mao's regime at least promotes the belief.

There was a grave danger that Chinese officialdom might overlook the importance of the peasantry, even as recently as 1955. Peking saw it as a time when Wicked Landlords reared their ugly heads again. Secret land transactions were taking place. The people had forgotten their curious classifications: out of 500,000,000 who lived by farming, 60 per cent were labeled "Poor Peasants" which meant they had little or no land. There were still some Middle Peasants with enough to live on that they need not hire out as laborers and there survived some Rich Peasants with so much land they could pay for outside labor. This Communist division gave the impression of wealth and poverty living side by side. In fact, a *mu* or one sixth of an acre would support a single peasant and it was a rich man indeed who worked seven acres.

Mao in that same year cocked the trigger of a gun that would propel his peasants into a revolutionary upheaval such as the world had never seen. He made a personal investigation into the condition of the countryside and some say he strode across the rice paddies much as he had done as a youth when he stripped to catch the sun's rays in accordance with his theory of "absorbed energy," and tuned his ears to what the peasants were saying. This time, though clad, he had more energy than some of his faithful followers can have appreciated.

"What still lingers in the countryside is capitalist ownership by rich peasants and individual peasant ownership — an ocean of it. As everyone has noticed in recent years, the spontaneous tendency in the countryside to develop toward capitalism is daily growing stronger and new rich peasants are springing up everywhere. Many well-to-do peasants are striving to become rich ones." Thus spake Mao when he returned home to brief his ideological commandos.

His attack was directed not so much against offending peasants as against the officials who were forgetting the lessons of history. Some observers believed that when Mao got out among his own kind, they were quick to accuse his regime of not pursuing the revolution. This may be true. On the other hand, it seems much more likely that Mao could see the countryside drifting back into capitalistic habits and that he manufactured these complaints and accusations in order to respond to them. If this seems a tortuous theory, it is worth remembering that Mao's own official record reveals this pattern of devious methods for calculated plans. His own slogan, in fact, was this: "Cadres Should Use the Poor Peasants, Unite with the Middle Peasants, Gradually Eliminate Rich Peasants."

He took great pains to avoid a further terror. Grim memories still stalked the placid countryside. To an onlooker, it seemed changeless and unhurried. You recoiled at the spectacle of so much energy applied with such diligence to tiny tasks: a man scratching a furrow only five inches deep with the universal plow which consisted of a bent piece of wood and a rusting blade: the use of harrows in the paddies, mere bits of wood armed with a single row of teeth; the painful stealing of fertile land, step by step, up every steep hillside.

But the peaceful pastorals were misleading. The executions had shocked the peasantry and it is doubtful if many drifted into capitalistic ways except from sheer expediency. For instance, a Kunming city executive told me it had been necessary to introduce a controlled "free market" to encourage greater production among peasants who otherwise kept some of their produce for private sale in order to live. "Now," he said, "our Kunming free market is getting 40,000 more chickens, 20,000 more eggs and 120,000 more catties of charcoal and firewood for the State than would have been previously available — *every day.*"

Devices like the free market were brief nostrums to heal injured feelings after a convulsion of petty tyrannies. While the butchery was ended, the technique of mass arrests was still employed, usually for a short time after each harvest. Sometimes statistics were published that revealed a great deal. They were given by officials who quite clearly suffered no sense of shame and when it was admitted, for instance, that many innocent people were jailed, the Minister of Public Security blandly submitted the argument that it was better to inconvenience temporarily a few innocents than allow many offenders to escape. "Temporary inconvenience" might be anything from a few months in a cell to several years' hard labor on the Yellow River. Madame Shih Liang, then Minister of Justice, even more blandly declared that during eighteen months prior to mid-1955, there had been about one million criminal cases brought for preliminary hearing before People's Courts, mostly in the countryside. One third of these cases she identified as counterrevolution and sabotage. The lady Minister regretted that not enough attention was being paid to the current class struggle; not enough arrests and trials were made; serious crimes were dismissed with light sentences because of "Rightist, pacific and lethargic thinking."

All this was said to the accompaniment of police action shortly before Mao launched his campaign, casting himself and the Party in the familiar role of heroes acting solely on behalf of the peasantry. Thus, having frightened the countryside and revived memories of the earlier phase of mass executions, Mao could send forth his battalions of persuaders.

I asked how their arguments were phrased. Briefly, peasants were cajoled by endless discussions lasting far into the night, conducted by tireless and garrulous young men previously briefed (in the case of Yunnan) at Kunming. These briefings were no less gigantic than the mass trials and they brought to the provincial capitals the battalions of youths whose job was to execute new policy.

"We called into Kunming many thousands of Land Reform cadres," the municipal secretary general, Chin Chu-ju, told me in explaining why Kunming's population showed a sudden increase of twenty thousand in one year. "These got special training and were then sent down to lower levels of government in the countryside."

I inquired later about the kind of briefings that were given. It appeared that these took place as often as twice a year, and that the "agricultural bureaucrats" at a given signal would trek into Kunming from their remote stations on foot, by bicycle or in carts. Once assembled, they were given Mao's latest directives to study *and discuss*. The discussions were most important of all. They kept each man's mind politically pure and drilled into him a set of automatic reactions to ensure that he could operate independently until the next assembly.

A typical follow-up lesson appeared in *Hsueh Hsi (Study)* for January of 1957, when a campaign was in full blast against the cadres themselves whose heavy-handedness might be causing discontent. The case is quoted of a village Party secretary mobilizing peasants for a collective farm.

"Do you know what Communist society is like?" he asked. "If you are annoyed with cold in winter, you take a plane to the tropical seacoast. If heat annoys you in summer you can go to the North Pole. Isn't that good?"

The peasants said: "Good."

"Well, sign here," said the secretary, coming to the point.

"Joining the collective calls for further consideration," they said.

The secretary was enraged. "If you do not join the collective, you do not support Communism." And so he produced his pistol and forced them one by one to sign.

This behavior was called Commandism and the revealing comment was made that another campaign had been launched "to do away with this practice of using force."

To correct it and other bureaucratic faults, a nation-wide drive was already under way. It became known to the outside world through official references to a speech made by Mao Tsetung early in 1957 in which he warned against differences that might arise between the people and their own regime: an impudent heresy, by Russian standards (see page 377). In the countryside, the young and garrulous officials descended like magpies with a new set of slogans to apply to their own behavior this time.

These slogans became known of course to the peasants who were naturally glad to see Mao taking up the cudgels on their behalf. It was good to hear the insufferable wiseacres from town being told: "Go into the Fields Barefoot," and "Non-Productive Cadres Should Spend Half-Day in Fields, Half-Day in Office."

Better still, the men responsible for organizing collectives were instructed: "Stop Playing Poker! Tear up Playing Cards Which Estrange from Countryside."

Much was done to encourage oral and written denunciations against village officials. This could be done through a network of people whose tasks were to gather information. The uncharitable might call this a secret-police system, composed of: (1) Residents' Committees comprising between 100 and 600 households; (2) Street Offices to "carry out systematic social investigations" and thus leave the police to "devote full strength to combating secret agents, ruffians, bandits and other saboteurs"; (3) Security Substations which also conducted "publicity work regarding the elevation of revolutionary vigilance."

In Kunming there were 9000 men and women in a total population of 700,000 whose job was to run the local network. There were also Security Defense Committees: one for each of ten State-owned factories, one attached to each of twenty Middle Schools, the local university and technical colleges. There was one of these committees to each of seventy-nine farm co-operatives, and to each village. These Committees were set up in units of three to eleven adults "with a clean history, upright in work style, adept in linking up with the masses and enthusiastic in security work."

Besides all these precautions, there were People's Supervisory Correspondents, also known as Popular Reporting Agents although I doubted that many of them were overwhelmingly popular.

Their task was to watch for signs of political backsliding or laziness on the job: either one of these "crimes" could be made the basis of a charge of sabotage or counterrevolution. The charges were heard by People's Reception Offices, military tribunals or mobile courts. To help in the framing of charges, there were information boxes everywhere so that the accuser might remain anonymous.

Now all this vast apparatus was functioning smoothly by the time I was in Kunming. It had grown out of the original terror and it reinforced the new policy of persuasion.

Persuasive techniques were necessary from every practical viewpoint. As one rural official explained: "It used to be said that three sentences of soft words were not as good as a blow with a stick. It was also said that the masses could not be moved without pressure. But what happened when we used blows and pressure? The grain output went down."

Another said: "There is an old Chinese story. A farmer buys a donkey. He is told that it will work extremely hard but only responds to kind treatment. But the farmer discovers he cannot make the donkey do any work at all and he complains to the former owner who at once flogs the donkey into action. 'But you said this donkey responds to kind treatment!' protests the farmer. And the former owner replies: 'Yes, but you've got to catch its attention first.'"

Having terrified the peasants into an attitude of the strictest attention, the regime moved smoothly into another gear. But where was it getting China? To take this tiny corner, and more specifically this sleepy rural city of Kunming, as an example it seemed to me *nothing* of any practical value had been achieved in the previous seven years. Yes, there had been elimination of certain evils, but every capable Chinese was now engaged in watching his neighbor and echoing senseless slogans.

I went to a former aircraft factory outside Kunming. For a time it had been producing simple farming tools, a commendable endeavor at a time of crisis and food shortages. Then it stopped production altogether for three years while its skilled machine-tool workers underwent "political reform."

This was stated to me without much embarrassment by the directors. I could hardly believe my ears. In China, in the middle of the twentieth century, in a period of grave shortage of technical ability, these revolutionaries between 1950 and 1955 had in their possession 500 mechanical craftsmen and another 3000 semi-trained technicians, plus American precision machinery capable of copying Western aero engines and of making gears, instruments and machine tools. Yet their total production was two horizontal, Soviet-type boring machines, one Soviet-type vertical boring machine, two Soviet-type milling machines, two Soviet-type universal-tool milling machines and four copies of East European milling machines. They had also made steel plows of a pattern that later proved inapplicable to China's agriculture, helping to waste about one third of that year's modest steel production.

This factory had been set up by American engineers for the Central Resource Commission of the Chiang Kai-shek Government and had been regarded as one of the best in China. I wandered through its dilapidated sheds. Now, at long last, it was in brisk production and about 3000 men and women were making Soviet-style precision machinery.

I said they seemed to have been sacrificed to the worship of all things Russian. There was an English-speaking executive who walked with me, providing unofficial comments. He nodded and pointed to a large and idle American planing machine. "It is still in perfect condition after almost twenty years," he said and then looked significantly across at a new planing machine, copied from a Soviet model and built in a Chinese factory at the mouth of the Yellow River. The problem of breaking it down and transporting it to this distant rural scene must have been colossal. It had come two thousand miles on the backs of trucks, in trains, over rugged country trails, and I suppose it satisfied some official planner shuffling his blueprints and stabbing his pen here and there over the vast map of China.

"First an army officer was put in charge," said a director. "We studied from the Soviet Union the three-levels system of administration. We had to remold thoughts and style of working."

This gobbledygook boiled down to the fact that the crucial years had been wasted in a vain attempt to copy the Russians. A typical example of inefficiency and bad tutelage by the Russians was the case of Tao Hsih-chuan, a fourth-grade lathe worker. After his thoughts were "remolded" he learned of a Soviet technique for high-speed lathe cutting.

"When I tried it though," he said, "my tool kept burning out. Then one day a Soviet youth delegate visited us and he said I should polish the tool after sharpening, and thus my later work was a success."

What would have happened but for this accidental encounter, Tsao did not say. But I presumed that instead of being an Advanced Worker as he now was (entitling him to a bonus equivalent to $11.20 every three months) he would have ended up a confessed saboteur. This had been the fate of his bench mate who also consistently broke his tools.

It did seem to me, however, that some ruthless self-examination was now in progress. Where, before, there would have been no admission of these failures and certainly no frank discussion of production figures, there was today a growing disgust with the total incapacity of Communist officials (no matter how persuasive) to produce material results, better living standards or even a little more food.

This disenchantment was most widespread among the people who mattered most. They had been chivied, harassed and shepherded into the collectives with promises of startling increases in food production. But other urgent matters were being neglected while the extra grain and cotton were won at the expense of subsidiary crops like sweet potatoes and fibers, and pigs, poultry and handicrafts. There was no compulsion in the old sense: only the steady, relentless pressure of arguments. Meanwhile the real task of education went neglected. In Kunming, which seemed characteristic of the whole country, twenty out of every hundred children were without schooling of any sort. There were 80,000 youngsters who started primary school at seven years and were working in the fields at the age of twelve. Another 20,000 who should have been getting primary education were helping on the farms instead from lack of teachers.

Little was being done to relieve the pressure of overcrowding. Grandiose buildings had been erected while citizens multiplied in Kunming's warrens of curved-roof houses. The official figure for accommodation was four square feet of floor space for each person. It was certainly true that every citizen had now got a label and the city's 2000 pedlars had been miraculously transformed into "commercial units," but all this amalgamation and control simply meant that individuals ceased to show any enterprise. In the place of many energetic and ambitious workers, shopkeepers, farmers and coolies, you now had regimented cyphers. Instead of private enterprise, you had State planning. And the Chinese, while they will slave for themselves in the hope of making a little extra, are not inclined to sweat more than is necessary when their wages are fixed and assured.

The same problem had arisen here too, as in other parts of China, of administering the big new co-operatives and collectives. They required skilled staff, men who could manage what were in effect large business enterprises. The result was that almost all the Party officials and assisting cadres were forced to spend much of their working time running these new organizations. In at least two provinces, so I was told by a dejected and disheartened East European farming expert, the entire cadre force was involved in trying to run agricultural affairs which were previously the instinctive work of thousands of individual peasants. These were affairs of bookkeeping, not affairs of higher productivity.

For instance the overworked bureaucrat was constantly conducting surveys. Here are some definitions taken from the 1956 handbook for rural cadres:

> *Production value of subsidiary production* refers to the value of types of production undertaken by members of agricultural-producer co-operatives, such as digging or hunting of wild animals, plants or minerals; processing fees obtained by peasants during leisure hours from processing their own raw materials. [Thus was the venturesome poacher reduced to a dull statistic.]
>
> *Working days* are units for computing the amount of labor spent on a working norm. One working day equals ten wage points.
>
> To establish number of mixed tractors [there were no tractors within a hundred miles] count the number of tractors of different brands and different capacity . . . large Stalin eighty caterpillar-tracked tractors with 60 h.p. or more, medium and small tractors . . . Number of standard tractors is worked out by the following formula . . . Thus can we compare the actual number of tractors used for different enterprises in different areas and for different purposes and work out the total volume of work done by tractors, thereby reflecting the utilization of tractors in agriculture.

This was indeed bureaucracy gone mad. Where were the helpful hints on ditch-digging? Where were the hundreds of useful tips and pieces of advice that might have been disseminated over the same network of officials? There was paper available, printing presses were rolling, and if Peking had a mind to do so, there might have been a steady flow of practical information to bestir the peasant. Instead, he was swallowed up by yet another Table of Contents, his spirit crushed between stout volumes of the Yearly Index.

Perhaps I am being unfair. Perhaps my reaction was no different from that of a Chinese confronted with a by-law referring to the municipal drains of Manhattan. However, to me it all sounded far less useful than municipal drains and a good deal more like government by the insane.

Mao may have felt the same way because already he had some very sensitive antennae projecting into the rural regions. These were provided by yet another network of agents. They represented eight pseudo-political parties. Each party took care of some strata of society and belonged to the People's Political Consultative Conference. These men and women were encouraged to voice limited criticism and they were sent on investigative tours. They were the megaphones as well as microphones of the regime because they broadcast new measures in addition to picking up and reporting any trends of public opinion.

I found one of these human instruments, vibrating away in his capacity as a microphone, on one of the new collective farms.

CHAPTER THIRTEEN

The Loyal Opposition: Mister Sa Explains

◉ ◉

"Other party propaganda is forbidden and thus The People's money is saved . . ."

THE MAN in the wheel chair patiently listening to harvesters was Kao Ssu-chi, favorite writer on science among Chinese children.

"Kids are space-crazy in Peking," said Choirboy Ma. "They talk about little else in school these days."

Comrade Kao wrote about rocket ships and felt, perhaps, some sense of escape from his crippled body. Chinese children talked about space travel with possibly similar emotions. Their country was still badly crippled. It seemed unlikely, however, that the writer's audience this day would have much time for flights of fancy. They were members of a new, giant collective on a semi-mountainous plateau, two thousand feet above sea-level in Southwest China. The women, some with babies lashed to their backs, continued to bang sheaves of rice against huge round stones while the men talked. Kao, as a People's Deputy, had made the arduous journey here by air and a British Land Rover, and his chair had been wheeled to the front of an abandoned temple.

I looked down on the curious spectacle from a vantage point above the *hsiang*, a minor civil division which in this case embraced some thirty-five hundred tribal Yis and Chinese.

There was a straggling lane with tree-shaded homes of bamboo
and mud, five broad and shallow pits where the women
pounded stones or winnowed the grain by flapping carpets of
woven straw; three new whitewashed public buildings with
red stars, and a maze of worn brick houses that crept terrace
by terrace up a gentle hillside. Small boys with red Pioneer
scarves round their necks jogged across the wide expanse of
paddies, their carrying poles weighted at either end with
bulging panniers. An old woman picked bugs from a padded
cotton jacket she had split open. A small girl chopped vegetables on a flat stone behind a tumbledown hut.

There was something timeless about the scene. The harvesters thumped their stones with an insistent rhythm. Their
patched rags blended with the lovely yellows and greens; distant hills in a blue haze turned their smooth bellies up to the
luxurious December sun. Christmas was only ten days away
and here it was a time for gathering crops, for spreading the
golden grain under the hot sun and curling your bared toes
around the path-finding stones worn smooth by generations of
naked feet.

"And that concludes the statement about the miserable life,"
Party secretary Pi Liang was saying when I reluctantly joined
the others who were solemnly noting that ten years earlier the
wretched Kuomintang preyed upon these villagers.

There followed a barrage of statistics. I wandered away
again. Suddenly, in a walled garden, I found ten bent old men
crouching wearily on narrow wooden benches. In another
corner squatted eleven aged ladies in embroidered caps, black
jerkins and heavy woven skirts. Their faces were puckered
and wrinkled, their clothes were stiff with many impregna-
tions of mud and dust and the sticky mixtures of the sty and
stable. Like everyone working in the collective, they were as
much a part of their surroundings as a fox that runs on bent
legs belongs to an English coppice.

And yet there *was* something that made them alien figures
on a Chinese landscape. They were idle. They sat nodding in
the sun, the men sucking on empty long-stemmed pipes, the
women examining their thick, dirt-ingrained fingers or rocking

slowly back and forth in time with the *thump-thump* of the harvesters. A teen-age girl, sleek black pigtail dangling over one shoulder, danced in among them with a shower of words and they were instantly alert. Comrade Kao was coming to hear complaints.

Heaven knows what he was told. I could not imagine that these dear wooden figures had anything to say at all. They were the Black Pond village committee, however, and not carvings round a cuckoo clock.

I asked later if it was not difficult to squeeze something better than jargon out of people who must be petrified by the memory of earlier purges. The claim was put forward that by education, more and more peasants were persuaded to utter intelligent criticism.

I said: "Free criticism? Upholding the rights of landlords, for instance?"

"Yes, criticism is permitted on any subject. But who in China today would want to uphold landlords?"

In theory, Mao Tse-tung had found a novel way of preserving the revolution without stifling ideas. Deputy Kao was assigned an area for investigation, like his colleagues, and would report back to Peking. Meanwhile, eight full-time teams moved around China checking the work of local committees. These investigators were responsible to the Standing Committee of the Chinese People's Political Consultative Conference (C.P.P.C.C.). There were 690 provincial committees. Thus the organ provided Mao with eyes and ears to discover what millions were saying, doing and thinking. The work teams probed into every kind of activity; the political integrity of students, for instance, or the abuse of authority by rural cadres. They made sure that the self-critical autobiographies of every man, woman and teenage child were kept up to date. They checked to see if the correct line was being promoted in the study of international events (pursued in even the lowliest cottage).

There were eight non-Communist parties in the C.P.P.C.C., which may seem at first glance to be heresy. Some devilishly ingenious mind, however, saw the necessity for providing a controllable outlet for doubts, fears and deviations. These could find expression on many platforms licensed by the Government, and indeed most of the revelatory criticism published in the official press had to be inspired by the cadres in order to encourage others to voice their true feelings. Thus what appeared to be a spontaneous wave of criticism swelling from end to end of China and echoed in the local newspapers proved on closer examination to be cleverly sparked by the eight C.P.P.C.C. work teams, touring deputies, or handbooks for cadres.

In one village I found a middle-aged cadre bringing his records up to date. Five years earlier, he was illiterate and bound to his own small patch of land. Beside him was a booklet issued for the guidance of field workers in gathering rural statistics.

> Agricultural statistics do not consist in random use of figures to explain and study social phenomena [it stated]. Marxist-Leninist truth must be employed. [Only then] can these figures become flesh and blood, be lively and capable of solving problems.

However lively they might appear in Peking, the requested statistics sounded a death knell to personality in the paddy. The booklet had been issued by the Peking Publishing House in 1956 and outlined a technique for analyzing the productive capacity of a country district:

> Livestock acquires a dual significance in the process of production. Animals are fixed assets when they yield products. They are floating assets when they themselves become products.

Poor Peasant Li, the cadre studying this bewildering guide, stood in great danger of being identified himself as a floating asset. Indeed, while he filled in a column headed *Female animals capable of procreation*, his cousins in the cities were carrying out similar surveys on the human race. We shall be hearing more about some of the results. We glimpse their purpose in a statement made by a former Nationalist leader, Shao Li-tzu, to the C.P.P.C.C. some time later:

> In East Germany seven children are allowed to be born to ten

couples. This gives a slight but satisfactory increase in population. As to China it would be satisfactory if the birthrate can be regulated at seventeen per mil per year. We are willing to do our utmost under the Central Government Birth-Control Committee.

Chief of the non-Communist C.P.P.C.C. parties was the Revolutionary Committee of the Kuomintang, headed by Li Chi-sen whose revolt in 1948 against Chiang Kai-shek ended in failure. Li and other Nationalists of similar sentiment fled eventually to Mao's side. Others of the intelligentsia joined the China Democratic League which was headed by the Minister of Timber and Light Industry, Shen Chun-ju. Four parties claim to represent business, educational, labor and rural interests. There was an Overseas Chinese party and a cunning little organization called the Taiwan (Formosa) Democratic Self-Government League founded to "oppose American imperialism and liberate Taiwan."

It was a long time before I discovered, in Peking, how a vast and vigorous dictatorship could accommodate these dissentient voices.

"We are in opposition but we do not oppose Communist Party policy," explained Mister Sa Kuang-liao. "We engage in mutual supervision. That is, we help the Government and the Government helps us not to stray too far to right or left of the correct road to socialism."

Mister Sa might be described as a leader of the loyal opposition. He was a glib gentleman. His party, the China Democratic League, made room for students and professors who in the early part of the regime hoped they might remain undisturbed in a state of benevolent neutrality toward Communism.

"We are all enriched by China's new political system," declared Mister Sa. "No money is wasted on election campaigns, for instance. Candidates are selected beforehand. There are never *mistakes* in Communist Party policy although there may be differences of opinion — which we all work together to correct. Thus The People's money is saved because other party propaganda is forbidden."

The opposition leader wore a vivid necktie and business suit to emphasize his role. He reminded you a little of those slim, nervously voluble Chinese who sometimes accompany Western V.I.P.'s on Formosa. He giggled at the thought of Communists being attracted to his own party.

But the question was pressed. Suppose the Communists should find they were in a minority?

"It does not matter," said Mister Sa. "This may puzzle you. But China is different from the West. We esteem minorities."

This was an unanswerable piece of Oriental logic. Mister Sa possibly detected doubt on the face of his listener. "Many things are different here," he said with magnificent understatement. "Our elections . . . We have consultations first and draw up a list of candidates. Since I work for the Government as a member of the Democratic League, I make suggestions. But I discuss these suggestions beforehand to avoid unseemly public disagreement. If there were no prior consultations, there would be public controversy. This would waste time and The People's money besides letting rich people exert their influence."

Then how were the people's wishes represented?

"Our Government generously pays the fares of all deputies and their friends to travel round the country twice a year," he replied. "Our Government then makes it possible for us to discuss any sharp differences of opinion revealed by these tours. We are permitted to discuss until all agree. Our agreement helps forward the common task, to build socialist society and transform China from agriculture to industry."

Who achieved agreement with what?

"Well, non-Communist parties endeavor to follow the correct road. Therefore we try to reach agreement with the decisions already made by the State Consultative Council."

What differences arose? How were they settled?

"Take my own case," said Mister Sa, eager to bear witness to his own conversion. "I was once a prisoner of Chiang Kai-shek. I opposed peaceful liberation of Formosa. I was bloodthirsty and wanted it liberated by war. I opposed giving Chiang Kai-shek a high post in our Government. I wanted him shot.

"Then I consulted and by a process of mutual supervision I came to see that Formosa should be peacefully liberated and Chiang Kai-shek allowed to surrender in return for a job here."

It may seem hard to visualize in the heart of Red China a political leader straining at the leash, hungry for action against Chiang Kai-shek, while calmer comrades of the Communist Party restrain him from biting a chunk out of Formosa. One is reminded of a time when China's celestial emperors used an inverted phraseology bearing no resemblance to their actions. In this case, however, it would be rash to dismiss as mere fustian all the claims of a man speaking under official license. Mister Sa had been worked up to a pitch of aggressive anger by earlier campaigns against Formosa; when the Party adopted a new line, it was not difficult to cool Mister Sa's ardor by "mutual supervision."

The existence of Mister Sa and "opposition" parties is essential to Chinese Communism. Even Yugoslav Communists insist that for any country now governed by a Communist regime, admission of opposition parties would be a backward step. However, it is worth repeating that China's internal policies have always remained her own affair. Even while attacking Tito's criticism of Russian intervention in Hungary in 1956, the official Chinese press was also reporting domestic policy more heretical in its superficial aspects than Titoism. Thus a speaker at the 1957 C.P.P.C.C.'s conference, Lu Kan-ju, talked of continuing Mao's tolerance toward intellectuals although "some friends in fraternal countries do not much approve of this policy."

Mao, it seemed, was not so complacent as the Russian Communist Party which believes it embodies by definition "the dictatorship of the proletariat," no matter what the proletariat feels about it. Such has been the mystic power of the Russian Revolution, however, that this doctrine has been seldom questioned by Communists of other lands.

By the end of 1956, it appeared to some observers in Peking that Chinese Communist theoreticians were paying close attention to the challenges thrown out by leading Communists in

Europe. Pietro Nenni, the Italian Socialist leader, in explaining his break with the Communists, quoted the words of the
Italian Communist Party founder, Gramsci, that once the party
ceased to function democratically, it becomes reactionary instead of progressive and its description as a political party
becomes mere camouflage for a police state. Polish Communists, during a visit to Warsaw by Premier Chou En-lai, were
recalling a prophecy by Rosa Luxembourg, a Polish-German
Marxist, that any attempt to build socialism without democracy would result in a state where only bureaucracy remained
as the active element.

One great fear among Chinese today is that with receding
memories of the hardships and iniquities of pre-revolution
days, there may be a gradual backsliding among officials and
Party cadres. The gigantic bureaucracy of modern Russia, with
its special privileges and lackadaisical working habits, has not
passed unnoticed in Peking. I found my own Government
guides were familiar with Western criticism that Russian officialdom was like the European bourgeoisie in the middle of
the nineteenth century.

So there are cycles of self-criticism, of public mockery and
ruthless introspections. The fiction is maintained that all
Chinese want to build a socialist nation irrespective of their
feelings about Communism — all, that is, except "counterrevolutionaries." The margin is dangerously narrow and ill
defined, however, between legitimate criticism and the expression of seditious thoughts. Consequently, despite all pretense,
the waves of harsh criticisms aimed at ministries, the armed
forces and individual cadres are officially inspired and controlled. To keep on the safe side, officials closely follow Peking's current line; but this, too, is not good enough. They
are accused of echoing the views of their superiors without
understanding them.

Mao administered the first stiff dose of a new mental purge
at a Supreme State Conference in February 1957, preparatory
to the C.P.P.C.C.'s third conference. There he referred back to
speeches made in the Yenan days of 1942. These are incredibly detailed examinations of how a Party cadre is in

danger of becoming a bureaucrat instead of a crusader. Mao warned against subjectivism, sectarianism and the Confucian "eight-legged essay"; that is, a stiff and formalistic exposition of policy. "The ruling class," said Mao, "used to indoctrinate students with Confucian teachings and compelled people to believe reverently in the whole Confucian caboodle as if it were religious dogma."

A modern version of this was given in *China Youth*. A senior group leader was accused of making his followers successively rise, work, rest, play, listen to newspaper-reading and even start eating, in drill fashion. "One of them was marked down for evening criticism for writing an unsupervised letter home."

The same magazine published a complaint from Szechuan province:

> If you express opinions, you are accused of contempt and required to make a self-examination [complained the writer, Pa Jen]. The poison of feudal ideas lingers. Bureaucratism finds its market. Officials prefer to be dragons in a rural area than tiny insects in the city. These dragons call mass meetings to drown voices of criticism.
>
> These dragons forbid love affairs. Boys dare not approach girls at school, men on committees dare not talk with women. What is to be done? Write notes? We would be suspected of writing love letters.

All of this makes boring literature. The visitor to modern China would prefer to ignore it all, and write about the colorful aspects to the exclusion of all else. He is just as guilty of one-sided reporting as those Western experts, often existing on fat state subsidies, who sit in Hong Kong, Formosa and Japan, and ruminate on the translations of official Chinese press and radio. Their conclusions often leak out to the Western press and give rise to predictions that Red China is on the point of economic collapse, or about to become the scene of a vast uprising. It seems not to occur to their sponsors that their speculations are based largely on the revelations of the Chinese Communists themselves; and that these revelations expose the growing political strength of the regime, even while admitting physical weaknesses.

One great fault of Western propaganda is that it leaves the impression of a China groaning under terror and the use of brute force. Visitors to the mainland, with this impression in mind, are surprised to see a placid countryside, smiling faces and an appearance of bustling purpose. They report this and are then either accused of being fellow travelers; or persuade their readers that modern China is the victim of vicious canards. The truth is that no casual tourist will see forced-labor camps in operation, nor will he notice large numbers of security police. If he is a reasonably sharp observer, however, and if he will submit graciously to tedious hours of political incantation, he will perceive certain peculiarities of speech and behavior. He may then come to the reluctant conclusion that the most populous nation on earth is undergoing a daily indoctrination of extraordinary thoroughness.

Once, when I was mistakenly directed to two different offices for an important interview, my interpreter said: "We are the victims of bureaucrats. There are too many bureaucrats in China today, including Communist Party members who think they enjoy a special security against criticism. I am going to write to the papers about this."

One of my companions was greatly impressed. Like myself, he remembered that in China two years earlier, nobody would have dared express this opinion. But the interpreter knew he was on safe ground. The Party cadre in his dormitory (he lived with ten colleagues over the China Travel Service bureau) had lately read out an interminable series of lectures on the need to combat bureaucracy.

It may be difficult to visualize, but the entire Chinese nation is divided up into small units of ten or a dozen families, and these families are in turn involved with other political groupings; Father in the factory has regular supervision and Mother is tied in with the local street committee; each of the children has a class "study group." These groups are like water in a pond. When a pebble is thrown, when a campaign begins, the ripples move steadily and inexorably outward to agitate the whole surface. But what happens in the silent dark depths?

Most Westerners are unwilling to believe that intensive indoctrination can really disturb the deep wells of tradition, of Chinese family life and personal pride. We are inclined to grasp at straws. For instance, comfort is taken in the apparent promotion of family loyalties after a prolonged attack upon them. "How to treat your counterrevolutionary father" was a typical example (published in *China Youth* in 1956) of glamorizing the youngster who denounced his parents for seditious thoughts. But then, most unexpectedly, China's Red Army chief, Chu Teh, published "Reminiscences of Mother."

Tough old Chu Teh, close companion of Mao for thirty years, was the son of a wealthy farmer. His tribute of parental love was accompanied by a series of pronouncements to Chinese youth. Articles appeared under headings like this: "Love and support of parents is also necessary virtue in socialist society."

I talked with enough young people in widely scattered parts of China to believe that parental ties are the last consideration of doctrinaire officials. The usual story was that the youngster studying in Peking had a father working in a Manchurian factory, a mother in a Shanghai cotton mill and very possibly brothers or sisters pioneering in the borderlands. In extolling the virtues of family, the regime carefully pointed out that loyalty to Marxist-Leninism still came first and then urged youngsters to write home regularly and in cases of necessity, help support their parents. This was an apparent reversal of the earlier, harsh campaign to break up the family; and it might be taken as a move toward more liberal tendencies. I am cynical enough to believe, however, that this is a good example of a determination not to push things too far. Family life *has* been broken up to the extent that the regime feels quite capable of ferreting out the skeletons in any cupboard. Why go further before present gains are consolidated?

Just as he had become patron of the arts, all religions and science, so Mao also took over Chinese family life to mold it and utilize its inherent strength. Meanwhile, in its role of lord protector, the Party began in 1956 to describe the horrors of family life outside the fraternal circle of Communist states. So we found Master Teng Heng-lin, a former student in the United States, describing in *China Youth* how money alone held American families together. He recorded this conversation with an old lady in New York: "I myself don't like to see the queer way of life of my own children. They spend too much money. They get drunk, turn crazy and dash around naked."

Teng tells his presumably horrified readers that unwanted American parents commit suicide, while others let their children starve and widows go insane trying to pay rents. He wrote: "There was even a son who in his desire to become rich, murdered his mother and killed forty others by putting a bomb in a plane." (This did in fact happen but one would hardly call it typical.)

These tales leave some strange mental images in Chinese minds. They carry little weight with older Chinese or students at many universities and schools of higher education. Parents living overseas get surprisingly frank comments on such propaganda from children at mainland schools. This is sometimes taken as evidence that letters are not censored. They are not slit open and pieces cut out. They are read and the contents noted for future reference.

Thus Chinese Communists display far greater audacity than their Russian comrades. "Auto-criticism" is part of Communist life. Bolshevik self-criticism for the group ensures that lessons are learned from past mistakes; it helps forestall complacency. But in China everyone is put through the mill; the soul is publicly bared. The objective is not to punish the nonconformist so much as to discover *why* his faith faltered.

Mao's goal was to make submission to a Party will so natural that it became essential to personal happiness. This has been explained often enough. One can only suppose many foreign observers who ignore it have simply omitted to read the Party press. The old China hands who persuaded Britain to recognize the new Peking regime with undignified haste and who later advocated free trade as a means of "winning over" Chairman Mao or converting him into an Oriental Tito were possibly guilty of a greater sin than mere omission.

Greed for profit in the China trade has left unsavory memories in the history of Western enterprises in Asia, and one is reminded of the case of a British gunner in the *Lady Hughes* who in 1784 accidentally killed a Chinese boatman while firing a ceremonial salute. The Chinese demanded that the gunner be handed over so they might strangle him by hand. British authorities complied, although the wretched sailor was performing his duties in firing the gun. The innocent Briton died in lonely horror, betrayed by his own countrymen and, many years later, a British newspaper in Canton, *The Chinese Repository*, alleged that such a policy of conciliation amounted almost to subservience and was the infamous result of an obsession with trade at any cost. And it was a fact that the British had been threatened with a stoppage of all Chinese trade unless they gave up their man.

So today there is lingering suspicion of Western businessmen who cling to a sentimental faith in Chinese individualism. There is an underlying contempt in the attitude even of Communist trade officials as they sit back and await the scurrying traders. "Old China hands" should know better than most that during many years' submission to the formality of Confucian ideology, the ruling scholar-gentry class of China developed some useful automatic reflexes which makes them close allies and obedient servants of any strong and centralized government. To pretend the Chinese are not amenable to modern discipline seems to many observers a calculated deception.

It was Confucianism which provided a blueprint for Mao's educational plans within the Party. His flinty Number Two, that ascetic-looking patriarch Liu Shao-chi, quoted it in discussing "How to be a good Communist." He was preaching to comrades during the Yenan period. There must be continual study and self-criticism, exposure to false ideas and submission to Party inquisitions before a true Communist could become active in the Faith.

"At fifteen I had my mind bent on learning," said Liu, echoing the famous Confucianism. "At thirty I stood firm. At forty I had doubts. At fifty I knew the decree of Heaven. At sixty my ear was an obedient organ for the reception of truth. At seventy I could follow my heart's desire without transgressing right."

These became the six stages of modern Party training. Cadres were "steeled" against hardship, violence and anti-Communist arguments. There must be instinctive obedience to a collective will. But this must not become slavish. The whole purpose of repeated campaigns within the expanding Chinese Communist Party was to produce millions of healthy and energetic workers who had technical imagination, practical ability, but utter spiritual devotion to the one true cause. Liberal trends in China were an essential phase in the training of Party leaders.

This was explained in the official magazine *Hsueh Hsi* (*Study*) which guided ideological thinking and was edited by Ai Ssuchi, a brilliant Chinese theoretician almost unknown in the West. He popularized Marxism for the masses. This particular issue of his magazine was circulating while I was in Southwest China. "People," it said, "are surprised that we now introduce into classrooms the study of theories by Russell, Kant and Hegel. We also suddenly publish books incompatible with Marxist views, to the surprise of comrades . . ."

Then he added, and his words have been strangely overlooked in the West:

> Marxism is science and truth and it grows through struggle against erroneous theories . . . If we confine those who seek truth to the greenhouse and impart by scientific planning only, the knowledge of Marxism . . . then they will wither and die if moved outside and placed in the sun and drenched by rain. Marxism and non-Marxism should be placed side by side and the broad masses will know what to choose.

The divergences between Russian and Chinese methods of applied Communism inside their respective frontiers were not likely to lead to conflict. But there were differences in foreign policy which arose almost from the very moment that Mao Tse-tung took power, although at first they were not apparent.

In domestic policy, Mao was resolute and patient. When his more impatient followers questioned the strange policy of slowly absorbing capitalists into the State system instead of liquidating them as in Russia, they were told: "Continue the policy of *buying out* the capitalists. We need technicians and managers and our buying-out policy is sincere from the long-term angle."

In foreign policy, Mao was slower to exhibit such caution. According to experts on Stalin, such as Tito, the Russian leader until his death was exercising a profound influence over Red China's foreign relations. This seemed to be confirmed in 1957 by General Lung Yun, vice-chairman of the Communist Defense Council and a former Yunnan warlord.

"It is totally unfair," he said, "for the Chinese to pay all Korean war expenses. The U.S. gave up her claim for loans granted to allies in war, yet the Soviet Union insists that China even pays interest." He would like to know, added General Lung, whether Russia meant to repay China for industrial equipment taken out of Manchuria.

Naturally General Lung was publicly reprimanded for this disloyal sentiment, but obviously he had not spoken merely for the sake of saying something. His masters seemed anxious to give an impression that Russia had impatiently pitchforked them into the Korean War with disastrous results for the Chinese.

They began more confidently to preach their own traditional, Oriental approach to the defeat of enemies. "Yes, buy out the capitalists," said Mao. "And in areas like Tibet, also move slowly. Move slowly, slowly, comrades. Only when the time is ripe should we act with swift resolution."

He was addressing the 1957 Supreme State Conference and he added: "We should not be impatient. Conditions in Tibet are not ripe."

All this suggests the Chinese have always rejected force, and that Communist leaders fought in Korea because badly advised by Stalin. They may wish to give this impression in these days of piping peaceful coexistence. But their full philosophy has been expounded by Mao in his *Problems of War and Strategy:* "Every Communist must grasp the truth: 'political power grows out of the barrel of a gun' . . . the whole world can only

be remolded with the gun. As we are advocates of the abolition of war, we do not desire war; but war can be only
abolished through war — in order to get rid of the gun, we
must first grasp it in our hand."

This is an extraordinary assertion, characteristic of Mao's inverted logic. It is still the creed taught to twelve million
Chinese Party faithful. But because of a temporary lull in Peking's aggressive attitudes, many are misled to suppose the
philosophy has changed. The gun was used, however, to deliver shocks in Korea and Indochina. Mao's dictum that after
each shock there should be a period of calm reason shows no
sign of having been abandoned. "Impatience is harmful . . ."
he wrote. "Ten years' revolutionary war may be surprising to
other countries but for us it is only the . . . preliminary exposition of the theme with many exciting chapters to follow."

Some of these exciting chapters undoubtedly have involved
Russia, and will affect her even more as Red China grows
stronger. The area of conflicting interests is Asia. Already the
Chinese have become something of a barrier to Russian ambitions there.

2

Shocking the Neighbors

CHAPTER FOURTEEN

On the Chopping Block

◉ ◉

THE SHOCK TREATMENT that put the rest of the world in a sweat began when Mao scarcely seemed installed in Peking. His new Government was proclaimed on 1 October 1949, and it faced colossal tasks. Chiang Kai-shek had still to be forced off the mainland with his Nationalist armies. The southern port of Canton awaited occupation and the semi-tropical island of Hainan had yet to be invaded.

These and other problems were hardly solved when the Korean War began. Four months later a battalion of the Seventh South Korean Regiment, Sixth Division, won the race with American troops to be first on the Yalu River and the frontier of this new land of Mao. The entire battalion promptly vanished. Two days later, on October 28, 1950, survivors escaped with tales of Communist Chinese troops in sandy quilted uniforms, of Russian "Katushka" rocket launchers and Mongolian cavalry. Their reports were received with derision in General MacArthur's headquarters. It was a well-known fact that Communist China was in no shape at all to wage war. Earlier "warnings" relayed from Peking by way of Indian diplomats were examples of Chinese bluff. This was the General's "home by Christmas" offensive and the General had himself assured President Truman there was very little chance of Chinese or Soviet intervention in Korea.

But the General was wrong. On another peninsula at the

other end of China, similar miscalculations had taken place. Worried French intelligence officers in North Indochina had a good notion of what was happening. Sitting in a map room of the Citadelle, French military headquarters in the northern capital of Hanoi, one of them told me: "The Chinese have been training the Vietminh in Communist guerrilla tactics for years. Now they are prepared to support them with modern Russian weapons, with regular training in technical warfare at bases just over the border."

But in the winter of 1950 there were few to believe these French reports. Traders and their colonial government cronies in Saigon were reluctant to face the unpleasant truth. Like British colonialists in Hong Kong, they preferred to wallow in a sentimental mélange about the Chinese who were said to be incapable of soldierly discipline, far too fun-loving for Communist austerity and unable to act decisively as a nation.

Vietminh forces, drawn from the seemingly languid peasants of Indochina, were commanded by General Vo Nguyen Giap. When Chinese troops swept out of the frigid plains of Manchuria and delivered the first shock in Korea, the second major shock was being planned by General Giap two thousand miles away in the sweltering Tonkin jungles. He had with him a veteran of the Battle of Stalingrad, General Nguyen Son, and a former divisional commander in the Chinese Eighth Route Army, General Ho Lung. They consulted a Chinese military mission from nearby Nanning, the capital of Southeast China's Kwangsi province, where Vietminh regulars were now training: each graduation class caught a train straight back to the battle zones on a conveniently located railroad.

Mao was starting to electrify all the borders of China. As a young man, he helped draft the Manifesto of the Second National Congress of the Chinese Communist Party back in 1922 which listed as one of its objectives: "liberation of Mongolia, Tibet and Sinkiang." It might have seemed arrogant then, were it not merely funny, that a handful of ragged plotters meeting in a Shanghai hide-out should indulge such dreams.

Now his troops began to move into Tibet. On October 26, 1951, the first units entered the secular city of Lhasa. Plans were made to convert other armies at the time fighting in Korea into colonization brigades for Inner Mongolia and that legendary land of Tatars, Sinkiang. It seemed the ambitious men of the early twenties, having just achieved power, were willing to take on the United Nations in Korea *and* challenge Soviet Russian interests in Sinkiang and Mongolia *and* begin to colonize relatively unexplored, rugged borderlands equal in total area to Europe.

They knew, it was clear, just where they were going. So much cannot be said for the victims of their new propaganda. Inside China it was "Hate America and Aid Korea." In Malaya new instructions were issued to the Communist Party there for a politico-military struggle to replace the terrorist campaign in which the Malayan Races' Liberation Army had killed 1275 soldiers and policemen, and abducted or murdered 2319 civilians.

Each group of victims considered itself a separately injured party as it became a target for the ferocity of Peking. British businessmen, who were bundled unceremoniously out of Shanghai, complained to one another in their Hong Kong clubs, but were prepared to trade wherever possible with Communist firms. Their countrymen fighting in Korea knew nothing of the war in Indochina. American military leaders in Korea paid belated attention to the French plight in Indochina, while the French merchants of Saigon bitterly resented interference in their trade with China by American-sponsored embargoes.

This total lack of co-ordination, the individual's refusal to admit a common danger, and the greedy search for profits, all of which assisted Peking, were symbolized in a flight I made in those days from Saigon aboard an amphibian plane chartered by Chinese Nationalist bankers in Hong Kong. Crates of processed gold, freighted from Paris by the Bank of Indochina, were transferred from an Air France plane and we flew this precious cargo to Portuguese Macao (a few miles west of Hong Kong) where it was delivered to the purchasing agents for Peking.

At this very time, agents of another kind were pushing into Burma and Thailand. They were active wherever the Chinese were living abroad: in Indonesia where eighty-two million people are spread along a tropical archipelago of three thousand islands; in Singapore where one million Chinese dominate two hundred thousand others of all races.

Their allies were not fifth-columnists in the usual sense of the word. Many had never moved from their places of business in Bangkok or Sarawak or Rangoon. They were not necessarily Communists. They were Chinese. Some supported Chiang Kai-shek and the Formosan garrison, though more and more were fascinated by Peking's rising prestige. They were the Overseas Chinese: hard-working, ambitious, irrepressible and tough. In Thailand they numbered three million; half a million lived in the Philippines. There were a million in South Vietnam and three million in Malaya. They trickled across the Burmese border in countless numbers.

Among them, ideas took root and grew. Sometimes there was no need for outside encouragement. The Singapore schoolgirl who horrified her teacher by reciting, "We shall drive out the white monkeys," only quoted from a Chinese textbook. Among Chinese students there was little necessity for a direct representative from Peking. But among the peasants in hidden valleys almost isolated in the mountains and rain forests of Southeast Asia, the busy evangelists from mainland China could work undisturbed.

These agents possessed formidable mental armor. They came to free Asia from imperialist oppression. They blamed Western exploitation for the survival of feudal societies. They quoted Mao Tse-tung and set up schools at which the study of Marx and Lenin was obligatory. Their minds were streamlined, packed with Communist lore and sealed against argument. Any peasant who opposed them was guilty of treason because they came as liberators of the people. They were grains in the Yellow Wind. The Party was a living church, they proclaimed: an incarnation of the historic will. Its members were part of a living entity which transcended its human cells.

In North Indochina, one man in three of the regular Vietminh armies was such a cell, self-disciplined and prepared to endure all hardships in conformity with the Party will. Few among nine million peasants of the Red River delta dared to quarrel with this formidable mass mind. They lived in a wedge which opened on to the Gulf of Tonkin, fifty miles on either side of Haiphong port. The wedge pointed one hundred miles inland with Hanoi near the apex.

By the beginning of 1954, this triangle was held by the French Force, Terreste du Nord Vietnam. For years French newsmen had tried to catalogue for their people at home the disasters which were piling up. French colonial authorities arranged their recall to Paris. The French reporters frequently had read Mao Tse-tung's works, were familiar with his tactics in China and recognized the same pattern here. Officialdom preferred to believe the old myths which colonialists are apt to invent about the natives whom they dimly perceive through thickets of privilege and wealth: "The Vietnamese hated the Chinese, the Vietnamese were not military minded, you could control them by pampering their barons and playing off one power group against another."

Perhaps the value of a free press was seldom better illustrated than in Indochina as the stage was set for stark tragedy.

General Giap had some 170,000 regulars and guerrillas in the north. Their bases were deep in the surrounding mountains, but their lines of communication ran right into the Franco–Vietnamese network of forts and auto-defense towers. The French now understood the nature of the enemy, his infiltration technique, his use of peasants and his ability to operate independently of a supply base. The knowledge had been there some time but its application came too late, for the men who made policy were far to the south in Saigon.

In Saigon a typical servant of the French Empire was a short, shrewd boss of what the French called a "politico-religious organization." General Le Van Vien commanded 8000 terrorists, the Binh Xuyen. He purchased for a reputed million dollars the Saigon police force from the absentee Emperor Bao Dai. Like other warlords in the area, when stuck for ready cash, he could shake down the French for a few thousand dollars by stirring up trouble and then offering to suppress it. Son of a cattle rustler, he ran one of the East's worst

red-light districts. His private army and his own police protected his bordellos and the spectacular gambling casino Le
Grande Monde. He shared with Bao Dai an estimated daily
take of $25,000 from smuggling, piracy, kidnaping and sev-
eral exotic rackets. But he wore the French Legion of Honor
on his powerful chest. His sins were washed clean by the
purity of his hatred for Communism.

General Giap was also a stocky, crop-haired son of peasants.
Like other Communist leaders, he was first a product of French
education. He struggled through school, helped by the French,
and became a lecturer in political economy at the University of
Hanoi. He also had a formidable French police dossier for
subversive activities.

Giap joined Chinese Communist forces across the Tonkin
border in 1941. Soon the Japanese were flooding into Southeast Asia to demonstrate the weakness of the hitherto superior
white colonialists. Giap's wife died in a French jail and his
sister was executed by the French. When he returned to North
Indochina, it was to fight for two years as a Communist guerrilla with U.S.-supplied arms against the Japanese.

"General advance on all fronts" was his Vietminh Military
Order Number 1, and now, nine years later, the campaign
had brought him close to victory. His leader was Ho Chi-
minh, a frail-looking intellectual whose name rallied the people. But his inspiration was Mao Tse-tung. Many years ago,
Mao argued that conquest of China was possible once the Red
Army had a good base of operations, and his words could be
applied to Indochina:

> There exists an uneven political and economic development
> and this is indicated by the coexistence of a frail capitalist econ-
> omy and a predominant semifeudal economy of a few seemingly
> modern industrial and commercial cities and boundless ex-
> panses of rural districts in medieval stagnation; of several mil-
> lion industrial workers and hundreds of millions of peasants
> living under a decaying regime; of great warlords administering
> the Central Government and lesser warlords administering the
> provinces; of a regular army and a variegated collection of local
> armies; of great steamship lines, motor roads and railways, to-
> gether with field trails and wheelbarrow paths . . .

Facing Giap early in 1954 was General Henri Navarre who was impatient with events. Already the Vietminh had crept so far into the Red River delta that nearly one village in three was under Communist control. The green plain stretched smooth as a billiard table to north and west, ending abruptly where saw-toothed mountains brooded in the sultry heat.

Navarre decided to draw the enemy out of the mountain caves by sending his best troops to the fort of Dienbienphu. The move was made to order for any student of Mao, and General Giap had already proved himself a star pupil.

So long as the French Expeditionary Corps sat tight in the delta, Giap could only toy with that dream of conquest. He had always to face the one factor missing in Mao's analysis of the situation in China. Amid the "medieval stagnation" of Indochina was a French army which, now that the United States was footing one third of the bill, could afford to experiment. The lessons of Korea had at last begun to take effect. One million Catholic peasants in the south of the delta were tightly organized and had the weapons and moral fiber to defend themselves. More local Vietnamese troops were being raised and sent into action. The drain on French lives and money was heavy. It still took 88-mm. tanks to clear the roads each morning, mined at night by guerrillas. Most of the forts beyond the delta were lost to the Vietminh but nevertheless, if the French stood firm with allied support, there was nothing more that Giap could do.

Instead they chose to challenge him. Nothing could have fitted more smoothly into the classic Chinese pattern of conquest by cleverness. Mao had delved deeply into national legends to dramatize his point that guerrilla warfare was merely the servant of political stratagem. His favorite novel, *Romance of the Three Kingdoms*, possibly provides more clues to Maoist plans than all the turgid works of Marx and Lenin. It also happens to be more readable.

One technique described in *The Three Kingdoms* is to "capture the Emperor in order to control the lords."

Emperor Bao Dai was on the Riviera when his people needed him in Saigon. He had been approached in 1946 with offers of a job in Ho's revolutionary government. He was ap-

proached again with a warning that events might soon make
him see the force of Vietminh arguments. He refused.

For such a moment, devotees of *The Three Kingdoms* can
find alternative advice. The tales of battle between warlords,
bandits and kings are case histories of psychological warfare
in an age when Ancient Britons fought in woad. If the Emperor ran away, his kingdom could be toppled by giving the
lords a bad fright. Mao had already explained (in *Problems
of China's Revolutionary War*):

> A quick decision . . . requires: thorough preparation, correct
> timing, concentration of a preponderant force, the tactic of en-
> circlement and outflanking, favorable positions . . . A battle is
> not basically decisive that ends only in routing the enemy . . . To
> wound all ten fingers of a man is not so effective as to chop one
> of them off; to rout ten of the enemy's divisions is not so effective
> as to annihilate one of them.

While the quick, decisive battle was being carefully prepared, the international machinery for a conference at Geneva
began to creak into motion. There was little enthusiasm for
the Indochina war in Paris and hopes of an armistice ran high.
France had 26 per cent of all her military officers and 46 per
cent of all her troops tied down in an eight-year-old conflict
that had cost the French Empire some 71,500 dead.

Navarre was putting his finger on the Dienbienphu chop-
ping block when rumors of Communist "willingness" to discuss an Indochina truce were heard. Coolies were trickling
down hidden mountain trails by December 1953, dodging
daylight French air patrols as they carried the massive guillotine piece by piece. Soviet trucks jerked and slithered over the
roads from the Chinese border in the wake of long columns
of bicycles bearing bamboo containers and panniers in which
were secreted the meaningless screws and tubes and bolts that,
reassembled, became radio transmitters or camp kitchens or
mortars.

On March 12, 1954, General Giap lowered his sights on the
rice bowl of the mountainous Thai country some two hundred

miles west of Hanoi. It had taken him three patient months to concentrate his preponderant force. In Peking, Premier Chou En-lai prepared for his patient and reasoning return to the sophisticated Europe he had left forty years earlier as a fun-loving student: only this time he meant to win back (through peaceful negotiation backed by force) China's former vassal adjoining Dienbienphu.

For fifty-six days and nights the French poured the cream of their Expeditionary Corps into Dienbienphu through the parachute-exits of Dakotas. There were the 1st, 2nd, 5th and 8th Colonial Paratroop Battalions, the 5th Vietnam Para-Battalion, the 9th Mobile Group; there were Algerian and Moroccan Tirailleurs, and little Thai paratroopers who blew like thistledown into Communist lines. There were Foreign Legionnaires, some of them Germans, who feared that as prisoners they might be sent via Russia to their homes in East Germany to stand trial as "traitors." Giap chopped them down with heavy artillery, 120 mortars, recoilless rifles and other weapons nobody thought his peasants could use, let alone assemble on the encircling mountainsides.

At dawn on May, 7, seventeen Flying Boxcars were loading ammunition for Dienbienphu. To the squat concrete radio tower at Gia Lam air station came a faint radio message from the underground headquarters of the garrison commander, Colonel (later General) Christian de Castries. It asked for drugs and food instead of bullets. The end had come.

Mao's earnest young disciples had executed their task in the approved manner. After careful preparation, they had severed the one important finger. They had sprung out of medieval surroundings, armed themselves with rocket launchers when experience spoke only of slingshots, and annihilated "16,000 troops and all the French Commands," as they themselves rather meekly confessed.

In Geneva the news softened French resolve. Premier Chou En-lai arrived with the smile on the enigmatic but handsome face that made thousands of European women swoon. The great Chinese mystique went to work. People remembered

that Mao Tse-tung was also a professed lover of peace and
here was Chou, his resourceful and charming henchman, to
prove it.

Mao had said, echoing both Clausewitz and Lenin, that war
was the continuation of policy by other means. There were in
France at that time more than a million sympathizers to echo
his words: "We are advocates of the abolition of war . . . but
war can only be abolished through war — in order to get rid of
the gun, we must first grasp it in our hand."

It was agreed at Geneva to leave the Communists in sole
control of the gun in North Vietnam. Late in June, I caught
the Air France flight from Paris to Saigon. At Karachi five of
us were escorted from the plane and placed in quarantine because we carried no yellow-fever papers. The other four were
the Vietnamese Minister of Defense, Dr. Phan huy-Quat and
his wife, his *Directeur Adjoint de Cabinet* and the aide-de-
camp.

The Defense Minister was a victim of red tape, but nothing
would induce the local French diplomatic staff to help him out
of the baking oven provided by the Pakistan Government for
our ten days of purgatory. His brother had been a minister-
without-portfolio with the Communist Vietminh. Dr. Quat
was a socialist whose avowed mission now was to plead that
his own two Catholic provinces in the south of the Tonkin
delta should be saved.

He was detained long enough for French forces to evacuate
the two provinces. Then together we flew to South Indochina
where he was accorded the military honors due to a person of
his position. Next day he resigned.

It may have been coincidence that he was delayed in Pakistan. Dr. Quat did not think so; if the Air France air liner had
carried yellow-fever clearance papers, there would have been
no demand for documents from individual passengers. As it
was, he fretted in quarantine, unable to reach even a telephone
and denied any opportunity to warn his people of the territorial sacrifices France had made at Geneva in the name of Vietnam in order to salvage what remained of her Expeditionary
Corps. In our long conversations, lying on the stone floors to
keep cool, Dr. Quat repeated with great vehemence his con-

viction that the only real resistance to Chinese Communism had been available in the north. He should have known. His supporters were led by revolutionaries who had become disillusioned with the Vietminh; who were themselves from the villages of Tonkin; who knew, after varying periods of service in Vietminh battalions, that they were serving Chinese and not their own national interests. They believed France abdicated any claims as a protector by betraying them twice in fourteen years, first to Japan and then to China. Some called themselves "patriotic Communists" and believed Ho Chi-minh might once have been detached from Soviet or Chinese sponsors before his utter indoctrination. Some were self-styled socialists. They made up the young, virile Dai Viat Party which was determined to rid their country of the French, but not at the cost of absorption into a new Chinese empire. But Dr. Quat's delay in Karachi proved fatal and very soon he found his movement under suspicion for subversion.

A Catholic figure was brought to power, a resolute anti-Communist Ngo Dinh Diem, who tackled corruption and moral decay with the aid of U.S. dollars, some 57,000,000 of them for refugees and 100,000,000 annually on defense. Dr. Quat was placed under house arrest and his Party's supporters either detained or advised to forget their socialistic dreams.

And in the delta to the north, people waited anxiously to hear what had been agreed at Geneva. When the details were broadcast from London on July 21, it was too late for many to escape, although thousands tried and succeeded. Priority was given to French military forces and the roads and exits were clogged with army traffic.

Mao's shock treatment was over. The sweating patient had become most of Asia where Eisenhower's words of August 1953 now echoed ominously:

> Let us assume [the U.S. President had said] that we lost Indochina. If it goes, several things happen right away. The Malay Peninsula, that last little bit hanging on down there, would be scarcely defensible . . . all of India outflanked. Burma would be in no position for defense . . . if we lost all that, how would the free world hold the rich empire of Indonesia?

But China had made all the progress she could with guns as her argument. Now it was time to talk, to persuade, to administer to the sick peoples of all the underdeveloped nations.

The microphones of Peking Radio began to vibrate with relentlessly reasonable voices in the yellow languages of Burma, Thailand, Malaya and Japan. "Asia," they said with gentle insistence, "is sick from the exploitation of Western imperialists."

CHAPTER FIFTEEN

"Think of Every Rock You Crush as an American Head"

◉ ◉

I saw the final act of the French tragedy in Indochina from the Communist side. My companions were wiry Vietminh troops whose iron self-discipline commanded my reluctant admiration. I understood why they had survived eight years in the jungle and I shuddered to think of our utter ignorance in the West of their capabilities. Their minds were steeled against heresy; their bodies were dedicated to the Party and The People. If one of their comrades questioned an order, displayed an eccentric sympathy for the enemy or misbehaved with the peasants on whom they were billeted, he was immediately subjected to harsh and interminable sermons. These blank-faced soldiers were human missiles to be launched against the West: and once they defeated the French they became armed evangelists for the conversion of the peasants they had "liberated." Each one was a Communist textbook with arms and legs and a mouth from which spilled the words that would have been meaningless when printed and set between stiff covers for distribution among illiterates. Their leader, they were told, was Ho Chi-minh. They called him "Uncle Ho" and because he sprang from the same soil as themselves, they felt a bursting pride that concealed their true status as servants of China and Russia.

I entered their ranks as a newspaperman attached to the

Canadian members of the Indochina truce commission whose
melancholy duty was to help preside over the last rites of the
French Empire in Asia. Once inside Vietminh territory, however, I spent that summer of 1955 with Communist army officers.

It was Friday the 13th in the Red River delta when the last
scenes were played. The first sweat of the day trickled down
our faces and early mists dissolved above the brilliant squares
of paddy, or lingered in villages embattled behind walls of
bamboo. There were Russian trucks on the road driven by
Chinese and this should have been their day of victory. The
day was given instead to small soldiers in jungle-green uniforms who waited outside the port of Haiphong. Some held
bouquets and others let droop between them the banners reading: *Long Live Ho Chi-minh! Long Live the Party!* They
stood silent, rigid and watchful while across the filthy river
littered with sampans General René Cogny prepared to bury
seventy years' French rule in North Indochina.

Some miles away and several hours earlier, I had talked with
a young Frenchman. His name was Claude Drault. He wore
the blue uniform of the Chinese Railway Volunteers. As he
stared at me with emotionless blue eyes, his home in the 14th
arrondissement of Paris seemed distant indeed.

"What is my future?" he echoed. "To work. To work and
work — for The People."

Two jars of drinking water were placed between us. His
hand shot out, then hesitated. His eyes shifted over my shoulder to a Chinese in a rice-straw helmet who gave him a sharp
nod. The hand finished its movement.

"You ask me what I do in my spare time? I study — how to
serve The People better, how to improve work style."

I looked down in embarrassment. There was absolutely no
point of contact. My questions were going in circular motion
around a central theme. Since Drault had been in Communist
captivity, he faced for the first time another product of his own
civilization. There was no hint of recognition: his mind was
in some mysterious deep-freeze. He need only say the word
and his captors must release him, but no sign came.

"You ask about my politics," he said. "You cannot put politics into a book."

For the first time his body showed animation. He lifted both hands and described the shape of a book.

"Politics are The People. Politics means to work for The People."

His hands dropped back and then he began all over again like a cracked record. Again he outlined the shape of a book, again he said: "You cannot put politics into a book. Politics are The People . . ."

This memory stayed with me throughout that day in May 1955, when a proud French general put his last troops and tanks into landing craft while his late enemies marched softly on rubber-soled feet into what had been the headquarters of the Force Terreste du Nord Vietnam.

The Vietminh moved forward street by street, advancing without the thunder of tanks or the crunch of boots, without even cheers or shouted orders. The French, burly military policemen in steel helmets, faced them across each road and fell back as the time came to relinquish a new sector of the town. The Communists swept forward, their few Molotov trucks purring down the main thoroughfares, their slippered platoons infiltrating down the lanes and several thousand more of them flooding slowly and quietly into houses, shops and the bistros where the bottles of Pernod would gather dust and the gay signs fade.

"This is like attending your best friend's funeral," said the Canadian army officer who brought me in with the new occupiers. General Cogny evidently thought so too. At the very end, he asked Canadians and other members of the Truce Commission to avoid a bitter little ceremony on the Haiphong quayside.

Eight buglers sounded *descente des couleurs* but the last lament was played by a solitary Moroccan on his mouth organ after Legionnaires and men of the Garde Republicaine trooped aboard the supply ship *Jules Verne*. It was a mournful melody he played alone on the deserted dock, keeping guard over the stained knapsacks, the scattered bedrolls and the notched rifles of the last French colonial army to fight in the Far East.

He was playing, though he never knew it, a requiem to the French Empire in Asia. The dirge was "*Malbrouk s'en va-t-en guerre.*"

Around the war memorial to French dead, townspeople had assembled since dawn. They had watched that humiliating retreat, the French walking backwards and full of bitterness. Now as French destroyers and evacuation ships glided into the Bay of Tonkin, the Vietminh began the new task of education.

There were the Eight Points of President Ho with Regard to Newly Liberated Cities. (*Those who commit sabotage will be punished*); the Eight Political Wisdoms of President Ho (*All clergy will fulfill duties as citizens*).

And there was a local version of the Three Cardinal Rules of Discipline and the Eight Reminders, first formulated by Mao Tse-tung for the Chinese Workers' and Peasants' Red Army:

> (1) Obey orders in all actions. (2) Do not take a single needle or piece of thread from the people. (3) Turn all booty over to H.Q. (a) Talk to people politely. (b) Be fair in all business dealings. (c) Return everything you have borrowed. (d) Pay for anything you have damaged. (e) Do not beat or bully people. (f) Do not damage crops. (g) Do not flirt with women. (h) Do not ill-treat prisoners of war.

This was not only an echo of Mao. It was, in its way, classically Chinese. Similar disciplines were promulgated by Hung Hsu-ch'uan, leader of the Taiping uprisings one century earlier. His armed peasants were ordered to befriend the local citizenry; pay for everything used; enter private houses only when asked; avoid damaging crops; use persuasion rather than brute force. Rape was punishable by death.

Clocks were turned back one hour in conformity with Peking time. The victors brought rice and salt, and a booklet which listed their achievements of the previous ten years.

The booklet recorded as the climax to those triumphs:

The Battle of Dienbienphu . . . wiped out 16,200 enemy

troops, including seventeen battalions of infantry and para-troops, three battalions of heavy artillery, ten puppet Thai companies and many units of motor vehicles, transports, anti-aircraft and aircraft; all the staff officers including one brigadier general, sixteen colonels, 352 officers from second lieutenants to majors, and 1396 noncommissioned officers;

Brought down and burned sixty-two planes of various types;

Captured all arms and arms dumps concentrated in the French cluster of fortified positions, consisting of twenty-four cannons of 105 and 155 millimeters, ten flame throwers, sixty-four motor vehicles, 542 radio sets, fifty-one machines including five bulldozers, 5915 rifles, 5000 gallons of gasoline, 21,000 para-chutes, twenty tons of medicines and medical instruments . . .

The newcomers brought the jungle with them. Patrols moved into the streets at dusk, each with its distinctive whistles and cries. They moved like phantoms between the twisted trunks of banyans. The evening chorus of cicadas made the air vibrate like an orchestra of telephone wires humming in a breeze. But there was no breeze and the frenzied song drowned conversation and plucked at taut nerves.

That night the citizenry got their orders. The Military and Administrative Committee issued a proclamation:

One half of our country is completely liberated. The port of Haiphong, the collieries, rice fields and 700 kilometers of our coast are restored to our people . . . The present task is to pre-vent all sabotage . . . The American imperialists, the French colonialists and their clique are plotting . . . Unity is not yet achieved and South Vietnam, Laos and Cambodia are being turned into American military bases for a new war.

The war cries were muted, however. General Giap, tem-peramental and impetuous, was under restraint. For him, the overthrow of French rule was the first example of a colony achieving its freedom by Communist revolution. The task was incomplete. Below the 17th Parallel remained another twelve million of his people.

For the Chinese, most of the former kingdom of Annam had returned to its previous state of vassalage. Eighty years earlier, the French forced the Annamites to transfer allegiance from China to France. Now that honor was satisfied, it would be foolish to provoke the Americans further, since their aircraft carriers had come perilously near to intervening at Dienbienphu with atomic weapons. Of course this New People's Democratic Republic owed allegiance to nobody and the Chinese went to great pains to conceal their presence except on occasions when their advertised appearance coincided with some munificent gesture. Nevertheless, they were undeniably there.

I was allowed to roam around the interior, using an old Citroën and official "black market" gasoline. My movements had to be planned in advance, although an efficient "jungle telegraph" gave adequate warning to area commanders if I changed plans abruptly. My companions were two former university teachers who explained how their early Boy Scout training taught them the rudiments of guerrilla warfare. Both were hollow-chested, emaciated young men with senior commands in the 42nd Vietminh Regiment which held down three French Union mobile groups for an entire year on a short road between Hanoi and defense headquarters in the north delta sector. They said gleefully that in all this time the French had been their sole source of supplies for food, ammunition and weapons.

Comrade Duc, the senior, suffered like most Vietminh veterans from malaria. He spent hours tracing the progress of old battles on the backs of my notebooks, sketching steadily in the hired Citroën as we bounced and bumped over slippery tracks cut through the jungle.

Life looked grim. Columns of coolies were everywhere seen, spurred in their tasks by slogans pinned to their Aladdin straw hats: *Think of every rock you crush as an American head,* was a favorite among railroad workers. French was still the language used in remote mountain schools whose pupils had played truant to run messages through the French lines.

One day I arrived at Ho Chi-minh's former underground headquarters at Thai Nguyen. It was concealed in the forested hillside above a tributary of the Red River. We reached it by queuing for hours behind Soviet trucks to cross on a

wooden barge. This ferry was waterlogged after each crossing and needed baling out. Its total capacity was two donkey
carts and one truck, plus the ten men required to haul it across
by pulling hand-over-hand on a cable. The bombed remains
of a bridge lay twisted in the river.

"Our President has a joyful wit," said Comrade Duc, leading
the way through breadfruit trees to Ho's advance base during
eight years' campaign. He gestured to neat wooden huts with
thatched roofs, bamboo-latticed doors and an effective over-all
camouflage provided by mottled parachutes.

"He calls this mutual aid," said Duc. "The French provided
the parachutes at Dienbienphu."

A stocky figure invited me to sit in a blackwood chair with
inlaid mother-of-pearl. Young grass shoots grew out of the
packed earth floor. My host advanced into the light. He was
General Chu Van Tan, president of the Executive Committee
of the First Inter-Zone. He might just as easily have been a
waiter. He wore no insignia but he did carry a tray of soda-
pop bottles.

According to the general, it was at this shelter that Ho arrived with reassuring news for his aides, who were worried
about the French build-up at Dienbienphu.

"Uncle Ho was asked what he felt about the situation," said
General Chu. "He took off his sun helmet, inverted it on this
table and pointed into the crown. 'Down there,' said our
President, 'are the French. We are all along the rim. This is
the opportunity we have awaited.' "

I said it was lucky for Ho that several thousand Soviet trucks,
artillery, mortars and anti-aircraft guns were available at the
time. The general angrily stubbed out his cigarette.

"All these years we fought with weapons stolen from the
enemy or forged in our mountain caves," he said. "Look
around here! This was our advanced headquarters for eight
years. The French bombed it regularly and claimed three times
to have killed Uncle Ho. They used napalm — all *that* did was
win our side more friends among peasants. This is what we
were fighting with before Dienbienphu . . ."

He took me outside. In a clearing beside the river were

several elephants, dwarfing the tiny Vietminh soldiers who scrubbed them down. A stream of earnest young men wheeled bicycles out of an adjoining compound. Each had a satchel thrown over one shoulder. Rusting in the tangled undergrowth were small, finned bombs somewhat like the incendiaries dropped on London by Nazi bombers. They were easy to identify. Three years earlier, I had been in a French outpost when the tower was shattered by these "flying bombs." They were launched from ramps of split bamboo. The fort's outer defenses consisted of barbed wire and a "moat" of stone chips to inconvenience the barefoot peasant army. Suicidal youths broke through the barriers with homemade bangalore torpedoes, danced across the sharp stones and breached the walls with crude grenades lashed to the tips of bamboo poles.

"Yes," the general was saying. "That is how we fought before Dienbienphu."

The sky was turning black. The air was heavy. A blue magpie flashed its brilliant tail and rose steeply with a cry of *pit pit pit churrah* that sounded like the mockery of a victory cheer.

Suddenly the valley was bathed in the awful, steely blue flash of tropical lightning. The scene etched itself on the memory with the clarity of a photograph: an elephant with trunk upraised, panniers of military supplies on either flank; another elephant still at its ablutions, a silly red flag tied to the head harness. The seemingly unending column of officials, held for a brief second, each with his bicycle and satchel as symbols of bureaucratic power in this jungle. General Chu fondling a crude bazooka from his private war museum . . .

Comrade Duc with bloodshot eyes betraying his illness tried to focus on the river where logs drifted. The lightning transmuted the water to quicksilver and the logs, chained together, were revealed as railroad sleepers with their own floating village of thatched huts.

Then the light went out. I felt unexpectedly sorry for these people with their incredible self-discipline and their pride. You admired their courage and grit while deploring their foolishness. They had fought to Dienbienphu and then, in the moment of triumph, their true inspiration revealed itself in the flood of Soviet and Red Chinese aid which must have been waiting there on the northern marches.

This was a poor reward, to be given jargon and cant to mutter. Yet even the most intelligent of them echoed the gray porridgy language. There were no stirring words to match their valor. A remarkable war was already reduced to drab gibberish. I asked a leading Vietminh "hero" how he lost one arm. His name was Le Van Cau which he disclosed reluctantly. He said: "I lost it fighting for The People." That was all.

Who were The People?

"Victims of an American imperialist plot," said Comrade Nam Dang when I went to his security headquarters in Hanoi. He hauled three wretched youths out of a jail cell. "These were lackeys used to seduce their fellow students."

Security Chief Nam was a short, dynamic man. He made statements that outraged the Western mind. He was blissfully unconscious of the effect of his words.

"Our security police conducted the trial of these three lackeys before twelve thousand people at Hanoi University," he said. "We had loudspeakers everywhere so that all could hear. We had to instruct the people, you see, not to be seduced by American agents. The defense lawyers had to plead guilty of course. They were there to ask for clemency after sentence was passed."

He pushed forward an old, bent man who was father of one of the convicted boys. Shoemaker Nguyen Van Tan mumbled his piece to me, eyes fixed on the ground: "I am one of hundreds of loyal parents who have urged the public authorities to take these measures," he said. "I am glad my boy has been arrested as an example of how Imperialist Agents are luring children to go south."

I recognized the glazed look in his eyes and forbore to question the poor fellow. Instead I listened in fascinated horror to the calm, incisive voice of the secret police chief: "And so security depends on The People themselves and upon their vigilance. We must make The People always aware of enemies who try to undermine all we have suffered and worked to build.

Thus in this very street every neighbor keeps watch. This is collective vigilance. If something suspicious is seen in the adjoining house — meetings at midnight, for instance, or the arrival of a stranger — it is the citizen's duty to maintain observation and report to security agents."

Shortly after this I got a salutary reminder that even a sophisticated European, engulfed in this atmosphere where outrageous ideas become acceptable routine, loses all sense of balance. The wife of a Communist journalist produced a child in the former French military hospital set aside by the Vietminh for senior officials, East European diplomats and military casualties. She was Bulgarian, from a cultured family. The new baby was scarcely twenty-four hours old and might be expected to soften even the flintiest mother's heart.

I went to see her, clutching a large box of French chocolates tied in pink bows and wrapped in gay paper. Such luxuries were rare. I had paid considerably to find this one and was not at all sure the contents had stood up well to the heat. I walked through packed corridors, reflecting that when the French had been in possession the overcrowding was no worse, but the confusion and dirt infinitely more depressing. Considering how many people were in that hospital, it was now unnaturally hushed. And considering the few materials that its new owners had to work with, it was also unnaturally clean. A Swiss Red Cross official, in fact, had been trying for almost a year to break down Vietminh pride and *give away* large quantities of drugs, disinfectants and medical equipment. He was regarded with dark suspicion.

But suspicion could have been nowhere darker than in the large, airy room in which I found Madame X. Whatever was happening to The People squashed in the corridors outside, Madame was having none of it. Later it was explained to me how The People never objected to relinquishing their comforts for foreign friends like Madame. It was a long and involved explanation and I have forgotten most of it.

The young mother was turning her pink little baby for my inspection when she suddenly froze. I was placing the French chocolates on her bedside table.

"Are those — " she choked. "Are those for me?"

I nodded, rather proud that an ignorant old capitalist had discovered these rare delicacies in this Communist stronghold. I imagined that her voice was choking with gratitude and glad surprise.

Her face set into a mask of intense revulsion. "French — !" she spluttered, pushing aside the gaily wrapped box.

She never touched the box again and neither did I. For all I know, it may be there still, the pride of The People who can point to it from their corridors as proof of how well they look after their foreign friends. It sits there, I suppose, the ribbon faded and bedraggled and the chocolates quite moldy.

CHAPTER SIXTEEN

Breakfast with Uncle Ho

◉ ◉

THE AIR of conspiracy was strong when the comrades came for me. They bore an invitation to breakfast with Uncle Ho. I was lying under the mosquito net in my room at the Métropole, pressed down by the stifling heat and wondering if it was really a lichee bird crying plaintively outside, or just another exuberant patrol leader looking for the rest of his Vietminh scouts and a good deed to be done for this day.

"Mr. William Seemen!" cried a familiar voice. I pretended not to hear. There was an urgent rapping on the door. "Mr. William Seemen — plea — se!"

Comrade Duc was in a flap. He had flapped before, yesterday at exactly the same hour and in precisely the same way. On that occasion I dressed hurriedly, skipped the nauseating coffee in the steam bath they called a restaurant, and rushed out under the firm impression that I was about to meet the uncrowned heads of North Vietnam. Instead I was subjected to fifty minutes' exhortation by two tame Buddhist priests on the enlightened religious policies of Uncle Ho.

I lay still. If I answered Comrade Duc, he would never release me until we kept whatever appointments had been arranged without my knowledge. If I stayed silent he would scuttle down to the reformed bar boy, a lad who reeled home on the dregs of other people's drinks in the days of French imperialism and tolerance. Somewhere in the mysterious labyrinth of basement rooms occupied by Vietminh, he had found his redemption. Now, to prove the cure, he presided over the hotel's liquid assets and disapprovingly served members of the Truce Commission.

That bar boy was keeping a sharp eye on me. In the old days, French colonels on leave from the outlying forts would argue with us. Now the stools where they sat were empty. Their beautiful secretaries were gone. Only the boy remained, meticulously wiping the dry counter, watching my exits and entrances under lowered lids.

"Mr. William, you are ten minutes late already."

Wearily I raised my voice. "For what?"

"The President."

I jumped from bed, cursing. The touch of a laundered shirt on my bare skin started the awful flow of perspiration. My socks were missing; so was my belt. I thrust my feet into sandals and used a necktie to hoist my pants. Unshaven, disheveled, I presented myself before Comrade Duc.

"President Ho Chi-minh has been waiting," he said accusingly.

I staggered off to the former imperial palace. It had the air of being occupied by usurpers. A man on a bicycle wobbled round the courtyard. Inside the entrance hall there were camp beds, two steel chairs and an enamel washbasin.

I was ushered into the high-ceilinged reception room by two small men in shabby blue tunics. Duc, looking lost, waited at the great, studded main doors.

"We got you up early," said Ho Chi-minh, entering behind me. He spoke English in a soft, hesitant voice. He gestured to one of the bright pink easy chairs, peering at me through smudged spectacles like an elderly professor.

"Let us just talk," he said, offering a Chinese cigarette. Tea was brought, and some tasteless biscuits. We sat alone in a room furnished like a spare bedroom in some seedy London suburb.

I had long ago submitted several questions. He ran down the list with a gnarled finger, answering each point, glancing at me inquisitively when he was unsure of my meaning. A

breeze stirred the muslin curtains. The cigarettes went out and
were relit. The tea in thick china mugs turned cold.

Uncle Ho was indeed a strange man. Every whisker of his
straggling beard coiled and writhed out of the sickly yellow
skin as if independently planted. He fumbled often with his
spectacles, taped across the bridge. He wore a khaki tunic,
buttoned at the neck. His trousers were threadbare and
baggy, short at the ankle, and his socks were obviously hand-
knitted. The socks flopped over black sandals cut from truck
tires.

"We hate the American Government for poking into Asia's
affairs," he was saying. "We do not hate the American people.
It is clear the American people do not support their government policies here. The American people are our friends and
like us are opposed to propping up puppet regimes of the
dictators Chiang Kai-shek, Syngman Rhee and Diem."

He expressed bewilderment at the rigid opposition of the
West to his regime. "We had to help wherever it was available
to win our revolution," he said.

I pointed out that disagreeable features in his government
were typical of Communist regimentation. There had been a
parade of youth only the previous Sunday. Youngsters were
assembling long before dawn and marched throughout the
day, chanting "Long Live Ho Chi-minh!"

"You may be reminded of Fascist regimentation," replied
Ho. "But this is not the case here. This is a question of
bringing our youth together for tasks to be accomplished on
behalf of The People. We are not committed to regimenting
our People as a pattern for the future. The children you saw
marching behind the drums . . . before they had nothing. Those
children the West — er — expends? . . . Is that the word? Yes,
the West expends its pity on those children now . . . what did
they have before? The privilege of cleaning the boots of
Frenchmen?" His hands trembled. "In the countryside, the
French gave these children little showers of napalm."

Sharply, jerking his head back on its scrawny stem: "We are
in a state of emergency. During war you accept restrictions
on liberty. Here it is the same.

"Do not forget in Asia we have not had the time to gain your perspectives."

He seemed an extraordinary complex of naïveté and great subtlety. He said: "I would like to have visitors from the West. But you see, if I had businessmen coming here they would report in an antagonistic manner because they had to."

I said this was not necessarily true. He blinked at me, adjusting the broken spectacles. "Well, you have in your country a peace-loving committee no doubt? Let them come."

"You can invite peace-loving committees until the end of time," I said. "It won't help you and it certainly won't impress us. We consider such committees are manipulated by international communism in a way that discredits them at home."

Ho stroked his bewhiskered chin. "But nobody will ever report truly about us if he believes in capitalism . . ."

We discussed economic problems. Ho said he would consider joining in schemes for mutual aid between small Communist and non-Communist nations.

"Remember we have been in the jungle a long time," he said. "We need time to study such questions. In the jungle you lose touch."

He rested one hand on my shoulder. "Try to understand."

I left, considerably puzzled. This beggar on a throne would have appealed to popular imagination in almost any other age. This tubercular, frail old man (he was then sixty-five) trailed his rags through Bao Dai's palace with dignity.

In almost any other age, his burning compassion would command respect. You wanted to clap him on the back, admit his peasants' skill had proved superior to Western technical strength, and propose terms for future collaboration. Ho seemed like a man who, given the chance, would respond to a genuinely friendly gesture. The fanaticism that drove his sickly body was fed by a raging love of his own people, but too much of the fuel was supplied in hard nuggets of cold dogma from Peking.

This barefoot mystic, like Stalin and Mao Tse-tung, was in his youth eager to devote his life to religious observances. Unlike the other two, he was still inspired by some tremendous urge toward self-sacrifice and to me it seemed he was a troubled man.

One month later he was summoned to Peking and Moscow. The Chinese granted him the equivalent of three hundred million dollars and Russian aid was offered at more than ninety million dollars. The Russians shipped a further 150,000 tons of rice bought in Burma. This avalanche came like an answer to Ho's swift interest in my casual suggestions that North Vietnam might seek aid among small Western nations of goodwill and no imperialist ambitions.

"It is a good idea," he had told me, adding wistfully, "but there is little we can offer in return for outside help."

Now, with such promises of Communist help, his half of Vietnam was on the road to recovery. It was also just as certainly reduced to the status of a satellite. General Giap would have preferred to drive south to win the rice surplus of the Mekong River delta. The price of "fraternal" aid was that his peasant army should make the best of Tonkin's ravaged paddies where even in good times the annual production of 100,000 tons of rice was inadequate.

Ho remained a figurehead. None of his books had ever been published. His contact with the masses was confined to explosive little slogans. Yet the Chinese could not dispense with him.

Early in 1956 Mikoyan brought word of "de-Stalinization" to Ho's territories while a senseless reign of terror was sweeping the countryside. Then Mao Tse-tung launched his campaign for controlled "free discussion" and at once the seething intellectual community of Hanoi seized its chance.

"In the jungle you lose touch," Ho had admitted. It seemed sure that he would welcome the relaxation, perhaps even show surprise at the excesses now revealed.

It is due to the lack of a legal code that our agrarian reform has bitterly failed [complained the Hanoi newspaper, *Nhan Van*] and that our army does not yet have a rational military service. It is due to lack of a legal code that a security agent can ask for a marriage certificate from couples on the bank of Le Petit Lac waiting for the moon to rise, that a census operation

cadre can watch at the door of a house, making its occupiers uneasy so they cannot eat or sleep; that a tax cadre can search a
house any time he pleases; that cases of kicking out tenants from
their houses . . . can occur . . .

The Vice-Minister of Justice, Nguyen Van Huong, wrote:

The People's life and property, The People's basic interests
such as democratic liberties . . . have been injured, sometimes
very seriously. In some places the law was not respected, in
other places the law was trampled underfoot.

Lonely deaths from hard labor and starvation were now
exposed and the blame placed on ruthless officials conducting
the program of land reform.

Protested the Party organ *Nhan Van:*

Cadres at battalion level, being afraid of Right deviation, have
made too many arrests and have persecuted The People a great
deal . . . in all not less than 100 persons were wrongly jailed (in
one village) . . . brothers from the same family dared not visit
each other and people dared not bow or talk when they met in
the street . . . Comrade Ngon, middle peasant, President of the
Administrative Committee and Party cell secretary was denounced
as a cruel landlord and executed. Other Party members were
executed one after another . . .

As I read this, my mind flew back to the chief of security
police and his flat denial to me: "No, we have not executed
anybody."

During the autumn and early winter of 1956, these revelations made astounding reading. They proved how dangerous
it is for Western observers to trust their eyes and ears inside
any Communist camp. It suggested to me, too, that a man like
Ho Chi-minh, driven fundamentally by a fierce desire to help
his compatriots, could be tragically fooled. The artists and
writers of North Vietnam who shared Ho's early instruction
on the inviolability of individual rights had for a time expressed in moving language the same aspirations, the same
hopes and fears as their comrades in Hungary whose rebellion
was being crushed.

But on November 5 *Nhan Van* went too far. The editor,
Phan Koi, was previously known for his trenchant writings,
and his grandfather had been a famous patriot opposed to
French rule. Phan wrote: "A customer asked a bookshop
owner: 'Do you sell *Nhan Van?*' The reply was 'No, sir.' The
bookseller slowly twirled his mustache. 'In selling *Nhan Van*
you run the serious risk of dying early.'"

Phan Koi was hauled posthaste to Peking. University students and professors kept up the attack. In its last issue on
November 20, *Nhan Van's* acting editor, Tran Duy, wrote:
"We ask for Democratic Freedoms in order to build up man's
life, to restore man's right to live and man's dignity in society."

A decree was issued over the signature of Tran Duy-hang,
President of the Executive Committee: "Article 1. Close the
newspaper *Nhan Van* from the date of issue of the present
decree. Immediately after the issue of the present decree, the
circulation of all copies from the first issue to the last of the
paper *Nhan Van* is forbidden . . ."

The brief respite was over. While it lasted, the Chinese-
trained ideologist and secretary-general of the Lao Dang
(Communist) Party was obliged to make a self-criticism. He
was Truong Chinh whose pseudonym referred to the Chinese
8th Route Army's Long March. He was regarded as second
to Ho and leader of the pro-Peking faction in the Party.

Truong in other circumstances would have certainly replaced
Ho Chi-minh. But instead, Ho took his place as Secretary
General. It was apparent that for the time being Ho must be
utilized to camouflage Chinese determination to fashion North
Vietnam in their own likeness. Premier Chou En-lai flew down
from Peking and was carefully photographed on November
18 beaming confidently beside Ho. By the end of December
his Cabinet had discussed the policy for 1957 and the irrepressible Truong Chinh declared: "In the work of leadership
it is necessary to use the army and security forces firmly."

Ho mounted the rostrum to face his National Assembly the
following month. The intellectual opposition only a few weeks
earlier called it "a rubber-stamp assembly . . . neglecting its
principal duty, which is to make law."

But all Ho said was that the Assembly's most important tasks included "the increase of dictatorship." Its most important achievement, said this ghost of a great revolutionary, was its arrival at "unanimity of views."

The newsreels showed him staring vacantly ahead, flanked by silent, tight-lipped Party men. He reminded me, oddly enough, of poor Claude Drault.

CHAPTER SEVENTEEN

Tibetan Lullaby

◉ ◉

RED CHINA's mopping-up operations were accomplished wherever possible without conflict. While Indochina's fate was shaped by use of the gun, it was sealed by peaceful consultation. The new Peking regime had been struggling with infinite courtesy to get rid of ambitious Soviet Russian agents in Sinkiang (Chinese Tartary) and other areas of the former Celestal Empire in Inner Mongolia and Manchuria. Those Russians who were permitted back had to sign short-term contracts and were selected on the basis of their technical knowledge and ability to help promote Chinese plans to colonize and later industrialize the interior.

I have already described what an inquiring traveler could see of the new Chinese tactics of painstaking discussion in the southwest border regions. Their most subtle schemes for conquest, however, were directed toward Tibet which waters the lower territories of Burma and Indochina and defends the Indian subcontinent against invasions from the north.

The greatest barrier to China's capture of Tibet (or, as many Chinese geopoliticians would say: "its re-occupation") was the young independent nation of India. However, by their military exertions in Korea and Indochina it was possible for the Chinese Communists to deliver a considerable shock to the Indian Government of Pandit Nehru. It became perfectly clear that Indian officials were fearful of Chinese military power and would avoid conflict at almost any cost. Thus Mao Tse-

tung was able to talk calmly and reasonably about his desire to
take over Tibet, having first adopted a fierce mask of military
resolve during preliminary communications with Nehru during the Korean War. I was lucky enough to witness the moment when Nehru was finally confronted with reality.

The scene took place in the Sea Palaces of Peking. The
time was November 1954, some months after Premier Chou
En-lai won his diplomatic victory at Geneva and before his
satellite Vietminh troops completed their occupation of North
Indochina. It should be pointed out that India was a member
of the Indochina truce commission and held a controlling vote
on matters of dispute, since the other two members were Red
Poland and Canada. I had already seen how skillfully the
Chinese made use of India's fear of further hostilities in the
Indochina arena, but I was unprepared for their bold exploita-
tion of Nehru's goodwill.

The principal player was the fourteenth Dalai Lama of
Tibet, reincarnation of Lotus Thunderbolt, patron deity and
founder of the Yellow Hat Lamas, "The Great and Precious
Prince of the Faith, Noble One of Soft Voice, Mighty in
Speech, Excellent of Knowledge, Absolute in Wisdom, Holder
of the Doctrine, the One without Equal, Powerful Ruler of
Three Worlds, the Ocean Wise."

Behind him in red robes stood his proposed replacement:
the Panchen Lama, reincarnation of the Dhyani Buddha, leader
of the Red Sect in Rear Tibet.

The holy young man in saffron robes had led the way into
the crowded pavilion. Nobody at first recognized him as the
Dalai. He was propelled gently by a beetle-browed statesman:
Premier Chou En-lai. The stage was set with characteristic
care some while before the arrival of Nehru who was on his
first visit to China as Indian Prime Minister.

The audience included foreign diplomats whose reports would
be carefully read in Western capitals. The bit actors were Red
Army generals, bulky and anonymous in plain brown uniforms;
a scattering of political chess players led by Politburo strategist
Liu Shao-chi, cold and aloof; the governors of Communist provinces, all ex-military chiefs; and that former Cinderella among

the famous Soong sisters, Madame Sun Yat-sen, widow of the revolutionary and second sister of Madame Chiang Kai-shek.

For me, the dramatic highlight of that chilly afternoon came when the Dalai and Panchen Lamas were conjured up without warning so that they were flanked by the two men most interested in their destinies. Facing each other on either side were Premier Chou En-lai, sponsor of the Panchen Lama: and Nehru of India, backer of the Dalai Lama. Thus was Nehru confronted for the first time since the Holy One flew to the Indian border two years earlier, as Chinese troops occupied the insular city of Lhasa. Communism had breached the armor of isolation, opening the hermit land and placing itself on the 1800-mile border with India.

I stood directly behind Chou En-lai that moment as he said, speaking English to Nehru: "I believe you may like to meet our friends from Tibet?"

The encounter had been cunningly contrived. Chou, having strategically located the Tibetan leaders inside the packed pavilion, then went out to meet Nehru. He led the Indian premier slowly through the dense throng, pausing here and there to make an introduction. The show was billed as a "tea party" in honor of the Indian Premier, but most people sipped lemonade. Nehru, hot and perspiring, blinked savagely at the blinding floodlights. Suddenly the crowd parted and there was Chou with a firm grip on the Dalai, the Panchen trailing obediently behind.

A silence fell upon the assembly. Every head had turned. The Chinese generals stood in clusters, moon faces attentive. Ice melted in a glass and tinkled softly. A foot shuffled.

Nehru glanced round. There was General Chang Ching-wu, first Chinese Governor of Tibet, smiling gently. There was the immobile figure of General Tan Kuan-san, Political Commissar in Tibet of the Chinese "liberating" armies. There was the trio of Long March heroes, chiefs of modern Chinese military power: Chu Teh (The Bear); one-eyed Lin Piao; and Peng Teh-huai, arms hanging loose, fingers dangling like sausages.

"I'm very pleased," murmured Nehru, politely extending his hand in a gesture as foreign to India as to Tibet. "Very pleased. After all this time . . ."

There was another awkward pause and then Chou, beaming in all directions, whisked Nehru away. Attention drifted from the two young Tibetans. Someone asked the Dalai for his autograph. The Holy One scribbled on the back of an old envelope, thin spidery characters like Sanskrit. The Panchen leaned over, took the paper and added his signature. The Holy One retrieved it and handing it back, said gravely: "Dalai Lama — on top!"

And indeed his name did come first. Close at his heels, however, was the young Panchen, almost totally a product of Peking. A weaker man than the Dalai might have been eclipsed. Instead, he survived until 1959 as an obstinate and lonely figure whose only strength was a mysterious moral and spiritual power. Against his slight person, and his 100,000 loyal lamas, the encompassing Chinese generals had not so far prevailed. Other hostile forces went to work instead. The full story of the Dalai Lama's ordeal, if ever it is told, will reveal the formidable nature of Chinese patience when combined with Communist wile.

The Chinese have always insisted that Tibet was their province and their present rulers wait with ill-concealed impatience for Tibetans to accept their plans for improvement. But — and this was the most significant thing — they still waited.

When Nehru found himself publicly acknowledging the Dalai Lama's existence as a free man in Peking, his mind must have flown back to the strange and sometimes angry exchanges between himself and Peking that began only two days after India recognized the new Communist regime. The Chinese Red Army announced that one of its basic tasks was the liberation of Tibet. Nehru told his parliament in Delhi, rather tartly, that he wondered: "Liberation from whom?"

The Chinese replied, in a note to the Indian ambassador on November 16, 1950: ". . . liberation of the people from oppression . . . for the sake of world peace, to maintain Chinese independence and prevent imperialist aggressors from dragging the world towards war."

In Tibet alarm was widespread. The fourteenth Dalai Lama was only sixteen and his Regent, Tokra, organized missions to India, the U.S. and Britain to rally support. From Peking came

a blunt warning: any country that received such an illegal
mission would thereby demonstrate its hostility to China.

Ancient prophecies were coming true. The thirteenth Dalai
Lama, before he departed to the Heavenly Field, wrote a letter
to his people known as the Precious Protector's Last Testa-
ment. He warned:

> The present is the time of the Five Kinds of Degeneration in
> all countries. In the worst class is the manner of working among
> the Red People. They do not allow search to be made for the new
> Incarnation of the Grand Lama of Urga. They have seized and
> taken way all the sacred objects from the monasteries. They have
> made monks work as soldiers. They have broken religion . . . It
> may happen that here in the center of Tibet the religious and the
> secular administration may be attacked both from the outside and
> from the inside.
>
> *Unless we can guard our country it will now happen that the
> Dalai and Panchen Lamas, the Father and the Son, the Holders
> of the Faith, the glorious Rebirths, will be broken down . . . All
> beings will be sunk in great hardship and in overpowering fear;
> the days and nights will drag on slowly in suffering.*

Tibetans believed for many centuries that there would be a
crisis when they must fight for their religion. They had been a
fierce people once. They skirmished with China for two thousand years, invaded India, Central Asia and China in the
seventh century A.D. and made alliance even with the Caliphs
of Baghdad.

Their books predicted a decisive battle with "Shambhala of
the North," a mystical country often identified as Russia. In
Tibetan houses were faded paintings of this future struggle.

In fact, three great nations have been rivals for control of
Tibet. It is a vast land, seven times the size of Britain, and
it varies in height from 9000 to 29,000 feet. Its tormentors,
often known as the Lion, Bear and Dragon, were at different
times Britain, Russia and China. But during the later years of
imperial rule in India the British did much to protect Tibetan
institutions and preferred not to interfere so long as it remained a neutral Himalayan buffer. Few tried to exploit its
natural resources. British explorers found evidence of radio-

active materials. A crude system of washing gold out of
Tibetan soil earned $112,000 every year in gold exports to
China. Official records of the T'ang Dynasty show that ores —
silver, copper and tin — could be mined with little effort.

The young man who fled from the 300-year-old Potala
palace as Chinese People's Liberation Army units entered
Lhasa on October 25, 1951, is the incarnation of a god-
king to the three million people estimated to live in Tibet.
To them, the Dalai Lama is a symbol of all the virtues. Where
a Christian talks of The Saviour, they speak of the Dalai
Lama. They believe in Reincarnation and Retribution. When
the body dies, the spirit escapes by one of nine holes; this
spirit goes through many earthly forms before it attains what
we would call salvation. We speak of God the Trinity, but
they say: "God the Buddha, god the whole canon of Buddhist
scripture and god the whole body of the Buddhist priesthood."

It descends to the level of mystical mumbo-jumbo for the
peasants perhaps. I often watched the long-haired hillmen,
daggers in their sashes and legs bound with Anglo-Saxon
strips of cloth, shambling round the great lama temples on the
Tibet border. *"Om Mani Padme Hum,"* they murmured, "Jewel
in Heart of Lotus," as they spun the copper prayer wheels set in
the circular walls.

The foreigner may sneer and call it idle superstition. Many
bloody fights were waged by Tibetans before Buddhism turned
them into recluses. As a great military power in Asia, they
overran West China in the eighth century and forced the
Chinese to accept Lake Koko Nor as their northeast boundary.
Later their influence became religious. They converted Mongolia and it was the great Altan Khan who invented the title of
Dalai Lama Vajradhara, All-embracing Holder of the Thunderbolt, for a Tibetan god-king.

Modern China's anxiety to control the fountainhead of
Lamaism is understandable. Ties were strengthened between
Tibet and Mongolia (a traditional enemy of Peking) when a
Dalai died in a Mongol city and was reincarnated there. Twice,
Tibet's spiritual rulers forced emperors of China to recognize
their independence. They were known as The Great Fifth and

The Great Thirteenth. The fifth Dalai Lama, as leader of the Yellow Hat sect, subdued the decadent Red Hats and traveled to Peking where the emperor stepped down from the Dragon Throne to greet him. It was a rare gesture, an admission that this man ruled an independent state.

But later emperors maneuvered Tibet into the position of a vassal. They worked through Chinese Resident Agents stationed in Lhasa. Tibetan monks who thought themselves the spiritual teachers of China were often unaware of the subservient status imposed upon them. Even as recently as 1945, Tibetans paid little attention to Generalissimo Chiang Kai-shek's insistence that their country was an outer province. Thus, unworldly to the last, they provided by their negligence an opportunity for Mao Tse-tung to embrace them in a comradely but crushing hug.

Mao could remember how, allied by their common faith, the Mongols and Tibetans once worked together to overthrow Chinese rule in 1910. Their strange supporters were the Russians who sent a Siberian lama from the shores of Lake Baikal (to which the Tibetan religion had spread) to Lhasa. This romantic figure, Dordjieff, interested Tibet in an alliance with Russia. It was a time of great jealousy between the Lion and the Bear over who should predominate in the Himalayan regions. Dordjieff took The Great Thirteenth to Urga, capital of Outer Mongolia.

From there the Dalai went to Peking where his pride was badly bruised. He was obliged to kotow before the Empress Tz'u Hsi and her son the Emperor Kuang Hsu.

Chinese troops stormed into Lhasa two years later and The Great Thirteenth fled to India. His Mongolian colleague, Hutukhtu, thereupon attacked and vanquished the Chinese in Outer Mongolia and made himself the local emperor. With pressure off Tibet, the Dalai Lama returned and through the Russian Dordjieff, negotiated a treaty of friendship and defensive alliance with the Mongolian.

Three years after the death of the thirteenth Dalai Lama in 1933, Chinese troops were back in Tibet. This time, however, they were Communists who, in retreat and savage with what

seemed impending defeat, sacked the lamaseries and so realized
the dead man's prophecy contained in the famous Last Testa-
ment:

> Land and properties of the monasteries and priesthood will
> be destroyed . . . Officers of State, ecclesiastical and secular, will
> find lands seized, property confiscated, and they themselves made
> to serve their enemies or wander about the country as beggars do.

All Tibet was in ferment in 1936 because the Dalai Lama's
reincarnation had not yet been found. The State Oracle was
consulted. The embalmed body of The Great Thirteenth was
examined. The face was mysteriously turned to the northeast.
In this direction went the searchers. In a province annexed by
the Chinese, they found a small boy with certain physical
marks — two pieces of knotted flesh on the shoulder blades and
a shell-like imprint in the palm of one hand. The boy with-
stood all the mystical tests, including the selection from a pile
of objects of The Great Thirteenth's personal possessions.

This boy, the True Incarnation, is the present fourteenth
Dalai Lama. He was then two years old, but a Chinese governor of the region demanded a heavy ransom. It was paid in
1939 and the boy was borne away for the arduous training
that would keep him remote from his family, celibate and
holy.

On that day when I listened to his halting English, flanked
by Chou En-lai and Nehru, I wondered if the redoubtable
spirit of The Great Thirteenth stirred behind those smoldering and presumably reincarnated eyes. For our meeting took
place in the Pavilion of Purple Light where, forty-six years
earlier, that other Dalai Lama endured two banquets given on
the eve of her death by the Empress Dowager, Old Buddha,
but which she refused herself to attend.

After this encounter, I contrived another trip to the southwest and made enquiries about the Chinese governor who
blackmailed the Tibetans before giving up the young lama.
His story illuminates some of the mystery of the border regions
between Tibet and China, and tells something of the Chinese
there up to 1949, when the last recorded Western travelers

passed through the region. It gives us some idea of the problems faced by any moralizing regime that followed.

The culprit in the blackmail case seems to have been a major warlord, General Liu Wen-hui. His rule extended out from the Szechuan capital of Chengtu to the edge of the Tibetan plateau, into a romantic frontier-land where opium was common currency, at least until the Communists arrived and possibly after. It was a wild country of outlaws, bandits, gun runners and fierce tribes. There are records of at least five hundred major battles being fought there in a period of twenty-four years.

General Liu had a force of ten thousand men, the 24th Division. They were known as the Szechuan-Sikang Frontier Defense Force, armed with fourteen bolt-action rifles to every sixteen men and two mortars to each company. His brigades had artillery of a sort and the unit commanders were either relatives or close friends of Liu. His own title was Pacification Commander and he reigned over what was known as Sikang province for five years after Communist occupation.

His troops' predations reached as far as the *kuan wai*, literally "beyond the customs barrier." From there onward stretched the Tibetan plateau of rounded hills rising to fifteen thousand feet from pastoral, alpine valleys. This was the land of the "Gold Sand River" which we know better as the Yangtse, and west of it were the Tibetan lamaseries with their interlocked princedoms.

The Chinese of those pre-Communist days held the official posts, professed contempt for the "natives" but nevertheless kept to the well-marked roads or remained within the packed-mud walls of towns, while using such derogatory terms for Tibetans and other tribesmen as "tottering" and "weak-minded."

Their sense of superiority is reflected in the boasts of General Liu's assistant, *before* Communist chieftains took over. In 1948 he was still telling visitors: "We shall have educated these natives so that within twenty years they will have forgotten even their own names."

Marx seemed less effective than the mandarin mind of the Chinese in inspiring these confident promises to convert their neighbors. General Liu himself held a conference which sounds surprisingly like those I heard in 1956 in nearby Yunnan. He met tribesmen who were inclined to be rebellious and promised them: "All disputes will be solved by peaceful means and not by resort to arms. We, the Hans, the Chinese who are your close relatives, assure you that every tribe shall be equal, that slavery shall be abolished." Observers at this meeting noted Chinese certainty that rebellious or independently minded tribes would only have to be exposed to superior Chinese methods to see at once the advantage of voluntarily becoming members of the Chinese nation.

This attitude is reflected now in the official pronouncements of Peking's envoys today in Lhasa. "Social reform in Tibet," said the Peking journal, *New China,* in 1957, "must not be implemented before, and can be only carried out after, conducting serious and repeated consultations with upper-strata Tibetans . . ." But there is never any doubt expressed that the consultations will eventually lead to conversion.

Whether you call it Communism or Chinese nationalism, however, the fact is that this invasion of Tibet's privacy was rebuffed. After examining Chinese techniques among other national minorities (for of course Tibetans are now such a minority, with their own ludicrously large *autonomous region* extending for 1240 miles eastward along the Himalayas and 740 miles across, from north to south) it seems plain enough that China will conquer by cleverness if not by force.

Her first attempt at occupation was a masterpiece of timing. The only rival interest was that of India. The former Indian ambassador to Peking, a geopolitician named K. M. Panikkar, wrote in 1955:

> The fact that the Chinese were unable in the past to organize a strong military area in Tibet should not blind us to such possibilities in the future. It may not be a danger in the immediate future but there is no doubt that an organized state in Tibet will alter the character of the Himalayan problem. True, neither the Himalayan passes nor the climate and resources of the country would enable Tibet to threaten seriously the security of its neighbors. No major danger to Indian defenses can develop from a

country which is so sparsely populated and whose resources are
so meager . . .

But the Chinese are already eliminating the factors from
which Mr. Panikkar drew some comfort: colonization has
started to fill up the empty areas; road builders, technicians,
farmer-soldiers have made a start in improving her resources.
A big colonization plan is underway. Just how big, it is
hard to estimate, but I have seen truckloads of cadres taken
to the edge of the Tibetan plateau. There were perhaps five
hundred to a convoy. They were not settlers: they were the
youngsters who would whip up "high tides of enthusiasm"
among several thousand colonizers.

Indian leaders never had illusions about Chinese occupation
of Tibet, perhaps, but just after the outbreak of the Korean
War there were many advisers around Nehru who advocated
treating the new Peking regime with gentle care. Sir Sarvapelli
Radhakrishnan, the Indian Vice-President, held the view that
Communism might one day become more flexible than Western
policy makers could foresee. The great Indian philosopher
told me one day, sitting on the lawn behind his Delhi home:
"In China the main problems are poverty, starvation and
natural calamities. If the Communist regime can solve these,
we may expect many changes and modifications."

This sentiment led India to advocate Communist China's
entry into the United Nations. But several things happened
at this time: October 1950. In Korea, troops of the United
Nations "police force" drove north of the 38th Parallel and
Indian diplomats immediately warned the West that this might
provoke Chinese intervention.

In Tibet, the first Chinese troops advanced towards Lhasa.

In the Himalayan kingdom of Nepal, closely linked with
Tibet through religion and trade, an internal feud laid open
India's northern frontiers to the new danger.

And in Delhi, Nehru told Parliament of his "surprise and
shock" at the news of Tibet's invasion.

But when Nehru was asked by Tibetan leaders to sponsor
their case before the United Nations, he refused. The Tibetan

complaint was cabled to the U.N. Secretary-General, Trygve
Lie. No sponsor could be found until El Salvador got the
item included on the General Assembly's agenda. A tiny Latin-
American republic thus came to the rescue of the lamas living
on the "Roof of the World." It was a curious alliance and
one which cannot have eased the Indian conscience. But
Nehru had at least affirmed Indian support of the Tibetan
complaint. When the General Assembly's steering committee
took it up, however, India reversed her stand.

Why? The most charitable explanation is that Nehru feared
the outbreak of a general war.

Once again, it seemed that Mao Tse-tung's shock tactics were
working. Communist Chinese troops were just beginning to
push down the Korean peninsula. It was a demonstration of
Peking's military strength: a frightening display of warlike
skill which left a permanent impression on the pacific government of India. Nehru, knowing he could do nothing to stop
Tibet's invasion, felt that he should pursue much more crucial
talks about Korea. One is forced to admire the broad vision
of China's new leaders: they were fighting a tough and modern
war only a year or so after their own guerrilla war had ended,
but they already saw that by exploiting India's goodwill they
might achieve greater victories in the field of international
politics. While they employed brute force in Korea, they applied brute reason to India.

Their skill was demonstrated within a few weeks when, in
January 1951, they warned India to prevent the passage in the
U.N. of an American resolution branding China as an aggres-
sor. If the resolution passed the General Assembly, Premier
Chou En-lai informed the Indian ambassador to Peking, there
would be no further hope of negotiations to end the Korean
War. Alarmed at the prospect of the war spreading, India tried
to stop the passage of the resolution and altogether dropped
the Tibetan question.

Yet the resolution did go through, China was branded, and
still her Communist leaders entered into negotiations with the
U.N. in Korea.

During this critical period of alarms and excursions in the

corridors of the U.N., a curious and ominous event took place in Tibet and Northern India. It was the Tibetan Year of the Earth Female Tiger.

The skies over Tibet turned scarlet. The headwaters of Asia's great rivers, which take their rise in Tibet, turned a sulphurous green. Great Himalayan peaks shuddered. A dramatic account is given by a young British missionary, Geoffrey T. Bull, in the remarkable story of his imprisonment by Communist troops in Tibet, *When Iron Gates Yield:* *

> Suddenly there was a tremor . . . Wooden pillars began to crack apart . . . The reeling of the earth went on, it seemed an eternity . . . Then came a new terror. Out of the cloudless star-filled sky came the most uncanny noises. Not thunder, not gunfire, but a new noise unlike any other. We all felt somewhat unnerved as the great cracklings reverberated through the heavens. I racked my brains for a scientific explanation but the Tibetans in great consternation exclaimed: "The gods are fighting! The gods are fighting!"

The whisper went round: "Such noises mean war with the Chinese."

Violent earthquakes threw one of the world's biggest rivers completely out of its course. The Brahmaputra, called Tsangpo in Tibet, was hurled into a river bed it had abandoned one thousand years ago, and floods took a great toll of life. On the wild borders of Tibet and Assam, the great river switched direction and the mighty waters cascaded down from a height of twelve thousand feet in a plunge that swept away villages all the way to the Bay of Bengal.

Six months later an astonishing agreement with Peking was said to have been signed by Tibetan leaders. They would "unite to drive out imperialist aggressive forces from Tibet so Tibetan people may return to the big family of the Motherland, the People's Republic of China."

This agreement permitted the "return" of the tenth Panchen Lama. He was a boy sponsored by the Chinese as a genuine

* London, 1955

reincarnation of the previous Panchen Lama who died in exile
in China in 1937. His education had been entirely in the
hands of Communists and he was installed as traditional ruler
of the Tashi Lumpo monastery at Shigatse, the second largest
Tibetan city. He was Peking's favorite; a sort of decoy elephant who would lead the wild herd safely into captivity.

The Chinese, of course, deplore any sinister interpretation
of this subversive activity. They display the same baffling self-
righteousness to be found among officials working with Yunnan's national minorities. In time, they say, the Tibetans will
be talked out of their backward, medieval superstitions. Nevertheless, Tibetan resistance has been much firmer than was
anticipated, particularly in regions traditionally ruled by the
Dalai Lama.

It became general knowledge in Peking early in 1956 that
military action was taking place in Tibet. I asked to go there.
As usual, instead of giving a direct refusal the Chinese simply
did not reply. Reports came from many quarters of fierce fighting between Communist troops and soldier-lamas. The Abbot
of Gyangtse, a provincial administrator under the Communists,
said 200,000 square miles were in the hands of rebels. He implied that Chinese officials were safe only on their new highways and in the garrisoned towns and lamaseries. Tibetans
had turned the tables by resorting to guerrilla war against their
oppressors, who themselves had used it recently with astonishing success.

Mao displayed his usual skill, ordered a full enquiry into the
behavior of his own officials and (according to Peking sources)
advised certain deputies: "We must proceed slowly and patiently, educating first and then slowly working up to a high
tide of enthusiasm. Then act!"

Vice-Premier Chen Yi led a Peking delegation to the Tibetan capital. A Preparatory Committee for the Tibet Autonomous Region was established. It was decided not to pursue
land reform. Religious worship was encouraged and work
started on the repair and extension of the chief lamaseries. A
Tibetan leader was quoted by Peking Radio as saying: "Worries and doubts about social reforms among Tibetans have been

removed by Chairman Mao who said they would not be carried out *in the second Five-Year Plan period.*"

Meanwhile, eyewitness reports were being brought out from the rebel areas by Tibetan and Nepalese traders who claimed that at one stage in hostilities a new Chinese motor road to Lhasa had been cut.

Word came that the Dalai Lama's court merchant was on his way to Nepal. Since I could not get into Tibet, nor talk freely with dignitaries like the Dalai Lama, I decided to meet this Lhasa official on the caravan trail that winds out of Tibet, passes under the shadow of Mount Everest and meanders into the Nepalese capital of Katmandu.

To whet the appetite for news, there were circumstantial reports of bombing raids by piston-engine aircraft of the Chinese Red Air Force against the chief rebel monastery of Litang. From Lhasa came an official Chinese news agency account of a curious conversation between the Dalai Lama and Peking's emissary, Chen Yi. The Dalai Lama, by then twenty-one, had ended a speech with the words: "We appreciate from the bottom of our hearts the meticulous solicitude and care shown by the Central People's Government and Chairman Mao for Tibetan people."

Then, turning to Chen Yi, the god-king added: "Tibet used to produce good serge. But our industry seems not to be making any headway."

Chen Yi: "Do not worry, Excellency, soon we shall be starting our own textile mills in Tibet."

They talked about the new Tsinghai-Tibet highway.

Dalai Lama: "I do hope some day there will be a railway to Lhasa."

Chen Yi: "Yes, yes, Excellency, the Tsinghai-Tibet highway will be surely converted into a railway. We shall do it."

It seemed the Chinese might have met a match for their indoctrination tactics in the Dalai Lama. During the ten-year regency before he assumed full power in 1950, the Dalai led a secluded life, but there were limited Western contacts who reported his keen interest in technical matters. These foreigners emphasized that his control extended over that part of East

Tibet known as Kham, with its center at Chamdo. This was territory shown on Chinese maps as part of their own Sikang province. When the Communists took control, they set up the *Mimang Tsoka,* or People's Assemblies, throughout the Kham region. But their Tibetan audiences used passive resistance. They sat through the long indoctrination lectures, telling their beads and murmuring like bees in a hive: *"Om Mani Padme Hum . . ."*

Angry and frustrated, but under strict orders from Mao not to provoke the lamas into armed rebellion, the Chinese abandoned the *Mimang Tsoka.* Soon the word *Mimang* became a symbol of defiance, a rallying cry for what the Tibetans called "peaceful obstruction" in a neat reversal of tables against Peking's "peaceful liberation" tactics. But to punctuate their resistance, the warrior lamas challenged Red Army troops to open guerrilla warfare.

The *Mimang,* the rebellious monasteries and the Khamba warrior lamas were all native to the Dalai Lama's home ground.

Fortified with this knowledge, I took off for Katmandu.

CHAPTER EIGHTEEN

Skirmish in the Land of Everest

◉ ◉

THE MAN you should see is the Robin Hood of Nepal," said my friend from World War II days. "His name is Singh — Doctor K. I. Singh. Used to be a wandering herbalist, then turned into a flaming revolutionary."

We were talking on the outskirts of New Delhi. My friend, a senior Indian Air Force officer, had unrolled a map. It showed India's northern frontier anchored at the eastern end by the kingdom of Nepal.

"The Chinese have infiltrated right through here," said my friend. He jabbed at areas of Northern Burma, the adjoining Assam frontier and some of the more remote, mountain-locked valleys of Nepal. "And," he added, "they've swept Tibet out of our influence entirely.

"Now they've sent K. I. Singh back from Peking after he went into exile under the protective wing of Premier Chou En-lai. He's back in Nepal calling himself 'The Liberator' — or rather, that's what many Nepalese now call *him*. Far as I'm concerned, he's a fully fledged political agent from the Chinese Communist politburo. If he can capture Nepal by peaceful political methods, Red China will control the Himalayan crest that was supposed to be our impregnable barrier against invasion.*

* Dr. K. I. Singh briefly became Premier of Nepal in July 1957, having been called upon to form a government by the same king who once placed a

But my purpose in visiting Nepal was not to hunt for Chinese agents. I wanted to see for myself what the new Chinese regime was doing in Tibet and one way of getting there was through the adjoining territory.

There were two routes into Nepal. You walked or flew. I tried walking once, and was glad of the excuse to fly. It was important to intercept the Dalai Lama's court merchant on the road from Tibet if I was to get a visa to Lhasa. Later he would be joined by a former Red Army general, the Chinese ambassador in New Delhi, and my chances of extracting even a verbal promise of a Tibetan trip would be poor indeed.

I flew up in an Indian Airline's Dakota with their senior pilot on the hazardous Nepal network, Bob Chater. Some of his fliers were making an aerial survey of the Himalayan kingdom, a tremendous task. Before World War II, Nepal was more of a forbidden country than Tibet, and five thousand square miles of the world's steepest country was not easily explored, even by air.

It lies like a spiked steel doormat at the back entry to Tibet. Twenty-two of the spikes are more than 25,000 feet high with Everest as greatest of them all. The legend of the Abominable Snowman was bound to grow in such a land where naturalists have long supposed there must be unusual forms of wild life. I knew already about some. There was the dzoz whose milk when fermented, produced some heavy hangovers. Close chum of the dzoz was the dzum, both hybrids of the mountain yak. They produced between them just about all a man could need for survival: milk, meat, cheese, beer, dried dung for fuel, hides for clothing and shelter. And their tails, of course, were highly prized as whiskers for our department-store Santa Clauses.

There were biological wonders like the mouse hare (a sort of fat guinea pig disguised in rabbit skin) and the snow leopard which prowled at the impossible altitude of twenty thousand feet. In some hidden valleys were primitive tribes like the Kushundas who wear animal skins, live in caves and refuse to

price on his head. Singh's progress from exile in Red China to the premiership was accomplished in the record time of two years.

have anything to do with cows. Hiding in lowland forests were the Hanhankri tribesmen whose hair grew so long that they resembled walking sheepskins.

But it was the people of the valleys who were most extraordinary and lovable of all: the Sherpa, the Nepalese peasants, the Gurkha, of whom a British professor once wrote: "[In battle] you endured hunger and thirst and wounds; and at the last, your unwavering lines disappear into the smoke and wrath of battle. Bravest of the brave, most generous of the generous."

As Chater flew steeply up the vivid green undulations of the Terai, a strip of jungle which hugs the Himalayan foothills, I checked the notes made in Delhi on the tug-of-war beginning between India and China.

There were eight million people here under Buddhist or Hindu influence. Indians had just decided to recognize that the thirty-six-year-old King Mahendra was a reincarnation of the Hindu god, Lord Vishnu.

The Chinese had made the equally fortunate discovery that in acquiring the Dalai Lama, they gained control over Nepal's only traditional system of education: the network of lamaseries of which the biggest was in the Katmandu valley at Bodhnath. In charge of the Bodhnath temple was the Dalai's representative in Nepal, the Chini Lama.

There were rumors of offers to Nepal of Chinese aid amounting to nearly fourteen million dollars (later confirmed) and a new Chinese highway built by Red Army labor gangs from the Tibetan capital to the Indian border. This road did, in fact, exist and reduced travel time between Lhasa and Calcutta from four months to two weeks.

The Indians gave scholarships, welfare schemes and seventeen million dollars' worth of technical aid. *Their* army was building a road from the Nepalese capital of Katmandu to India which would make it possible in time to drive all the way to the southernmost province of Kerala (which unfortunately acquired a Communist government the following year).

For years, Nepal's link with the outside world had been a donkey trail and an ancient ropeway. I remembered only too clearly that path, climbing over two 7000-foot passes and plunging for fifteen miles through dense jungle. It was reached after crossing the Ganges at Patna and journeying to Raxaul. From there the only railroad in Nepal, all of twenty-eight miles long, deposited you at Amlekhganje, after which you walked.

My porter on that trip was paid the equivalent of one shilling daily from which he provided his own food. A good boy could carry fifty pounds on a ten-mile climb up mountain trails each day. Mine did slightly better. He was hired from a coolie contractor whose written guarantee promised, "If a coolie leave before end journey, fee will be refunded." There was no mention of compensation should the baggage leave with the coolie. But in those days, there was no need. Doubled up under their heavy burdens, hollow-chested and old at the age of twenty, the porters of Nepal still hung on to their one possession: pride. No self-respecting porter would steal. However, we have an unhappy knack of tarnishing that which is splendid in Asia. Nepalese politicians have since complained that foreign aid has altered the scale of values because half of it is spent on salaries and raises local prices. Money, they say, has become more important than pride.

Across the Great Valley between Bimphedi and Katmandu is the ropeway on which has been slung during the past thirty years a flood of supplies from brass cannon to steam rollers and a Rolls-Royce. Sixty tons of goods flow into Nepal each day, as much as fifteen hundred coolies would carry in two days. The alternative is to fly goods in from Calcutta. Either way, imports are costly and an old, prewar car still fetches up to five thousand dollars.

We flew above the ropeway and slipped down on to Gaucher airfield, a flat-topped hillock overlooking the temples and pagoda roofs that cram the Katmandu valley. From this angle, I could understand why this was called the Land of the Gods. There are 2733 temples in that one valley alone and their spires and golden tiles stretched endlessly.

I was whisked off to my own surprise to see the Prime Minister, who was then Acharya Tanka Prasad. The jeep hurtled down crazy back streets, between high red walls and around temples where Hindu and Buddhist gods borrowed each other's shapes in jolly confusion, finally depositing me at a vast and crumbling mansion in time for tea.

There were other evidences of an alien influence; retainers in jodhpurs, white nightcaps and bare feet; faded pictures of anonymous kings and queens hanging crookedly; and a gloomy reception hall full of stuffed animals. You could, if you were careless, catch your elbow on a rhinoceros horn, fall over a tiger's carcass, narrowly escape the yawning jaws of a crocodile and finish up staring at the point of a Gurkha soldier's kukri knife, while sawdust oozed gently out of the belly of a black bear.

I was marched without formality to a back bedroom where the Prime Minister sat in striped pajamas before a tarnished teaset. He was a small, pleasant man who enjoyed the full backing of the Indian Government: so much so that while we talked, a first secretary from the Indian Embassy joined us without explanation or apology and effectively limited the scope of conversation.

Neither the Prime Minister nor his Indian sponsors wanted to provoke the Chinese in Tibet. "We will take help from any country provided there are no strings," he said. "Our policy is independence for Nepal."

I moved into an inn kept by a Canadian, Mrs. Elizabeth Mendies, and her husband Tom. It must have been a strange transition for her, from the steel town of Hamilton, Ontario, to this wooden hostelry built around a packed earth courtyard where coolies often assembled at dawn. Her staff consisted of peons in wrap-over jerkins, crooked hats and lopsided grins. At night, when it became very cold, pot-bellied stoves blazed away in each small room and from the pitch-black night outside came the low murmur of many families at prayer. The prayers went on long into the night, rising and falling in a muffled chorus from inside the dark mud houses. It was a wonderfully soothing change from the banalities of radio.

Nobody seemed to know about the Dalai Lama's court merchant, but there were still many good stories to be written from Nepal and at night I dropped in to the Royal Hotel to pick up the gossip from Boris.

While my own quarters were the very epitome of respectability, the Russian's establishment was always a circus of strange and unlikely characters. His cook, Pietr, came from Latvia and produced dishes never invented in that cold Baltic clime. But Boris was the ringmaster, a confidant of the local princes, host to Everest climbers and eccentric artists, a boisterous *bon vivant* who had once been a ballet master in Leningrad.

At that time, Boris had an odd collection staying in his cavernous rooms. There were ten Argentinian climbers with no peaks to climb because the Peronist dictatorship had toppled and with it their orders to conquer a mountain in the name of Eva Perón. There was a Russian painter who claimed to be *walking* through Asia, and who carried a growing volume of water colors rolled up in cylinders and tied to his back under a flowing cashmere cloak. And very soon there arrived General Yuan Chung-hsien, former Chinese Red Army guerrilla chief, now ambassador to India and Nepal, with his smiling entourage. Among them was his Oxford-trained first secretary, a plump and complacent young man whose popularity among Indians was soon apparent.

Boris treated them to a lavish, seven-course dinner on the night of their arrival. But he served it himself, wearing a turtle-neck pullover and stained corduroy pants. It was his very personal way of expressing his feelings.

The bumptious young Chinese diplomat got into conversation with me. We discussed the mystery of the Abominable Snowman.

"Ah yes," he said. "There are many strange things in the world today. For instance, Flying Saucers . . . aren't they really unmanned American high-altitude balloons photographing our territory?"

"How do they recover their balloons and the exposed film?" I countered.

He shrugged. "There are ways," he said darkly. (I thought

of the industrial magnate whose engineers protested that his design for a water-driven automobile was impossible: "Look, I get the ideas . . . your job is to make them work.")

I switched topics. "How do I get a visa to Tibet?"

He smiled. "If you are Nepalese, you don't even need an identity card."

"But I'm not Nepalese."

"Then I suggest you write to Peking through some approved Friendship Society, like the Sino-British Friendship Society — just to prove good faith."

He returned to his boxes which had just arrived in the doorway of the smoke-filled dining room. The boxes contained works on Hindu art, printed in Peking; lavishly illustrated volumes on Asian religions, also printed in Peking; and a pile of magazines containing an article on the physical improvements brought to Tibet by the Chinese.

"About one thousand pounds overweight, that little lot," said the Indian Airlines pilot who brought this cargo in. "Reckon the Chinese'll be wasting the same amounts of money on propaganda as the Americans at this rate."

He looked thoughtfully at Boris. "'Course, if I was a Russian — I mean a Commie Russkie — I'd want to know who was really paying for all this. After all, there's nothing about Russia in all this bumph, is there? I mean, China's a poor country, isn't it?" And he walked off whistling.

Later Boris and I stood under the red umbrella of the monkey-god Hanuman in the city square, keeping a sharp lookout for the police in their jodhpurs and hobnailed boots. "Come," said Boris. "Nobody will make arrest."

It was curfew time in Katmandu, one of the few survivals of a recent era when feudal laws kept the people in a medieval state of fear. Boris seemed pretty sure of himself so we left the umbrella's protective shadow and chanced a night in jail.

"Yes," growled Boris, pursuing our interrupted conversation, "jail here is very boring." Then he told me why.

Some while back, the Russian had gone into the brewery trade. There is a good deal of heavy drinking in Nepal and Boris saw a big market for his own brand of animal spirits.

He invented four brews: Monkey, Elephant, Tiger and Yak Beers. A license was issued which gave Boris a monopoly in the valley. He began on a generous scale and was soon brewing 2500 gallons monthly for a thirsty population of less than 40,000 male adults.

Then the bootleggers and moonshiners ganged up. They found police allies. Boris set up his own organization of agents. There were some brisk battles. His trucks were overturned. Their stills were smashed. Finally the inland-revenue office slapped a tax on him so enormous that he could not possibly pay it.

"I got to tax office," said Boris, "and I tell them I will not leave their premises until they cancel that tax. They refuse. So I stay."

He remained ten days there, in one of Katmandu's fifty converted palaces. At night he slept in the tax director's office. By day he stood as immovable as any statue in the public hall. Morning and afternoon, peons from his hotel brought buckets of hot water which they poured into a tin bath. In full public view, Boris stripped and bathed, singing lustily.

After ten days there was nothing else to do but either revoke the tax or jail Boris. He was jailed. Peons brought him sumptuous meals cooked by Pietr. He brightened the evening hours with a homemade catapult, firing mud balls at the guards. Finally the authorities sent him to the hospital.

Came his birthday and Boris threw a party. Among his guests were some members of the royal family, Indian dignitaries and their Nepalese friends whom Boris suspected of having engineered the tax.

The party lasted until the early morning hours, with Boris conducting ceremonies from his sickbed. Just as the chief guests prepared to leave, he held up a hairy arm for silence. "I am," he announced, "going on a hunger strike."

Boris was out within twenty-four hours, the tax suspended. Some say the threat of a hunger strike was too much for his enemies who had reason to know what an effective weapon it proved in India during the days of the British raj.

There were other genial characters around. None of them seemed to have seen the court merchant but all were rewarding in other ways. My favorite was Raj Bhandary, the only banker in Katmandu. He was a passionate collector of oddities, perhaps because he had lived forty-eight years in the most difficult place in the world for such a hobby. His office was reached through crooked lanes. There was a shrine at the end of the street with a brass-studded door, bright paintwork and a great god bristling with arms. Two dragons supported a mighty brass bell. Stone animals littered the squares overhung with balconies that displayed ornate carvings. Wherever you looked there were devils and deities and on the cobbles squatted stone elephants, winged horses and rhinos.

In the middle of this museum sat Mr. Bhandary, amassing fountain pens. His other collections were of secondary importance; they were, indeed, often for the purpose of obtaining yet more fountain pens. He kept thick Tibetan bank notes folded like concertinas under the mountain of ledgers on his desk. Behind the safe were wonderful treasures: rare maps, yak tails, prayer wheels, wooden gods and, in a prosaic cardboard box, glistening pieces of Nepalese gold. His reputation as a man who could produce almost anything had traveled far and wide. Everest expeditions relied a good deal upon his ingenuity. One expedition of British climbers needed some $2800 in small coins urgently to pay the Sherpa porters. A runner came back from their distant base with the request. It was the local day of rest, a Friday, and the bank was closed. The expedition's local man stressed the urgency of the matter. But even the bank's vaults seemed empty. Banker Bhandary promised nothing but next morning there was a pile of money bags, each holding one hundred coins, ready to be borne up to the camp by coolies. Without time to count the silver, the climbers' agent dispatched coolies and cash. Not a coin was missing when they arrived.

An atmosphere of intrigue was inevitable in a buffer state like this one. Sinister and unexplained figures floated around. The Newars, a powerful clan that controlled the Katmandu valley, gave the Communist Party its biggest support and their spies watched the Indians with undisguised suspicion. The Indians, ignoring charges that Nepal was their satellite, kept a sharp eye on American-aid officials. Everyone watched the climbing expeditions since a party of Welshmen had got themselves jailed by Chinese troops after they wandered into Tibet.

"Our biggest worry is the Abominable Snowman. Everest comes next," a Nepalese official confided to me. "Both give foreigners an excuse to spy on Tibet. We don't want to provoke the Chinese but we don't want to stop the expeditions. With Everest — well, it's been climbed and anyway it's there in one spot and immovable.

"But the Snowman. We get applications from all over the world now to chase *him*. We can't refuse them all. There's a Texan oilman wants to hunt with a helicopter. I'm petrified that he'll get on the trail of a Snowman and chase him right into a Red Army camp."

More real than the Snowman, though almost as elusive, was Dr. K. I. Singh. He was the only leading politician who, until then, had still not made the Nepalese premiership.

Singh was chased into the Red Chinese camp by Indian troops who helped the revolt in 1950 which ended the despotic rule of the Rana family. King Mahendra like his forebears for a hundred and fifty years had been a virtual prisoner of the Ranas and at the time of the rebellion took refuge in the Indian Embassy. When peace was restored, Dr. Singh continued to defy authority and seized Katmandu Radio. For a while the air waves were blue with Singh's angry denunciations. Then he was routed and escaped across the frozen Himalayas into China. For a time in Peking he enjoyed enormous success. A "liberation army" was created on paper and placed at his disposal. He broadcast demands for the overthrow of the reactionary regime in Katmandu.

Then the beautiful friendship seemed to sour. Dr. Singh claims he went on hunger strike to force the Chinese to let him return home. He arrived back in Nepal to become leader of the United Democratic Party, and loudly protested his intense love for India.

I was looking for Dr. Singh and keeping a sharp lookout for travelers from Tibet when Narendra Saksena brought me news of the Dalai Lama's party.

Saks was an Indian newspaperman who seemed able to wander into the King's palace, or some humble mud-brick cottage and get an equal welcome. His sensitive antennae probed tirelessly into every nook and cranny, bringing back news of Sherpa "Tiger" Tensing on the lower slopes of Everest, or of suspected murder in a climbing accident on some more remote peak. He knew the state of the palace plumbing (in fact, he warned there could be no Coronation that year unless the toilets were properly overhauled) and he knew very well how to organize an expedition. He knew, perhaps, a little too much about too many people, but nevertheless he enjoyed some astonishing confidences.

And so it was Saks who finally found Lord Ten Semba, court merchant to the fourteenth Dalai Lama, and his strangely colorful party.

Near the biggest Tibetan sanctuary of this Hindu kingdom I shared a dish of wild boar *shashlik* with the Red Chinese general and Ten Semba, while demons and water monsters beat gongs around our heads and blew thunder through immense silver trumpets.

We were assembled at Bodhnath, not many miles from Katmandu but a long way in time from the Hindu monarch who lived there. Two thousand years before, when savages roamed Europe, Emperor Asoka erected a Buddhist shrine. Now it was the spiritual home in Nepal of the Tibetan god-king. His faithful cardinal was the stout, gold-robed figure beside me, the Chini Lama. He was explaining to me why Tibetans stick out a pink tongue in greeting.

"A tear fell near this spot from the eye of a god," he said. "It turned into a beautiful girl. She stole flowers from Paradise and was punished by being born into a swineherd's home. But she became rich by selling geese and built a monument right here. An elephant was used to build the temple and when the girl died, she forgot to reward him. All her children were rewarded by being reborn in Tibet. The elephant was angry and turned himself into King Glan Darma, the enemy of Buddhism. He was killed more than one thousand years ago and when they examined King Glan's body, they found he had a black tongue. So now, to prove you mean no harm to a stranger, it is customary to show your tongue."

The Chini had just accepted 18,000 rupees drawn on the People's Bank of China from General Yuan Chung-hsien. He shook the ritual bell. The sun glanced off the tiny, embossed Buddhas on the golden miter he wore pushed slightly back from his broad and glistening forehead. The temple magician ran before him, waving fingers above his tall black hat covered in mystic signs. A boy ogre, tattooed in blue, shook the yak tails hanging from his wig as he crouched before the shrines with their guttering candles of clarified butter. Conch shells blew their shrill notes through the three thousand worlds of Buddhism. Drummers beat a thunderous roll with human thighbones used to ward off evil spirits. The noise was terrifying.

The golden spire of the temple towered above the surrounding lodgings for pilgrims. It rose in thirteen stages to the sky, each step another paradise through which the liberated spirit must ascend. Its tip was buried in the royal parasol of gold from which fluttered hundreds of ragged prayer flags of white and blue, saffron and red, descending to earth. Below the spire was the white hemisphere streaked with yellow, called by Tibetans a *chorten,* and over its rim peered two hypnotic great eyes. Between the eyes was the Chinese symbol of power — an emphatic question mark that told of mighty rains and a bolt of thunder. In a great circle around this vast tumulus ran a wall of prayer wheels.

Beyond the wall was a concourse of poor wretches such as I had never seen before. There were hillmen with long matted hair and ugly goiters under their chins or swelling up between neck and shoulder. There were blind children turning sightless eyes to where the temple orchestra stood below the *chorten.* Women stood, arms dangling, mouths open, eyes almost hidden by the black hair that fell around their shoulders. Some sat on the hard earth, thrusting forward their swollen legs wrapped in strips of cloth.

Encircling all were the double-storied houses with tumbling, tiled roofs and parched timbers. Inside dark cells, craftsmen beat soft silver metals into religious objects.

Ten Semba, a tall figure in an ornate, conical hat, left the feasting to distribute the Dalai Lama's largesse. A turquoise pendant dangled from one ear and behind it the end of a red ribbon woven into his plaited hair. He almost stumbled over his ankle-length brown robes as the beggars began to crowd him. His son, a child lama called Champa Jilla, leaned anxiously forward, his narrow eyes dancing with curiosity.

Beside me sat a pretty, gorgeously robed young woman. Surya Kumari was a daughter of the Chini Lama. "I've been invited to Peking," she said. "Daddy may come with me too."

A keen hockey player at her English boarding school in Darjeeling, she wanted to know more about this new China which offered to finance Buddhism in Nepal and already seemed to be approved by her Tibetan superiors and even the Dalai Lama himself. The fact that I had met the Dalai Lama made a deep impression. I was shown with pride the temple's golden book containing the graceful handwriting of the Dalai's mother, sent here earlier by the Chinese with an offering of 5000 rupees.

The Lhasa court merchant was dispensing walnuts, rice cakes and silver coins for the poor. He took good care, naturally enough, to emphasize from where it came. General Yuan was returning to Peking from his diplomatic post in Delhi and had brought with him more of the lavishly produced volumes of Hindu art reproductions printed on Communist Chinese presses. It was an interesting, two-pronged attack in the new battlefield of propaganda. From the Dalai Lama, under Chinese auspices: food for the poor. From the Chinese Foreign Office: food for the mind.

Pilgrims from the Tibetan borderlands were hobbling past to be touched on the head by the Chini Lama. Behind him rose the tumulus. Its square base represented the earth; the hemisphere was water; the flamelike spire was the symbol of fire; a crescent meant the sky's vault and a topmost circle with radiating snakes was ether. These are the five elements into which the body must resolve after death, say the lamas. It was a majestic thought, suited to the great mountains among which it grew and took root. But the Chinese, I knew, would not see grandeur in this perfect match between geographical sublimity and spiritual inspiration. There was a zealous look in their eyes as they regarded the squalid temple grounds and the surrounding poverty.

There may have been a gleam of triumph too. For scrawled in Gorkhali on many walls were the words: *Chinese are our blood brothers.*

I visited Ten Semba, the court merchant, after he reached Katmandu. His two hundred porters brought nine tons of Tibetan salt and some $11,000 in loose coins scattered among five trunks bound in yak hide. With him was a Tibetan provincial governor, Dela Chitung, a strapping soldier-lama who told me his appointment followed five years' "education" in Peking. That is, he was one of many Tibetan officials indoctrinated before the Chinese entered Tibet. Among Ten Semba's entourage were twelve servants, three small boys and a tiny, lank-haired "lion-dog" called Bhato.

They occupied stables in a temple courtyard and Ten Semba sat on the edge of his hard, wooden bed in their communal room, swinging his legs and beaming from ear to ear. They were on a shopping tour, he explained, mainly to buy two years' supply of Nepalese rice for the Dalai Lama, who regarded it as a delicacy, but also to pick up a few trinkets for the Potala palace back in Lhasa. To illustrate his words, a giant valet, dressed like an Elizabethan potboy in jackboots and yellow jerkin, poured the day's purchases on the stone floor. They included several pots of Yardley's foundation cream, a tin of toffee, a framed *Esquire* painting of a long-limbed blonde wearing black net stockings but little else, and a heap of pink plastic combs.

Sitting with his back against the bare wall, Governor Dela was telling his 108 Buddhist prayer beads. Beside him were silver filigree'd trays. These were portable "temples" for use on the road and stuck inside were photographs of the deities.

We talked about Tibet under Chinese rule. They seemed most impressed by the fact that the Dalai Lama had a telephone and eleven cars.

"There has been no land reform in Tibet," said Ten Semba. "I myself am a landowner with wide interests." He pulled his hands out of his long sleeves and rubbed an eye with the multicolored ring on his thumb. "It clears the sight," he explained. "The magnetism draws out dust thrown in the eyes."

He saw that I was interested and opened a battered chest. It was a Tibetan medicine bag. Inside were black leather pouches. One held balls of fluff which, placed on rheumatic joints, carried away the pain on being blown off again. There was a pierced copper disk for headaches: the disk was applied wherever the pain hurt most, the hole was struck with a tiny hammer and the headache vanished.

Governor Dela drew his skirts tight and stood up. He pinched the ends of his down-curved mustache, took up an umbrella and kicked aside a wolf skin with his thick-soled, red kneeboots. Framed in the doorway, he suddenly demanded: "Why did you ask how much money we carried?"

I replied, through an interpreter, that it had seemed an obvious question. He beckoned me into an adjoining room. It was filled with trunks, yak hides and a monstrous prayer wheel. He opened a trunk and shook out some silver, passing me a few coins. Not to be outdone, Ten Semba called for a bowl of yak curd which he pressed upon me. Monks were bustling around the golden griffins of the temple as I sipped from the bowl, and these two racy characters nodded and smiled to each other and at me.

The court merchant then explained that he had not brought the customary tribute from the Dalai Lama to the King of Nepal. This had amounted to 10,000 rupees annually since Nepalese troops defeated a Tibetan army almost a century earlier.

The last tribute was paid when Ten Semba made his previous trek, three years earlier. When the king asked Lhasa for an explanation of the abrupt end to these payments, he was referred to the People's Democratic Republic of China. There the matter rested, although at least one Nepalese rajah was said to be collecting tribute still from tribes on the Tibetan side of the border.

I took Champa Jilla, the boy lama, on sightseeing tours. He expected to go soon to Peking to "complete the educational process." Well, I thought, it wouldn't hurt to lay up some treasure in heaven. So we bounced around the countryside in my jeep, escorted by a strapping Tibetan who spoke better English than he admitted.

We approached one of the sacred cities as it came to life. Women bathed under the wooden dragons spouting water in memory of rich benefactors. Children cradled stones wrapped in rags, pretending these were dolls. Among the temples and towers came the tapping of the metal-smith's hammer and the wheeze of his goat-skin bellows.

A hidden radio shattered my impression of a fairy-tale town. "This is Radio Ceylon," it whistled and shrieked. "We now bring you Temple Time . . ."

Temple Time in Bhatgeon seemed liable to come at any hour. There was an old man drowsing under a banyan. He was the local magistrate. I asked if it might be possible to see the local and justly famous Lion Dance. He nodded eagerly and told me to wait.

So I waited, staring up into the mysterious depths of that giant banyan. The trees are fantastic, providing shelter for woodpeckers and squirrels, hairy-crested drongos, lizards, bees and delicate little sun birds. Some banyans become living temples and almost all are thickly encrusted in local legends. The shiny, tough leaves are said to bring bad luck, and from the branches were tied the heads of slaughtered enemies in times past. The banyan has always fascinated me, arousing childhood memories of mythology and textbooks studded with etchings of fiery bushes and trees festooned with the grinning heads of giants.

The magistrate returned and insisted that we go to his house. The bottom floor was a stable. We reached the living quarters by mounting a shaky ladder. Most of the upper floor was occupied by wooden chests secured by brass Tibetan locks. The keys were screwed into the locks, the notches being cut in a spiral. The women of this dark little household were making a thick gruel from maize flour, kidney beans and chopped potatoes.

By signs and snatches of English, sometimes speaking through Champa Jilla's guardian, the magistrate indicated that messengers were now out in the rice paddies to recruit the dancers. He opened up the chests and revealed monstrous wooden masks painted in grotesque colors. There were wigs and costumes, waistbands and silver ankle bells. He brought these out carefully and laid them on the sooty floor. What with the smoke swirling up through the wooden rafters from below, we seemed to be looking down on splendid dead giants.

The dance itself was a disappointment. It had hardly started when the police chief interrupted and asked for my authority. It had become necessary, he explained, to obtain special permission from Katmandu before holding the Lion Dance. We wrangled a while in his office next to a wayside inn. There were tubs of bitter beer outside and men sat in tiny balconies, looking much too big for their wooden dolls' houses. After we had tried the beer a little, I showed the police chief my passport with the signature in it of a Nepal Embassy official. He declared himself quite satisfied and the dance was allowed to proceed, accompanied by more beer.

We visited later one of those temples where statues of Lord Buddha and Lord Vishnu get so inextricably confused that they look alike. Champa Jilla was feeding the huge monkeys which haunt such places when one of them took a sizable bite out of his thumb. I had to return him to Lord Ten Semba that evening looking slightly the worse for wear.

This carelessness on my part did not help. When I finally asked for a permit into Tibet, the reply was oddly familiar: "If you were a Nepalese trader, you wouldn't even need a passport." However, I did wring out of the court merchant a reluctant invitation which I felt sure he would never honor.

By this time, information on the revolt in Tibet was beginning to flow in. A lot of it was suspect; and often the facts were wrong because the informant was a simple traveler with little knowledge of the geography beyond his own movements. But there were reliable witnesses too.

The picture built itself up, and doubtless there were vast omissions and some inaccuracies. But the reader will recognize a similar pattern of Chinese action in Tibet as was described in earlier chapters: undermine authority; bribe officials, convert others; take over religious activities in the guide of a benevolent interest; indoctrinate the young and above all things, proceed slowly, mixing leniency with harsh resolve.

The plight of the Dalai Lama was fairly clear. Each day he came under intensive attack by his Chinese advisers. This was a verbal assault and anyone who knows much about Communist indoctrination methods in Asia can imagine the nature of this ordeal. On the one hand, the Dalai Lama was said to be anxious to preserve at all costs the Tibetan religion. On the other hand, he was described as mentally sick of the endless arguments.

What he faced was the issue confronting all great religions, now that Communism is becoming increasingly influenced by its Oriental exponents. Should they compromise in the hope of salvaging something? Or should they resist at the cost of seemingly starting the bloodshed? The Dalai Lama, as leader of the easygoing and tolerant northern Buddhists, was unable to follow the example of Pope Pius XII, who could call on Roman Catholic bishops to remember the Polish saint who suffered torture and death rather than submit to the Cossacks.

Nor had the Dalai any means of knowing this same crisis which faced Catholics in East Europe. Twice he had turned to India for advice. Twice he was told to return to Lhasa. Now he was getting the full blast of a merciless campaign to win his friendship and support for Chinese policies. He was being moved out of the Potala, with increasing authority given to the Panchen Lama. The streets of the secular city which had known nothing noisier than a yak now reverberated to the roar of motorcycles driven by court officials in full regalia, with their robed retainers riding pillion. There were new Chinese highways, new Chinese postal stamps, a new Chinese newspaper and the People's Bank. Sometimes the Chinese went too far with all this (for instance, their original colonization program called for the settlement of Chinese peasants amounting to the same number as the total Tibetan population). Then a well-publicized retreat was made. After the Tibetans were hammered into an efficient army with its own political commissar and Chinese commander, the worried Indians were informed that Peking was withdrawing large bodies of troops. This news was greeted with acclaim by Indian newspapers and you wondered how far self-deception could take a nation: and how long it would be before Hindus were being drawn into making similar compromises.

I left Nepal amid rumors that the Dalai Lama might seek refuge there. Back in Peking when I saw him with Nehru, there had been a brief discussion with Mao Tse-tung. The Indian premier heard Mao promise that Tibet would be given an autonomy more distinct than anything granted to other Chinese provinces. On the strength of this, Nehru was unwilling to give sanctuary to runaway Tibetan dignitaries or undertake any other action which might provoke Mao and imperil the limited freedom which Tibet appeared to be offered. But when the young god-king saw that passive resistance could never succeed against Chinese arms, he fled to Assam and testified in mid-1959 to China's relentless conversion tactics.

However, when the Dalai Lama visited India at the end of 1956 it was a test of good faith. The Chinese knew they must let him visit the birthplace of Lord Buddha in what was a holy year, or stand accused in the eyes of millions of Buddhists as captors of the young god-king. But the Dalai trembled on the edge of a decision to remain and toward the end of his tour his Chinese escort became increasingly nervous. Finally they whisked him home after his Indian tour became so prolonged it provoked speculation. He had marveled at Indian industrial projects like the Bhakra–Nangal dam, the Chittaranjan locomotive factory and the Madras Integrated Steel Coachworks. He had shown a deep absorption in mechanical matters. His companion, the Panchen, talked only of world peace. Right at the end, the Panchen was allowed to fly into Nepal but the Dalai was sent directly home. Millions in the Katmandu valley then became convinced that their spiritual leader was in distress.

It was common knowledge that the Dalai was persuaded to go back by the Indian Government. Nehru's view seemed to be that by his mere existence in Lhasa the Dalai could stem the tide of Communist ideas.

While the unhappy youth in 1956 debated whether to return, I was back inside China in the Tibetan autonomous regions of the southwest. It seemed impossible to get into Tibet proper. Premier Chou En-lai had blustered to Western newsmen that he knew of "no law that prevents anyone from visiting Tibet." Nevertheless, the Chinese showed positive genius for discovering ways in which the journey would be impossible — at least until they were ready. The roads were blocked, or planes were delayed by bad weather, or there had been some other breakdown in communications. They kept an ace up their sleeve. Any traveler to Tibet, they announced, would have to pass a medical examination since the trip was a rough one at high altitude. There was little hope of passing for a traveler whose views were old, diseased and decrepit.

So, exasperated by these deceits, I gathered up all the notes of the previous year and cabled my story from inside China. And once again there was no reaction from the Chinese; no censorship; no delays. Just as they knew it would, this unexpected tolerance made me wonder for days if I had been a little too harsh in my judgments . . .

Tibetan rebels have forced Red China to change her timetable for making that Himalayan retreat an efficient Communist colony devoted to a new God of Production [I wrote]. I have just left Mekong River territory where hundreds of Tibetans are to be seen on guided tours with their Chinese commissars.

It is in the great canyon country of the Upper Mekong that Tibetans are apparently holding out five years after the Chinese entered Lhasa. The chief rebel monastery at Litang was bombed by Red Chinese aircraft earlier this year. Revolutionary leaders there are now said to be negotiating with Peking's emissaries who confess to errors of calculation.

Released from their Lhasa jail cells are Alo Chondze and other ranking Tibetans who resisted. The rebels remain in possession of heights in the Chamdo region, six days' truck travel east from Lhasa.

To lure them into a more co-operative state of mind, Peking has selected trained cat's-paws to conduct negotiations. These include Lama Tsurpu Kamapa who sold out last year by signing a treaty that formalizes Tibet's subjugation.

This reporter is the first Westerner to meet Tibetans from the troubled area with their jovial Chinese "hosts." The Tibetans are simple and honest men. They may find it difficult to match wits with their subtle neighbors.

What appears a victory for the rebels is in reality a demonstration of Communist technique for making a temporary retreat in the face of heavy opposition. The final objective is still to tame those who resist. But the weapons are now guile, bribery and indoctrination.

Chinese troops are being withdrawn but there is no letup in the settlement of Chinese colonizers in the sparsely populated northeast. Plans still call for colonization of parts of Tibet by some 3,000,000 Chinese peasants within ten years.

To reduce overt signs of Chinese occupation, thousands of Tibetan youngsters are being pushed through special courses in China. On the pretext of furthering their education and by the expenditure of large sums of money on the trappings of Lamaism, the Chinese hope to beguile them into a belief that Peking is the protector of their religious faith and the champion of their patriotic ambitions. In this way and with the same formula applied to all "minority people" the Chinese hope to seize key positions within the complex system of monasteries which since time immemorial have guided Tibet's destinies.

Two major factions in Tibet have discussed the policy most likely to regain genuine freedom. Those who advocated open revolt have been superseded by leaders who believe in awaiting some more opportune time.

Rebellion first broke out, however, in the Kham region which ironically enough was first to fall under Chinese control. Mao Tse-tung has seen the danger of further eruptions. He ordered officials to proceed at an even slower pace of "socialist transformation" than the one set by his political commissar in Lhasa, Tan Kuan-san, and assistant Fan Ming.

Changes have been made in the personnel of the so-called "culture stations" and the Patriotic Youth Cultural Associations which were in reality training centers for converts. At the same time, though badly equipped to undertake such costly ventures, the Chinese are speeding up their prestige projects.

One immediate objective is to make Tibet a more efficient center of production. In the revealing words of one Chinese official, describing to me the benefits brought to the region: "We are introducing medicine and clinics so that production can be increased. Old superstitious remedies are wasteful of working time and labor."

I concluded this effusion by saying: "It would be idle to accuse Peking of imperialism in Tibet. Her leaders are acting in the sacred names of Marx and Lenin and any territorial benefits gained by China are, of course, purely coincidental."

But I heaved this rock into a pool of unnatural tranquility. It brought no reaction; no recriminations; no defensive arguments. And not even a visa to see for myself.

Only months later, as the spring snows began to melt and swell the great rivers that flow out of Tibet, a small item arrived on my desk in Hong Kong. It was a New China News Agency report of a speech given by the Dalai Lama in Lhasa. He reviewed the past year: new highways had been finished; the Peking–Lhasa Airline was inaugurated; work was progressing or completed on hydroelectric power for Lhasa, thermal power for Shigatse; an auto-repair works, coal mines and medical laboratories.

He then admitted many defects and mistakes; food had been short and prices high; Chinese officials had gone rough-shod over local customs.

This speech was in utter conformity with the self-examination at that time taking place throughout China, even to the penultimate paragraph approved for all 1957 speeches: *Should I make mistakes please give your corrections directly.*

I remembered Ho Chi-minh and other less exalted people as I read the final appeal that came from the mouth but not the heart of the twenty-one-year-old youth who fought a lonely battle against Peking's persuasion brigades:

> Obey the will of the Chinese Communist Party and the great leader, Chairman Mao Tse-tung.
> Let us shout at the top of our voice:
> "Long live the prosperity of Buddhism, the Root of Happiness.
> "Long live the Chinese Communist Party.
> "Long live Chairman Mao, Great Leader of All Nationalities in China.
> "Triumph to all work of the Preparatory Committee for the Autonomous Region of Tibet."

CHAPTER NINETEEN

Trumpets for a Chinese Jericho

◉ ◉

> We have had too much liberty. We have become a tray of loose sand. We must break down individual liberty and become pressed together into an unyielding body like the firm rock which is formed by the addition of cement. . . . In order that all members may be united spiritually, first sacrifice freedom.
>
> DR. SUN YAT-SEN, FIRST OF CHINA'S MODERN REVOLUTIONARIES.

NOBODY UNDERSTOOD Chinese Communist methods for overcoming opposition at home or abroad better than the Chinese Nationalists. Perhaps the best proof that Mao knew how to use all the tricks of an Oriental despot was to be found in Formosa where his own countrymen and his most bitter enemies employed similar devices whenever they could do so without incurring the wrath of their American sponsors.

I moved from Red China into Formosa and back again sufficiently to be trapped sometimes into thinking myself in the other one's territory (although this only happened during long and drowsy interviews when my eyes were closed and the flow of words became disembodied).

For instance, when an alleged Nationalist spy from Chiang Kai-shek's famous offshore island was caught in mainland China he might find himself at the Prison of the People's Court in Peking whose governor once said to me: "Our aim is to remold the mind."

Similarly when an alleged Communist was caught on Formosa he might draw the sentence known to the Nationalists as "indoctrination." This took place in prisons like the Panchaio Experimental Institute whose governor had also told me: "Our objective is to correct their wrong thoughts."

On either side of the war in the Formosa Strait, I found Chiang and his enemies agreed about one thing: there could never be room for Incorrect Thinking.

The reason for this might be found in several factors common to the contestants whose policies grew out of the confusion and chaos that followed the breakdown of traditional Chinese society. That society had existed for hundreds of years without the slightest exercise of what we call "democratic" ideas. Both sides inherited a revolution begun by Sun Yat-sen who sought a new political ideology for twentieth-century China. Finally they turned to Russia for guidance. It is not widely understood, for instance, that Stalin dictated the new constitution of Chiang Kai-shek's Kuomintang when there was already a two-year-old Chinese Communist Party.

News was flowing freely between both sides of the Formosan war so that I never doubted my movements inside Communist China were known to the Nationalists, and vice versa. A nice exotic touch was the fact that postal authorities in Hong Kong were handling in 1957 some one million pieces of mail each week between the two enemies: Communist hogs fed Formosan soldiers: Formosan sugar sweetened the dreary mainland routine; and even at the height of the shooting a cable dispatched from the island fortress could be routed through Shanghai to the United States.

Once I landed at the Formosan capital with a Communist "chop" in my passport. Two men in Hunnish steel helmets and sinister black uniforms spotted this simultaneously and put their armored heads together with a resounding *clang*. I tried to read their badges of office. They might have belonged to any one of several police forces: the Peace Preservation Corps, the Anti-Communist Salvation Youth Corps . . . the possibilities seemed endless. I shuffled my feet nervously as they slowly raised their eyes. One said: "You were in Canton recently?"

I gulped and nodded. They whispered together. "Then tell us . . ." demanded one of the steel-heads. He was interrupted. When he returned to the subject I was supporting myself with both hands firmly braced on the customs' desk. "Tell us," they said, "*what is it really like there now?*"

In Formosa the political commissars still survived along with mass propaganda organs, disciplinary orders in place of a legal code, all under command of Lieutenant General Chiang Ching-kuo, eldest son of President Chiang Kai-shek, who spent nine years of study in the Soviet Union and now has a Russian wife. When Nationalists retreated to the island shaped like a tobacco leaf, only one hundred miles from the China mainland, there was a sharp reign of terror. Some hundred thousand Formosans were killed by the Chinese, who then imposed their government with Chiang as supreme authority, and his eldest son in control of secret police.

I saw Chiang Junior's masterly touch early in 1955 after sailing with a Nationalist Chinese evacuation fleet to the Tachen islands clustered together at the northern end of a Nationalist island chain strung for 322 miles along the coast.

Communist military chiefs directed a modern military operation against a tiny island near this group. It was called Yikiangshan and it perfectly illustrated Chinese tactics, old as Methuselah and yet modern as the MiG. The plan was to smash this solitary island and then retire to leave all the other offshore islands to collapse like dominoes, partly under the pressure of military expediency, partly by frightening the West into discouraging Formosa from offering further provocation. To some extent, this scheme worked and Chiang Kai-shek was obliged to shorten the island chain drastically. For a time, a vast armada of U.S. warships and aircraft maneuvered close to China's Communist defenses while the pacifists trembled and the Peking planners sat back patiently and with formidable calm.

But there was no extension of the war in the Formosan Strait although public opinion forced President Eisenhower to leash Chiang's large forces and to refuse support for any "Back-to-the-mainland" adventures. The name of the tiny target of Yikiang-shan crept into late night bulletins transmitted to

Hong Kong on January 18. For six hours, stuttered the news-agency teletypes, this hitherto unknown island had been under heavy aerial attack from 80 Tupolev-2s, some 60 MiG-15 jet fighters, 50 La-11 ground-attack fighters and 40 Illyushin dive bombers. Later a Communist naval force of two destroyers, two gunboats, three frigates and thirty-five small craft laid down a steady bombardment, assisted by artillery from a neighboring dab of rock occupied by Red Army units.

There was one small beach from which the defenders were driven, and under cover of the artillery and naval bombardment, some twenty-five hundred invaders jumped ashore from motorized junks and landing craft. A second wave landed in similar strength before nightfall. During the second day, Red artillery and engineers were put ashore under air cover. On January 20, after a fourth wave landed, all Nationalist resistance ceased. This left 6000 Communist troops, sixty landing craft and seventy motorized junks within striking distance of the main Nationalist bases in the Tachens.

I flew to Taipeh, the Nationalist capital, where heated debates were taking place on whether Chiang Kai-shek should evacuate all his garrisons in the Tachens area. A vast evacuation fleet was hastily assembled. There were high-powered conferences with a formidable team of U.S. Naval and Air Force chiefs. Admiral Felix B. Stump spared the press enough time from these urgent cogitations to announce that British Commonwealth newsmen would not be permitted to set foot upon his Seventh Fleet warships, presumably because British ships running the China blockade were being attacked by American warplanes and warships operated by Nationalist Chinese crews, putting us into a slightly hostile position. So we sailed instead in rusting Nationalist landing craft whose amiable and versatile commanders suffered no inhibitions.

But Chiang Ching-kuo had got in ahead of us. Two days after the fall of Yikiang-shan, some 17,132 inhabitants of the Tachens were told to register for evacuation. An intensive campaign was launched to persuade them to leave. By some inscrutable legerdemain, the gods of the temples were made to

predict impending disasters. Three old people were permitted
to stay behind as proof to foreign correspondents that no
coercion had been employed.

The removal of these simple fishermen and their families was
hailed as a great propaganda victory. It was not the first time
I had seen an Asian army drag away refugees in an attempt to
make political capital out of defeat. It was saddening to watch
yet another mass evacuation. Their junks, we were told, would be
towed to safety. Communist sources said they were piled together and burned. I saw the hasty exit made by Chiang's ships
and doubt very much that anyone bothered to drag the Tachen
junks across two hundred miles of ocean under Communist survey. There were however a number of gaudily colored, diesel-
powered junks with whipping radio masts and concealed guns
and it was obviously imperative that *they* be salvaged or sunk, together with their unfishermanlike equipment covered in U.S.
military markings. There was about this operation an un-
pleasantly sinister atmosphere. With Lachie McDonald of the
London *Daily Mail* I trudged through the main village on
Upper Tachen. Crooked lanes ran down to the wooden quay,
zigzagging through stone cottages built in terraces up the
steep, gray hillside. These lanes were crowded with ragged
figures carrying all their belongings in small bundles. They
shuffled step by step down to the sea where scores of U.S.
landing craft buzzed like angry bees.

This scene must have made the same impact upon the islanders as a sudden descent by Martians upon Corsica. In the
shrouds of a dawn mist stood the big ships of the evacuation
fleet, ominous dark shapes upon a vague horizon. Inshore
came the steel-gray craft with flat bottoms and blunt bows that
fell open like the gaping mouths of stranded whales. Sailors
bloated with life jackets scrambled to haul on board the wailing women and timorous children. Beach masters, looking
and sounding like school bullies as they roared orders over
loud-hailers strapped to their padded chests, kept the traffic
moving. Without doubt, three groups of people regarded this
day's work from three quite separate points of view. American sailors, handing out candy bars and comforting distraught

mothers, felt they were on a mission of mercy. The islanders felt they were engulfed in a nightmare. And U.S. and Nationalist naval commanders felt they had carried off a successful operation with slickness and scientific efficiency.

But those of us with time to stand and stare wondered if the journey was really necessary.

Madame Chiang Kai-shek was torn by no such doubts. I stood beside her a few days later in Taipeh as eighty-four Tachen orphans raised their tiny fists and cried in unison: "Thank you to the Minister of Financial Affairs." Then they sang: "Let us return to the mainland. We will devote ourselves to career of anti-Communism."

Madame Chiang smiled carefully and waited for the three mobile floods to quiver into light. Seven newsreel cameras began to whirl. Behind them flashed twenty press cameras. Out of sight were forty foreign correspondents, thirty members of the Chinese Women's Anti-Communist League and a number of Chinese gentlemen in American baseball caps.

An eleven-year-old Tachen "survivor" stepped forward. Madame Chiang turned a gracious head, lifting one soft and manicured hand but stopping just short of the little boy's rather grubby scalp.

"Thank you for food," said the small warrior. "Thank you for clothes. We will repay when we grow up by fighting Communists."

This was the signal for another chorus of "Return to mainland." Then each of these singularly talented orphans raised his right fist in the air and chanted: "Thank you Madame Chiang. Long live Madame Chiang! Thank you President Chiang. Long live President Chiang!"

Before the floodlights flickered and died there was a final chorus of "We must struggle for ever for existence of our nation." In the subsequent darkness there was a general exodus from the hall during which the orphans, heavily outnumbered anyway, seemed to disappear.

Madame Chiang took some of us into another room. She kept her voice sweet and low, and just the right amount of pity infused her words: "The fate of these children," she said, "was important to us. As indeed, it is important to all the Free World."

She gestured to right and left where several officials stood in attitudes of deference, dedication and deep humility. "These gentlemen are very important, too. They have weighty matters to discuss in these parlous times."

The men flanking her looked about them in a weighty manner.

"But," said Madame Chiang in a thrilling, throaty climax, "they have put aside their heavy duties to inquire into the fate of these little children."

We all bowed respectfully as she swept out. Her counselors fell in behind her. We fell in behind the counselors. Madame Chiang passed into the murky street, doors flinging wide at her approach, and was assisted into a blue-curtained Cadillac. The counselors stepped into a pursuing fleet of black limousines. We caught pedicabs. What happened to the orphans I never discovered.

Inquiries into the fate of their parents led eventually to the Panchaio prison where suspected critics of President Chiang are "indoctrinated," to use the word employed by General Wang Chieh. The general is a lanky, six-foot Northerner who runs the Peace Preservation Corps and he is answerable to President Chiang's eldest son, who seems to keep a pretty tight grip on the thoughts of Chinese as well as of the colonial Formosans. General Wang described the prison as an experiment in ideological reform and talked about "de-Communizing" the inmates in rather the same casual way that one would propose to decarbonize a car.

As I wandered through the compound, listening to the general and the governor explain the President's generous policy of correcting erroneous ideas, my mind boggled at the implications.

For the words of my Nationalist hosts required very little alteration to become the words of the Communist jailers I talked with only a few months earlier. Here was the same philosophy of "thought regimentation" which today spreads through much of Asia, striking down roots in the military dictatorships of Syngman Rhee in South Korea, and President Ngo Dinh Diem in South Vietnam, and always justified as a necessary defense against similar techniques in the Communist north. It seemed strange that despite the propaganda in favor of Western democracy, politicians in Asia should think in terms of mental dictatorship. Was the West so bankrupt in ideas that all it could do was propagate anti-Communism among its Asian dependencies? Had we nothing better to offer than political commissars along with the guns and tanks, soft-drink concessions, Cinerama and air-conditioned hotels? The answer seemed only too obvious unless you had a blind faith in Christianity. And how did we recruit the bulk of Asian Christians except by subtle methods of bribery; by the offer of education among illiterates, of charity to the destitute and of hope to those whose idols failed to provide the material benefits so clearly enjoyed by Christian foreigners?

It would be untrue to say there seemed nothing to choose between Chinese Nationalist and Communist methods of indoctrination. Americans were able to restrain Chiang Ching-kuo on Formosa just as they harnessed the zeal of Rhee and Diem, with purse strings for reins. I doubt that any Western observer would argue honestly that if the United States were to withdraw its money from the Asian territory it has supported since World War II, there would be any strong native resistance to the emergence of full-blown dictatorship. In this respect at least, the British record is better. With far longer in which to sow liberal ideas, Britons withdrew from their Empire in the East but left behind a working knowledge of intellectual freedom. Unfortunately it is this very spirit of independent thought that is considered nowadays to be the weakness of "neutral" nations like India.

The paradox is that Communist China is more exposed to these influences than some other parts of Asia. It would be foolish to suppose, for instance, that Nehru the former English public-school boy is entirely without an audience in Peking. A major source of information on world events for Mao Tse-tung was, at least in the first years of the regime, the British Broadcasting Corporation. When anniversary services were held for Sun Yat-sen in 1956, British visitors were unctuously reminded by Communist flatterers that Sun had once called their country "the most cultured of the modern world."

However, this lipservice did not spread as far as the Peking jail, whereas the proximity of Americans in Formosa did exercise some restraint on police boss, Chiang Ching-kuo. Here is a summary of what I found in these two camps.

Dateline: Peking, November, 1954:

"Our policy is reform through labor," said Governor Liu Hsiang-chun. "Punishment is inflicted by Social Rebuke; by the indignation of the Group against the Transgressor. They come to their final Redemption through the Purification of Labor."

There were 1400 "counterrevolutionaries" held prisoner. Among them were Kuomintang agents from Formosa, former generals and senior officers from the Nationalist armies and men identified as bandits and saboteurs. The main object seemed to be to squeeze every ounce of labor from this assortment of political criminals. They worked from dawn to nightfall weaving cloth, or making, dyeing and packing socks. There was hot rice water for breakfast; for lunch, a quarter of a kilogram of vegetables and one sixth of an ounce of edible oils, plus hot rice water; for supper, a repeat ration of lunch. Once a week there was a distribution of fat, or meat, "or its equivalent."

Governor Liu had a withered arm and a crooked smile. He called his jail "a daring experiment in education." He implied that it went somewhat further than similar Soviet institutions by giving people "The New Outlook."

He explained, sweeping open a door to the weaving sheds with his withered arm: "This is a battlefield of the mind, a workshop of political ideas."

A giant clock ticked above the clattering machines. Red strips of paper fluttered on the peeling walls. *Clack-clack-clack* went the shuttles. *Tick-tock-tick* went the clock. The weavers moved arms and legs in swift, jerky movements: One-two-three-bang.

It was, as the Governor said, an ingenious design. Each of the weavers was under suspended sentence of death. They could win remissions by exceeding the production targets brushed in graceful black strokes on the fluttering red papers. They could escape the executioner by beating the clock.

"You see, our problem was to find enough people for essential tasks," said the Governor. "Skilled craftsmen with technical knowledge mostly came from families with reactionary or feudal backgrounds. So the People's Government solved the problem of keeping them in production and at the same time achieving their Redemption. What goes on is a complete overhaul of a student's moral and mental equipment, carried out by the student himself."

He referred to them all as students. In fact, he said, 135 of them were free to go into the outside world but preferred to remain. Evidently they preferred the prison they knew to the larger one they did not know. But I refrained from saying so, while Governor Liu patiently interpreted the slogans on the walls and the whispering loudspeakers: Remember Duty! Disgorge Bitter Fluid! Overcome Harmful Work Styles! T'an-pai Quick! T'an-pai: Confession is Road to Life: Resistance is Road to Death.

Dateline: Formosa, September 1955:
"Here we convert enemies to friends and lighten the nation's burden by utilizing their ability or training them for useful jobs," said Colonel Huang Shiang-jen, in charge of the Formosa Provincial Vocational Training Experimental Institute. "Punishment is inflicted through Honorable Discipline: that is, the moral indignation of the Group is aroused and directed at anyone who breaks the code."

The colonel called *his* prisoners "trainees" and said there were now 506 of whom one third were Formosans, all convicted by military courts for political sins. Some were Communist agents and the official phraseology in sentencing them was that they should serve a certain "period of indoctrination." Among other prisoners were university students found passing handbills detrimental to President Chiang. It would be fair to say that any criticism of the Chinese colonial government on Formosa would result in a charge of "Communism." This was distinct from licensed criticism such as leaked into the Formosan press from official sources, which was a controllable safety valve for public indignation.

"We want to change their thoughts so they will ask for those things our government wishes to give them," said the colonel, unconsciously echoing one of enemy Mao Tse-tung's model thoughts. "We teach them the kindliness and lovingness of the President. We provide them with safety from wrong thoughts."

Stubborn cases were dispatched to Green Island, a melancholy
lump of rock about eighteen miles off the southeast tip of Formosa. The more wicked cases of Communist Wrong Thinking
were kept there. "They expect to be executed," said the colonel.
"When they find they are still alive, they become more male-
able." The camps gave intensive training in the great philosophies and the new political concepts of President Chiang. These
were: a New Birth, a New Life, a New Spirit and a New Action.

Of course the first three were dependent upon the New Action,
which was to recapture the mainland. The New Life, etc.,
would come later.

"When that happens," said Colonel Huang, "we shall set up
prisons — er, Institutions like this one, behind the advancing
armies to de-Communize our people."

His eyes crinkled into a smile. "Yes, it is indeed a great experiment. It is the way to rebuild a nation and teach the great Chinese people to think loving and kindly — not incorrect —
thoughts. Perhaps one day the whole world will have such
camps to protect humanity from wrong ideas."

It was no coincidence that reformers in Peking and Taipeh
all wore high-buttoned tunics of similar material and cut. The
uniform was known on the mainland as the Liberation Suit
and in Formosa as a Sun Yat-sen Suit. Both sides claimed Dr.
Sun as their inspiration but Peking had an undeniable advantage in also owning his widow. Skeptics may ask why Nationalist leaders did not rejoin the Peking regime if there was so
little difference between the two. Cynics would reply: money.
This was not the answer, however, for there were many scholars who felt gratitude for the modest academies sponsored on
their behalf by Americans.

Nevertheless, between 1951 and 1955 over half a billion
U.S. dollars were spent in direct economic aid to the Nationalists
and about $300,000,000 U.S. went annually on military equipment.
The stability of the American dollar had been admired for
many years by the ruling family of financiers, the T. V. Soongs,
who were known in Shanghai as the Soong Dynasty, and nobody had a greater respect for the value of hard currency than
little Mei-ling Soong, younger sister of T.V. and now Madame
Chiang.

On a straight cash-and-carry deal, the impoverished Communists were unable to compete with Washington. They applied instead the well-tried philosophies of Chairman Mao, concentrating first on the delivery of shocks that would put the future patient into a sweat. The amphibious attack on Yikiang-shan was meant to have this effect. It certainly shook Western military men and sharpened a few Nationalist wits because it was a demonstration of Red Chinese ability to fight a modern island-hopping war. The operation was a precision job, accomplished with swift timing and co-ordination between land, sea and air: and this destroyed the myth (wherever it survived after Korea) that the Chinese were hopeless warriors with no talent for organization.

There then followed a period when Peking, using powerful transmitters and small newspapers in non-Communist areas, told the Nationalists they were ill and prescribed the treatment: "Come home among your loved ones."

Peking leaders maintained a pose of kindly forbearance and on every possible occasion talked of the inevitability of Formosa's "peaceful liberation." Meanwhile, Communist roads and railways were driven through to the so-called invasion ports opposite Formosa; new airfields were built and old ones modernized; and groups of visiting foreigners were allowed "accidentally" to wander into military areas like Foochow which they dutifully reported "looked like southern England on D-Day."

The potential target for these preparations was Quemoy, a Nationalist island with an hour-glass figure whose local name means "Golden Gate." It was a gate that opens two ways: into the natural harbor of Amoy, the former treaty port and a good launching site for invasion of South China; or into the Formosan Strait. In 1949 the Red Army tried to take it, floating fourteen thousand troops in sampans and bamboo rafts across the narrow strip of water from the mainland, but the invasion was smothered by Nationalist forces.

When I first landed there on a small dirt strip just beyond the range of Communist artillery, both sides were exchanging bombardments, or shouting insults at one another through loudspeakers. But as Peking switched to "peaceful" tactics, the propaganda themes became stronger and Communist shells were fired only at long intervals to show the guns were still there. They were not only there: the numbers had increased and their range was extended to cover the entire island, including the airstrip and tiny dockside which provided lifelines to Formosa.

There were now many prominent ex-Nationalists working for the Peking regime and a stooge Kuomintang. In the province of Fukien, closest to Formosa, some of President Chiang's former followers broadcast messages of love and friendship to their friends and relatives in exile. They included the provincial vice-governor, formerly Chiang's Minister of Navy, whose recorded pleas reinforced those of the generals, ex-ministers and intellectuals paraded through Peking Radio studios.

These trumpets blew outside the walls of Chiang's Jericho with increasing force. The notes were sometimes off key but the listeners were often in a mood to hear only sweet music. This was not a case of Lord Haw-Haw, a traitor, broadcasting from enemy country to Britain. These appeals came from many well-known figures inside the Fatherland to exiles whose hopes of returning faded with the passing years.

A sample of Peking's propaganda shows the effort to persuade Chinese intellectuals that a new era of liberal thought had begun.

Peking Radio interviewer: "How are you, Mr. Lo?"

Lo Lung-chi, Vice-Chairman of China Democratic League: "Such big fun we have had this Spring Festival. Our Peking branch gave a big party — four thousand members and families."

"Are there famous stage performers in your League?"

"You are right. Teachers, professors and opera stars too."

Mr. Lo described the tens of thousands of Chinese scholars in his League. "They are very much excited since the Communist Party mapped out a program of co-existence and mutual supervision for democratic parties."

This was a glib introduction and Mr. Lo hastily turned to contemplate tragic separations among distinguished intellectual families. "I have real sympathy for those stranded in Formosa.

Old friends — too many to be counted." He sighed, recalling names like Liang Shih-chiu.

"Ai-ya!" The interviewer sat up sharply. "Did he not write a book on the art of cursing people?"

"The same," sighed Mr. Lo. "His eldest daughter is now a judge of Peking district court. She told me how she misses Father very much. Seven years she has been separated from parents. Very miserable. She must have been most sad in Spring Festival when all families get together. Ah, if only Formosa were peacefully liberated, many family reunions must follow."

There was a discussion on the liberation of Formosa:

"Premier Chou En-lai indicated that for the sake of complete unification of China, issues between us can always be settled by negotiation," said Mr. Lo. One could visualize him being led away from the studio, eyes blurred by his final peroration: "We Chinese are patriots and are surely united in our good wishes for development of our country!"

There was more than an island and a million exiled troops at stake. Perhaps more important in the long run was the loyalty of about twelve million Overseas Chinese. Traditionally, they were a source of income. Technically, they were badly needed in a country with great ambitions to become an industrial power but with limited skill. So long as President Chiang and his Nationalists existed, there would always be some rivalry for their attention. Politics were less important than success. To commercially minded Chinese, the men on Formosa were successful in hitting an American jackpot. Mao's regime merely made some doubtful deals with Russia.

Traffic in and out of mainland China was extensive. Many went back to see how the new government was faring and came back with tales of Russian exploitation. A common complaint was: "Why did we have to pick up such a poor Big Brother? The Russians are poorer than we — and certainly more stupid. And yet — one ton of our silk buys one ton of their useless pig-iron . . . *Pi-se*, that's what they are. Bedbugs. *Pi-se* suck the blood of the poor: not the rich, the poor."

Thus President Chiang scored in his choice of sponsors.

CHAPTER TWENTY

Aspects of a Myth

◉ ◉

THE IMPERMANENCE of Communism was an article of faith on Formosa so that the myth of an impending return to the mainland could be maintained. While American money may have won many allegiances, it also bought time for the Nationalist government to reform itself. In a period when the Formosan population soared from seven and a half million to ten million, the Chinese regime increased food production, carried through a sweeping land reform and turned the island into a self-sufficient community with a rising and healthy export trade. American aid developed power resources and communications, built water reservoirs, irrigated the land and sponsored light industry.

These achievements, the result of a more realistic alliance between the Chinese Nationalists and their American backers, were frequently pooh-poohed in the West. This was a pity because on the mainland there was greater concern (and respect) for these constructive aspects of Sino-American co-operation than might have been suspected. Communist leaders who once hoped to drain American strength by encouraging the flow of arms and aid to the Nationalists now understood better the tremendous resources at America's command. They were fascinated by American techniques and while they vilified their neighbors across the Pacific, it was perfectly plain that they also secretly admired their industrial knowledge and power.

Peking could hardly care less about an American way of life but its citizens were surprisingly better informed than the Russians about American Cinerama, nuclear reactors and fish-tail cars.

Most Chinese, like anyone else, love gadgetry. So long as the Peking regime could not win American technical help, it must distract attention from the gadgetry on Formosa. There was a danger that a majority of the Overseas Chinese would believe the myth of a Nationalist invasion of the mainland simply because they were dazzled by the shiny mechanical devices showered upon Formosa, ranging from guided missiles to sugar refineries.

Since Mao's government wished to command all Overseas Chinese loyalty, it appealed to the patriotism and the urge for national independence of Chinese everywhere. It called Chiang and his men on Formosa mere stooges of America.

This was successful among a neglected but important group, the exiled intellectuals. After the defeat of Nationalist armies on the mainland, thousands of scholars, writers, artists and scientists poured into Hong Kong where their welcome was a chilly one. Intellectual refugees all over the world have never been popular: few countries can be bothered with men and women who cannot be bought cheaply for mines, lumber camps and factories. In Hong Kong there was no exception to the rule. Even doctors found difficulty in making a living in a colony where disease could spread with frightening rapidity among the million or more refugees.

The phrase "return to the mainland" took on a new significance for the adult intellectual and the many thousands more youngsters who were able to get abroad the basic education they were denied at home. This growing force was spread right through non-Communist Asia. They listened cynically to the valid claims that in Formosa the Nationalists had ended most of the old evils, that the number of farmers owning their own land had risen from 57 to 75 per cent, while the proportion of tenants had dropped from 36 to 19 per cent.

These Overseas Chinese did not share the unshaken Nationalist belief that somehow they would reclaim the mainland. Al-

ready there was less talk from Formosa of an actual military
invasion and more vague speculation instead about a collapse
of the Peking regime from within.

And so the myth of an impending return assumed new aspects. How would the exiles return? As saboteurs and agents?
As converts to Communism?

By far the greatest number of rebels against Communism
had voted with their feet, trudging wearily into the sanctuary
of Hong Kong. Their plight was ignored by their own wealthy
countrymen and belatedly recognized by British colonial authorities. A curious combination of Chinese ingenuity and British phlegm did result in many finding work of a sort. Housing
programs helped a growing number of fugitives to leave their
squatters' shacks that scarred the Hong Kong hillsides like
leprous sores. But for the intellectuals it was a period of short
commons. Seldom in history had a great nation's best thinkers
assembled in such a tiny area and in such an atmosphere of dis-
interest. The greatest storyteller in South China was glad to
earn $98 monthly in recorded broadcasts. Playwrights turned
out literally dozens of scripts a year for films and opera to
maintain a decent living standard. Art was judged by commercial standards. Rich Chinese patronized programs of American cultural concerts to please their influential friends, but
ignored their native entertainers. The line-up for American
entry visas was jumped by a film actress with hips and
bust to win Hollywood's approval, while other Chinese with
fewer allures continued to wait through the long and dreary
months. This may have been good propaganda in America
but it was poor psychology in Hong Kong. Big empty countries
like Canada ignored the problem altogether. Disillusioned, frustrated and unhappy at being labeled "white Chinese," the
architects and engineers began to turn their eyes toward Peking.

The situation was crystallized one day in Hong Kong when
Leonard Lyons, the American columnist, visited a refugee film
studio. The studio worked twenty-four hours daily on a shift
system. We arrived at midnight as one producer ended his
film and another began a new one. Ng Chor-fan, a famous

Cantonese actor, told us it was necessary to shoot films like machine-gun bullets to stay alive.

"After a month's circulation," said Ng, "the film is useless. It won't make another cent. Our takings barely cover expenses. Standards are necessarily low. Yet we have some of the best actors in Asia working here. But you see, nobody cares about art. Building? Yes. Put up apartment blocks — make money. Put up cinemas, maybe make money too. Only if they make money, they will be interested."

He shook his head sadly. He was a tall, handsome product of the old Chinese theater. As chairman of the Board of the China film corporation, he knew his business. His companion made it clear to Lyons that he had no sympathy for the Communists. But the wife of a distinguished script writer whispered to me: "We have to talk all the time against Peking, especially to Americans."

After Lyons had left, the *Peking Daily Worker* announced film awards in which Ng Chor-fan was named producer of the two second-best films of 1956, and fourth best film star, in mainland China.

Actors and opera stars were under almost daily pressure from Communists and sympathizers in Hong Kong to return to the mainland. It says a great deal for the bitterness of their memories that so few responded, despite neglect and hard times. Those who did go back, whether professionals, businessmen or students, were quickly sorted out. Many came from Kwangtung province, which adjoins the colony. They were vigorous and shrewd like all Chinese emigrants, and the Peking Government was smart enough and practical enough to find ways of exploiting their varied talents.

Some commentators have called the Chinese "the Jews of Asia." It may be true that they are often feared and resented in the same way as Jews, for their superior sense of business and their amazing tenacity. But a Chinese who lives abroad has a permanent homeland he never forgets. Eurasian children, with one parent who is Chinese, are admonished never to forget their true nationality. Pride of race is perhaps nowhere stronger. You seldom find a Chinese raising his family in an

exclusively foreign community. He usually seeks a neighborhood of his own kind. There have been Chinese emigrants
for many centuries. They undertake all kinds of labor and
commercial enterprise, and they go for big profits. They are
quick to learn a craft and you find them as tailors, smelters,
jewelers, cobblers and mechanics throughout Southeast Asia.
The rags-to-riches saga is a familiar one for the Chinese. There
are millionaires who began by peddling "thousand-layer Shantung flat cakes"; rubber tycoons who moved slowly up from
a noodle barrow to a Malayan estate. The Chinese in their
time have been pirates and bandits who terrorized their neighbors; ruthless businessmen who worked out the most intricate
rackets to destroy competitors. Today there is still piracy and
banditry, in the fishing grounds as much as in the marbled
halls of commerce. Most of them, however, bring great talent
and inexhaustible ambition to the areas they colonize.

But the call of the homeland is strong. Rising nationalism in
Asia makes life increasingly difficult. Overseas Chinese discrim-
inated against in countries like South Vietnam and the Philippines began to feel they could hope for protection from the
powerful regime in Peking, after it demonstrated its military
strength so spectacularly in Korea.

And so they drifted back. Many were youngsters who were
offered scholarships. They got priority at Communist schools
which sometimes aroused local jealousy. Some were arrested as
spies and agitators. Once inside China, they were subjected to
a cold-blooded examination. Those who could be useful to the
regime were treated gently. The rest were sent wherever their
labor was needed.

I watched some of them one day as they took the plunge. I
was standing inside the Communist customs' shed a few yards
from the British border of Hong Kong. Green paint and gay
posters gave the outside woodwork a festive veneer, when
seen from the narrow iron bridge which crosses a muddy river
and links China with the outside world. A stream of youngsters swaggered through the silent sentries. I had seen their
sort before, pouring into ships at Singapore and defiantly singing "The east is red . . ." as they roughed up Europeans who
got in their way.

I had seen them in their rubber sneakers, white shirts and blouses and Yenan bobs, rioting out of Singapore schools. They sang "Tillers of the soil, unite!" to Slavic rhythms, and "Our China is so big and wide." The Irish policeman straddling the entrance to China on this particular day had a sorrowful look on his red perspiring face and I remembered his words on a previous occason: "Nothing wrong wit' 'em that two years in the Red Army and a dose of salts won't cure."

Unfortunately the purge was administered after the fatal walk across the bridge and, although I could see Paddy's sad spaniel eyes watching the young innocents from his safe position under the British flag, I could also see what was invisible from his viewpoint. Customs officials had segregated those who were returning for good and these luckless arrivals were given special attention. One boy was obliged to open his coat while a grim-faced girl of his own age fished swiftly through his pockets. She yanked out ball-point pens, wrist watches and other trinkets, and made a painstaking list of each item while the youth's face grew longer. Possibly he hoped to make a killing with his modest treasure-trove, or he may have had relatives on whom to bestow these coveted items. At any rate he was now permanently separated from them. Others in his group were similarly stripped and, further down the platform, peasants opened up their multifarious packages while the inspectors (mostly aloof girls in mob caps) disdainfully turned over plastic combs, cheap mirrors, oiled paper umbrellas and assorted gimcrackery. Some peasants had bought oranges, but this happened to be a time when Yunnan oranges were a glut on the local market and so the imported oranges were taken away and receipts issued. Later, in at least one case, the oranges were returned in a rotten condition, together with a bill for storage. This happened to a farmer's wife returning to Hong Kong but for most students there was no prospect of an early return, and the Irish bobby with the British crown on the lapels of his uniform was within a stone's throw, but also a world away.

There was one of those eager Englishmen with me at this time, the sort of determinedly kindhearted politician who oozes with sympathy for the poor, and makes a very good

thing out of his charitable instincts. He was plainly inside
China in a bodily sense, and it was his first visit, but his mind
had been made up long before and nothing that now happened to him physically would alter his prejudices. These
were not so much pro-Peking as anti-American: and if the
United States had been backing Mao Tse-tung I feel reasonably
sure my friend would have transferred exactly the same emotional attachments to Chiang Kai-shek on Formosa. In other
ways this newcomer was a sane, sensible man with a nice little
family in Hampstead and a seedy office near the Old Bailey
but now, confronted with smiling Chinese officials, he was
undergoing the strangest transformation. He refused to believe this was VIP treatment as formalities were waived, bags
were left unexamined, and beer and steaming bowls of food
were brought for his refreshment. I pointed out to him the
severe examination given to returning Chinese, but by this
time his eyes were able to record only the sights which fitted
his preconceived ideas.

Privilege blinds even the most observant traveler, and by the
simple device of helping foreign visitors into trains, escorting
them to hotels, and greasing their passage through customs,
the Chinese have won paeans of praise. Their hypocrisy in
lauding The People while catering to a privileged minority is
curiously overlooked. The only jarring note in the customs'
questionnaire handed to my English friend was its unexpected
demand: "Have you an accordion?"

He came to me later, deliriously happy because girls in the
street had held his hand. "Those little warm hands of friendship," he babbled. "Just wait till I tell my public about *that*.
And the Americans tell us these people want war!"

There is no harsh treatment of returning Chinese and it
would be wrong to suggest they become victims of brutality
and force. If they can be led gently into prearranged spots, if
they can be persuaded to desire that which the regime desires
for them, so much the better. Mao abhors resistance.

One of the most successful jobs of persuasion is done a few
miles from the border scene just described, at Canton. This is
China's fifth biggest city with the longest record of contact

with the West. Its arcades and broad streets look today as
they appeared at dawn in more prosperous time: that is, they
wait. They wait for the bustle of trade, the roar of traffic, the
shouts of hawkers, none of which has been heard for many
years. Noon in the middle of the week is tranquil as a wet
Sunday afternoon in Brooklyn or Trafalgar Square. There is
a difference. On Sundays the streets here fill with uniformed
figures wandering slowly through the exhibition grounds, the
solitary tall department store, or along the banks of the
swirling Pearl River. They are a disciplined crowd moving
softly through spotless streets like gray snowflakes drifting in
a petrified forest. There are no beggars, no prostitutes, no
flies. But they have all died a little, one suspects, from bore-
dom.

On the river bobs the biggest water-borne community in the
world. Old crones appear at one end of their tiny sampans in
the morning to feed caged hens, cook on open fires amidships
and move into the stern at night to sleep. Babies crawl under
bamboo canopies. Fifty thousand human beings live on the
frail craft, while swift midstream currents carry down junks,
ferries of violent colors and long chains of rafts.

If you turn your back on the river and proceed west you will
pass through the old Factory Area where Western traders were
confined after Britain's King George III was informed by the
Chinese emperor in 1793: "Our Celestial Empire possesses
all things in prolific abundance . . . needing no manufactures
of outside barbarians . . . But as Celestial Empire products are
absolute necessities to you, we have permitted as a signal mark
of favor that foreign *hongs* be established at Canton . . ."

The foreign concessions look eerily empty and forlorn today
except for a few State trading agencies. The names of streets
like Chinese Green Pea Soup and Respondentia Walk have
changed. The famous old gin shops have long since departed:
Ben Bobstay, Old Sam's Brother, Tom Bowline, Old Jemmy
Apoo. But there are a few fresh delights. One of Canton's
senior officials was known as Patrolling Soother, Member of
Court of Universal Examiners, Imperial Censor and Attendant
Officer of Board of War.

Where his office once stood is the China National Animal
By-Products Export Corporation which offers the trading descendants of George III: "Ducks' feathers, hogs' bristles and
human hair."

It is planned to make this city an international trade center
again and already it has become busy with visitors on short
trips from its rival, Hong Kong, which will be left (the Communists hope) to wither on the vine. Some are Chinese thinking of returning home permanently. They are taken up beyond
the old foreign settlements to Overseas Chinese Village Number One.

The happy family of Engineer Li Yi-quang lives here in
evident comfort and at small apparent cost. I went to see him
with a Canton city official, formerly a warden in a British jail
in Hong Kong.

Engineer Li had a gaily painted, two story house with *servants' quarters* occupied by two amahs who stood out from the
crowd because they looked sleek and well fed. The roof was
gaudy red and the veranda from the master bedroom looked
down into a neat crescent of similar houses.

We might have been in a shrill new suburb of some American boom town except for the Russian MiG-17's screaming
out of a nearby airfield.

Engineer Li had just arrived from Indonesia. His neighbors
came from Malaya, Burma and Vietnam. They included a
doctor, another engineer and two architects. They all had
what Peking required: technical knowledge or businesses
abroad. Some lived on the profit of these foreign enterprises.
They owned the houses, purchased from the State for about
$9800. They often had more room than they needed and they
paid a nominal tax.

It all sounded unlikely — or expedient. "Don't you resent
the privilege these people enjoy?" I asked my guide. "They
get better wages, possess their own property, enjoy preference
if they want to see opera or go to an exhibition . . ."

He lived with his wife and three children in two rooms on
the fourth floor of a tenement. He earned $14 monthly against
Engineer Li's $78.40. But all he said was: "Overseas Chinese

worked hard in foreign lands. They deserve the best for coming back to work for us."

I said perhaps maliciously: "Isn't an Overseas landlord
wicked? Isn't an Overseas businessman an exploiter of the
people?"

He gave me an old-fashioned look. "They did not exploit
our people," he replied with finality.

Engineer Li was an affable man with a quick laugh and
watchful eyes. He found the stores cheap, he said: a fur-lined
U.S. army parka cost $5.60, a pair of shoes could be had for
as little as $2.80 and a Shanghai-made bicycle was $39.20. A
night at the Cantonese opera was twenty-one cents. There
were puppet shows and an amusement park. But his enthusiasm
lacked conviction.

He denied any attempt to convert him by direct political
discussion. His son went to school across the road, however,
where Marxist-Leninism and the works of Mao saturated the
curriculum.

Li Junior had an identity card which he dropped into a
basket each time he left the school premises. In the entrance
hall of his school was a blackboard with a big poster: *Our
Little Five-Year Plan. It seemed simple: (1) Take rest according to timetable. (2) Collect scrap iron. (3) Protect
library books, repair toys. (4) Raise chickens, ducks and rab-
bits. (5) Save waste paper.*

There were 760 students. Their 300 parents were among
200,000 Overseas Chinese who have taken jobs in and around
Canton. If the parents were treated gingerly, their children
were soon introduced to the ways of the new society. Li
Junior was scrawling on a blackboard to his teacher's dictation
when I looked in. He wrote: "I hope Papa and Mamma are
working properly."

CHAPTER TWENTY-ONE

Mao Takes a Lead

◉ ◉

This is almost tantamount to trampling underfoot the principles
of Marxist-Leninism, yet in actual fact it is creative Marxist-
Leninism in operation, a masterful application of the Marxist
dialectic to the concrete conditions of China.

> SOVIET FOREIGN MINISTER SHEPILOV SPEAKING OF
> MAO-ISM TO THE TWENTIETH SOVIET PARTY CON-
> GRESS. (HE WAS, HOWEVER, LATER DEPOSED.)

PERHAPS the biggest and most absorbing mystery in world
politics today is the question of China's relations with Russia.
Western observers in Peking and Moscow were always willing
to predict conflict between the two at some future date, but
these were drawing-room speculations. It was a great deal
more exciting to roam as far afield as possible both inside the
Soviet Union and China in the hope of picking up more
tangible clues. I remember, for example, flying in a Russian
air liner along the Crimean coast and snatching a glimpse of a
large and sinister guided-missile launching ramp. With me
was a young Chinese scientist who craned forward eagerly as
the steel girders and deep storage pits came into view. The
Russian air hostess hastily moved him to a seat on the other
side of the plane in what could be hardly described as an act
of trust in her Oriental ally.

On another occasion, the political leader of a non-Communist state relayed to me the word of Mao Tse-tung during a long and private conversation. "We do not fear H-Bombs," declared Mao. "Let the Big Powers wipe each other out. China will survive."

This bold utterance was in character with most of what was said about Mao. He was opposed to Russian bellicosity and prepared to stand back if his partner's belligerence met with fatal results. The whole concept of a frontal attack on a potentially superior enemy was alien to Chinese thought and tradition. Mao regarded the Party as a gigantic, low-pressure tire which would yield to any sharp resistance, flattening itself out and rolling over the obstacles just the same.

Whether the Russians appreciated this view or not, there were many like Shepilov anxious to reassure Mao of their admiration. Stalin had almost broken the Sino-Russian alliance by his attempts to ridicule the Chinese Communist Party and later to restrict its power. When he died, Mao launched a veiled attack on the dictator with an exposition on the theme of "collective leadership" which it took the Kremlin almost a year to swallow and finally publicly to endorse as a Russian-made idea.*

Russian leaders began to adopt Mao's policy of gentle persuasion in Asia when they realized just how effectively Red China's military adventures had won widespread respect. Marshal Bulganin and the Soviet Party Secretary, Nikita Khrushchev, essayed a tour of India and nearby states; it became apparent that they were clumsier performers than the Chinese.

Their efforts followed the Bandung Conference of twenty-

---

* A resolution proposed by the Central Committee of the Chinese Communist Party said personal dictatorship must be fought as well as "conceit, self-complacency and tendency toward worship of individuals." This followed the purge of Kao Kang, former chairman of the State Planning Commission, once head of Manchurian affairs and ex-Politburo member. Kao was suspected of selling Manchuria out to the Russians. Thus the principle of "collective leadership" was affirmed over the body of a Stalinist recruited within the Chinese Politburo . . . and almost one year before de-Stalinization had everyone in Russia singing the praises of nonpersonal dictators.

nine Asian and African nations in Indonesia. There I saw
Premier Chou En-lai score heavily in favor of Red China at
the very outset when he flew into the volcanic plateau in April
1955, a few days after his Chinese colleagues were killed in
the sabotage of the Indian air liner *Kashmir Princess*. Horrified delegates quickly assumed the plane had been destroyed
by "American agents" and this stimulated the general atmosphere of anti-Western feeling.

Chou En-lai was too shrewd a campaigner to try any histri-
onics. He got off his own plane, his handsome face dark with
what appeared to be suppressed anger. One week earlier, he
had warned the British charge d'affaires in Peking that he had
information that secret agents were ominously active while the
Kashmir Princess was waiting at Kai-Tak airfield in Hong Kong
to fly Chinese delegates to the Bandung meetings. This warning
was relayed to British security officials in Hong Kong, who
failed to take it seriously enough to ground the aircraft. It
blew up several hours after take-off and all passengers were
killed.

This incident had put the Indian delegation and their newspaper companions into a receptive mood. As Chou allowed
himself to be corralled in a corner of the airport building, the
Indians pressed forward eagerly. Chou flashed a scornful eye
over the handful of white reporters present and said: "Attempts are being made to sabotage this conference. My country has already suffered a grievous blow. But nothing can
prevent . . ."

His words were lost in a low rumble of approval. He smiled,
made a joke or two and was gone. Later he faced the delegates. "Yes," he said. "We are Communists. We do not deny
it . . ."

Like the old Chinese sport of "the Great Circle" in which
you use your opponent's own strength to throw him off balance, so Chou utilized attacks against his regime to discredit
the West. He became the martyr, the injured party, as he skillfully reminded his listeners that the West had kept Communist China out of the United Nations. "But we exist," he said
softly. "Nothing can alter that fact."

By the end of the conference, Chou had established his government in many minds as strong, anti-colonialist and willing to champion the cause of oppressed peoples everywhere. The climax came on the last night.

Under the concealed lights of the Savoy Homann Hotel, the Russian ambassador gave Chou a fleeting smile and then moved back into the shadows. The crowd was thickest around the Chinese Premier, whose unshaven face was dark with fatigue. The leaders of all twenty-nine nations had just condemned colonialism in the single voice that signified one and a half billion colored people on the march. A few delegates had tried to make it a march against Russian Communist imperialism too, but you had to be wildly optimistic to suppose they had succeeded.

Chou's face lit up. The tall handsome man thrusting across the ballroom was Colonel Nasser of Egypt. His aides whispered to me later that although he suspected the Russians, he admired the Chinese.

Behind came Krishna Menon of India, prehensile fingers wrapped around a cane, his great sad eyes liquid with emotion. Nehru stood by the door, withdrawn and haughty, a little hurt by his lack of popularity. Outside, in festive streets lit by a tropical sunset, children offered 300 rupiahs ($19.60) for Chou's autograph and only half as much for Nehru's.

In the world of colored people, Chou represented success. Sir John Kotelawala of Ceylon had drawn attention to a renaissance of Russian and Chinese colonialism, but the whispers went round that he was a colonialist lackey. So he stood back with Pakistan's Premier, Mohammed Ali, both of them reluctant but self-confessed admirers of the Chinese performance. Nearby the burnoused figure of Saudi Arabia's Prince Faisal bumped against plump little Norodom Sihanouk, the on-again-off-again ruler of Cambodia.

In that aviary of rare tropical birds there flapped twin crows of hate. Archbishop Makarios of Cyprus admitted that Cyprus was neither in Asia nor in Africa. "But this is a conference against colonialism," he said. "I'm here to talk about Cyprus under British bondage." He waggled his square black beard and waddled off for a glass of lemon juice.

The Grand Mufti of Jerusalem, Amin El Hussein, patted his

tall white hat with its scarlet crown, gave me a fierce stare and said: "Give Kenya back to the Mau-Mau." This dignified old man, Hitler's guest in World War II and supporter of Nazi plans to exterminate all Jews, now lived on an Egyptian subsidy. What was he doing here, far from Cairo? "Britain," he said, "has started an annihilation campaign by expelling Kenya tribes from their homeland. I am here to protest."

They were all there, leaders of movements against the wicked West, chiefs of states that were recently colonies, dominating the few troubled Turks and fervent Philippinos trying vainly to break this new partnership between the anti-colonialists and Communists. Once again you were reminded of that other famous alliance between the Walrus and the Carpenter: for the Chinese had effectively salvaged Communist prestige just when the Russians were losing it.

> "The time has come," the Walrus said,
> "To talk of many things:
> Of shoes — and ships — and sealing wax —
> Of cabbages — and kings —
> And why the sea is boiling hot —
> And whether pigs have wings."

By the end of that year a vaudeville act from Moscow had hit the Asian stage. Some who followed them around India and Afghanistan called them "The Marx Brothers." But although Nikolai Bulganin and Nikita Khrushchev had a brand new, colorful line of patter, they were very far from comic.

"Tigers eat meat, buffaloes eat grass," growled Nikita. "You cannot make buffaloes eat meat and tigers eat grass. Nor do we want you to change your way for ours."

This was the folksy language of Mao Tse-tung and it went down well among India's peasants. "Come," said the Soviet Communist Party Secretary, taking the sickle from a peasant working in a Bengal rice paddy, "let us always work together like a good team of oxen."

Khrushchev never minced words. I watched him convert a fashionable Bombay audience one evening on the race course. Sitting at our table were richly dressed wives of businessmen, diamonds flashing under the stars, saris slipped bewitchingly from dusky shoulders. The accents were clean, clipped British accents; the jokes and banter of a sort you might hear in the pubs around Threadneedle Street. Then Khrushchev stood swaying under floodlights and told us: "When the first proletarian state was born, it was not greeted with the ringing of church bells."

Russia and India, he proclaimed, had together faced the same colonialist enemies. Britain had interfered in the Bolshevik Revolution, said the Party Secretary, lifting his fists. The Hitlerite war had been a plot by Russia's enemies, led by Britain, to turn the Nazis into a machine of destruction against the Soviet Union. "We learned the hard way and we got bruised," he said. "Profit by our experience for we don't want you to get bruised in the same way."

There was a thunder of applause led by my table companions who so recently behaved like recruits to an English drawing room. These wealthy men and women, raised in British schools, lovers of English literature, cheered loudest when Khrushchev described for them the imagined miseries caused by British "oppression." At first, following these two formidable performers around the great subcontinent, I thought they had misjudged their audiences. It was easy to sneer at their sallies but suddenly the act became familiar and you remembered Mao Tse-tung and his simple approach to simple people. Stalin had never really learned Mao's lesson but his successors were trying hard.

Early next morning I was tempted out of bed by a gathering rumble of childish voices. The streets around the Brabourne Cricket Stadium were flooded with perspiring Indian youngsters, their large, melting eyes darkened by mascara smeared upon the lids. About one hundred thousand of them were crammed into, around and even under the stadium. By 8 A.M. I was lost in their ranks, although few reached above my waist. They were woefully thin and their little voices chirped in dismay at the rising pressure of bodies around them. Every child seemed confused and unhappy. When the barriers broke, spilling toddlers into lower sections, I became a prisoner of each wave of semi-hysterical motion. Every school in Bombay, and many from several miles around the city, had dispatched these children to greet Bulganin and Khrushchev.

Why? I kept asking myself. The only answer came from a school principal conducting a juvenile brass band in the middle of the field. He turned his sweating face, still waving his baton, and said: "The Russians gave Mr. Nehru an even bigger reception in Moscow. We cannot do less." He was echoing, unconsciously, the words of Nehru's daughter, Indira.

Khrushchev appeared clutching white doves, flashing his gold teeth at a procession of small flower bearers but making no apology for keeping his multitude waiting nearly an hour in the baking sun. The brass band never missed a beat, never altered a note. I asked its conductor what they were playing. He was an elderly man with one of those open, friendly Indian faces you find among the B.A.s, Oxon (failed). He waved across to a woman holding aloft a device consisting of crossed Indian and Russian flags. "What is this called, my dear?" he shouted, still beating time.

She shouted back. He turned to me, eager to help a foreigner: "It's 'Good night, Irene,'" he said.

The Indian subcontinent was by this time under diplomatic assault from both Peking and Moscow. The vast Indian nation of four hundred million people was straining to break the fetters of poverty and industrial backwardness. Its problems were almost identical to those of China.

To the northeast, the Chinese were already approaching the Himalayan crest. At the northwest gate, Russia was wooing the King of Afghanistan, Mohammed Zahir Shah, who was carried away by the festivities sufficiently to proclaim "historic bonds of friendship" between his rugged mountain monarchy and the Soviet Union.

The difference between the Russian and Chinese courtship of India itself was fascinating. Time and again I stood and shared the embarrassment of Indian engineers as Khrushchev told them in the bluntest language just how badly outdated they were. "Come to Russia," he kept insisting. "See for yourself how we do these things the modern way."

But the Chinese were humble and attentive. "Please show us," they would murmur politely. "We are so far behind you in all industrial matters. Please tell us where we go wrong and permit us to study your advanced methods."

Khrushchev boasted about his new H-Bombs while Chou En-lai folded his hands and said: "China is poor and backward."

And yet there persisted in my memory the words of Mao Tse-tung as he told his biographers: "As a young man I felt depressed about the future of my country after I read of Japan's occupation of Korea and Formosa, of the loss of suzerainty in Indochina, Burma and elsewhere." These were areas he regarded as rightfully Chinese. Presumably he did still.

3

Back Through the Looking-Glass

◉ ◉

A nation is an association of reasonable beings united in a peaceful sharing of the things they cherish; therefore, to determine
the quality of a nation, you must consider what those things are.

ST. AUGUSTINE: *The City of God*, XIX, xxiv

CHAPTER TWENTY-TWO

The Year of Truth

⊙ ⊙

In 1956 small numbers of workers and students in certain places went on strike. The immediate cause was failure to satisfy certain of their demands of which some should and could be met while others were out of place or excessive. But a more important cause was bureaucracy . . . A small number of agricultural co-operatives created disturbances and the main causes were also bureaucracy and inadequate ideological education.

> MAO TSE-TUNG, LAUNCHING HIS 1957 CAMPAIGN TO
> "REMOLD" CHINA'S BRAINS

WHEN YOU CROSS the great divide between East and West you step through Alice's Looking-Glass which transformed left into right. In modern Chinese jargon it often happens that Peace does mean War, Freedom *is* Slavery, Liberation spells Invasion.

By the year 1956, however, it was difficult to label all Russian or Chinese actions as "wicked." Nor could you always reverse Communist statements to arrive at the truth. For one thing the peaceful revolution sweeping through India achieved results which impressed the Chinese. They were impressed because they saw India gaining prestige, building up socialism and advancing her development plans with Western aid (and even the Chinese Communists were by this time bound to admit that Western technical assistance was greater, more mod-

ern and flexible, and dispensed more freely than anything the
Russians had so far offered). The Chinese were also learning
for the first time that Gandhi's methods of passive resistance
could be made to work against a softhearted enemy.

As for the Russians, their rulers conducted bold experiments
to "liberalize" the regime they inherited from Stalin.

I returned to China through the Soviet Union, looking for
contrasts. Russians living close to Western Europe were obviously anxious to broaden their horizons. But in the interior
many said they would like to see Stalin come back: they were
the petty officials who required some form of Oriental despotism to buttress their feeble powers.

The mood among European Russians was demonstrated by
an odd incident in Kiev, the capital of the Ukraine, where
technical progress has been dramatized most. I wanted to interview the President of the Academy of Sciences. The local
press officials made excuses: he was busy, he had a cocktail
party, he was entertaining a Danish atomic scientist. With
Welles Hangen, then of the *New York Times,* I found the
Dane. We used him as a protector to get into the Academy
and we asked him to help obtain the interview.

As a result we were told about Sputnik I a year before it was
launched. When the Kiev press officers discovered our stratagem they were highly indignant. But so far as we could see
the Russian scientists had been only too eager to talk to visiting Westerners about their achievements, though not in order
to boast. They were enthusiasts and had little time for political considerations.

New winds of reason were blowing, particularly among
writers. It had all started about the time of Khrushchev's
famous speech in February exposing Stalin's crimes. The result was, for literature, the "Year of Truth."

Writers were preoccupied with the threat of becoming robots. There was a short story by Alexander Yashin which described a group of individuals who, subjected to Communist
indoctrination, became mere levers in the State machine. There
was a poem by Semyon Kirsanov about a mechanical heart
which made a human being "uncomplicated, convenient, always ready to take orders." The most famous work was

Vladimir Dudintsev's *Not by Bread Alone* which attracted
the widest attention by protesting against the Soviet system
in frankest terms.

A flood of writings by Soviet writers against the iniquities of
the regime ended later with a recantation of their "errors" by
two of the most fiery rebels, Emanual Kazakevich and Mar-
garita Aliger. But this was not to take place for several months
and meanwhile, the relaxed attitude of the Kremlin led to the
first public wave of revolt against dictatorship in many years.

The Chinese had launched a "free speech" movement too
but with the expressed aim of correcting the wrong thoughts
of intellectuals. While their Russian comrades sharply exposed some of the darker side of Soviet life, the Chinese merely
fired off some deft criticisms and remained firmly bonded to
Mao Tse-tung. In Moscow, readers were excited to find at last
an honest portrayal of their hardships and poverty in Anna
Valtseva's story *Apartment No. 13*.

In Peking, however, literature took this familiar form:

> Chairman Mao Crosses the Yangtse River [declared the Pe-
> king *Chung Kuo Ching Nien Pao*]. Winds were strong in May
> (1956) on the Yangtse . . .
>
> A plump comrade asked: "Comrades, do you know who is go-
> ing to swim the Yangtse with us? Well, it is Chairman Mao, our
> respected and beloved leader." All jumped for joy. Their exulta-
> tion was beyond description. Chairman Mao, being at an ad-
> vanced age, might not find it possible to swim the dangerous wa-
> ters and they wished to help the Chairman make the crossing . . .
>
> Several automobiles arrived. Out of one stepped a stalwart
> giant. All shouted: "Here comes Chairman Mao."
>
> Chairman Mao looked round smilingly and then dipped into
> the river. His companions were Wang, Wu and Yu. Behind in
> an escort boat was Li who so envied the other comrades that he
> finally jumped in.
>
> He found Chairman Mao serenely lying on the water taking
> a rest. With a few gentle strokes, the Chairman glided with ease.
> Li tried to do the same but he began to sink like a piece of heavy
> rock. When he came up again, he found the Chairman still smil-
> ing serenely as he floated on his back, examining each bank of
> the river.
>
> All were impressed by the Chairman's health and courage.

After swimming one hour, Chairman Mao looked at his watch and said: "We have not reached Hankow yet!" Later the comrades all agreed the Chairman's determined will was really touching. He would not give up until he reached his goal!

The goal had been over twelve miles away and according to this account it took Mao a record two hours to get there.

By contrast, it appeared that Russia's new leaders were yielding to the pressure exerted by intellectuals and the growing columns of technicians: that at long last the oldest and most powerful Communist state in the world recognized the truth of the assertion made by Adam Wazyk, whose poem on the degradation of youth had just been published in Red Poland: "When students are enclosed in textbooks without windows, when the lamp of imagination is extinguished, then truly oblivion is dangerously near."

In China by comparison there was a much more cynical approach. Chinese Communist observers inside Poland and Hungary had reported on the ferment among scholars and students. They openly warned Mao Tse-tung that in the Soviet Union itself there were fifty million young people whose intellectual revolt could smash the system, unless properly handled by the provision of officials and controllable safety valves.

These safety valves were more common in China where the language itself was better adapted for the exercise of mental dictatorship. Writers were encouraged to express practical criticisms and at the same time to inject into their work certain fundamental ideas that conformed with Party policy.

To appreciate this, some features of the Chinese written word need to be understood. The use of a picture language leads to a combination of ideas wrapped up, sometimes, in a single ideograph. A complete political thought can be reduced to a simple sign. In Russia (as, for that matter, in the West) there are slogans and phrases which plant attitudes of mind into the unwary reader's head. The Chinese were able to go a step further because, to quote the Western sinologue, Bushell:

The picturesque nature of Chinese writing . . . demands of

those who wish to excel in its practice an education of hand and eye such as are required by draughtsmen. The strokes of the ordinary character are replete indeed with light and supple touches, sudden stops and graceful curves, waxing energies and gradually waning lines such as only long apprenticeship of the brush could give. The Chinese *lettré* is firmly convinced that the characters of a perfect writer convey something of their graphic beauty to the ideas they express, and give a delicate intrinsic shade of meaning to every thought enshrined in them.

The thought enshrined in the simplified characters adopted by Mao's regime was usually highly political. For a time, it was hoped an alphabet based on either Cyrillic or Latin characters might be employed, but this would have destroyed the ready-made apparatus of language which Mao was already putting to good use. He had experts condense thousands of ancient ideographs and he was able to get remarkable results in teaching soldiers the basic combination characters that were evolved.

But being a pragmatic Chinese, Mao tossed this early system overboard when he found it froze the minds of military scholars into a state of utter rigidity. He had wanted a system that would make it possible for thousands of peasants to learn quickly and easily to read and write. Now when he got such a system, he discovered that while it gave him access to the minds of his followers and enabled him to plant his theories there, it also prevented these controlled minds from displaying any initiative at all.

A young soldier could read certain orders and he could write them for the consumption of others, because he had learned by heart the ideographs involved. But — and this was officially admitted — he was incapable of acting on instructions or of passing along any directives that did not exactly conform to the simplified characters taught to him.

This raised a crucial question. When Mao's spokesmen talked frankly about "brain-washing" did they understand the *practical* consequences of building a robot nation? In Russia there was an outcry against the development of human robots on purely intellectual grounds. But the Chinese, anxious to achieve industrial equality with other powers, could see certain practical obstacles created by mechanical thinking.

Yet the Chinese were also aware of the consequences of allowing too much intellectual freedom. They wanted to create a nation whose citizens were all agreed upon philosophical matters but who could individually contribute ideas of technical value. Mao saw the need not to *extinguish the lamp of imagination,* but he also wanted to create his collective mind with its millions of human brains working in harmony.

Mao defended his method: "Ever since 1927, we have used it," he reminded Russian observers thirty years later. "I made an initial remolding of my ideas from books but it was mainly through taking part in class struggle that I came to be remolded. And I must continue to study if I am to make further progress. Can capitalists be so clever as not to need more remolding?"

What was Mao driving at? Well, he had to face the unpleasant truth by 1956 that his methods of indoctrination worked only too well, so that China had become virtually as stagnant as it was when Confucianism instead of Communism ruled the minds of the educated elite. He was defending those methods and also seeking some means of galvanizing the minds of his limited number of scholars and literate officials. For it was in this year that his economic planners faced up to reality and made drastic reductions in their industrial objectives. Once again, the Chinese Communists may have felt themselves to be alone responsible for their own salvation just as in the days of the Yenan caves.

They were particularly worried about the growth of bureaucracy. They saw how in Russia an entirely new ruling class of managers had arisen. This managerial class enjoyed privileges denied to everyone else. The Chinese strongly disapproved of this and their leaders were anxious to prevent such a phenomenon developing in their own country. China had already suffered too much from a ruling class versed in the authorized literature of the time but professionally incompetent.

This difference of attitude toward bureaucrats was most evident in the Crimean holiday resorts to which I went before returning to China. Here the Russian civil servant lived royally. Here I encountered more of the many Chinese to be found roaming East Europe and Russia. Some were going home from a scientific conference when we discussed the problem of bureaucrats in the seaside town of Yalta. It was a day in late September 1956, when the air had a tang to it, and the sunshine danced on vivid green vineyards and gave a pinkish tinge to the snow-capped mountains rising almost as aloof and remote as the somber bronze statue of Stalin glowering across the town square.

CHAPTER TWENTY-THREE

Seals and Fakirs on a Russian Beach

◉　◉

Two elderly and gentle Chinese astronomers from the Purple Mountain Observatory in Nanking were with me on this fine autumn day. I fastened on them unashamedly after that prolonged and solitary journey through the Ukraine. They were friendly and never got drunk; they were infallibly courteous; they spoke good English and discussed news of the outside world with grave curiosity. All these virtues were the more valued for being somewhat rare in my present environment.

We were discussing the evils of bureaucracy. Both were returning to China from a gathering of Communist astronomers. I rather hoped that star-gazing, far from encouraging belief in dreams, might make them more realistic observers of their life on a semi-Marxist earth. I said none of the Communist prophets had foreseen the emergence of a new ruling class, the expanding civil service.

"Chairman Mao foresaw the problem," said one astronomer, Comrade Fung.

"He has fought valiantly to solve it," added Comrade Tang.

They folded their hands while I said this was encouraging news. But how did the Chairman propose to abolish the privilege and power of bureaucrats when their numbers increased and their power grew with the expansion of State ownership? Was it not true that Marx and Lenin both overlooked the fact that bureaucrats always had ruled China?

"No," said Comrade Fung. "The People are strong. The People rule."

"Yes," agreed Comrade Tang. "Bureaucrats are servants of The People."

We gazed thoughtfully at the speedboats skating across the harbor. On the gray, wet beach, young Russians stretched on the sharp pebbles as patient as fakirs, while their elders turned fat white bellies toward the sky like blubbery Arctic seals awaiting winter. The girls wore bikinis. Their mammas favored the more conservative blue bloomers of Tsarist days. There were no ice creams or lollipops, but nevertheless I thought of the luckless women in the pounding steel mills nearby, working into late pregnancy, and sometimes giving birth to deformed children. There seemed to be more cripples in that area than anywhere else on earth, although when you asked about this there was always one bland Russian official who would talk vaguely about Nazi atrocities and the harshness of war. But if you stole more glances at the deformed children, not wanting to stare, you found it hard to believe that even the Huns could stunt the growth of an arm on a ten-year-old child in a war that was now twelve years gone.

And I said to my Chinese friends from Purple Mountain: "These are bureaucrats," gesturing toward the beach. "You won't find a manual laborer among them . . ."

Jazz blared from Yalta's only radio shop, drowning my voice. Through the leisured promenade crowds twisted the small, alert figure of Harry Goldie, self-styled "Russia's Only Real Jazz Crooner." With him was a blond interpreter from Moscow and a movie actress in an old raincoat and whose hair was in tatters. We had previously met aboard a Soviet luxury liner, the *Lensoviet*, crossing the Black Sea and I had asked the actress why she was going to Yalta. "For my health," she replied.

Goldie's answer was similar. "Resting," he said. "You don't know what it means to be a jazz king in Russia. Work all day, work all night and never time to play." He gave me a hard look. "Now don't get me wrong," he added. "I never was born in Brooklyn like some people say. Why I'd be a gone

gosling if my wife here thought I wasn't just one hundred
per cent Russian."

Aboard that ship I tasted some of the crumbs of comfort
that come from living as a bureaucrat in Russia. "Make room
for our foreign visitors," boomed the dowdy headwaitress in
the crammed dining saloon, shoving me ahead of the mealtime
line-ups. All passengers had similar priorities, classified in
the same way, I supposed, as myself. My travel coupons were
marked *de luxe,* but they could have been *superior,* or one of
three inferior classes, depending in the worst capitalist way
upon how much money I had to spend. The equivalent *de luxe*
Russian usually turned out to be within the court circle of
pampered poets, artists and other intellectuals.

In Yalta later I said to Mr. Fung, or it may have been Mr.
Tang, that Russia's ten million or so bureaucrats might be
reckoned a new class of exploiters. But their attention was
fixed on an open Zis parked near a restaurant.

A face appeared in the doorway opposite. It was the familiar
calm face of Ivan Serov. British papers had nicknamed him
"Ivan the Terrible" only a few months previously, hounding
him out of London while Bulganin and Khrushchev were already on their way to take tea with the Queen in Windsor
Castle. It was said that Serov had been expert in liquidating
large non-Russian communities. I had stood beside him frequently enough in the year just gone: with his Soviet leaders in
India, Afghanistan and Britain. He hardly seemed to fit the
character of a Soviet secret-police chief.

Serov glanced slowly round. The Yalta crowd thickened.
They were strangely quiet. The Security Chief, eyes shaded by
a broad-brimmed fedora, swiveled his head and gave a sharp
nod. There was a pause and then a clattering down dark
wooden stairs before Khrushchev appeared, a lewd grin on his
round face. Beside him ambled the corseted plump figure of
Tito, head back and chin out, a patronizing smile beneath the
cold hard eyes he cast down on Khrushchev's gesticulations.

That scene remained clear in my mind for long afterwards.
We did not know it then, but Tito was in conference with Russian leaders because a crisis had erupted in Eastern Europe.

Already Poland's anger with Russian domination had spilled over, and in Hungary the October Revolution of the anti-Bolsheviks was already brewing.

Tito stood there amid unexpected applause. Khrushchev clowned. Serov's pale blue eyes swept the waterfront. Down on the beach, the seals and the fakirs lay oblivious with their copies of *Pravda* folded into triangular hats and the stubs from their vacation coupons clipped to their noses to save them from sun blisters.

Poor seals and fakirs, poor little bureaucrats who never knew that they would soon become the targets of scorn, the objects of heresies uttered by the rulers of my two Chinese astronomers tracing patterns in the sand with their black Shanghai "Kwik-Open" umbrellas.

I met the movie star on the plane to Moscow. Why was she going home? "I have a dreadful cold," said she.

"But you said Yalta was the place for good health."

"Ah — well, only Mamma can cure my colds, with hot milk and honey," she said with a sigh of great resignation.

In Moscow the first faint ripples were felt from the Eighth Congress of the Chinese Communist Party. I knew a cameraman in the Soviet film unit and he sounded enthusiastic about China: "More Party members there than anywhere else in the world."

I reminded him of some advice given to her emissaries by the last Empress Dowager of China, Old Buddha: "In converting the barbarian, be careful not to be converted yourself."

He winced, then unfolded *Pravda*. Its columns were devoted almost entirely to a report from the Chinese Eighth Party Congress, thousands of miles away in Peking. "You see," I said. "They're converting *you* already."

It seemed a sensible plan to return to China. The growth of the Chinese Communist Party was erratic and this Eighth Congress had about it an air of singular importance. It was twelve years since the previous congress and the six before that were held in the 'twenties. Chinese leaders had held power and concealed their differences, while following a devia-

tionist policy that dated back to the meeting in 1935 when Mao
Tse-tung apparently took command.

The Russian airliner that took me back jogged across Siberia
like a country bus. Our tousled pilot flew in and out of muddy
airfields with glamorous names: Sverdlovsk and Omsk, Nov-
ossibirsk and Kanoyask. At each stop, stout waitresses in frilly
caps and rumpled aprons served dull but ample meals. The
hotels were heavily Victorian with brass-knobbed bedsteads and
velvet curtains. White busts of Stalin lurked in the bushes
wherever we reboarded the plane.

At Irkutsk on the border we climbed out of our tired old
Ilyushin and entered a spanking-new one. A smart Chinese
steward handed out chewing gum, scented paper fans and
route maps. The crisply uniformed Chinese pilot moved back
among the passengers from time to time, reporting our progress. Some hours later we were over Ulan Bator, the capital of
Outer Mongolia. It looked no more romantic than a Canadian
mining camp.

Next to me sat an aromatic young man from Tibet. He pulled
a wooden bowl from his robes which, overhanging the tight
waist sash, fell into huge pockets. One arm was bared and
around his partly exposed chest was a picture of Lord Buddha
enshrined in a silver amulet. A pouch for flint and tinder rested
in his lap. A long-stemmed pipe with a tiny metal bowl was
thrust into one of his red and blue boots, reeking of rancid
yak butter.

His brown Homburg had fallen into the aisle. You could
read the name of a famous London hatter in the crown. He rejected the proffered chewing gum, preferring *tsamba* which he
kneaded in his bowl from a paste of barley meal mixed with
tea and rancid butter. When he passed the bowl across, I took
it willingly. *Tsamba* is the staple diet of Tibetans who farm
twelve thousand feet above sea level and my ears were popping
with the changing altitude. Chinese gum has a rubbery flavor
and anyway, if you had to unblock your ears the ancient
Tibetan technique provided nutrition as well as exercise for
the jaws.

We left Ulan Bator behind and our shadow raced across the

blinding snow, interrupted at long intervals by forlorn camps of Mongolian tents that looked like black spiders spreadeagled on a white counterpane. Patches of earth appeared, then yellow hills and at last there was no snow but only an expanse of sand. We were crossing the melancholy Gobi.

My Tibetan companion nodded and pointed excitedly. A funnel of wind whirled across the sad, flat desert and sucked into its vortex millions of grains of sand. A diminutive caravan vanished under the twisting cloud.

"In a great land of grass without memory, the boundless unreckoned year, squared out with dawns and fires . . ." The haunting words from T. S. Eliot's translation of the *Anabase* of St-John Perse came back to me. ". . . O traveller in a yellow wind."

We were losing height with great dignity, the wing flaps trembling and the earth sliding below more rapidly. A russet snake, scaly with weather-worn stones, wriggled from under the trailing edge of one wing. The Great Wall of China made its entry with watch towers on the hilltops and crumbling arches in the valleys. Was the Pyramid of Cheops still a Pharaoh's dream when this incredible defense work rose to link the deserts of Inner Asia to the Gulf of Chihli? Where was the Colosseum of Rome when the Chinese scratched this line along their northern marches? Genghis Khan and the Mongol Golden Horde conquered Russia fourteen hundred years after it was built. Mohammed, a Prophet of God, had not yet spoken and Nebuchadnezzar had still the Temple in Jerusalem to destroy.

Somewhere down there Confucius, the First Holy One, had himself looked back two thousand years, even as I now looked back two thousand years at Confucius. He had seen at the far end of that long corridor of time the Golden Age of China, when the legendary Yellow Emperor ruled a happy and contented kingdom.

Confucius preached that China might recover that halcyon age if individuals who composed the state were cultivated personalities. But he died in a time of harsh realisms and the Great Wall was a monument to those who denied his teachings.

Its constructors were expedient and ruthless men who argued that one state might conquer the world and thus bring peace by superior discipline. They ordered the burning of books in fear that cultivation of the individual might bring disorder and weakness.

As we slipped into Peking airport, I wondered what it was the new rulers of China really hoped to achieve. They were different men from Bulganin and Khrushchev. They were old comrades, veterans of harsh adventures and determined champions of the peasant. Many resentful Russians had said to me that in the Kremlin were leaders who were simply enjoying the fruits of Stalin's labor. No such charge could be made against Mao Tse-tung and his seemingly changeless circle of aides. Among them were sensitive and sensible men. Did their thoughts go back to the Yellow Emperor of antiquity, and his faith that tolerance and liberal thought must always produce happier and more prosperous societies? Or did their minds dwell on magnificent but useless achievements like the Great Wall, erected by slave labor to prove China was the greatest power on earth?

Martial music blared from a corner of the aircraft park. Banners flapped lazily and voices sang the new national anthem of China:

Arise, you who refuse to be slaves,
Our very flesh and blood will build a new Great Wall.

But perhaps the real answer was in the smiling welcome of the Chinese astronomers I had first met in distant Yalta.

"It's warmer here," they said. I shivered. There was snow in the shadow of the drab hangars and the temperature was falling.

CHAPTER TWENTY-FOUR

More Than the Grave to Cure a Hunchback

◉ ◉

FEVER AND FRET spread like a plague through the colleges and universities of China. Uprisings in Hungary had been crushed by Soviet Russia. All the hate and anger for Russia which had survived seven years' barrage of propaganda now surged again. If it was only a handful of Chinese who betrayed their emotions, they belonged nevertheless to the vital group upon whom grandiose plans for national industrialization would either soar or crash.

In a crucial week of November 1956 it was exciting and enlightening to be in Peking. Night after night, East Europeans listened secretly to broadcasts from London. About one hundred Hungarians were visibly in distress. Other delegates from "friendly and fraternal countries" made clandestine contact with nonfriendly embassies in the hope of finding some other exit from China than the road to Siberia.

Then, by a curious coincidence as we shall see later, an incident took place at memorial services to Dr. Sun Yat-sen whose erratic and oversimplified interpretations of modern Western society gave energy to the Chinese revolution, and provided a shaky bridge between old Imperial China and the Red China of today.

Present were some of the hundred thousand "intellectuals" (writers, technicians, professors and doctors) composing the entire force of practical and creative men able to carry out ambitious plans handed down by a Politburo ruling the world's most populous nation. They were asked to approve two resotions. One condemned Anglo-French action in the Suez Canal and this was applauded. The second resolution was submitted three times and each time it was received in dead silence. It supported Russian action in Hungary.

News of this rare demonstration spread like wildfire through the ancient capital. Already many students and professors were getting news of the last agonies of the Hungarian rebels by listening to London on short-wave radio, just like their European comrades who crouched in the bulky Hsin Chiao Hotel near the Temple of Eighteen Hells.

The tragedy in distant Budapest was having an even greater impact than most of us then in Peking could possibly know. Premier Chou En-lai was overheard at Nanyuan airport telling a Russian colleague: "The high walls of Peking are likely to separate the leadership from the masses . . . If we don't change *our* bureaucratic ways, some day the peasants will break through the walls."

Hungary was the last piece of evidence needed by Mao Tsetung to prove certain Chinese interpretations of Marxist-Leninism were correct. He took literally the warnings that a Communist Party must not build walls between itself and the public. He also repaired an oversight in the Marxist analysis of Asian problems by renewing his attack against a ruling bureaucracy.

But for the time there was official silence. It had been a typical week when the capital was treated to an average amount of political panache and few concrete developments. The new municipal airport was ready for trial landings by a Russian jet airliner said to bring London within Peking's reach in a single span of daylight. Workmen were tearing down some of the central *hu'tungs*, crooked and high-walled lanes that were old when Kublai Khan moved his imperial seat here. Where Prince Kao Hsü was roasted to death in the Iron Pagoda, there now rose the skeleton of a radio-tube factory. Little else of a practical nature seemed in progress unless you counted the soaring dormitory blocks that marched west from the old Execution

Grounds, block by dreary block, as if the builders had run out of control.

In this same week a delegation of Japanese swelled to five thousand the number of foreigners living on Chinese bounty. The British Embassy was plastered in posters and slogans of protest against armed intervention in Suez. Egypt was ceremoniously awarded 24,170,000 Swiss francs from the Chinese Politburo acting in the sacred name of The People who probably never knew they had that much in the Swiss kitty. The mayor was in Moscow. Premier Chou En-lai prepared to tour China's former tributaries and some of the neighbors: Vietnam, Cambodia, Burma, Nepal, Afghanistan, Pakistan and India. The usual weekly exposure of spies and saboteurs had taken place, this time in Manchuria among Taoist priests. And in the Hsin Chiao Hotel where there is nowhere to pay your bills, there lived 348 official guests who never would pay their bills and one other foreigner who unfortunately would.

Near the Altar of Silkworms, within the Sea Palace walls, the taut figure of China's chief dogmatist, Liu Saho-chi, led the debate on Suez and Hungary in the Second Plenary Session of the Chinese Communist Party's Central Committee. It was to take seven months for the ideas then tempered to become known officially to the outside world, and then only through the mystic medium of Mao Tse-tung.

A sort of Chinese Doctrine was being prepared. It was presented as a 17,000-word speech by Mao in the following February and released publicly in late June after official revision. What he said should come, chronologically, at the end of this narrative. But since his policies were already being practiced and therefore arise naturally in the telling of this story, we may take a preliminary glance now at this extraordinary document.

Its effect on the West was on the whole good. Yet the speech was in fact an exposition of the Chinese way with heretics, knaves and fools. The basis of politics was production and everything must be measured against this yardstick. Heretics might be tolerated if their ideas would help increase production for The People. Knaves should be deprived of what was amusingly termed their "freedom of speech" until The People's agents had wrestled for their souls.

In fact, "Not to have a correct political point of view is like having no soul," proclaimed Mao.

As for the fools, they should be gently guided into efficient production. They should not be mistakenly executed. There were differences between the Communist Party and the public and it was necessary to analyze the causes of these differences and, where they proved to result from legitimate complaint and not from mischief-making, to correct the errors thus exposed. A man should not be regarded as a fool simply because he taught at university, misunderstood Party doctrines and preferred to devote more time to his science laboratory than to his dialectics.

All this left a good impression wherever modern communications rushed a condensed version to the breakfast tables of readers in London, Paris and New York. However, in Moscow where there is no great haste to be first with questionable news, many Russians had time to digest in detail what Mao had said. Not all liked his line.

The difference can be summarized by quoting the two men of different temperament and background who each prescribed his own medicine for Communism's enemies. One was bureaucratic king in the Kremlin and the other was battle-scarred peasant on the Dragon Throne of China.

"It is impossible to re-educate capitalists," said Nikita Khrushchev with his usual robust grim humor. "Only the grave will cure the hunchback."

This black philosophy was challenged humbly but firmly in the Oriental tradition by Mao who invoked the name of The People sanctified by the dialectic and beatified by dogma: "Use only . . . methods of criticism, discussion, persuasion and education . . . It is very harmful to use crude and summary methods to ban wrong ideas because the wrong ideas will still be there . . . Fighting wrong ideas is like being vaccinated and develops greater immunity."

Then Mao put his finger on the damning proof that Khrushchev's approach was not, to put it as courteously as possible, wise. "Certain people in our country were delighted when the Hungarian events took place," he said. "They hoped something similar would happen in China, that thousands upon thousands of people would demonstrate in the streets against The People's Government . . . These events caused some of our intellectuals to lose their balance a bit but there were no squalls . . . Why? We had succeeded in suppressing counter-revolution."

It had been possible to expose future enemies by Mao's campaign to "let one hundred flowers blossom and one hundred schools of thought contend." This introduced a licensed freedom and scholars were persuaded to reveal innermost doubts. Useful criticisms were heard and a major aim was to bring down those bureaucratic walls which kept the Party and The People apart. Mao, acting on behalf of the collective deity called The People, himself identified which flowering thoughts were beautiful and which were merely what he labeled "poisonous weeds."

Some cautious Chinese scholars found Mao rather vague on this question of identification. How would they be sure not to succor a poisonous weed? The answer was simple: weeds were harmful to The People. But who *were* The People? Well, said Mao, this collective term could change according to circumstances but in general it referred to an attitude of mind. An antagonistic thought was a weed, and its perpetrator betrayed an antagonistic attitude toward the Party which represented The People.

Round and round went this singular argument. China was a kind of democracy "such as not to be found in any capitalist country since it is democracy under centralized government."

Mao's classic speech was full of such paradoxes. It was a bold attempt to create an efficient and vast colony of worker ants whose movements were directed by a collective intelligence. Terror had reduced the country to a malleable condition of mental exhaustion and it was now time to inject kindly and happy, collectivized thoughts which would release a mass of productive energy, none of which would be wasted in antagonistic criticisms of the regime.

Mao pointed out that there was nothing new in his argument. He affirmed the correctness of Chinese policy as long ago as 1942 when Stalin regarded him as a hopeless upstart.

Once again, as in Sun's day, the Chinese revealed their quest for a new, expedient and successful faith to replace but not entirely to discard the old Confucianism. Like Sun, their leaders mistook the nature of democracy. Like Sun, they rejected foreign ideas until they underwent a Chinese transformation.

Mao denounced any doctrinaire acceptance of unsuitable Russian methods and advised his people to "learn things which suit conditions in our country, that is, to absorb whatever experience is useful to us."

The ferment in Peking was a natural one where Hungary was concerned but was artificially stimulated on Egypt's behalf. I had been expelled from Egypt during the Suez crisis. A cable from the Canadian Broadcasting Corporation asked for comment on Chinese reaction to the Suez affair. Peking Radio agreed to transmit the broadcast. This had never been done before as a service to foreign correspondents. I wrote an ironical, critical script, pointing out that few Chinese knew where Egypt was until told by Party leaders.

> The growling, angry mob which descended on the British Embassy to desecrate its walls with slogans and posters swept up a visiting Frenchman [I reported]. They chanted "Down with the wicked French!" with their arms around the Frenchman's shoulders . . .

At the radio studios I sipped hot tea with senior Communist officials while they outlined plans for transmitting my voice to Canada. They were polite, painstaking and embarrassingly generous with time and equipment. The script began to burn large holes in my pocket. The comrades offered to broadcast a tape of my voice each morning on two wavelengths until notified by Canada that this had been successfully monitored. They asked humbly if I would object to their preceding this with a few bars from Radio Peking's station signal.

My face was red as we paraded to the control room. I had to

consider what might happen if a Chinese Communist asked to broadcast from Ottawa to Peking. I had to consider that Canada did not even recognize Peking. I had also to reflect that in Moscow it would take six months merely to discover who could authorize an antagonistic broadcast by a capitalistic reporter to a nonrecognizing imperialist stronghold.

The script being tightly screwed and slightly damp, an obliging official uncreased it for me. Five courteous Chinese made me comfortable at the microphone, brought water, demonstrated control-room signals, and then stepped politely back. Their earnest and attentive faces formed a smiling semicircle and I felt like a wolf in missionary clothing about to snarl obscenities to some unsuspecting ladies' Christian Half Hour.

I cleared my throat, gathered up my shredded resolve and croaked through my notes. The smiles were a little fixed when I finished and the senior official said, "Thank you for your criticisms," and then glanced significantly at each of his assistants.

Thus bloomed another flower in Mao's floral dance. The effect of my words in Canada was of no consequence to the Chinese. They were discussed, however, among those Chinese exposed to contamination. My alien views were welcomed as a further test of faith and it was agreed that I had given birth, as a matter of objective fact, not to a blooming flower but to a miserable specimen of stinkwort.

The Chinese are a naturally courteous people and seldom if ever say No. This we were taught at school, although later the illusion was shattered when you struggled to squeeze into an elevator behind twenty jabbing Oriental elbows. But in the matter of denying requests, the present Chinese Foreign Office in Peking is to be admired for its dexterous avoidance of negatives. My long list of projected trips and interviews was whittled down — but only by my own wish. It usually happened like this:

Me: "I should like to go to Tibet."
Official: "Ah, yes. And what else?"
Me: "Nothing else."
Official: "But you may have to wait for a plane to Tibet."

Me: "Okay. Here are some other things I could do in the interval."

Some days later: "What about this trip to Tibet?"

Official: "You must make out an application."

Me: "Well, why didn't you tell me I had to fill out a form . . . ?"

Official: "You never asked."

Me (*some days later*): "What about this trip to Tibet?"

Official: "Ah, yes. Now, about this request to see the new automobile factory at Changchun . . . Your air ticket is booked for Saturday."

Me: "But I don't want to go to Changchun unless it's impossible to visit Tibet . . ."

Official in strongly disapproving tones: "Ah, I see. So you do not wish to see the automobile factory although we have made arrangements and . . ."

Me: "Okay, let's go to Changchun."

On my list was a request to see Mao Tse-tung and an inquiry about agriculture. Could I drive around the countryside, preferably in some hitherto unvisited area?

"But you have already met the Chairman," I was reminded.

"Well, I'd like to again."

"There may not be time if you wish to do all these other things."

It was usually about this stage that you found it expedient to exploit the opening given in this reference to "other things." Quickly you demanded to know what these might be. And of course the Chinese, knowing you would not risk losing all facilities for the sake of this crackpot scheme to interview the Chairman, would dangle several genuinely attractive offers: a trip to Chinese Tartary, perhaps, or a tour of Inner Mongolia. Travelers in modern China sometimes pretend that there are no restrictions. "We were free as birds," they often proclaim. It seemed to me they must have referred to domesticated ducks.

However, to be perfectly fair, there were many opportunities for travel, and interviews with officials could be astonishingly frank on occasion. Expenses were something like one quarter the artificial rates in Russia: one tour that cost me about $1100 included 2000 miles of air transport, two weeks of accommodation and food, and some 1500 miles of driving by private car.

There was a lot of amusement to be derived from poking around the back alleys of Peking itself. Sometimes it took several weeks for the authorities to set up the "spontaneous" journey that one had requested. Then, to kill time, you tried again to interview Mao. Richard Hughes, a tenacious veteran of Far East reporting for the London *Sunday Times,* dashed off a fluent and persuasive telegram to the Chairman, acquainting Mao with his presence in the capital and urging an early audience.

He delivered the cable to the main post office outside the Forbidden City. The girl unfolded the message and stared disapprovingly at the word PERSONAL which preceded Dick's communication. "This word," she declared, scrubbing it out, "would cost you an extra half yuan." She glared into Dick's sanguine countenance. "Also it is unnecessary. Everything is personal that goes to Chairman Mao!"

CHAPTER TWENTY-FIVE

Peking: Past Historic and Present Indicative

◉ ◉

"OUR PUBLIC TRANSPORT has increased by many thousands per cent," intoned Director Fung Ke-jeung. "In the department of motorized traffic there are now eighty times as many vehicles as Before Liberation."

"*Eighty* times?" I made a hurried calculation.

"Eighty," confirmed Peking's chief city planner in a firm voice. He waited for the prim stenographer to complete her notes on the conversation, check his figures against her handbook and finally give him the brief and customary nod.

"You mean," I said, "there were only five vehicles when you took over?"

He looked surprised, even crestfallen. The girl grated her boots on the marble floor. "And now," said Director Fung, "let us consider the Cultural Amusements of our capital . . ."

Later my escort said: "How did you know there were only five vehicles?"

"Because the transport department gave me the hard statistic. *They* stopped handing out those ridiculous percentage increases. They said Peking now has 403 buses."

He shook his head sadly. "We must practice better mutual supervision between the departments," he said with the earnestness of youth.

His words were as mystifying as Peking itself. The ancient capital keeps its high walls and inner secrets despite Marx, the great leveler. Many have tried to suppress its irrepressible citizens. Chiang Kai-shek moved his Nationalist Government south to Nanking and renamed the old city Peiping ("Northern Peace") in a subtle attempt to introduce a name which meant, when freely translated, "flattened out": it was his way of destroying its past associations. Before him came invaders with other labels. The Kitan Tatars called it Yenking. The Golden Horde re-entitled it Chungtu. Kublai Khan moved here and while his Mongols called it Khanbalyk, the Chinese went right on referring to it as their own Tatu. By the time Marco Polo arrived with the fancy variation of Cambalue the inhabitants must have suffered a chronic bewilderment about exactly where they did live. So they adopted a frank and unassuming name: Peking, "the Northern Capital."

The gray walls of the city record these moments of history as the rings in a tree stump give away its age. There is an innermost Forbidden City. Around it is the rectangular wall of the Inner City and along its top you can take a brisk fourteen-mile walk that begins and ends above Human Hair Lane. If you look south from the Eunuch's Cemetery containing bones of the men who made palace plots, you see the Chinese Outer City and the sublime architecture of the Temple and Altar of Heaven, separated from the Temple of Agriculture by the flourishing Thieves' Market.

Chinese are alarmingly vague about the geography of their own capital. Curtained taxis driven by Korean War veterans bounce slowly down the middle of the main thoroughfares while their drivers search myopically for an address which has been in existence probably for seven centuries. There are four hundred such taxis, mostly Russian-built and reserved for foreign visitors. When two happen to get on the same highway, heading in opposite directions, it becomes a game of who will swerve aside last. Each plods steadily and inexorably down the crown of the road. No doubt this won medals in Korea, but it leaves the stranger breathless. The only signals are given by means of an illuminated arrow fixed inside the windscreen and turned manually to indicate direction. The arrow is visible only to someone dead ahead.

The vagueness of directions helps Peking retain its privacy
and mystery. The place is a rabbit warren of narrow lanes
lined by windowless walls and inward-facing houses. The passion for secrecy caused emperors in the past to have themselves buried in unexpected and unmarked areas of their gigantic tombs; and the Empress Dowager in this century even
found a means of closing and bolting the door behind her
after her body was borne into its burial place: doors to the
vault were pulled shut by the departing mourners and giant
stone balls rolled along grooves behind the closing portals,
thudding into shallow holes to lock the scheming old lady
securely in her last abode.

One of the few men ever able to make a detailed and accurate map of the labyrinthine city was Father Hyacinth of the
Russian Embassy in 1829, and in the end it was *Father
Hyacinth's Description of Peking* which, despite its great age,
finally revealed to me the unsuspected lives of three million
people who make this the world's fifteenth largest metropolis.
With the ecclesiastical guide in hand, alone and apparently
unsupervised, I wandered into odd byways and fell in love
with its medieval atmosphere.

Some find it dull, shabby and destitute. I always thought it
fascinating, endlessly amusing and comfortingly old. Even in
their silliest moments of denouncing the past, Peking's planners have been restrained by some deep, historical and irresistible sense of pride. They tempered their dogma much as the
emperor moderated his enthusiasm when he built the Altar of
Heaven. This was to be the pivot of empire, a dazzling central
millstone with outer balustrades of marble. This would concentrate the lustre of China's vast domains which saw the sun
set in the west as dawn came to the east.

The Altar was built and carefully erected *outside* the northern part, called Tatar City. The grandeur of the universe must
not interfere with the greatness of Peking. So today Red
China's leaders acknowledge the enormous superiority of Russian technical knowledge, but they have put the Soviet Exhibition Hall with its spires and minarets outside the city walls and
next door to the zoo.

When Mao Tse-tung reveals himself from the top of the Gate of Heavenly Peace, he stands opposite a far more modest little gate where each successive dynasty engraved its name upon the lintel. This is the famous Dynasty Gate and there is a legend that workmen, who in 1912 were replacing the last inscription with a new revolutionary tablet to "The China Gate," took down the old label: "The Great Manchu Gate," just as previous signs had been removed, but being canny and cautious craftsmen, they agreed to hide it in the archway overhead as an insurance against its being needed once again. They were true Peking citizens and were not being carried away by every wind that blew. Their ancestors had seen the Golden Horde, the Tatars and the Manchus come and go, and they had passed down through the ages a small but significant piece of advice: "It is important only to survive. Martyrs never make fortunes, never sire big families nor pleasure their ancestors. Therefore obey the victor but never underestimate the loser."

In accordance with this sage counsel the workmen prudently hid the discredited tablet. In the same attic, they stumbled upon two more stones proclaiming previous dynasties still longer dead, placed there by equally prudent hands.

Mao never encouraged such precautions. His dynastic tablet is a granite column engraved with his own square handwriting in gold and it interrupts his view of the little gate. Nobody is likely to conceal *his* shingle as a form of insurance against future changes.

Those who find modern Peking dull would agree with the London *Times* correspondent who complained:

> Distractions of the foreign colony have been severely restricted . . . Horse-races, riding, the cross-country and point-to-point races are only memories of a happy past. To-day one hardly sees a horse. Gay picnics are rare. Temples which foreigners used to hire as summer residences are empty and deserted.

The young man who showed me this carefully preserved clipping enjoyed my embarrassment. We were sitting in The Three Tables where officials pop in for lunch from the Foreign

Office hidden in a neighboring *hu'tung.* Children peered through misty cracked windows on their way home from school. The floor was uneven cobbles. Diners in winter kept their thick padded jackets over their shoulders and warmed up with the fiery Manchurian grain spirit, *mao t'ai.* In this medieval, cozy corner with the freezing wind howling outside, officials sometimes shed their cloaks of reticence. Conversation blossomed. Formality vanished.

It was said Mao liked an evening's conviviality and had designated twelve Peking restaurants to uphold the best traditions of Chinese cooking. Just as Chou En-lai declared: "We are China and nothing can alter the fact of our existence," so these smoky little restaurants tucked in narrow lanes announced quite simply: The Steamed Dumpling Shop or Peking Duck Eating Place. For the equivalent of $11.20, four people could sit down to a series of delicacies ranging from force fed, crisply roasted ducks to a final dish of lotus soup, and all washed down with beer and several stone jars of *mao t'ai* which could make some people drunk on its aroma alone.

Near the Gate of Military Proclamations during the regime's first five years was a black cave which became warm and cheerful when a large and very round Moslem could be persuaded to light up his ancient firepot for a Mongolian supper.

Kao Jou Wan, whose name was burned into the blackened rafters and meant "The Roast Meat Man," was enclosed in black, stained robes, a skullcap perched on his head, spectacles on the tip of his warty nose and a gray beard that waggled as he talked. Old Marshal Chu Teh, a cheerful and wart-ridden man himself, ate there often. Revered as a great soldier, the marshal would pick his way between bicycles stacked outside an ironmongery next door and crouch as he stepped carefully over the greasy floor bricks. His favorite dish was cooked in a *huo kuo,* a sort of copper firepot. The pot was fed with charcoal, and a moat of water round the shining chimney boiled away above the flames. The pot was quite small and squatted in the center of a circle of six or eight diners. When the water was bubbling you tossed vegetables into it, then cooked your strips of meat by dangling them on the end of chopsticks. Kao Jou Wan mixed piquant sauces and you ate, standing with one leg hoisted on a narrow bench. It was a good start for a party and no doubt Chu Teh knew where to take it from there. But the average citizen was denied such pleasures and the city pulled the blankets under its chin long before midnight.

If you could hover over Peking as the majestic bands of light caused by the aurora borealis flicker above Mongolia to the north, you would see a stranger sight below. From all directions converge the muleteers and camel drivers with bricks and stone that will transform the city's ramparts. As sections of the ancient walls come tumbling down, new factories rise in the east, new colleges and dormitories to the west. The humble donkey follows age-old trails to the sites of cotton mills, machine tool and agricultural equipment plants, to iron and steel factories, mines and railway repair shops.

At the center of all this activity is the geomantic portrait of a three-headed monster with six arms, laid down a trivial five hundred years ago as the basis of Peking City. Necromancers drew up the plan and, although the incrustations of industry and dormitory towns lie thick around, old Monster No can be clearly distinguished as you fly low overhead.

Monster No's three skulls are the main gates into the city. His digestive system is the Ditch of a Thousand People. His hands clasp the Temple of Confucius to the east and Hsi-chi to the west. Above his heads are the northern Bell and Drum Towers. At his feet lies the Temple of Heaven itself.

If you are lucky and first arrive by air with a Chinese pilot who takes pride in the capital, the plane will fly over the Forbidden City. Beyond this rises Coal Hill which was built as a protection against evil spirits, using earth scooped from the Pool of Great Fertilizer Spume.

This is where Mao Tse-tung and his aides work. They look out upon the Hill of Ten Thousand Years which is in reality an island in the Pool, adorned by the White Pagoda, the pavilion of Perpetual Southern Melodies, the Tower of Felicitous Skies and Wisdom's Fragrant Terrace.

To Mao's credit, nothing has been done to substitute numbers for these decadent titles. This causes the Russians a good deal of perplexity.

Looking down into the Forbidden City you find it crammed with gardens and courtyards, magnificent halls and pavilions. Communist officials are immensely proud of having completed the restoration of palaces. Here you find peasants and students strolling where once emperors strutted on built-up boots, and where until less than fifty years ago concubines groomed their black tresses with elephant dung and eunuchs bustled forth on palace intrigues.

However, if your pilot comes from Shanghai he may harbor an odd resentment against the capital. Many like him regard Peking with all the embarrassment of ambitious young men obliged to escort a doddering old maiden aunt. They dislike the bucolic habits of Peking's citizens and they carry this to excess. So you may land from quite another direction, irrespective of wind, and float down over the Summer Palace with its temples and pagodas spread over small green hills. This is like a sudden descent into a Japanese dwarf garden, brilliantly studded with the glazed tiles of rooftops that sag in the center under their own weight. Red pillars and fretted marble walls end abruptly. With your back forcibly turned to the old city, you slide over scarred brown earth to land at Nanyuan or another new metropolitan airport.

Peking's masters are well aware they live only forty miles from the Great Wall but more than a thousand miles north of the realities of Formosa. They shrewdly preserve the color of history and resist attempts to make them imitate Soviet Russia. There was a time when their architects were forced to compromise: the result was a line of unsightly semi-skyscrapers with pagoda roofs. The mayor once boasted he would lay an airstrip in the city center, just across from the former Examination Hall where scholars sought entry into the emperor's service.

Since then, a serious effort has been made to strike a balance between the practical requirements of a modern city and its cherished traditions. Life inside the Tatar city has changed surprisingly little on the surface. Tinkers with small brass gongs search for customers; tailors squat against the crooked walls to play Chinese checkers. Dealers still sell caged linnets and jade earrings in the Street of the Happy Phoenix. At the junction of the Street of a Thousand Lanterns and Fire-Spirit Street stands a mannikin traffic cop who bellows at the ragged pedicab boys through a megaphone. You can buy satins on Embroidery Street where a tailored silk shirt costs $5.60. The brothels that once attracted the young princes have been abolished, but you can still see a Chinese film which documents this purge of the prostitutes. It is called *A River Flows for a Thousand Years and Now Is Dispersed.*

Pedicab boys are a stubborn relic of the discredited past. Early in the regime, they were being squeezed out of existence. But the Chinese are unlike other political dogmatists: although they felt that three-wheel bicycles were a poor advertisment for the new era, they also realized these bath-chair conveyances were the only immediate solution to problems of public transport.

These wheeled versions of the rickshaws are found at designated corners of the main thoroughfares. Their owners crouch in a row, voluble and cheeky, looking like a flock of chattering starlings in their black rags. The last pedicab boy to join the line takes over a megaphone and on the arrival of a customer he bawls the requested destination through his tin horn. His comrades decide whether they feel like going there, and the first in line who expresses his willingness to convey the would-be passenger then wheels his vehicle into the road and motions the applicant into its torn seat.

You will note a certain independence about this procedure. Pedicab boys are lone wolves, the only genuine eccentrics I ever found in a nation whose millions upon millions of people seem these days to think alike just as they all look alike. The pedicab itself is unique. There are machines like it all over Asia but none displays the same ingenuity or reflects the idiosyncrasies of their operators in quite the same way.

The carriage bounces on rusting springs, the brakes are blocks of wood chained to the axles and thrown into the mechanism in moments of emergency. The mechanism is a simple crank, chain and gear worked by pedals. There is often a string looped around the handlebars which, when pulled, jams another piece of wood against the rim of the front wheel. At night, a lantern made from bamboo and rice paper is hung in front with a lighted stub of candle flickering inside.

There is nothing quite so strange, if one has a sense of the romantic, as the journey by pedicab late at night down the Street of Eternal Peace. There is little motorized traffic at any time and Peking is the one capital in the world where a rural calm prevails after ten at night. Around you move the glow-worm lights of other late travelers creaking along in their own pedicabs. The drivers shout at each other, guttural voices growling out of the constellated darkness. Dark shapes loom suddenly ahead and resolve into more pedicabs loaded to the sky with wooden coffins, or bales of cotton, or mysterious packages topped by wicker baskets a-cackle with ducks. Sometimes a string of Bactrian camels plods across your path, sand from the Gobi Desert in their shaggy coats and cargoes of rugs and skins between their humps, shambling with steady disdain as if they were ready to continue another seven hundred miles southward across still further sandy plains.

Rocked gently in your squeaking cradle, occasionally alarmed by the sharp wheeze of a late tram, you nod comfortably in a world of phantoms.

The fantasy deepens in winter when black, padded hoods are pulled over the muffled passengers and the boys mount their saddles in lumpish, black, quilted coats, and caps with earflaps that turn them into panting monsters as they struggle over ice and packed snow. Even the children, normally dressed in gayer clothing, are converted into square little creatures who seem to have been stitched into large tea cozies. These gnomelike citizens can be seen on a December morning packed tight into what is known in Peking as a "school bus." The conveyance resembles a small packing case on wheels and carries ten kindergarten-size children whose tiny faces peer solemnly out of snow hoods. Closer examination of the packing case, which has a rear door, windows and a distinctive coat of vivid green paint, reveals it to be our old friend the pedicab in disguise.

American trucks also underwent conversion early in the regime. They provided the backbone of public transport and looked like mechanized packing cases of a larger kind. The Chinese stripped them down, mounted a simple wooden structure on the chassis, stuck enormous red stars on sides and back and attached metal plates that identified these "coaches" as products of the local auto-conversion works. However, they also left on the engine covers the names of the original makers. Some sort of perverse pride caused the drivers to polish these alien names so that you were constantly startled to see among the graceful Chinese characters and five-pointed stars the sudden declaration: INTERNATIONAL or GMC or even that name reeking of capitalism and the Wall Street conspiracy, FORD.

The paradox of Peking is that its exterior is pleasant while under the calm surface there is a far more ruthless mental struggle waged between the Party faithful and unenlightened citizens than anything known in Moscow. To the casual visitor, Peking offers more diversions and small delights. The majority of people have submitted to the dictates of their leaders, and therefore bear few signs of physical ill-treatment. They are poor, of course, but they are allowed more color in their daily lives. There are simple toys in the markets, sweetmeats and candied fruits; small luxuries can be found which are trivial enough but, being altogether absent in Moscow, are appreciated only by those who have had to make do without them. It is pleasant to be able to stand outside a motion-picture theater eating peanuts or huddle around a hot-chestnut machine. There are restaurants, often nothing more than wood and canvas with mud floors, where you can get draught beer and noodles between four in the morning and midnight. In one of them is an old man with a singular occupation: he stands over a caldron of crabs and each time an enterprising crustacean crawls over the backs of his comrades to reach the pot's rim, the old man wallops the individualist back to the bottom with a small cane. The crabs come from Tientsin by rail, tied up for the journey with stringy grass, and their residence in the caldron is a temporary loosening-up period before they are boiled. Probably letting them loose in the pot satisfied some esoteric Chinese culinary law but to me the old man with the stick was symbolic. He knew what was best for crabs, just as Mao knew what was best for the Chinese, and when one tried to elevate himself over the tops of others he was smartly rapped back into place.

The noises of Peking are medieval: the clatter of tinsmiths; workers chipping away at boulders with hammer and chisel; the distinctive cries of hawkers. One of the most unexpected sounds is that of laughter; in the early evening as the majority of workers trudge home by foot, they josh each other and shout, and sometimes break into roars of laughter. Once I traveled in a streetcar crowded with solemn faces. David Chipp of Reuters was with me, giving his imitation of an English yokel telling a long-winded yarn, and the harder I laughed the more people around me began to grin. Soon the Chinese, who even if they understood English would never have followed Chipp's false accent, were rocking with laughter in sympathy with me.

The most primitive noise is the Peking spit. Although there are spittoons in every public building, covered with wooden lids on the end of conveniently long handles, the pavements in winter become an obstacle course. During the cold months and early spring, dust blown by the Yellow Wind covers the sun and forms a permanent mist which irritates the lungs and penetrates everywhere. This is the origin of the spit and not even face masks seem to have defeated it.

If you could visit Peking at lengthy intervals you became aware of changes of a subtle kind. There were the blatant differences, of course, between phases when the regime was annoyed with the West and when it smiled upon us. But the deeper, uncontrollable changes were to be found in the way people lived and co-operated with the authorities. There was a slow decline in some standards: salaries remained at an average of $28 a month, and then rose a little in 1956 with a balancing rise in commodity prices. A woman who drove streetcars told me she found it more difficult to save out of the joint salaries of herself and her husband, but she estimated her monthly family expenses at 80 per cent of her own earnings. She said it was possible to go to the movies once every

two weeks, and added with a smile that films were more interesting and less political than before. She lived with ten
relatives in a house built on three sides of a walled courtyard
near the Thieves' Market, a bawdy hide-out for street entertainers and confidence men.

I went back to the Thieves' Market after an interval of two
years. Previously, sinister blue-tunicked men had followed me
while I filmed this gaudiest acre in all of Peking. Now I was
greeted with smiles. The sword dancers posed for pictures, the
tumblers hammed it up like veteran actors and a fat little
eunuch, who told stories while juggling on the end of a pole,
made it his business to provide me with a stepladder so I could
follow his movements from a perch above the ring of on-
lookers. Several times I was spoken to in English by shy old
men who grinned delightedly when I responded. Behind
white cotton screens were the same old sword swallowers, the
same seedy jazz bands pounding out a discordant version of
"Tiger Rag."

There were other changes of a less spontaneous nature. The
"freedom to worship" described to me by a complacent little
man, who called himself the Director of the Bureau for
Religious Affairs, sounded much more like a State licence to
perform certain rituals in places known as Churches. I went
to the famous Lama Temple which had been reconstructed by
the Communist Party at a cost of something like $196,000 in
a cynical attempt to reassure China's seven million Buddhists.
The lamas who prayed at the feet of the Buddhist redeemer,
Maitreya, a golden idol standing "seventy elbows high," were
dependent on State goodwill.

It was possible to see the outline of Mao's tender trap even
more clearly. Terror was replaced by a delirium of reason.
Fear receded before the brute force of endless argument. The
era of mass executions was yielding to the age of collective
submission.

Mao was setting up special work teams to begin studies in
mid-1957 upon the intellectual lives of Chinese who did not
fall into the broad categories into which society had been
divided already. The teams were selected from graduates of

the "Institute of Socialism" where students were heavily dosed
with "dialectical and historical materialism, political economy,
the history of the Chinese Revolution and current events and
policies." Their task after graduation was to find the best
means of indoctrinating those specialist groups of Chinese who
had so far resisted complete conversion including ". . . religious
circles."

Yet, with all this careful planning, I wondered if the trap
might become so tender that it ceased to be a trap at all.
Would its designers mold it too carefully to the characteristics
of their people? Could they unwittingly shape it into a mask
instead, concealing behind its rigid features a prolongation of
the past?

Item: A young Chinese official stands with me on the Great
Wall of China. We have skidded on an icy road for forty miles
out from Peking. Now we see an incredible landscape stretch
before us. The Wall dips and rises, wide enough to march an
army ten abreast, high enough to dwarf Mongolian battering
rams, vanishing into hollows and then crawling triumphantly
out again toward another barren peak. It unwinds for hundreds of miles.

"It was built on the bodies of Chinese workers," says my
companion bitterly. "People are China's cheapest commodity.
We have to be careful not to fall into the same trap again, but
you know, too many of us today forget the real meaning of
the Wall. It was built bit by bit to keep out enemies but it
cost us more in human lives than the worst kind of war.
What's the use of building great things at the cost of suffering?
Me, I want to study and learn before agreeing to grandiose
projects. My greatest wish would be to go to Oxford University in England and become a scholar. Already I know many
of Shakespeare's plays. I will recite to you from *Hamlet.*"

And to my astonishment he declaims the soliloquies of Hamlet right there, shouting into a mighty wind which gets under
our coats and threatens to balloon us all the way into Siberia.

Item: There are more domestic servants in Peking than you

will find in any other world capital. Not only do the authorities admit this bourgeois situation, they encourage it. There is even an unofficial Amahs' Guild which charges diplomats 10 per cent more than the Communist Personnel Department. In Russia, factory workers dump their children in nurseries, but here you find mill hands employing a baby's amah at a modest salary. Amahs are mostly old and garrulous. Complained one (in the Peking *Daily Worker*, too): "I have to work from 6 A.M. to 11 P.M. for a government official . . . do the shopping, cook and wash clothes for his wife and three children too . . . What sort of equality is this?"

Item: There is a form issued to foreign correspondents. It looks like this:

REQUEST FOR INTERVIEW OR VISIT
Person you like to meet....................................
Place you like to see ....
Things you like to know...................................
Other remarks ....

You could let imagination run riot on these forms but sometimes the most impossible requests got unexpected answers. Russell Spurr, formerly of the London *Daily Express*, filled the top line in thus: "Henry Pu-yi, Emperor of China." Chipp of Reuters had already made the same request and both were suddenly hauled off to Manchuria where they did indeed meet Henry — "the ex-Emperor," as he reminded them — undergoing reform through labor.

Item: A British economist, Nicholas Kaldor of King's College, Cambridge, came to Peking University to lecture on Lord Keynes's economic theories. Kaldor advanced before his class, chalk ready, and announced: "I could prove to you by facts that Karl Marx was wrong but this is an academic discussion so I shall prove it to you by pure theory." He proceeded to do so amidst attentive silence.

Taken at their surface value, some of these were among the good things that had happened. But there was an air of rehear-

sal about them all, and later the listeners to Keynesian theory
(for instance) had to repeat their own Party pieces to prove
that nothing heretical had entered their heads.

You can judge, therefore, how difficult it has been for honest
observers to estimate in just what direction Mao was taking his
country. He is the master of diversionary thrusts, zigzags and
sudden reversals. There have been previous crises in Mao's
personal affairs when he found it expedient to beguile Western
visitors. He never lost sight of his ultimate goal, however, and
this has been defined in his own speeches which are today
distributed in edited versions throughout the world on a bigger scale even than the works of Stalin.

To determine the quality of Mao's China, you must consider
events among a cross section of the people over a period of
time. In the next chapter you will find some account of what
happened to the boisterous people of Shanghai. When terror
reduced them to a state of trembling submission, Mao lost
their creative abilities and was obliged to relax tension in conformity with his own theory. Thus a visitor to fear-ridden
Shanghai in 1952 would disagree violently with a visitor to
the port in later years, when Mao was coaxing men of enterprise to use their ingenuity again within his political framework.

CHAPTER TWENTY-SIX

Shanghai's Reign of Terror

◉ ◉

To put it bluntly, it was necessary to bring about a brief reign of
terror . . . To right a wrong, exceed the proper limits. Wrong
cannot be righted unless proper limits are exceeded.

MAO TSE-TUNG

SHORT AND SHARP waves of terror swept the mainland after Mao
took possession. The rhythm was again that of the *yang-k'o*
folk dance with its simple pattern of two steps forward and
one back. There were features of Chinese life which had to
be labeled Wrong and these had to be eliminated. These
Wrongs were attacked with excessive vigor, and just when the
strain might prove too much, the regime relaxed in preparation
for another convulsion, and thus it advanced slowly and by
inches, only withdrawing a little in the face of heavy opposition. The entire nation now performed the simple step and
this was hardly surprising. For many years it was the framework of revolutionary plays. Slogans were chanted to its insistent rhythm. So the cycle for the first eight years was unmistakable: strict discipline, then slight relaxation, then iron
rule again.

For six million citizens of Shanghai this seemed like the erratic pulse beat of a bucolic regime composed of country
bumpkins. The world's fifth largest city was open to the four
winds of foreign ideas, driven by worldly-wise ambitions and

invigorated by international commerce. Its citizens had contempt in those early days for the northern rulers who had
shifted China's capital back behind the Tatar walls six hundred
miles away.

A rude shock awaited them. Peking was expert at handling
500 million peasants *en masse*. It was less sure of these six million individual human problems. So Marshal Chen Yi, Commander in Chief of the Red Third Field Army, was installed
as Mayor of Shanghai. One of his first actions was to inquire
from the French managers of two blocks of flats if he could
rent half of the "Picardie" on Avenue Pétain and the upper
three stories of the "Gascogne" on Avenue Joffre.

The Frenchmen agreed. They had expected pillage and wan-
ton destruction, the usual accompaniment to occupation by
Chinese Nationalist troops. Instead they were renting out
twenty-four apartments at a total of $8400 monthly. The new
mayor made only one request: that there should be no provision of hot water or central heating, even though these were
in the lease.

Next day eight hundred new tenants marched in. They were
simple peasant soldiers whose astonishment with Shanghai's
skyscrapers was only exceeded by the thrill of going to live in
one. They slept on the floors, packed like sardines. The only
clue to their presence, though, was the crash of their boots
by day and laundry instead of lace curtains in the windows at
night. At the end of each month the tenants left to make
room for another battalion. So it went on until several thousand troops had been redistributed throughout the land with a
message of confirmation: "It's true, comrades, we slept in
those great tall buildings in the heart of the French imperialist
concession, just as Chairman Mao promised we should."

Two years later, the Frenchmen had been taxed out of business.

The story of Shanghai is a condensation of Mao's empirical
methods within the limits of his theories and the demands of
Soviet Russia. He sought men with ideas and business talent.
Some he frightened into permanent silence. Others he remade
into servants of the regime whose knowledge could be employed in trade with the capitalist West.

He used them as a kind of yeast, to ferment and agitate among the duller bureaucrats. It was the kind of heresy to make Stalin, with the blood of Ukrainian merchants on his hands, turn in his glass coffin in Red Square.

But even if the yeast was frothier and the leavening lighter, the end of Mao's brewing operations would still be good Communist beer.

I traveled "soft seat" on the Peking-Shanghai Express No. 15 which thundered along a smooth railbed in a twenty-two-hour dash with some twelve hundred perfectly disciplined passengers. In the wheat-growing plains between the Yellow River and the Yangtse, we stopped briefly at wayside stations each specializing in food delicacies. At Ta-chu where floods covered the surrounding paddies and peasants paddled in baskets to rescue ducks, there were tiny roast chickens in paper envelopes dispensed by girls with their faces masked. They handled the wrapped food with chopsticks while a Comrade-in-Charge-of-Passenger-Comfort swatted flies. All these precautions against germs were impressive until I saw a coolie packing the chickens before they reached the platform. He had piled their little roast carcases on an open bench beside the kitchen lavatory where flies buzzed unchallenged.

It is not surprising that the Thirteen Wise Men of Mao's Politburo treat their subjects like children. Drill an instruction into the Chinese peasant's head and he will obey to the letter. "Kill flies!" intoned our train announcer. "Battle germs!" But you still had to specify which flies to kill and what germs to defeat. If we approached a river, the loudspeakers became positively martial: "Hwai Ho — Giant Bridge Ahead! Built by Comrades of Railway Brigade. Heighten Watchfulness. Close All Windows. Defend the Express."

Then, briskly: "Express Now Triumphantly Has Crossed Bridge."

In Shanghai I found the sort of sophisticated observers who could record the pattern of events and later complete the history of the great port. What follows is based on the evidence of Chinese and Chinese-speaking citizens. There is at the time of writing a considerable flow of solid information from Shanghai, and even a regular and uncensored column of news is

mailed for old residents to read in Hong Kong's *South China
Morning Post*. Some of my informants are faithful Communists and others are better not identified. One who may be
mentioned is Mr. Liu who was director of the Shanghai Port-
land Cement Works. When I saw him in 1954 he had dwin-
dled to joint owner, still drawing profits with the State for a
partner. Two years later he was down to submanager and sinking fast.

When the peasant armies marched into Shanghai on May 28,
1949, it was obvious that they were efficient robots. All their
thoughts and impulses had been classified and cross-indexed.
They knew only mass emotions. The ordinary citizen possessed
a nervous and chemical system which responded to current
American film posters showing a blond actress spreadeagled at
the feet of a man. The soldiers seemed only to react when a
slogan was shouted. They tore down the posters and expressed
hatred for Americans. "Love All the People" was the theme of
the thought signals they were receiving at this time.

These troops were the nucleus of the creation of a mass
mind. They began by classifying people. Black marketeers
were shot down in the street and cartloads of Shanghai's dockside ruffians were unemotionally executed, but the first months
were spent "taking the census." Dossiers were built up on
each individual. One copy was lodged with police of the Public Security Station set up in one's immediate neighborhood.
Each station had one household officer who appointed street
committees.

Many foreigners were favorably impressed. There was order on the streets, currency values had been frozen after the
insane inflationary days and there seemed to be an end to corruption (an abrupt end for some people, but the tumbrils
were not a disturbing spectacle to diplomats safe behind protective walls). By the end of 1949, optimistic reports were
being sent to London by distinguished British traders. At a
Far East conference of British experts it was agreed to recognize the Peking regime.

Mao had gone to Moscow. Meanwhile ominous changes
were taking place in that greater part of Shanghai life that

was hidden from foreigners. Mayor Chen's instructions were
to avoid causing any sudden panic but to prepare carefully for
a quick swoop on classified "enemies of the people." He was
working closely with Lo Jui-ching, Public Security Chief of
700,000 troops detached for duty on the home front.

Lo was a tall, middle-aged man with expressionless eyes that
seemed more sinister for being set above a mouth hooked into a
permanent grimace by a cheek wound.

Lo's men were patiently preparing for the holocaust. They
were mostly graduates from the indoctrination schools set up
in Yenan after 1942 to teach basic thought-control methods.
They had the civilian population catalogued and were now
developing "mutual supervision" among the different groups.
Mr. Liu of the Shanghai cement works, for instance, had been
inveigled into the Revolutionary Capitalists Association where
nightly meetings began to smudge some of his bourgeois
ideas.

Some clue to the situation was given by *People's China*. It
explained how the swiftness of victory created problems of
control.

> Greatest possible use must be made of students, Government
> personnel and intellectuals of the old society. But their minds
> are thickly encrusted with feudal ideology . . . Revolutionary
> colleges therefore specialize in transforming old-type students
> and intellectuals into new-type cadres. Retraining schools have
> turned the bulk of students into new people within six months.

Strange new ideas floated mistily through millions of minds.
During two thousand years, the Chinese had built up some
eighty thousand ideographs which often summarized a thought.
Now the people of Shanghai learned portmanteau words as
they watched hysterical parades of youngsters attending mass
meetings, or read the posters that appeared overnight in
the streets. *Exterminate Accidents!* they were told. *Beat Down
the Big Feudal Exploiting Landlords!* Factory workers who
had always worked in shocking conditions for as long as eighty
hours a week were gratified to learn they were entitled to
much shorter hours, fixed salaries, and health and medical

benefits. They then returned to their benches to perform *Patriotic Overtime!* which sometimes extended into *Shock Attack Overtime!* without noticeably affecting their wages.

Mao returned from Moscow. "People's security organs have discovered large numbers of secret service organizations and special agents," he announced.

The terror was on. Overnight through Shanghai swept Security Chief Lo's men.

"*T'an-pai* quick! *T'an-pai* is road to life. Resistance is road to death."

Into countless ears the pleas to confess were whispered. Anyone who had sympathized with Chiang Kai-shek and the Nationalist cause was urged to register before his neighbors denounced him. Meanwhile the neighbors must denounce suspected agents. Naturally, if an alleged spy were denounced before declaring himself the penalty was severe. And if a neighbor should denounce a mutual acquaintance while you remained silent, then you were open to suspicion too. Mutual spying thus spread into the home, organized on the same principles as the self-disciplined army.

It became dangerous to harbor a fugitive from "justice." This word, like so many others, had undergone a transformation. Justice, Mao explained, was an instrument by which Communism would prevail. Once arrested, a suspect could only plead for generous treatment. "Guilt by arrest" might be a fair summary of the law.

There was, of course, no legal code except such militant regulations as Mao's 1951 Proclamation of Punishment for Counterrevolutionaries. Even crimes carrying the death penalty were vaguely defined. Punishment could be inflicted for alleged crimes committed twenty years earlier. Article 9 revealed how a slip of the tongue might bring disaster by making it an offense to instigate resistance to the Government and "conducting counterrevolutionary propaganda and agitation, fabrication and spreading rumors."

If you were a *kan-pu,* a cadre, it was necessary not to spend too much time with a small group of intimates. Your job was to Follow-the-Route-of-the-Masses and to keep in touch with local people, transmitting to them the Party's wishes, and also Reflecting-Upward to higher official levels the secret grumblings of your neighborhood. If you kept to a clique, you might be guilty of Small Circle-ism. This might lead in turn to Using-Personal-Relations to protect a wayward friend from analysis.

The analysis was a psychological investigation into any mind suspected of hiding secret doubts or worries. It was eventually extended to all members of the population, an ambitious application of Bolshevik auto-critique. In Russia this had been confined to bureaucratic inquests in the hope of improving efficiency.

In China the regular group "criticism and self-criticism" provided a blueprint of public thought and impulse, known as the Cross-Flow-of-Experience. The danger was that leading cadres might become friendly with individuals and Commit-Tender-Emotionalism when trying to Purify-the-Ranks. The cadres were the most vital units of society. They initiated all campaigns by picking out "the politically pure, non-Party member, non-proletarian-originated" members in their community to spread word of each new policy.

"Hate America" campaigns focused public resentment of the past upon the foreign devils most feared by Mao. At the same time, Russians began to arrive by the thousands. They took over blocks of flats in Avenue Joffre, and prisoners from the notorious Ward Road jail began to erect, under their instruction, a vast Sino-Soviet Friendship Center which would tower above all the vast symbols of earlier foreign domination. A vigorous drive against foreign missionaries began to gather momentum, churches were closed and the official press began to publish long lists of arrests.

The *yün-tung* or Party Drive helped spread new policies, softening up public opinion, and in the first years also cleaning out potential enemies or those dissident intellectuals who could be converted. There was no attempt to conceal the terror between 1950 and 1953. Shanghai readers of the Party papers were kept informed of the numbers of executions and arrests. There were two kinds of execution. One was expedient and swift. The other was called officially "Suppression of Counterrevolutionaries with Fanfare."

A fanfare execution was held after a Mass Accusation Meeting. It was frequently broadcast. The intention was to give the public a sense of participation. There seems to have been no sense of guilt on the part of the organizers. Statistics were published of the numbers of people "deprived of existence" and in Shanghai, when I inquired for a total figure, it was freely estimated that in all China some fifteen million Chinese had been killed one way or another in the first five years of the regime. I was shown an official report of one trial. "Comrades, what should we do with these criminals, bandits, secret agents, evil landlords, heads and organizers of reactionary Taoist sects?" From the crowd came an answering roar: "Shoot them!" The convenor asked: "Should we have mercy on them?" And the crowd thundered: "No!" and "Mao Tsetung, Live Ten Thousand Years!"

The "judges" then rose while the convenor wound up proceedings: "It is our duty to do the will of The People. We suppress the counterrevolutionaries. This act we perform according to law. Those who have to be killed, we kill. In cases where we may kill or not kill, we do not kill. But when it has to be killing, we kill."

The dreadful cry of "Sha! Sha!" "Kill! Kill!" was heard daily as each drive got under way. I talked with many officials about these fantastic blood baths in which masses of normally placid people became killers. They discussed the matter without trace of embarrassment.

"You see," said one, "we had to stir people up."

There were many suicides during the period called in Shanghai "Hunting the Tiger." Wire nets were placed around some tall buildings so that falling bodies should not kill pedestrians, but there was a high casualty rate among rickshaw boys. One unsuccessful suicide said the worst part of his ordeal was the discussion afterwards.

There was plenty of propaganda material in Shanghai. You tired of hearing about notices in European parks: *Dogs and Chinese not allowed,* although you blushed to think of them.

Looking at the palatial homes later turned into Young Pioneer Palaces on the Russian model, you wondered how their Western owners could have remained blind to the catastrophe that waited to engulf them. Their ostentatious homes soared above lanes where thousands of fellow human beings groveled.

As each campaign blew gustily through Shanghai, similar tornadoes swept the rest of China. There was perfect coordination, as can be readily seen from reading provincial Communist papers. Each storm broke down a little more of the individual. There was a model Party mind and it seems to have been the function of certain officials to discover new ways in which the individual might deviate from this model. The officials were called "People's Supervisors."

The first hint of a fresh drive might come in the form of a "news story" from a remote part of the country. In earlier years, this might be an attack on missionaries or alleged spies. Then laborers who broke their tools, or lagged in their work might be quoted as examples of counterrevolutionary agents. Much later, however, the criticisms were aimed at Government officials and even at Mao Tse-tung himself. But where Party officials were the target of criticism, there was always some involved reason and a more distant Party objective to be attained. For instance, Mao might be accused of leniency toward bureaucrats who abused their powers, and he could then "yield to public pressure" and punish the men concerned without losing their personal loyalty.

Up to 1954, there were many waves of terror, each with its own label: The 3- and 5-Antis (against corruption and evils of public behavior); Study Campaign for Ideological Reform; Exterminate Imperialist Elements Wearing Cloak of Religion; Censure Putrid Life of Capitalist Class.

Some of these achieved worth-while results. Clem Attlee's famous "no-flies-in-China" judgment after a brief trip through Shanghai was perfectly fair. But decent men like Attlee could not (and still cannot) conceive of such a mass "spiritual" training responsible for phenomena like clean streets, reformed prostitutes and absent beggars. To the Attlees of this world, educated to believe and hope for the best in their fellow men, you could not explain that five minutes before he went on tour in Shanghai the entire neighborhood was placed on the alert. Citizens were not watching the distinguished visitor but each other, ready to report any untoward incident.

By that time, a global peace campaign had been launched hard on the heels of the Korean armistice. Shanghai's East China branch of the Resist-America Aid-Korea Movement had changed its title and was now devoted to consolidating the sense of collective punishment and collective responsibility. The next big step China faced was the elimination, *without* terror this time, of private businessmen. People's Supervisors were preparing for the "High Tide of Enthusiasm for Socialist Transformation of Capitalists."

The reign of terror prescribed by Mao was at an end. The proper limits had been far exceeded. Perhaps the weapon that Chinese Communists had forged got out of hand. They lacked resources and scientific knowledge to attempt fission bombs but they had started their own kind of chain reaction within the mass mind they were dangerously manipulating.

Something burst under all the strain. The Chinese people, resilient and energetic, went on working twice as hard as most other Asians. But now they were almost utterly subdued. Thousands of officials, it was admitted, suffered nervous breakdowns. How many more ordinary citizens collapsed? It became difficult to coax ideas out of people whose minds were paralyzed.

I made a collection of the slogans used up to this time in Shanghai. Taken alone, they sound as if China is governed by the insane. But these phrases cropped up in everyday conversation.

Any trial was known as a Struggle. Usually the Vigilance Section of the Cultural Bureau prepared the defendents, a process known as Brewing-Objects-for-Struggle.

At any mass meeting there were Positive Elements who stayed in the audience and shouted slogans at suitable intervals. Later these meetings were used for criticism and self-criticism. Every citizen was trained in the habit of a weekly confessional. When there was a drive against Guerrilla-Style-of-Behavior, that is, excessive informality, or Tendency-Toward-Freedom-and-Looseness, the planted officials would stir up the audience to shout comments about the poor wretch up for Self-Accusation.

Of the many groups into which all Shanghai's citizens were divided, *every* member had to face this ordeal. This included senior officials. The most frequent drives were puritanical in motive: Beat-Down-Depraved Elements, Stop-Obscure-Relationism (a lovely euphemism for free love), Halt-Tendency-Toward-Extravagance.

You could not merely plead guilty to such traits as Pleasure-Viewpoint, Isolated-Retrospection (which meant you had been indulging in some private thoughts about the regime). The whole purpose of the Self-Accusation was defined as "exposing the state of mind." Judged guilty, you might be lucky and come Under-Surveillance-by-the-Masses. This meant the evidence against you was flimsy and the punishment might be trivial, such as being last to pick up your chopsticks at the communal meals. These control methods were made easier since everyone belonged to some organized group, and the workers were easily grouped together because dormitory living was not alien to them.

Luckless victims went to Reform-Through-Labor-Camps. Whatever the Chinese may call them, these are forced-labor camps but the difference lies in the emphasis on indoctrination. Force is seldom used. Guards are not necessary. The Chinese for centuries have been accustomed to living in large organized groups and to mass labor methods of controlling rivers or building great earthworks. Once destined for the bleak interior, a wharfside coolie became resigned to his fate and this was the first stage in his conversion to obedient citizenship.

Once I was asked by a Peking Foreign Office man: "Why do you dislike slogans? I notice you get irritated with them and I have wondered why this is."

I said the slogans clouded independent thought and might ultimately destroy it. Temporary relaxations in the regime's grip on people were only designed to draw forth further deviationist thoughts to which new labels could be attached. I said: "You've even got slogans now to cover sloganism. Soon you'll have as many labels for the thoughts of human beings as you've got ideographs, and then you'll be able to control every brain in the land. Maybe you think that's O.K. but the prospect terrifies me."

He looked blank. He seemed an intelligent young man. Obviously he did not understand this point of view at all. "Slogans are the only way we can get anything done," he said. "And anyway, we like to shout things like 'Ten Thousand Years to Chairman Mao!' We like calling him a glorious leader who gives us the correct line."

I doubted whether many of Shanghai's sophisticates felt this way. Despite repressions, there were revivals of prostitution and *lao-mo-ping* or the Old Disease of black-marketing. The Yellow Ox broker gangs operated between purges. Rackets were still worked. The cemeteries on Bubbling Well Road and in the old French concession, for instance, were dug over, and unclaimed bodies were cremated and the coffin wood sold for firewood.

The coffin wood had a sweet odor and it was in high demand because it was resinous and inflammable. Hawkers found that a cartload of cheaper kindling was soon infected with this same identifiable smell if a catty of coffin wood was carefully mixed into it. Sold by twilight, the cartload of firewood then brought a much better price.

I went to a Shanghai people's tribunal where an old man named Chen was accused of converting thirteen gold bars (one "big bar" weighed ten ounces in those days) to his own use. Chen had shown considerable ingenuity. First, he found a prospective buyer for the shop where he worked as manager. He persuaded this victim to keep two sets of books, one for Government inspection and the other a personal financial record. Then he stated the black-market price for the shop, which was thirteen gold bars more than the price listed in the book kept for tax purposes. Later the buyer discovered Chen was not even owner of the shop. Meanwhile the owner went to the police.

When the police investigated, Chen blandly offered to repay

the money. "Yes," agreed the victim. "Yes," said the owner.
And the police thought the settlement would probably save
everybody's time and face. But all that Chen repaid was the
official price recorded in the first book. He kept the surplus
thirteen gold bars, confident the victim would not dare com-
plain and so reveal his own misdeed. Unluckily for him, the
victim risked embroilment with tax officials and did report the
matter. Thus Chen now stood in the dock.

The case was conducted in successful imitation of Western
methods. It was a model courtroom with model policemen and
model defendants. But of course there was no legal content to
the procedure. The case closed with the defendant's lawyer
pleading for leniency. But the lawyer was appointed by the
Public Security Bureau and his only function was to try to reduce the sentence. Chen was automatically regarded as guilty
once he appeared at the tribunal. The real inquisition had
taken place in the prison cells. After Chen was led away to
serve two years of reformation, a plump little man in the back
of the court jumped up and made this speech: "As a representative of the Association of Revolutionary Capitalists, branch
of Nanking Road, I wish to thank the People's Court for its
fair trial under the Constitution for protection of personal
property and its endeavors solemnly and earnestly to defend
the interests of Capitalists in accordance with the correct policy adopted by the Chinese Communist Party under the glorious leadership of Chairman Mao."

I found this mockery of a trial so disgusting that I left hastily. An official raced after me: "You were not pleased? But
you must understand that Before Liberation there was no law
and order and the wicked exploiting colonialist traders . . ."

There was a showpiece Institute for Reformed Prostitutes.
Many foreigners taken there have been impressed, as they are
impressed by the tribunals selected for them to visit during
halts on China's conducted tours. But there were still "wild
chickens" around, girls who refused redemption. Some of the
girls finished up with the army in North Korea. They were not
forcibly taken off the streets nor were the dance halls immediately closed. Most were gently squeezed out of existence

to the accompaniment of incessant argument. Those who resisted were mainly film starlets or young ladies of the "Great
World" amusement hall. They were a pathetic lot who seemed
to survive by some secret arrangement with officialdom. In one
or two cases they were in reality concubines, and their masters
were evidently permitted to continue these liaisons.

Even in its drabbest days, Shanghai was appalled by the gray
lumpiness of Russian women. There were perhaps ten thousand Russian and East European advisers at one time, many of
them with families crowded into a section near the municipal
airport. Worldly-wise city dwellers watched Russian housewives feverishly buying up small luxuries, invading in particular the silk shops.

"They knew what they wanted," a Shanghai tailor told me.
"They always went straight for the gaudiest dress materials."

There was general ill-will toward the *Lao Ta-ko,* which can
be translated as either Elder or Big brother. At the height of
the Korean war when another high tide of enthusiasm had
swept most able-bodied men and women out of Shanghai, the
work was nearing completion on the Sino-Soviet Friendship
Exhibition. This ornate wedding-cake structure had a tall
spire, and to the blank astonishment of the impoverished citizens this tower began to gleam bit by bit with a spreading coat
of gold.

At this time, they had helped buy 3700 Soviet fighter planes
at a cost of around $59,000 each. The war fever had not
blunted their sardonic sense of humor, however. "The People's
gold is gilding Big Brother's tower," was one popular crack.
People went in organized groups to inspect the Exhibition
which housed examples of Russian industry and arts. There
were some superb samples of Moscow's calendar art: huge oil
paintings in gilt frames, illuminated by ornamental light bulbs
and depicting matronly factory girls with their hair tied in
white kerchiefs as they bent over their machine tools. The
showroom furniture was fretted with little lace-edged anti-
macassars, but the joints were loose. There were balalaikas
(which play a kind of music foreign to Chinese ears) and
television sets on carved legs.

Author with Chini
Lama, representative in
Nepal of the Dalai
Lama, Tibet's spiritual
leader.

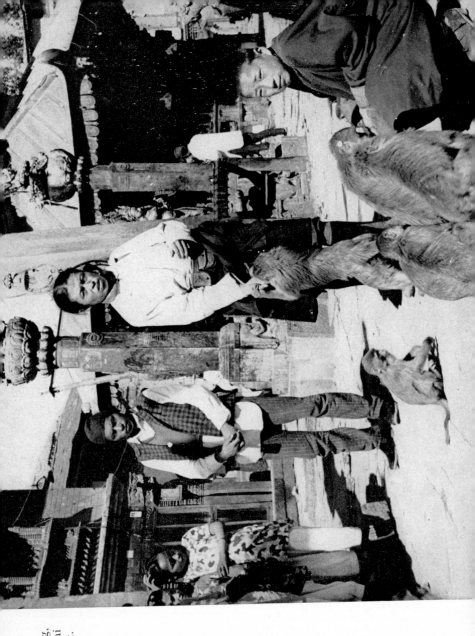

Champa Jilla, squatting, was the son of the Dalai Lama's court merchant.

Stone camel outside Ming Tombs near Peking disdainfully watches donkey caravan bringing bricks to new reservoir.

Lord Ten Semba was heavily guarded and his escort carried some alarmingly sharp knives.

Two old men of Peking. Their ancestors have seen the dynasties come and go.

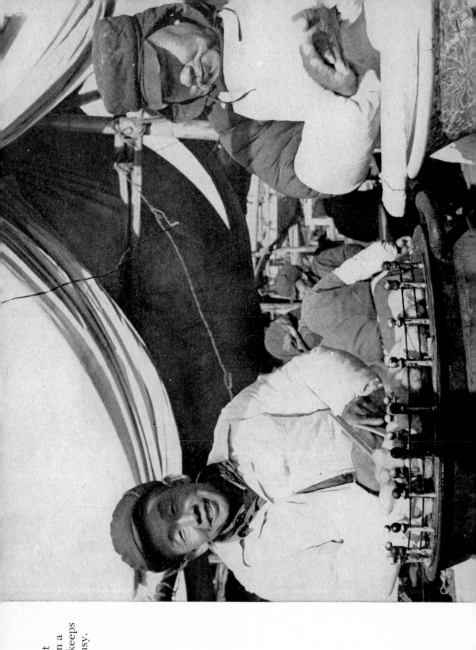

Hot-dumplings pot serves passers-by in a Peking street and keeps these two cooks busy.

Lunchtime for this small Chinese hawker means a bowl of rice in a Kunming street.

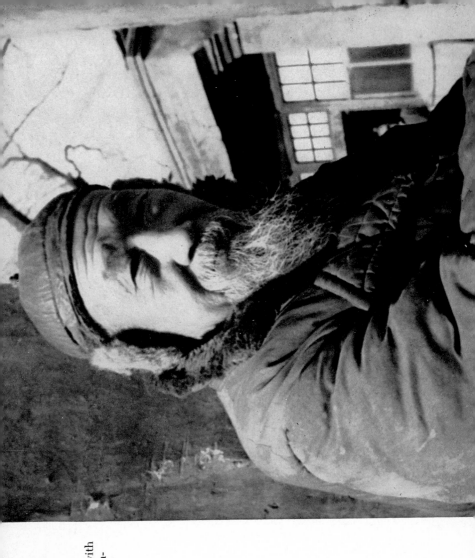

In Peking old men
regard the Russians with
benevolent condescen-
sion.

This Tibetan lama now works in the famed Lama Temple in Peking: he is paid by the Communists who thereby retain control of a powerful religion.

A Yunnanese bride and botanical research worker described in "Ladies Impudent and Mannish Grown."

Yunnanese fisherman.

December harvest
in Yunnan.

I glanced at my Shanghai-born companion when we toured this curious collection. "Why do the Chinese make this pilgrimage?" I asked. "Is it to learn the superior cultural techniques derived from the advanced Soviet experience?" He nodded his head absently.

I thought of classic Chinese art: the thousand delicate ways of brushing bamboo onto paper; the famous horses and frail goldfish, the simplicity of three chaffinches perched one below another down the center of a silk scroll that stretched from ceiling to floor. Suddenly I remembered a phrase used to describe carelessness in the new Chinese society, derived from criticism of a formal painting.

"Would you call this Rough-Branch-Big-Leaf Style of Work?"

My Chinese friend gave me a pleased look. Behind his head, a large crack had appeared in the white, ornamentally embossed plaster. There was a rumor the Exhibition was shifting on its foundations, and the building had ominous splits in the woodwork, while some of the doors seemed reluctant to fit in their frames. The Chinese, who are expert carpenters and building constructors, cannot bear a badly woven wicker basket, let alone a tilting skyscraper. They were also resentful of the high Russian salaries which rumor said came to around $700 monthly in some cases. There were stories of East Europeans who sought to buy American dollars, and I thought this boisterous city showed an unfortunate tendency to ridicule the comradely efforts of their Communist brethren.

For a long time it seemed that Shanghai would wither on the vine. Officials told me proudly of grandiose plans to depopulate the port.

This depopulation was accomplished originally by shipping off several thousand adults to Yellow River and railway projects. In many cases, this resulted from political "crimes" and the victims were sentenced to labor reform. Public Security statistics were released to show that by 1954 this mass labor produced 770 million construction tiles, nine million pairs of socks, 1,700,000 steam-radiator couplers and two billion bricks. Security Chief Lo added in a public speech: "Income from reform labor during the past four years, after deducting living costs of criminals and other necessary expenses incurred in work of reform through labor, has been accumulated in the forms of fixed and fluid capital and approximately equals the expenses."

It was nice to know that the debraining system worked. Instead of massacring the politically dubious members of the new society, you bludgeoned that part of the brain where the doubts resided. Even with costs deducted, this system paid for itself because you thus retained muscles and backs in good working order. The Chinese to this day are proud enough of this experiment to demonstrate it gladly to visiting Asians. "Treating the illness," Mao called it, "to save the patient."

In Shanghai the worst elements were removed in this fashion, and then came a new and unexpected turn of events. There was a sudden surge of genuine enthusiasm in Peking for plans to colonize the border regions. One distinguished visitor in 1955 recalled that Premier Chou En-lai "during lunch could not keep off the subject of mass migration." This time, instead of shipping workers away as criminals, mass meetings were called at which young people were once again worked up into a frenzy of excitement. This time, however, they were not condemning a friend or neighbor. They were volunteering to develop the virgin lands.

Mayor Chen Yi himself trekked off into Tibet, while thousands of pedicab boys were converted into truck drivers to work on the dizzy new highways slammed into the heart of that high country. In a single twelve-month period, it was estimated that some 63,000 Shanghai citizens joined the colonizers. Newspapers were crammed with names and addresses of mislaid relatives and friends. Almost daily, columns of youngsters might be seen excitedly marching off behind banners and *yao-kou* side drums.

But plans for Shanghai had been reversed. It began to feel and look big, bustling and boisterous again. Soon the red tiles of new housing blocks soared above the old gray slums. Factories began to march outward again, heavy industry to the east, textiles and light industry to the west.

Shanghai is often compared to Leningrad, because the Russian port was also a funnel for about half all national imports until revolution swept by. Then it seemed that each city must turn its back on the ocean and integrate large forces of skilled labor into the new economies. However, Shanghai was now different. In morale, energy and color it compared very well by 1956 with Leningrad, which I visited some months earlier. The Russians at home seemed lethargic, content to line up for daily necessities, drably dressed and unenterprising. Shops were dusty, poorly wrapped goods were taken out of grubby trays and the window displays were universally dull. All was stodginess and decay until you poked into the theater and schools, where it seemed that real initiative and imagination were beginning to show.

Now if you might have whisked several thousand Russian housewives from the chill Baltic coast to the torrid streets of Shanghai, the lady burghers of Leningrad would have most certainly rioted. The improvements were small, superficial, but significant. There were street puppet shows, a variety of operas, fun fairs, and hawkers of sweetmeats and tiny luxuries. Consumer goods were attractively packaged (I am writing, of course, in relative terms. They were attractive by any Communist standard.)

The dens of vice were gone for good. Of that, no doubt. The days were past when race tracks were always crowded, night clubs never closed, foreign amusement halls flourished and in the great port itself, ships of all nations nuzzled the wharves. But now there were, besides the haunts of virtue, "secret" factories and underground dance halls, with other evidence of private enterprise making fruitful alliance with Party yearnings.

There were submarine pens around Soochow Creek. Gone were the lumbering old junks I had seen previously, whose bridgework was heavily armor-plated, while troops squatted on cargoes destined to run the Nationalist blockade. Now freshly trained workers assembled prefabricated Soviet submarines on the slipways. But it was not this which seemed responsible for a new air of confidence.

"Made in Shanghai" products were beginning to flow into Southeast Asia. Cheap goods made by cheap labor, they sold outside China at less than domestic price. On the famous Nanking Road were silk brocades, gleaming new bicycles, tinned goods and grand pianos — but only on exhibition, marked *For export only.* Still the boom had raised spirits, for although it scarcely raised living standards, it did give an outlet once again for personal enterprise. Unfortunately, the people of Shanghai are too resourceful and many went at once into business as middlemen. Yellow Ox brokers were publicly denounced for buying up scrap iron at ten times the official price and still making huge profits. Irrepressible, high-spirited and irreverent, this wicked old rake of a city was all set to plunge back into its former habits.

"It's like riding a hunter," explained an American-educated official. "If the horse is not properly broken in, it gets accustomed to your heavy hands hauling on the reins. Very soon you dare not relax the reins because the moment you do, the horse bolts."

The reins on Shanghai did slacken, however, long enough to release some of the energy and imagination badly needed in a Communist state. Teams of artists got together to improve packaging of exports. Ideas bubbled up for better production methods. Some emboldened citizens lodged complaints against officials who knew nothing about factory problems but were authorized to direct industrial affairs.

Most businesses had merged into "joint ownership" with the State. Their owners, fully aware that this was only a step toward nationalization, surrendered their rights and continued to work them as partners in socialism. There was little choice. The "transformed capitalist" sold shares to the value of invested capital to the State. The State paid 5 per cent return on the owner's original holding plus a capitalist share of profits in equitably distributed dividends. Each enterprise was subject to State price controls and if it lost money, the 5 per cent was still paid.

Without knowing the hidden pressures upon him, you might suppose any businessman would approach his relationship with extreme caution. But when the "high tide of transformation" was rising in 1955, owners were clamoring for this salvation from a possibly worse fate. They *wanted* partnership with the State in preference to more political indoctrination. But the State took its time. Every owner was obliged to prove his enthusiasm for the new system. One told me: "I was sent home several times to reconsider my acceptance and to search my own conscience. Was I truly transformed, were my old bourgeois habits of thought really corrected?"

After the conversions were over, "secret" factories were permitted to function under a sort of unofficial license. They were technically illicit and untaxed. They flourished brass plates on their doors: *Unregistered.*

Vice-Premier Chen Yi, chief economic adviser, said: "Secret factories are generally doing useful things. They can increase the number and variety of available goods and are swiftly adaptable to local demand."

The regime, having taken two steps forward, had crushed opposition and badly winded even its own supporters. Now it stepped adroitly back.

CHAPTER TWENTY-SEVEN

Ladies Impudent and Mannish Grown

◉ ◉

A FUSSY AND WOMANISH obsession with the trivia of modern Chinese life was evident in the speeches of Mao Tse-tung as he grew older and more possessively in love with The People. He called himself Lao Tai-tai, meaning the family elder who figures in most Chinese operas. He used the term in the secret part of his key 1957 speech, and hinted that, like an old woman, he wished to potter about in the background of politics. Yet even here he could not escape paradox. For the more worried he became about his country's future, the more he seemed to indulge his old-maidish anxieties.

He was concerned about "contradictions" between the leaders and the masses, he said. His doctrine that such differences did arise was sufficiently startling an admission to bother his Russian allies and raise the hopes of liberals. But his methods of eliminating such differences seemed odd. He fidgeted with yet more labels: some differences were "antagonistic" and some were "nonantagonistic" to The People.

Mao reserved the right to decide what was "antagonistic" and who were The People and he claimed a woman's prerogative to change his mind when he thought it wise. With spinsterish care he laid down codes of behavior. If the ordinary citizen transgressed the code he had to be studied and placed in one of the two categories. "Nonantagonistic" culprits were condemned to ideological reform but the remainder got savage treatment.

Thus Mao was more than a father figure to Party youngsters who needed guidance on matters normally reserved for the judgment of parents. It would be fatal to scholastic ambition, for example, to be found guilty as a student of making love during a period when relations between sexes were strictly surveyed. However, it might later happen that the Party would experiment with some new theory suggesting happy mixing of boys and girls would heighten their intellectual powers.

It was obviously hopeless to look for parental help in deciding how to avoid trouble. The wave of intense puritanism that swept through China reflected Mao's harsh standards, but suddenly some of the taboos would be lifted for reasons of expediency.

In these confusing circumstances the emancipation of women could lead to many embarrassments. Mao had to lay down strict rules of conduct and yet he had also to listen to what was theoretically the equal voice of women. He made divorce possible but then heard a nationwide wail of protest from disconcerted husbands. He tried to curb the unexpected rush to obtain divorces, and at once there were feminine murmurings. As arbiter of morals in place of Mum and Dad, he had to pass judgment on the most intimate questions and then become embroiled with his lady colleagues who (we shall see later) were willing to exercise their franchise rather more extensively than Mao may have anticipated.

Mao could direct a guerrilla campaign. He was a superb strategist. He was master of the art of "uniting-with-one-enemy-to-overpower-another." He was many things but he was not a mother-father figure. The collective mind was not yet bisexual.

Whether women will influence national affairs in future depends in China on the true extent of their effect so far on Party policy. Women wielded more power in the home than legend would have us believe, but their influence within the family waned as the Party issued more and more domestic directives. So there was a compensating rise in feminine activities

outside the home and while Mao undermined the foundations
of family life, he also rendered idle the tongues of millions of
Elder Sisters, Number One Wives, and Mothers. All this feminine energy had to find an outlet eventually and it has already
taken some startling directions.

There was a jet squadron in South China whose MiG-15s
were flown by the dashing young ladies. Yet some had sisters who
still hobbled on crushed feet. Old China saw beauty in "lily
feet," the result of binding them in early childhood, and the
pitiful effects remained: elderly women supported by canes,
pattering along on what looked like goat hoofs.

New China is proud of its emancipated girls. You find them
driving trams, flying on aerial surveys and also, let it be said,
digging ditches. I watched one of the more glamorous ladies
descend by parachute into a Chunking paddy. Her canopy collapsed and she stepped out of the harness with the aplomb of a
New York model stepping out of her girdle. I captured her
expressionless face on a television camera. She betrayed no
surprise although she could have hardly anticipated meeting a
"long-nose" in U.S. Army trench coat and aiming a triple tur-
ret, 16-millimeter cinecamera at the end of her long drop. Her
father had been a blind minstrel who drifted from one teahouse to another singing ancient ballads. Women of China have
all jumped an equally formidable distance from medieval slavery
to some kind of independence in a scientific age. It would
be foolish to dismiss their emancipation as merely the right
to take an equal place in the chain gang.

At one end of the scale were women who were ministers of
Justice, Health, and Overseas Chinese Affairs. There was a
woman in the appropriate post of super-snooper: Madame
Chien Ying, Supervisor of "the People's Control," which
meant she ran the housewives' grapevine. Four women
were vice-ministers of Food, Water Conservancy, Labor, and
Industrial Textiles. There were 2400 women teachers in
Peking alone. One in seven of all judicial workers was a
woman. Every farm co-operative was supposed to include at
least one woman on the board of management. Three
women scientists held top places in the Academia Sineca.
Sun Yat-sen's widow was one of six vice-presidents of the

Republic.* Even red tape had a feminine touch and out of four million designated bureaucrats, more than 605,000 were women. Nor did feminine privilege conceal itself entirely behind desks. China had eighty Lady Model Farm Workers.

A common complaint is that leaping into the new age, women have left their femininity behind. Well, as Mao Tse-tung said: "Revolution is not a invitation to a banquet." Taking their cue, his womenfolk dress for a box lunch. They are not much inclined to shed their revolutionary boots and trousers. Some told me they were genuinely sorry when Mao hesitantly hinted at a return of the *cheongsan* with its side slits revealing slender legs from ankle to thigh. For one thing, not everyone had stockings and a thigh without its silken sheath is uncommonly exposed to the elements and other hazards. For another, side slits were simply not practicable in a workaday world of packed buses and tyrannical looms. "It's all very well for Mrs. Mao," said a Shanghai secretary. "*She* has no laundry difficulties. But for working girls, a male uniform and boots does cover many sins."

The current Mrs. Mao was, of course, a well-known Shanghai film star before her marriage.

There was a girl in a Manchurian steel mill who sat all day long before a panel of buttons. She typified the new female breed. When she pressed a button, a red-hot metallic worm writhed down the gangway, bounced over clanking rollers, squeezed itself through rows of steel jaws and, after crashing down a sort of metal waterfall, came to rest at the decidedly unbound feet of this redoubtable young person. While it sizzled and smoked and assumed the form of a fifty-foot length of seamless steel tubing, another girl gave it a nod of approval and her friend pressed the button again. The push-button artiste, under questioning, said: "My spare time is spent in political studies and how better to increase production. If I marry, it will not interfere with my production schedule unless I have a baby. If I have a baby, it will go into the factory nursery. And the State will give me thirty minutes every four hours to suckle it."

---

* By 1959 she was one of two vice-chairmen.

She was one of 2,800,000 women workers in China's expanding industrial areas, and her leaders at a Production Front conference early in 1957 proudly proclaimed that the fair sex
now performed more than half the work of textile mills, filled
one quarter of all railway jobs and clearly had overcome their
frailties. Women "impudent and mannish grown" were swarm-
ing into cooperative farms to the tune of *ten million,* but the
Chinese clearly did not share the Shakespearean judgment
that they were "more loathesome than effeminate men."

The prim and unsexed girl soldiers whose pigtails and
square faces lie embalmed in smudgy Party newspapers of the
pre-1949 era speak of it now as Before Liberation. Their
symbol since the Year 7 B.L. has been Madame Chu Teh,
wife of the Grand Old Man of China's armed forces. She still
tucks her hair under a peaked cap. Only her broad hips under
the belted jacket and coarse trousers reveal her sex. She married at seventeen when the Marshal was already forty-three,
an arrangement now frowned upon by the official judges of
modern matrimonial fashions who edit *China Youth,* and recommend late marriage for women on medical grounds, which
one suspects were discovered only after the birth rate got out
of control.

Madame Chu Teh previously lived in the home of her selected future husband, a fisherman who bought her as a child
from her poverty-stricken father.

This marriage has been in other ways a model for the new
generation. Given the Chu Tehs as an example, girls are urged
to seek mates from their own political class. But about the
Year 3 A.L. (*that is, After Liberation*), there was an unpleasant
surge of immorality. This was called *nao nan-nu kwan hsi* or
Getting-Up-Man-Woman-Relations. It was defeated by getting up a movement to Censure-the-Putrid-Life-of-Capitalist-
Elements.

There was trouble too about the ease of divorce. Young
men suddenly found their wives talking back to them. Some
who whipped their wives for such impertinence were staggered
to find themselves hauled before the kangaroo courts of divorce or charged with assault. Not all the rough justice of the

period was bad. Families who still tried illegally to arrange marriages were reminded of the new Communist Marriage Law. Polygamy and concubinage were abolished (although exceptions were made). Married women kept their family names. Child betrothals were forbidden and there was a strict injunction against drowning newborn babies. "Children born out of wedlock," it was stressed, "have the same rights as those born in wedlock and are protected from persecution and insult."

No grand and superficial judgments are yet possible on the effects of all this. Women in China always exercised far greater influence within the family than was apparent to casual observers. Young brides today have fewer opportunities. I visited one at Yunnan's botanical research center. Her name was Chang Yueh-ying. At the age of twenty-two she had poise, zeal and the forbidding title of Advanced Research Member of the Chinese Academy of Science.

"I live in a dormitory with my husband," she said. "We call it home. In our minds we have a real home and some day my group will achieve its housing plans. We do not worry. The superior organs will take care of us."

Mrs. Chang described her daily routine: "We have one hour for rewarding and refreshing activity in the evening. The rest of the day follows a strict schedule. Exercises before breakfast at seven. Research from eight to eleven. From lunch until four we consult our professor and discuss working problems. From four to six, lectures. After supper we have self-study like politics or foreign languages. Bed at eleven."

I asked about her rewarding and refreshing activities.

"My beloved plays the Chinese violin," she said. "I play the harmonica and sing."

I went back to see this pleasant young researcher some days later. The extent to which times had changed can be estimated from the fact that two years earlier it would have been difficult for me to take this initiative. There were two reasons for going back. First, the research center was dealing with strange hybrids found in Himalayan regions where animals and plants of the temperate zones mingle with those of the tropics, and

Mrs. Chang's tomato trees were only the first hint of potential discoveries. Secondly, she was an intriguing product herself of the collision between the past and present, between the hot-house atmosphere of an old society where evils flourished and this Spartan age with its equality of the pick and shovel.

Once she was initiated into the traditional Chinese Rule of Three. She was admonished to observe the Three Obediences: first to obey her father, then to obey her husband and finally, as a widow to obey her son. There were Confucian rules for divorce obviously framed by a dominant male. If a wife was sterile, adulterous, loose-tongued, leprous, disobedient to in-laws, or a thief, she could be driven out of the home. But the husband could be all of these things and more: his wife had no right to leave him. Her only escape was suicide, and then her own family could wreak revenge by going to law for compensation.

All this has changed. In the old China, it was said: "A woman married is like a pony bought — to be ridden or whipped at the master's pleasure."

The new marriage law states: "The arbitrary and compulsory feudal marriage system which is based on the superiority of man over woman and which ignores the children's interests shall be abolished."

Unfortunately, it seemed to me that the law frequently released women from one form of bondage to enter another. Feet were unbound but hands were placed more firmly on the plow.

Article 8 made this clear: "Husband and wife are in duty bound to love, respect, assist and look after each other . . . and to engage in production . . . and to strive jointly for the building up of a new society."

But Mrs. Chang seemed a vast improvement upon some of the priggish girls of earlier encounters. Immediately after the new regime took over, a puritanical wave swept the country. Some 760,000 women began moving into industry and 2,000,-000 were officially recognized as laborers, or served in the army. They were a formidable lot. They seemed to have lost all sense of humor or fun. They answered questions like children repeating their lessons.

Mrs. Chang was selected to marry into a science dormitory. It was natural enough that some of her answers should sound strange to Western ears. I asked how many children she planned to have.

"That is a matter for later discussion," she said with utmost solemnity. "It would not serve society to have babies now."

This chilling response cannot reflect the entire picture. Chinese family life still persists although youngsters are taught not to harbor foolish sentiments. Economic planners in their wisdom sent Mrs. Chang to serve the drive for higher production here at the botany center of Black Dragon Pond. Her parents did not protest. Meanwhile their daughter was inspired to feel that this betokened a new freedom.

I asked about her studies. "We are doing dialectical materialism now," she replied. "We get reports on big events like the Suez aggression by Anglo-French imperialists."

She took me through tranquil gardens and greenhouses moistly warm and vibrant with lush green life. The trees were neatly labeled and grew in their appointed places. The tea roses blossomed on time and the insect-catching nepenthes dutifully snapped up flies.

You felt that this was a model of what Chinese society should be, each rooted to a designated spot and performing with efficiency.

"The only trouble," said my hostess, explaining her research problem, "is that my fruit and trees cannot speak."

She fondled the delicate brown fronds of a skeletal tree. "This species grew one million years ago. It may be the oldest in the world. We discovered this one and are trying to grow more. It's the first living example of *Metasequoia glyptestroboides*."

A gardener spat noisily behind a juniper bush. "Some day," said Mrs. Chang, "we shall persuade them not to contaminate the ground."

She said her young husband banked forty to fifty yen a month, an average of about $196 yearly, out of their joint salaries. This I did not doubt. Several times while changing money at banks scattered about the country, I asked about individual savings. The answers varied: but it was always said that people in employment tried to put something by. This contrasted with Russia where the sturdy citizen would counter questions with: "Why should we save when all our needs are already met?"

The idea of collective responsibility seems to penetrate at all levels of Chinese society. "My group decides my salary which is a basic fifty yen monthly," said Mrs. Chang. "We all watch each other and report when we consider a colleague deserves better money — or is failing to pull his weight. You see, we who do the work know best if it is being done properly."

What about promotion?

"Well, it takes me four years to become an Assistant Research Member of the Academy and another six years to become Deputy Research Member. But my progress can be influenced by the reports of colleagues."

Did she have a boss?

"If you mean the director, he is Professor Tsai Si-tao, and of course we report on *his* progress too."

Her offhand statement thrust me into a contemplative mood. I found myself relaxing, like the White Knight, into an inverted position. From this viewpoint, the new world seemed to come right way up again. Otherwise, it seemed topsy-turvy nonsense to arrange promotions from below and recommend to high authority that one's workmate should get more pay. Professor Tsai, for that matter, was prominent many years ago as one of China's leading botanists and I fancied he would not take kindly to little busybodies signing his credentials.

When I suggested talking with him, however, Mrs. Chang shook her head decisively.

"He must get on with his studies," she said and whisked me into a perspiring hothouse. Pale red tomatoes, shaped a little like pears, hung under leathery leaves of what was undeniably a tree.

"This is my project," she said proudly. "We think almost anything can be grown in Yunnan. We are cultivating rubber too, and there is a fragrant grass useful for the Chinese perfume industry."

A smile lit her small, delicate features.

"Yunnan is wonderful for research," caressing a nervous little fern whose leaves closed under her hand. "We have found two hundred unknown plants already. There are twenty thousand varieties of tree, shrub and plant. The other day I saw a beautiful bird in shining yellow with a red head and green beak. When we go out on field work we find the strangest little animals."

The blue hills were throwing long shadows across this province where it is always spring. For the first time, Mrs. Chang's voice became excited. For the first time she looked and sounded like a young bride. I followed her gaze through magnolia trees to where her husband walked slowly, head buried in a book.

And I hoped most fervently that it would always be spring somewhere in the hearts of these youngsters with their baffling exteriors of prudishness and devotion to a cause.

It would be unfair to condemn them all as joyless. Women, anyway, understand their own sex better. My wife spent a brief time in Peking and got an impression that professional women did not share this somber mood. She recalled our return from a late supper with Chinese officials. We took the same tram with a couple I thought were dour and dedicated. They lived in a dormitory, kept their only child in a nursery and despite American educations seemed deeply resentful of anyone from the American continent.

I would have let this judgment stand. But my wife talked to *his* wife. They got on a peculiarly intimate plane shared by most women, irrespective of creed or color. The girl confided that dormitory life was certainly not her idea of bliss, nor did she like the tendency in factories for women to shelve family cares. "But what can we do?" she demanded. "In the old days I would have had a rich and easy life while all around me people starved. I don't want to go back to that again. No, in China we at least sink or swim together."

Over my head was a metal plaque. My wife asked what it meant. Her companion glanced at me mischievously. "He should attend our Family Planning clinics."

"Why?"

"Well, the sign says: *Seat reserved for pregnant passengers.*"
In Peking, of course, there is a certain sophistication. Most women with any authority have been under Western educational influences either at home or abroad. One would like to think that it is *their* urbane approach to life which will prevail. They succeed in persuading foreigners like myself of this. Their pretty, slightly American accents are beguiling. Their younger sisters make no secret however of their resentment of "American interference" in Far East affairs.

Some of the junior set met on Saturday nights in the International Club. This extraordinary and unlikely haven was formerly the exclusive haunt of foreigners. It squats in the old Legation Quarter of Peking, untouched by the bustle around but slowly sinking out of sight behind monstrous new cliffs of concrete. Nearby is the British diplomatic compound with seals on its underground passages into the Chinese Security Police Headquarters next door, its own soda-pop factory rusty with neglect, and its private powerhouse, now pressed into use with the State electricity board. There was a time when haughty young Hussars emerged from the Embassy and invaded the bowling alley, the paneled bar and the ballroom of the International Club. Now their descendants play badminton in the Embassy pavilion or dance sedately under lights that flicker and pop, prisoners behind ambassadorial walls that for a long time were plastered with *Save Egypt!* signs by Chinese demonstrators who scarcely knew whether Suez was a passage or a pudding.

At the International Club, of course, they knew all about Suez. Here were the gay sparks from the satellites, budding Chinese diplomats and a few of the twenty thousand Soviet and East European technical advisers who were in Peking at that time. On Saturday evenings they became determined seekers after Pleasure. The Slavs tended to block the entrance into the bar, nudging one another and eying the girls like village louts at the local hop. But here and there, some tortured young face might be detected, seated at a crowded table with Chinese wife or mistress, and usually identified as a Hungarian or a Pole.

The girls wore slacks, a few used lipstick, and I found them pathetically attractive. They reminded me of the third daughter of a Chinese landlord I once had. Her mother ruled the wretched child with an iron will. But from time to time the daughter was thrust into the harsh Chinese society of Hong Kong. There she stood, trembling and pale, literally unable to string two sentences together, while her mother glowered in the background.

"You *will* have a good time," the State had told these children. And they waltzed gracefully in the arms of the tunicked cadres, or sipped orange juice and watched the clumsy figures at the bar nervously under lowered eyelids. When the orchestra laid down its mixed bag of Chinese and Western instruments, the silence among these girls was embarrassing. But sometimes you encountered an older lass who was not easily frightened.

One took me bowling with her husband. At the end of the evening, he turned to go. "You forgot to set up the ninepins," she reminded him. He shook his head angrily, mumbled that the Club boys could do it in the morning, and went to the door. "Pick up those pins!" she rapped. "You have enjoyed your Pleasure. Now you must work for it."

It is dangerously easy to talk airily about "Chinese women" on the basis of a few encounters. The prevalence of blue uniforms has given rise to legends about blue ants. So the casual visitor to Peking, meeting a witch in blue, believes in the prevalence of witches. Or spending an afternoon with the kindly blue-clad ladies who run the children's hospital, he believes all women to be gentle and intellectually adventurous. But the Chinese have worn blue for a very long time and it is not necessarily a sign of uniformity.

I think it useful to make this point, because uniformity exists in other ways less obvious to the foreigner. Western propaganda speaks of blue ants. When a visitor finds women who are far from antlike, he feels foolish and resents the publicists who led him into false conclusions. He then quite often denies their silly prattling, instead of condemning their motives. He will say, on slender evidence, that Chinese women are free and unafraid. What he often means is that he did not meet women in mental chains, as he was led to expect.

In the countryside, women labor in much the same way as they always have. Their spare time, however, is fully occupied. A dozen memories flock to mind: of old women crouching over school desks at night, painfully forming their first letters; of the quiet mutter, leaking through trellised windows, as mothers in a requisitioned temple repeat lessons at midnight; and most often, when staying overnight in a rural rest house, of finding the ragged chambermaid hunched over a note-book beside a pig-fat candle in the early morning hours.

We are frequently told that the reason for Communist success in Asia is that poor people want their bellies filled before their minds.

The poor people of China, during the crucial three years covered here, were certainly no fatter than before. But they were given more than enough food for thought; so much of it, in fact, that to keep pace with the gargantuan meals they could only digest and not discriminate. The West gave their neighbors a cornucopia of material goods, but nothing to inspire a spiritual fervor. Mao offered blood, sweat and tears; and then, weaving his dreams, he created a wonderful paradox. He appealed to spiritual qualities, rode the tide of revulsion against corruption and harnessed that most impractical attribute of the Chinese race: pride. Mao could make the loaves and fishes stretch endlessly through a multitude of sermons. The West could only supply more loaves and fishes.

How else explain the submission of women to the industrial horrors, for instance, of Manchuria?

I have never in my life felt my spirits sink so low as the night of the Workers' Hall Dance in a suburb of Mukden. This former Manchu capital is bounded by a ten-mile earthwall. About two million people live outside. Beyond the earthwall are many lesser walls topped by barbed wire, surrounded with electrified fences, but whether as protection against intruders or whether to confine the inmates was never clear. The inmates are makers of guns, rocket-launchers, pneumatic tools, seed oils, chemicals, machine tools and unexpected creature comforts, like red-lacquered coffins.

Southeast from Mukden is the railway to Antung and Korea. Its station signs are in Russian, with Chinese as an afterthought. Great locomotives pound over the shiny steel rails, drawing enormously long loads; gleaming metallic mysteries for Korea mostly, with sometimes the recognizable wing of an MiG. Past this railway is a wide space and on the edges of this gray field sit snub-nosed jets. Beside the jets are tables and at these tables are anonymous figures in quilted uniforms, heads engulfed in helmets with gross rubber ears.

It is beyond this sinister little fighter base that we find a suburb with the imaginative title of Tiehsi, which translated means: "West-of-the-Railway."

Here I went dancing. My guides drove through unpaved roads, headlights dimmed, and between tall concrete columns. Each column concealed a row of workers' dormitories. There were three floors to a building, fifteen windows to a floor, and five buildings to a row. Each dormitory had a large white number painted at either end. There were four doors on each side of a building, and over every door there hung a naked light bulb and a loudspeaker.

We bounced between a score of these "streets" and stopped outside the Workers' Hall. Muffled strains of Slavic music emerged from the main block. Around the compound were old men who crouched beside baskets of peanuts soaked in brine. Flames of red and yellow burned loosely in the wind, sometimes blown into long ribbons and twisting the long shadows into grotesque shapes. These flares tended by the peanut venders were the only illumination outside the hall.

As a rule, I like the beauty of flaming torches and regret the technical advances of our age: the neon lights, the filthy smell of gasoline fumes, the constant endeavor to drown the creak and clatter of the horse cart, the anxiety to turn night into day. But here, among the ghostly numbers on the walls, the flares gave a most sinister aspect to the suburb of West-of-the-Railway.

There seemed to be hundreds of people pressing into the hall. The flickering yellow light played on their strained faces. Their shadows lengthened with one puff of wind, then diminished with another. The crowd in peaked caps and trousers was at once an army of heaving giants and a troupe of dancing dwarfs.

I began to push through them, urged forward by the guides. Faces turned up to inspect me. Under some caps, the hair was long. The eyes, the mouths, were all the same. But the hair was long, and I realized with a shock of dismay that these were the women.

The women held hands together until we had all squeezed into the dance hall. The band was playing a peculiarly insistent rhythm and a seething mass of uniformed figures, still wearing caps, swayed back and forth in time to it. I had difficulty in keeping my feet. Despite the freezing night, the pressure of human beings had turned the inside of this unheated building into a furnace. When it became known that an official stranger was present, a mass movement seemed to generate itself. Luckless couples were driven outside, men holding on to men, women with women. Slowly the atmosphere dissolved. Within twenty minutes, you could see clear across the hall, while outside rose a controlled murmur, rather like diesels in an MTB throttled well back.

Chairs were produced. I sat next to a girl and nodded and smiled at her. She shrank a little. Out of the remaining crowd there now appeared a number of boisterous youths. These were the inspirational cells of this particular group brain. There were three boys and three girls. They announced a sort of Manchurian Paul Jones, and themselves started it going, and then broke away to cajole others into joining in. The band pounded on worn temple drums, or plucked on Chinese two-string fiddles. The dance came to an end and six youngsters were led onto the floor. They wore Russian-style peasants' skirts, bright blouses and ankle boots.

"The Collective Farm Dance," announced my companion and these Chinese workers went into a Siberian routine that seemed utterly humiliating to national pride. My attention wavered and finally broke when a girl sang, to slow sad notes from a beribboned balalaika: "My comrade has gone to fight in Korea: he is now a Heroic Truck Driver." It was bad enough to be lost in this Manchurian nightmare without the bizarre addition of Soviet-style jollity.

I have no idea whether there blossomed beneath their thick jackets some higher aspirations among these girls who sang of war and production. Perhaps in that sweating mob outside there were some who longed for the day when hair might be grown to the nape of the neck and clothes cut to fit feminine curves; when there were lovelier things than curves of production to sing about. But I doubt it.

Years before, the women of China were chattels. They married into clans. A girl acquired more than a husband; she got the living and the dead; his ancestors were her responsibility, his mother became her mistress and she lost even her own name. The attitude toward women is summarized in the advice of a father to his son. Adultery was a waste of production. "You sow your good seed," he would explain, "in the plot of another."

All this has unquestionably changed. The Marriage Law struck fear in the hearts of many bullies. Women could and did take their revenge against their past oppressors. But others committed suicide and many more flocked to the two thousand "circuit courts" which in 1954 toured the countryside in an effort to clear up litigation of which one third involved divorce.

The anger of women was directed into more useful channels. They were encouraged to expose the secret feelings of husbands, fathers, lovers and sons. The glorious task of emancipated womanhood was to persuade their menfolk to bare their sins.

I often spent an evening at the opera. It was always superb entertainment. There were no props, only the barest furnishings, and the audience put flesh on the bare bones by interpreting each classic flourish of an actor's arm. You knew who the players were by their make-up: vivid geometrical designs on their faces, or grotesque masks, or long trembling peacock feathers set in gorgeous headdresses. The warrior horseman fluttered upstage with triangular flags flying from poles in his back. The general (a woman) swept her arms backwards and up, catching the peacock feathers and pulling them forward over her masked face, at the same time advancing sideways with slow, controlled movements of her booted legs. The women sang in high-pitched, quavering voices; and each lift of an eyebrow, each crook of the finger, was full of meaning to the audience. The majesty of emperors, the violence of warlords, the haunting beauty of a princess or the haughty tyranny of an empress were expressed by a classic pattern of costume, movement and music. The music was complicated: rattling *hsia* drums, cymbals, gongs, moon guitars and hardwood castanets played by consumptive-looking old men in caps.

I went backstage as I had often done before, and as so often happened, the cast lined up to greet me. The warrior horseman was still wearing the thick-soled Mongolian boots and he seemed to be the leader of the group. His wife, in the make-up of an empress, nudged him and he bent his head and said: "We humbly thank you for your interest in our too-hopeless performance and we request you to give us the benefit of your superior experience and give us your criticisms which we shall humbly seek to study."

It was not such a different speech from the kind you might have heard at this same theater a century ago, when actors were "the mean people." Their rank today is elevated but there is the same pretended humility. There was, however, a triumphant look on his wife's face which I doubt would have been there before.

I borrowed her copy of *China Women*. In it was the account of a girl who suspected her father of heresies. She had wrestled with his conscience, rather than denounce him to the police. But finally she had to call in the security agents. He was unable himself to see clearly his errors and the police assisted him. They put him in a cell where reflection was easier.

"Father," she wrote, "is a happy man now that he has freely confessed his problems. The Government has saved Father and I am happy to have assisted, thus benefiting my country and The People."

If Father was indeed a happy man, others of his sex might cringe. They faced the terrifying prospect of China's women with tongues unleashed as well as feet unbound.

CHAPTER TWENTY-EIGHT

Penicillin on the Yangtse

◉ ◉

WHEN A WOMAN of wealth fell sick in old China, her doctor interviewed the patient through curtains drawn round the bed. Then he handed a naked mannikin of ivory through the drapery and shortly afterwards, a slender white hand would return it with a mark showing where the pain hurt most.

Today these mannikins stand alongside hideous cut-away models of the human body in the front windows of Peking's medicine shops. They attract large crowds on Sunday morning after the Party devotions. The bigger mannikins are full of holes to demonstrate how acupuncture needles may be driven into the body without fatal results. Thus Western medicine meets the traditional remedies of the East, the dummies uneasily embracing before the public view.

Ever since Mao Tse-tung reportedly got a new lease of life from traditional Chinese medicine back in 1952, there has been a determined attempt to foster the ancient remedies of herbalists and the art of acupuncture. The latter skill is curious to watch: a long needle is twirled rapidly so that it drills its way to the nerve junction thought to be causing ill-health.

My first experience of Chinese medicine was fairly drastic. I boarded a Yangtse riverboat at midnight in Chungking, feeling my way to the landing down a steep flight of stone steps. Coolies moved endlessly under pale yellow flares, bringing provisions and chanting work songs, eerie for that hour.

The ship's decks were crowded with sleeping bodies. My crowded cabin was stifling with fumes from the engine room and chill river mists.

We were thumping through the five-mile Chütang Gorge in broad daylight when I discovered how ill I was. The river swirling beneath was chocolate brown, and the immense limestone cliffs heaved their flanks high until they seemed to fuse overhead. Steel Russian lighters were clamped to either side of the boat. Our siren was a mournful cry that echoed down the melancholy canyons. This was the first of the Yangtse gorges.

There were nauseating medical posters in the dining room and brutally frank diagrams on such matters as pregnancy and the use of stand-up toilets. For the first time I regarded chopsticks with suspicion.

Maneuvering through the tortuous Siling Gorge had a claustrophobic effect. A kindly Frenchwoman found me in the middle of the night hanging over the stern. A large and capable person, she drove the others from my cabin and kept watch. Among the two hundred passengers and a crew of twenty, there was no doctor. Or so it seemed until the Marquis chose to reveal himself.

The Marquis deserves his own chapter. He began to travel with me in Manchuria. He appeared to be Brazilian. Mentally, he was still in the Soviet Union and spent his time hammering out articles on a tiny typewriter. When we went together to the Great Wall, my enthusiasm for this colossal monument was dampened by the fact that he remained in our car typing a piece on the Gorki Museum. He was a small man of infinite resource, with a large red nose and trousers that persistently burst open at the front. His greatest difficulty was the language — any language. This helped him to maintain a pose of denseness. I never met a more determinedly dense man. Once, in Shanghai, he got wind of the Seaman's Institute. Only he misheard the initial word. "Is'oomans 'ere?" he asked me, rolling a lascivious eye. " 'Oomans in Institute? Vair' interesting. Is low life in Shanghai, is *most* interesting . . ."

It took me a little while to understand that his mind was dwelling on sex.

As a guest of the People's Government, he never quite understood, was never quite ready to leave and on one notable occasion never fully appreciated that the man he forced to pose for a photograph was Mao Tse-tung. But he was handy with his camera and he became most dense in the middle of factories or port installations. He also had the singular habit of keeping under his bed odd items of food saved from supper. When some of us found ourselves hungry and the hotel kitchens irrevocably shut for the night, we raided the Marquis, who yielded up a fine prize: an enamel plate filled with cold boiled fish.

So when the Marquis stumbled into the cabin, bewildered as usual, I was not too surprised to hear that he was formerly a doctor. One ear glued to my chest, he announced that what we wanted was penicillin. The ship was scoured without success. The Marquis said he would "cup" me instead. There were no tumblers but the ship's cook raked up an assortment of rice bowls and sake cups. By the time we reached Ichang at the mouth of the gorges, an audience of Chinese encircled my back, which was festooned with chinaware from which air had been exhausted. The cupping relieved the congestion, but did not restore prestige. In an emergency, the Chinese had been found wanting. Much worse, their deficiency had been demonstrated to a foreigner. The Frenchwoman's swift dismissal of hesitant suggestions from the comrades that it might be imprudent of her to watch over me that night was equally damaging. She drove them away with a flourish of her enormous knitted handbag. "Clearly you could not inflict harm upon a flea, *mon pauvre*," she declared, digging ointments and cough drops from the depths of her cluttered bag.

My protector fought off the captain, the ship's commissar and solemn comrades summoned from among the passengers. "You are all stupid," she told them pointedly. "This man is sick and you will make him worse."

What confused the issue was the fact that this generous-hearted woman was herself a member of the French Communist Party. Yet it was her utter conviction that the Chinese would finish me off with their incessant chatter about production, river control and the Five Year Plan. She was confirmed in this view when, having left the cabin a short while, she returned to find me gasping helplessly in a bronchial paroxysm while our chief interpreter continued relentlessly with a lecture on China's waterways.

But he won the final round. When we bumped alongside Hankow dock on the third evening, I was hustled ashore and into a waiting car. One hour later I was standing before a U.S. Army fluoroscope while a nurse in boots, blue trousers and threadbare white tunic took blood from my ear. Without quite knowing what had happened, I found myself plunged into thick woolen pajamas and laid out on an iron U.S. Army cot. Outside the night was black. Inside that hospital somewhere in central China all contact with reality seemed to have been severed.

A torch flashed on my face. "Chinese penicillin," announced a firm voice. Something was jabbed into my arm. I lay rigid. Boots grated. Another voice said: "Open mouth, please." A sleeping tablet disappeared down my throat and soon I drifted into sleep.

I awoke with a start. A prickling sensation traveled slowly down one arm. It was followed by itchiness and then a sense of numbness. This continued by inches over my entire body. Should I call for help? The prospect of trying to explain was too formidable. I let the odd sensations make the circuit and in an hour they were over.

This nightmare occurred after each injection of penicillin — "Chinese penicillin," barked the doctors each day when they assembled to prod me.

Pride in their product put me in a fix. On the one hand, it was not funny to become itchy and numb by turns, three times daily and once in the middle of the night. On the other hand, the hospital might hang on to me as an interesting specimen if I divulged the secret. There was an attached medical college and from time to time young people dropped in, ostensibly to make tests, but in fact to talk. I hit on a stratagem. "Much is heard in the West about traditional Chinese medicine," I said again and again. "It would be enlightening to see it in practice."

So they brought me a delightful little old man in a gown, black skullcap, and equipped with a beard. He wore black cotton slippers with rope soles, the kind you could buy in Peking for the equivalent of a dollar. He was a Chinese physician right down to the two-inch nail curving out of a little finger. I was willing to risk his herbs to dodge more penicillin.

I spoke to him of the great respect in which old Chinese remedies were held by many Westerners. He smiled and nodded. I said one should be careful not to absorb too much of modern cures — like penicillin. Even Chinese penicillin. He stroked his beard and felt my pulse.

One of the young medical students explained he was measuring my pulse rate against twenty-two categories, each indicative of a type of illness. I waited. The old man briefly smiled encouragement and went into a huddle with the more conventional doctors. Finally I was asked to roll over and bare my thighs. There was a familiar jab. In what little space remained they had impaled me yet again with the penicillin needle.

I was free to roam the corridors after the fifth day. The whole place had a faintly uncanny air. The wards were crowded with militant-looking youngsters. Nearby were new convalescent dormitories of stiff-backed men. Evidently this municipal hospital was playing host to the lame and the halt from the local Red Armies. The toilet arrangements were primitive, the nurses overworked and most of the equipment was American. The patients averted their eyes when I appeared. It was perfectly plain that the entire hospital was on its guard.

The days were long. I pleaded for reading matter and was brought a few dog-eared propaganda magazines. I began to write. The matron, a girl who looked only twenty years old, arranged for me to cable to my paper. In the first story, I described the unusual circumstances in which I found myself and complained that, in their zeal and patriotism, the comrades jolted the hospital at dawn with military marches played over loudspeakers and continued this cacophony with brief breaks for physical jerks until nightfall. This, I suggested, might account for my slow recovery.

The point was misunderstood. Shortly after a messenger collected this dispatch, a young man appeared in the quadrangle outside my window and played, "Oh where! and oh where! has your highland laddie gone?" on a trumpet.

Many members of the staff spoke English. Some of the nurses had attended missionary schools and remembered English and American teachers. One young doctor enjoyed dropping in for brief chats. "Yes," he agreed, "this is a hard regime and the revolution was cruel. But you can't make an omelet without breaking eggs. Life is less difficult than previously. It is a question of us all learning to think alike on political matters, share common objectives and then work together. There is no room for men who would destroy our new nation by unsupervised criticism. Individualism is a disease and must be cured as you would treat a patient."

These chilling words were spoken without emotion by a medical practitioner whose early education was provided by Catholic teachers at St. Xavier's College in Shanghai.

He took me to the outpatients' clinic to pay the modest bill. There were the familiar line-ups at a counter where two harassed girls dispensed powders. More striking was the docility of the crowds. A woman rocked one wailing child in her arms while another cried lustily from its perch on her back. Small children stood patiently, their polka-dotted overalls of padded cotton split at the middle to reveal pink little bottoms. Parents and old folk took their turn without fuss. "Please make way for a foreign friend," said my companion. The ranks of people magically parted and I proceeded to the head of the line, red to my ears, resentful of my privilege and ready to protest. Such traits might have been justly exhibited by the waiting populace. Instead they moved aside unprotestingly.

I had run out of local currency. The shroff (he was still called this) rejected foreign bank notes. I was due to leave early next morning and hated the thought of further delay. Could I possibly change money at the bank?

"Let's see," said the doctor. "It's too late this evening. However, our bank has a special service for patients. Your train leaves at eight? I rather think the bank's representative makes the hospital rounds at seven."

And sure enough, on *that* morning he did.

I saw many more hospitals. Russian influence was widespread. The Soviet Red Cross Hospital in Peking took care of high-ranking Party members and the capital's large population of Russian and East European advisers. Much lip service was paid to the superiorities of Soviet medicine in the earlier years. The Russian Hospital was superbly equipped and there were fifty-four Russian doctors whose training was based (it was stated with relish) "upon the teachings of Pavlov who gave us the foundations of Soviet medicine." What was glossed over was the fact that the hospital was originally built by Americans whose staff overflowed into an annex. Under the new order, the annex was not required and I stayed in it frequently under the impression it was a hotel.

But subtle changes took place. By 1957 Peking was publishing eighty-two volumes of ancient Chinese medical lore, including thirty-five hundred traditional remedies, under the authoritative imprint of the People's Medical Publishing House.

"Our Government attempts to blend traditional Chinese medical and acupuncture practices, after research and examination, with Western medicine," the vice-director of Chinese medical education, Dr. E. J. Wei, explained. "It is believed we have a valuable contribution to make. In the past, however, there were no proper schools or medical organizations for supervision and control of traditional methods which were handed down in a restrictive manner from masters to apprentices or family relatives."

In addition to conventional hospitals there were now centers of traditional Chinese medicine: four colleges, sixty-seven hospitals and twelve hundred clinics. Some five thousand doctors with Western training were learning Chinese herbalism; and it was hoped their investigatons would result within two or three years in a successful combination of Western and Chinese methods.

"We do believe acupuncture is superior to anything else in treating nervous disorders," said a Peking child-health specialist, Dr. C. J. Yang. "For instance, we treat infantile paralysis — polio — only by this method."

I want to see acupuncture in practice. Long needles are twirled between the fingers. "Like this," said a practitioner, showing me how he kept his fingers supple by revolving a burning matchstick between finger and thumb so the wood burned evenly.

"We get sixty per cent success with epileptics," said another nerve-puncture specialist. His explanation of the acupuncture theory seemed simple. Needles stimulated nerve centers, which in turn caused glands to release chemicals or make bodily organs work extra hard. He admitted that nobody seemed to know why needles inserted in certain parts of the body should produce good results; he only knew, from knowledge handed down to successive generations and now being assembled, that this was so.

The claim was made in Peking that Encephalitis B, which presents many problems to Western medicine, responded to a combination of Chinese herbs and acupuncture. Chronic inflammation of the kidneys showed some hopeful responses.

"We must be cautious in claiming good results," said Dr. Wei. "But we have definitely achieved a great measure of success with polio, and we seem to be making progress in research on cancer treatment with herbal remedies. We know it all sounds very unscientific, but don't forget that the traditional remedies have stood the test of centuries. We think these country cures must have had merit or they could not have survived."

Plagued by a cold, I tried one of these cures. Chinese friends took me to a snake shop. We weaved through crates of cobras caught in the monsoon rains sweeping in from the China Sea across Kwangtung province. In a slime-covered cellar, caged raccoons paced up and down restlessly, while an overalled assistant hauled one cobra after another out of the boxes. He slipped a thumb and forefinger down the belly of each snake, found the gall bladder and, in a quick, neat operation, cut it out and slipped the stunned snake back into another bag.

Three gall bladders were dropped into a cup, split open and the green-black bile mixed with snake wine. I drank this in a single gulp but still caught the bitter taste. It was supposed to fix a cold and stimulate sexual appetite. All it did was upset my stomach for a week.

However, I pursued investigations undismayed. There was always an immediate and enthusiastic response to inquiries. "Had I head that Chairman Mao kept in good health by the use of Chinese herbs?" I was asked. "Did I know that the Chairman was a prodigious long-distance swimmer and a formidable athlete at the age of sixty-four?"

I *had* heard, but doubted some of the stories. Even dried toads and snake bile could hardly be responsible for one claim made by the New China News Agency that in May 1956 "Chairman Mao swam twenty kilometers non-stop in two hours across the swift-flowing Yangtse River." This would have made him the world's champion.

It was curious that Mao should be linked with this resurgence in Chinese medicine. There seemed to be no exercise of critical faculties: the Chairman had spoken, his views coincided with surging waves of nationalism, and therefore (it seemed to me) everyone was determined to prove he was right. Oddly enough, this blind obedience to a Party attitude was exactly what Mao had attacked years before, employing the analogy of a Chinese chemist.

"Go and take a look at any Chinese chemist," he said in an important statement to Party leaders in 1942. "There you see a cabinet with innumerable drawers, each bearing the name of the drug: toncal, foxglove, rhubarb, saltpeter — indeed everything that should be there. This method has been picked up by our comrades . . . It is the method of formalism which classified things according to their external features instead of their internal relations."

I took a look at many Chinese chemists. My favorite was in Yunnan where traditional cures meant a great deal to country folk.

Yan Fung, the local physican in Pao Shan, held some large black objects in his hand that looked like deflated balloons.

"Dried bears' bladders," he said. "Our local output has gone up forty pounds a year."

"Good for rheumatism," grunted his bearded assistant.

I bumped my head on the low beams of their store. Queer shapes lurked in the gloom. There were dried toads, split lizards, the bones of local mountain leopards, a bear's great paw and the extended claws of a wolf.

It was like the inside of a witch's caldron. Here were, in fact, the "Eye of newt, and toe of frog, wool of bat, and tongue of dog," from Shakespeare's hellish brew. The street outside was narrow, unpaved and lined with little shops that crouched back from open ditches, exposing their few wares to the ragged passers-by.

"Sale of this medicine has risen fifty per cent here," said Yan Fung. "Chairman Mao himself ordered a big increase in production of herbs."

I wondered how you would raise the production of powdered deer's horn, tiger whiskers, ground fishbones and cicada skins. All these remedies where set out on wooden trestles and I hesitated to ask what macabre relics lay in the innumerable drawers covered in cabalistic signs.

For centuries Yan's store had stood here. He was justly proud of this. He scooped up some slender white stalks. "In winter," he said, "they live like worms. In summer they turn to grass."

I said this was obviously an old country superstition and surely the Party would disapprove of such nonsense. He absorbed this comment, sucking on a hollow tooth and peering at me from under wiry-haired eyebrows. Several long whiskers grew from a mole under his chin and he fingered these as he asked: "You are not Russian?"

Receiving a negative reply, he said: "Here we believe these stalks of grass turn into worms in winter." He repeated this in a flat and final tone of voice.

"Bears' bladders are very expensive," he said, in reply to my questions. His prices worked out at about $50 a pound of dried bladder. Cow's gall stones, ground into powder for fevers, cost close to $45 an ounce. He hammered at a subterranean plant called *ghu ling*, the sort of horrid dark shape you encounter in nightmares. "For indigestion," he explained.

"The root of a *ma-huong* plant is for perspirations, its stalk having exactly the opposite effect. Carrots are good for the liver; pumpkins help the spleen. Pine seeds are a tonic. Powdered scorpions cure fevers and tree fungus acts as a soporific."

There is a tremendous market for these oddities beyond China. A petrified root was shown to me as a popular export to Japan. Wherever Chinese live abroad there is a big demand for such physics as wildcat pickled (complete with fur) in alcohol. Snakes yield the ingredients for a variety of sorceries: their venom, meat, blood and organs all have a prescribed usefulness.

This demand in Asia is so great China cannot meet it. One of Canada's exports to Hong Kong is cows' gallstones. Another, not generally boosted in Ottawa's trade literature, is the male organ of the Arctic seal.

Opium is widely regarded as a sovereign remedy but, banned in China, is more commonly used among Overseas Chinese communities. It is responsible for much of the tuberculosis in Hong Kong, a Crown Colony of Her Britannic Majesty with the world's highest TB rate. A famous believer in opium was the Empress Dowager Tz'u Hsi until just before her death, when she was severely shaken to see a comet "large as the moon, with a tail like a broom five miles long." Taking this as an omen, she gave up the pipe; not a bad thing to have done since ten years earlier she had decreed that all court officials must stop smoking opium within a decade. Time was up, in more ways than one, and she died soon afterwards; some said a victim of the Dalai Lama's patent medicine, others said from the prolonged effects of dysentery.

By that time, acupuncture was widely revered. There was in Peking a famous bronze statue in the temple to the God of Medicine. The temple was razed to make room for the Russian diplomatic compound. Prince Uktomsky took it to St. Petersburg where it excited great laughter and vulgar comment. The statue charted all those holes which might be safely used by the specialist in nerve puncture.

Today Prince Uktomsky might laugh on the other side of his

face. The possibility looms that the Soviet Union will be obliged, in the interests of fraternal cooperation, to give Chinese herbs and needles a fair trial. Already the Soviet hospital in Peking has found room for the ancients who mix these magic philters.

In the earlier days when Russia still cast a spell upon these people, China's halls of medicine echoed to the cry for more children. My 1954 notebook contained the comment: "Object is to raise population from one-quarter to one third human race. Like industrial production drive, with Model Mothers competing to over-fulfil targets."

That was the time when several hundred million Chinese were persuaded to regard Pavlov as their hero and Soviet medicine their infallible guide.

With miraculous ease, Mao popularized the reverse view. Within two years, one quarter of humanity chorused that it had no wish to flood the earth. Abortion became law, the methods of contraception were vigorously promoted and the diagrams on the Yangtse river boats became even more revolting. And in the countryside, precious little was heard from Pavlov's disciples.

CHAPTER TWENTY-NINE

China Enters Her No-Baby Days

◉ ◉

IT WOULD BE just too easy to declare with an apocalyptic flourish that the Age of the Planned Baby dawned in China with a secret and urgent meeting in the Pavilion of Political Diligence. Such a conference, however, did occur. Mao Tsè-tung was there with his shadow, Comrade Liu Shao-chi, and the buxom Health Minister, Madame Li Teh-chuan. It was March 1954, and to the outside world this trio maintained an anti-Malthusian posture. Privately they discussed what seemed a major break with Russian orthodoxy. If China was to prosper, her estimated population of a billion people by 1980 must be drastically cut.

But how? There were three major problems and we know from internal evidence that these were shredded through the mills of pragmatic argument for two years. In the process, the Soviet Union repealed its own law against abortion.

The problems were these:

Could China break with all previous practice and launch a Family Planning campaign without annoyance to the Kremlin?

Would this terrify millions of peasants who, in the later words of Madame Li, "would think we were stopping them from sowing the seed of new life?"

And finally, could the cheaper methods of traditional Chinese contraception be used effectively?

A singular competition between two of Shanghai's cigarette

factories revealed to foreign observers how some of the answers might be found. In the summer of 1956, investigators reported to Peking that twelve tobacco factories were turning out babies almost as fast as cigarettes: about 3000 babies each year to 14,500 women workers. It was therefore decided to persuade the ladies of Number Two Shanghai Cigarette Factory to experiment with herbs and other concoctions used by Chinese medicine men to discourage pregnancy. In Number Three Factory, however, there was a free distribution of modern devices.

The surviving infants would be "planned" babies indeed, and their numbers would measure the merits of rival techniques. Soon this singular trial was being repeated with variations in other industrial areas. A model mill was found and publicly extolled: Shanghai Cotton Mill Number Nine had reduced *its* birth rate from 20 to 12 per cent by a little concentrated effort.

An old man, formerly one of Chiang Kai-shek's Nationalist leaders, finally took the fatal plunge at the 1957 People's Political Consultative Conference and uttered the words everyone waited to hear.

> According to my shallow understanding [said Shao Li-tzu] the view of Malthus, that population if left unchecked would increase at a geometrical progressional rate, is *correct* . . . China and the Soviet Union are completely different. Our population is about twice the size of theirs but it has a little more than half the land . . . The Soviet Union is underpopulated and the annual rate of increase is small and slow, so it adopts a policy to encourage increases in population.

This was strong stuff. Shao took the precaution of hastily adding: "I stand to be corrected if I am wrong," before he came to the heart of the matter. "In China," he said, shattering not a few die-hards, "the present rate of increase is too big and sharp. Therefore we should *dialectically* adopt a policy which seeks to plan for and control the birth rate."

So the Chinese quarreled with a favorite Russian myth. Other Communist Parties limped along with Kremlin rescripts that the nineteenth-century Englishman, Malthus, was utterly wrong in claiming that food production lagged behind population increase. The theoreticians even disguised Malthus as an instrument of British colonialist ambition.

Of course Shao, being a non-Party deserter from the Kuomintang, would be expendable if policy should change again. For although Soviet Russia of this time seemed opposed to family planning, Kremlin views on abortion were subject to the most bewildering revisions.

Madame Li* seems to have been the catalytic agent in breaking down Chinese prejudice. As widow of the former warlord and "Christian General," Feng Yu-hsiang, she had considerable influence. It would seem that her agitations began at least by 1953 and were fed by observations on tours through non-Communist Asia. She saw, and evidently reported, that Chinese Communist leaders might as well forget their dreams of an immediate uprising of the peasantry in undeveloped nations if they refused to face Asia's curse: soaring populations whose numbers grew faster than food.

And so, "with the greatest reluctance," she told the 1957 C.P.P.C.C. session that henceforth the strict rules governing induced abortion and sterilization would be changed. Such operations would be made on request and without restriction.

A massive campaign was launched at once, revealing that preparations had been long in hand. Exhibitions toured the country, films and lantern slides were circulated, posters went up in remote villages, all harping on the one great theme of birth control.

A symposium was conducted at Peking's Labor Cadre School. The chief topic was: "Control of the law of population."

"Man," said a *Peking Daily Worker* editorial, "is most valuable"; and it went on to discuss how to conserve this precious commodity, how to avoid squandering it by overproduction. "For control over frequency of impregnation," it concluded,

---

* Her strongest critic was Madame Sun Yat-sen, one of the famous Soong sisters, who decided to support Communism although her sister championed the Nationalist cause as Madame Chiang Kai-shek. Madame Sun opposed the whole idea of birth control.

"there must be advocacy of late marriage. Frustrate early marriage, promote late marriage and teach birth control."

These ringing words reverberated through the nation. A moody diplomat in Peking had already told me: "I expect to see officials ration out pregnancies among newlyweds. Their thought control is now so good that a young couple can be told where and when to have babies — and of course, how."

Old Shao Li-tsu, having stuck his neck out fairly far, now pushed it out further. "Men," he said, "must be taught the important political task of birth control . . . The right age for marriage should be twenty-five to thirty. Young couples should not fall in love or get married too early."

He talked a good deal about a mysterious "directive" from Mao Tse-tung. In the new spirit of anonymity, Mao as the nerve center of the developing mass mind of China had broken the news to the inner circle, and now the ripples were radiating outward. From all parts of the country came information on traditional methods of contraception.

Shao mentioned a few. There was said to be a medicine derived from a kind of toad (though some said it came from fungus) which taken orally would prevent conception. This ancient formula had been disclosed by the reformed prostitutes of Shanghai.

Death might result from the swallowing of tadpoles, however, said to be a sovereign remedy in the south. There were stories from Malaya that the raw juice of unripe pineapples was effective, and Madame Li herself sent for an experimental dose from the new plantations on Hainan Island.

She reported to the C.P.P.C.C. that one Shanghai textile mill produced (besides shirts) a total of "7000 babies in seven years out of 7000 male and female workers."

Some doctors objected. Special medical forums were held in Peking. We glimpsed the curious trend of debate from official reports. These were very revealing. A certain Madame K'ang T'ung-pi, for instance, called for prohibition of abortion by law. Evidently she failed to catch the spirit of the meeting. Doctors were assured beforehand that Chairman Mao was anxious to hear all views expressed. He wanted no slavish echoes of foreign doctrine. So Madame K'ang's impassioned speech was heard in relative silence as she quoted case after case from advanced Soviet practice to support her thesis that abortion and birth control were wrong.

Old Comrade Shao was given the delicate task of ridiculing her blind devotion to Russian methods. He was reported by the official New China News Agency as saying: "Comrade committee member K'ang has cited examples from the Soviet Union, but unfortunately she did not notice that the outlawing of abortion in the Soviet Union had been repealed in 1955, otherwise she would perhaps not advocate the prohibition of abortion by law."

How did this change come about?

The Chinese are a pragmatic people, otherwise they could not have survived. They took practical action while echoing impractical theories, and this was particularly true under the last dynasty, the Ch'ing. The authoritarian aspects of Confucianism were stressed in imperial edicts and it was more important to be orthodox than think. Instead of a real study of Confucian principles, the examination student who hoped to join the privileged scholar-gentry class would learn by rote the "eight-legged essay." In other words, to quote Mao Tse-tung in his attacks on "eight-legged" formalism, they knew the form but forgot the content. In rebellion against this torpid conformity, scholars began a re-examination of the classics in order to apply their teachings to modern society.

A similar rebellion against Russian orthodoxy hardly means, as some optimists would suggest, that the new China is less dangerous because it promises to give a new vitality and vigor to what was becoming a dying dogma. No theory in the past had unduly bothered the Chinese when circumstances dictated otherwise. The British found this to their delight when running opium into China in the nineteenth century. The story bears repeating for its revelation of Chinese habits.

In the Dragon Seat of the 1820's was Glorious Rectitude. One of his many edicts on the question of foreign devils began: "It is very difficult for the Barbarians to understand the proprieties of the Celestial Empire." Therefore, he admonished

his Hong contractors in Canton, every discreet effort should be
made to discourage the Outer Barbarians from undermining
the Empire of Lord-of-the-World with "foreign mud": opium.
The gesture having been made, the proprieties observed, Chinese officials proceeded to do tremendous business in opium.
British clippers in the Pearl River unloaded vast quantities of
foreign mud at the Island of the Solitary Nail, and were then
pursued by as many as forty men-of-war junks. The junks
clapped on all sail, the clippers were careful to give them fair
chase, and at an appropriate moment the Chinese discharged a
loud volley and the Barbarians were seen to vanish in defeat
over the far horizons. Horsemen galloped to Peking with tid-
ings of yet another glorious victory, and in Canton the chests
of opium were swiftly borne into the warehouses of Hog's
Lane.

Events today are less colorful and it would be wrong to
suppose that the moralizing fervor of the regime does not penetrate into most walks of life. But some time ago, the expedient and flexible men and women who group themselves around
Mao Tse-tung came to the conclusion that it would be fatally
stupid to copy the Russians in all things.

They pointed out that the Soviet Union was underpopulated
at the time of revolution: China, on the contrary, was over-
populated. And they set about methods of correcting this.
Some pointed out that more than half the human race was
Chinese back in A.D. 1644, and was likely to become so again;
at that time (the start of the Manchu dynasty) there were
estimated to be one hundred million people in China, and even
in those days there were alarmists who said the land could not
sustain such a pressure of population.

I talked about this one day with an elderly professor from
Peking University. As with so many Chinese intellectuals, the
point he wished to make was not immediately evident.

"Masses of people have always been a Chinese problem," he
said. "That is why you see this experiment in 'mass democracy' — the cynical call it dictatorship, but I think they're
wrong. From the start of the Manchu dynasty, China was the
only country in the world able to support a very dense population. How?"

He stroked his chin whiskers. "By using mass labor, on dikes and irrigation and roads; by putting ten men into a paddy instead of five; by living in crowded conditions, frugally; and by submission on the part of peasants to the directives of the labor-team organizers.

"You had to have Western industrial development before you could cultivate the land so intensively. We had no machinery but we did have organization. You had pioneers: individuals who explored new country. When we established colonies, we sent people in large groups led by public officials.

"You are going to say: 'Why, that sounds like China today.'" He smiled and continued to stroke his skimpy beard. There was a short silence and then he changed the subject.

Professor Wu Ching-ch'ao discussed this question of organizing the masses, using of course the modern idiom of Marxism, in the official publication *New Construction*. He was discussing the traditional Chinese belief that the three most desirable joys in life are Prosperity, Long Life and Many Children.

But prejudice [he wrote] can be removed by propaganda and education. The most deep-rooted prejudice in the world is probably that for private property. But in China the people gave up such prejudice through propaganda.

The same could be done with the prejudice for more children.

The Chinese can be silly and sentimental. No doubt it would take time to remove this idiotic prejudice. But Professor Wu had assembled his arguments. "Don't attack us and say we are New Malthusians," he warned. "We are not. We advocate birth control because it is believed good for the health of mothers, good for the care and attention and education of our children, good for prosperity, good for making our production fall in line with basic economic laws of socialism and good for relieving unemployment.

"If you want to object to this conclusion," he added, "explain your viewpoint from the angle of practical needs."

Once an expedient course of action is decided upon, a formidable array of statistics is fired at the unwary populace. This, I suspect, has been tried on the Russians too. As a leader

in the Kremlin, I would feel distinctly uneasy whenever I saw
an emissary from Peking come to resolve an argument.

A typical set of calculations was published in the *Peking
Daily Worker* in March 1957. It pointed out the wastefulness
of abortion with these figures:

> In six months last year 1593 people went into Peking's
> twenty-four municipal hospitals for abortions and occupied 10.6
> per cent of the beds available for gynecology. They used the
> equivalent of 4779 doctors and, assuming artificial abortion
> takes fifteen minutes, they wasted 1194 hours of precious pro-
> fessional time. On the basis of an eight-hour day, this amounted
> to 149 working days, which meant one doctor doing all the
> work would spend nearly seven and a half months doing it!

The case of Big Sister Ku was widely quoted. She had fourteen children. This was no disgrace. However, steps were
being taken now to curb other prolific Big Sisters with a
prejudice for big families. Midwives were spreading enlightenment in seventeen provinces. Another 12,000 midwives of
Inner Mongolia were "trained and reformed."

Mongolian midwives astride camels scattered illustrated
tracts around the Gobi and nailed the kingly nomads before
they squeezed in among their many wives for a night under
the yak skins. But for many minority groups, Mao's policy
was not to interfere in such intimate matters. Concubines and
extra wives, too, were allowed.

Once more, Mao's practical application of policies cloaked
with jargon suggested the cautious Imperial Dragon rather
than the bigot. I found senior cadres and the executive chief of
a tribal area who frankly admitted their adherence to second
and third wives acquired before the revolution. In some parts,
non-Han Chinese were allowed to maintain old customs of concubinage. Overseas Chinese returning to the homeland could
bring and continue to live with additional wives.

This, I am sure, has upset many doctrinaire Communists
coming from abroad. Mao's argument seems to be that provided such practices do not perpetuate themselves and even
become contagious, it is better in the long run to let them

flourish *among certain classes*. That is, among Overseas Chinese whose political feelings are neutral or friendly; and among minorities who might be driven into armed resistance if hastily converted. Meanwhile, of course, the daily persuasion meetings continue among all such people. Their conversion is regarded as purely a matter of time.

Another strong reason for taking the birth-control campaign slowly was indicated by Shao Li-tsu. "Contraceptives are too expensive and cost more than one yuan [about forty-two cents]," he said. "This is due to the profiteering of the China Medical Company."

Blank stares met my request for details about this profiteering. This was not unexpected. It frequently happens that the Party propaganda machine is ahead of senior officials, and even while the Family Planning drive was in preparation, the woman gynecologist in charge of Peking's maternity and child-health hospitals, Dr. C. J. Yang, was telling some of us that there was no official concern with the growth in population. Soon afterwards, her minister announced that China's population was bounding to the astronomical height of 15,000,000 more people every year. The number of babies born annually was more than 22,000,000. This at once conjured up a vision of the Chinese multiplying *each month* by more than the whole population of New Zealand.

This fearful prospect might influence Dr. Yang, previously unworried and preaching a different gospel, to reverse her views. But how would you make millions of housewives change their longing for "Many Children?"

Professor Wu spoke confidently of removing prejudice by propaganda. He had cause for certainty. In such personal matters as birth control, or forcing out the local prostitute, there are legions of little female busybodies. They belong to an intricate organization of housewives and once again, there is nothing new about their existence. The difference lies in technique. For centuries in China, as elsewhere in Asia, the local Neighborhood Association has been a means by which authority could spy upon the citizen.

In modern China, this roles assumes tremendous importance.

It is disconcerting to find so many visitors to Peking maintain that "thought control" does not exist; that stories of mutual spying are absurd. The fact is that the power of these small units is tremendous.

I cannot give you an example of how neighborhood groups changed the Chinese love of children into something more calculating, because my last visit ended before the campaign got under way. To show how pressure can be applied, here is what happened in the coastal industrial center of Tsingtao when it became overcrowded.

Thousands of peasants came looking for work and, in December 1956, the local People's Council became alarmed. There was widespread unemployment and some unrest. Men had been laid off at the local locomotive works. Work on harbor extensions had been stopped. The textile mills were reducing the number of shifts. All this was the result of economic problems that forced a reduction of ambitious plans. The influx of peasants from the Shantung hinterland only aggravated a local crisis.

It was announced that there would be "a mobilization of peasants who have blindly infiltrated into the city to return to rural areas for production."

This was to be done by gentle persuasion. A foreign observer in the city would have seen no dramatic migration, no forced marches under guns.

The pressure was applied in far more subtle ways. A document was circulated to leaders of neighborhood units. It reveals the technique for handling all unpleasant tasks.

> Public security men are to strengthen census control. Permanent residential facilities should not be granted to peasants who come here when they should be working on the land.
>
> Food departments: Strengthen control of supplies and restaurants. Temporary residents may have food for a limited time only.
>
> Labor departments must not give jobs to peasants.
>
> Persuade temporary workers in factories to go back to their villages.
>
> Attention should be given to the following: (a) propaganda

and education should show the importance of farm work; *(b)* those with permanent employment, registered as permanent residents and on the census may not be sent home; *(c)* parents and direct dependents with no productive power and who get subsistence from working relatives may stay.

This document sounds harmless. Read it again, however, and you will gather the mentality of its authors. The standard by which to judge a would-be resident is his productive capacity. If he fails to measure up squeeze him out by denying food and employment. There is one slender hint of kindness: provided an aged parent cannot work, and so long as he lives entirely off his family, he can stay. Yet, after the same instructions had been published in the Tsingtao press, a Western visitor to that city, who speaks fluent Chinese, hotly argued that the people there were free and motivated only by self-discipline.

The leader of a street group is no doubt high-minded. She is the local gossip transformed into an Official Snooper. In Peking they have one whose name pops into almost every account written by recent visitors. She is a sharp-eyed lady who weeps in recounting her memories of past miseries.

But I am being cynical. Any woman of Old China has justification for tears, shed for others if not for herself.

Madame Chiang is a street-committee chairman. She lives in a crooked, muddy *ho'tung* behind a red door and the usual high wall. When I went to see her, a street peddler had erected his stall outside. He sold Lux Toilet Soap, Camel cigarettes, Wrigley chewing gum and Gillette razors. When I looked closer, however, the word Lux had turned into a Chinese ideograph, the camel on the cigarette packet was an elephant and other brand names had undergone similar transformations. All were in fact Chinese products and retained American-type labels for ease of identification.

The wayward thought struck me that perhaps this symbolized China. The labels were changed but the contents remained the same. Or was it the other way around? The labels were the same but Sinified; the contents were different.

Madame Chiang, as one of almost three million directors of

street committees and neighborhood units in China, clearly suffered no such doubts. The Past had been Wicked: the Present
was a Struggle: the Future would be Glorious. Both wrappers
and contents were undergoing change. She was, it seemed, a
perfect piece of apparatus through which the *kung an* or public
security could transmit each new campaign. She knew all
about her neighbors: it was her job. She knew all about the
latest directives: that was also her job.

First, she said, came health and hygiene. Then came Happiness in Marriage (her eyes sharpened, her shrewd little head
nodded eagerly: "Often I have to talk to parents on behalf of
some poor young girl being forced into a reluctant marriage").
There were also the drives (she had been reading an article
entitled: "Should there be whipped up a high tide for changing the status of Capitalists?").

There was a lot about Madame Chiang and others of her
kind that I learned to respect. For I went back to see some of
them after an interval of two years. They seemed to have mel-
lowed — and yet . . . When the "high tide of enthusiasm for
contraception" began to roll, they snapped into action. They
were admirable women. There seemed to be about one to spy
into the affairs of every hundred females. They were formidable women. There were meetings at least twice a week which
they conducted, solely to propagate "high tides." They were
enthusiasts, fanatics: a terror to the girl student at No. 10
who liked to be paid for her favor; champions of the police
informer; digging relentlessly into the past of some poor, re-
educated bourgeois boilermaker; and wielders of great authority.
By the spring of 1958 their pressure and influence succeeded in
making any young couple indiscriminately producing children
feel positively bestial.

Tireless women, proud to be free from their old positions as
household utensils, they would love henceforth their Chairman, honor the State and obey the dictates of the Collective
Will. But they would make unrewarding companions.

To them fell the task of educating young brides and mothers in the fundamentals of family planning. The curious thing
was that they impressed me as the only successful solution to

CHINA ENTERS HER NO-BABY DAYS

the problem in Asia of popularizing this unpopular subject. There was, by contrast, an earnest spinster in India who had exiled herself from Western comforts in order to enlighten the illiterate peasants. She was an expert in her subject and spent a great deal of time persuading the Indian Health Minister, also a woman, Raj Amrit Kaur. Finally she got permission to test her scheme for natural birth control. Soon necklaces and score cards began to arrive by the gross from the United States.

"Whatever do they do?" I asked this well-meaning lady one day in Delhi.

"The beads are used to count the days," she cooed. "The cards are marked with 'those difficult days' in red. The housewife just ticks the card as she counts the beads daily. And here are the explanatory leaflets to precede our campaign.'

She flourished one in triumph. It was entitled: "Do you know what are your Baby Days and your No-Baby Days?"

CHAPTER THIRTY

Conspiracy in a Red Pavilion

◉ ◉

Marxists are still a minority . . . Marxism therefore must still develop through struggle . . . Ideological struggle is not like other forms of struggle. Crude coercive methods should not be used in the struggle but only painstaking methods of reason . . . Marxists must steel and improve themselves and win new positions in the teeth of criticism and the storm and stress of struggle. Fighting against wrong ideas is like being vaccinated — a man develops greater immunity from disease. Plants raised in hothouses are unlikely to be robust.

MAO TSE-TUNG *to a Supreme State Council in February 1957.*

INSTEAD OF political parties the Chinese had always their secret societies. The pulse beat of the nation prior to revolution was heard in the incantations of Buddhist and Taoist organizations, in the oaths between blood brothers as they swore to overthrow some tyrant. When life became intolerably hard the coolie could escape into his family and his secret society. He staggered uncomplainingly under enormous loads, submitted to oppressive warlords and kept his smoldering thoughts to himself and the family circle. The rickshaw boy fell panting between the shafts, shoulders bruised and back grooved, belly bloated and feet bleeding, and some unknown passser-by might touch his shaven head in a gesture of freemasonry.

Mao with the Mandate of Heaven in his hand, a road mender's cap on his head, came along as the father figure whose unseen touch consoled. He destroyed the family confessional and made the Party name a glittering, graceful symbol of defiance when painted in swift brush strokes on vermilion walls. By 1957 he was ready to test the claim that the need for compulsion had ended. He went farther than Stalin who said, at a similar stage in his career: "The function of compulsion inside the country has ceased, has withered away. The exploiters are no more and there is no one to exploit any more."

But Stalin did continue to employ suppression and terror. It led eventually to a denunciation of Stalin himself and it demonstrated in the most dramatic manner the emptiness of Marxist theory. This lesson was not lost on Mao Tse-tung, who made his bid for leadership of world Communism on an entirely different basis from that of physical power. Mao understood that terror creates enemies by its need for victims. So instead of prolonging naked force, he launched a Movement for the Ideological Education of the Masses which he insisted "must be carried out seriously yet as gently as a breeze or light rain."

However, it was not so easy for other Communist states to follow this example held up by the Chinese as a demonstration of how Hungarian-style revolts might be avoided. For one thing, terror could not be turned on and off like a tap in Eastern Europe. For another, the people were not Chinese.

Several factors favored Mao's belief that more could be accomplished by persuasion. There were the Chinese characteristics of submission to strong, centralized government; of avoiding open conflict at almost any cost; of echoing whatever dogma was fashionable; of agreeing with superior authority rather than becoming martyred in a hopeless cause. But these were essentially traits of Chinese character, and while Mao's methods were successful in a peculiarly favorable climate, they were not to be depended upon, say, in Poland or East Germany.

On the other hand, Mao's power was also threatened by purely Chinese characteristics. Under the bland exterior of a man who agreed wholeheartedly with official policy, there often seethed a caldron of hates and antagonisms. These secret protests inspired many men to join societies. And for this reason, Mao concentrated upon absorbing, subverting or uprooting such organizations.* He advised the Party at the very start of its career to "become the nuclear force of the Red Spear Society and the Big Spear Society and so gradually change their nature." These were large secret societies in South and Central China which he described as being "close to the masses and against the warlords."

He failed to uproot other societies. One of the more vigorous was the Triad of South China, which sprang from the attempt of 128 monks to overthrow the seventeenth-century Manchu Ch'ing emperors. The Triads later became an instrument of Chiang Kai-shek's Nationalists whose own Kuomintang began as a secret society too. If we are to understand how Maoism succeeds in regimenting so many millions of minds, we might consider the Triads and then possibly conclude that Mao's Communist Party has a great deal in common with the ancient secret rituals, and that its popularity is paradoxical, being based initially upon the influences of tradition. Many Party members mouth Marxist litanies as they might have sworn secret oaths. But to maintain this type of popular support, the Party has to remain a conspiracy *against* something. In the old days, it was secretly working to overthrow or may not have developed into an organization of spies and Chiang Kai-shek, to defeat the Japanese invaders, to eject Western imperialists . . . Later it launched popular campaigns against Americans in Korea, against missionary "spies" and against espionage agents.

The danger may be that if it runs out of "enemies" and becomes too securely enthroned, other societies will grow and conspire to overthrow the Party. This is not politics in any

---

* Mao's view of secret societies was expressed in the "Doctrine of Prepared Insurrection" which was submitted in his absence to the Sixth Chinese Communist Party National Congress in Moscow in 1928. He was absent because Stalin, busy smelling out Trotskyites, nursed the blackest suspicions of Mao.

Western sense, but in certain circumstances it can be more effective than a soapbox in Hyde Park.

"You must give up life to attain righteousness," admonished Liu Shao-chi in outlining the tests for Party membership during the late thirties. "Sacrifice your own life to complete your virtue . . . Speak not thoughtlessly to harm another comrade but instead endure the harmful words of others . . ."

There were even more thrilling codes. Mao described the maladies that might afflict the unwary member, and for each he prescribed a "Method of Rectification."

These mental diseases sapped the Party's energies and pierced its mental armor. They included Group Egoism ("a form of enlarged cliquism"). There were other horrors like Extreme Democratization; Non-Organizational Criticism; Hedonism; Absolute Equalitarianism and the most highly infectious Remnants of Adventurism.

One day while ruminating on the Rectifications and wondering how it might all sound as a Gregorian chant, I went to the Communist Canton security authorities and asked to see the old Triad headquarters at 14 Po Wah Road. There had been rumors that Triads were active again inside China.

The Triads were reorganized by Chiang Kai-shek's intelligence chief attached to Kuomintang army operations. He was General Tai Lee and he pushed thousands of Chiang's men into secret society branches. Apparently most fled, however, with the retreating Kuomintang to Hong Kong, ninety miles southeast from their Po Wah Road center in Canton. They became known as the "14K": the number was taken from their former address and combined with the letter K to indicate their fourteen-carat gold quality.

Communist officials were somewhat startled by my inquiries and they told me bluntly: "Triads are operating with Hong Kong as a base and as a branch of the Kuomintang. Their counterrevolutionary agents are constantly smuggling high explosives and other sabotage devices into our country."

They thereupon displayed a number of vicious little weapons which were said to have been discovered in the bags or on the persons of Chinese returning from the British colony.

There were imitation sugar-cane sticks crammed with explosives, plastic bombs no bigger than mechanical pencils and other "sabotage instruments." I was taken to an exhibition of such infernal machines. Bored citizens pushed buttons under a large wall map to illuminate "the American espionage route" from Formosa or across the Pacific. Parachutes, crumpled radio transmitters and other sinister gadgets littered the floor. The markings *Made in U.S.A.* were prominent on some of the equipment which might have been captured in Korea. It was not a convincing exhibition but it was difficult to dismiss with only a shrug.

Memories were still only too fresh of the warning issued by Communist authorities to the British chargé d'affaires in Peking, that an attempt might be made to sabotage the chartered Air India plane *Kashmir Princess*, one day before it happened. The airliner waited in Hong Kong for a Chinese delegation to the Bandung conference of Afro-Asian nations. It exploded on the way to Indonesia, and killed sixteen, including two of my former interpreters. British investigators identified the saboteur as Chow Tse-ming, alias Chou Chu, who escaped aboard one of General Chennault's ex-Flying Tiger planes to Formosa where Nationalist authorities gave him sanctuary. Chow was a Triad member, and British police said he was promised a modest reward to place a time bomb in the wheelbay of the starboard wing.

I returned from the Canton exhibition by way of the Memorial Hall to Dr. Sun Yat-sen. Lackadaisical officials were performing exercises in the grounds. On the adjoining airfield were three MiG-17's waltzing off and on the runway as their Chinese pilots practiced stream landings.

At such times you felt the entire Chinese nation was engaged in some gigantic and esoteric ritual. Loudspeakers announced, "Ten Minute Physical Interlude," and then chanted the liturgy to which the devout made their responses on bended knees. The ceremony occurred three times daily and I could always visualize it moving with the sun across China. It was not uncommon to hear the mechanical muezzins cry out in the middle of an official interview. Comrades would hastily assemble and lift their arms as if to invoke divine strength to cope with the rest of my barbaric questions.

In Canton they seemed less devout, although it was their native son, the good Doctor Sun, who introduced these public gymnastics. He also encouraged the Triads who became an ally of his own Kuomintang. The Triads in Hong Kong may or may not have developed into an organization of spies and saboteurs against Red China, but they helped keep the nearby city of Canton in a state of jitters and I had an opportunity of witnessing the extreme sensitivity of Communist officials to Triad activities, as I shall explain later.

There are, of course, many other powerful secret societies among Chinese, such as the semi-religious White Lotus which claims followers on the mainland, despite attempts at suppression. Hardly a month passed by between 1949 and 1958 when the Communist police did not denounce some secret organization. If their own propaganda was to be believed, the Party was waging a continuous struggle against rival groups. The difficulty was to judge how many of the official stories were true: some undoubtedly were, and others were embroidered or even invented to maintain the artificial sense of "the storm and stress of struggle."

I selected the Triads as an example because there is more documentary evidence available than in other cases, because they are quite openly used for political reasons and because so much of their mumbo-jumbo has its counterpart in Communist practice.

After Chiang Kai-shek's retreat to Formosa the Triads, having moved into Hong Kong in strength, were powerful enough to take over most local crime, which was as vast as it was ingenious and varied. They extended membership and became dominant among 1,500,000 Chinese in the tiny colony. Despite a large British-administered police force numbering 5000 men, Triad influence was almost impossible to eradicate. The vital area of police surveillance has never been more than sixty-two square miles, or one sixth of the entire colony. The rest is largely hillside or swamp. To this day, wherever people are densest (about 2000 to one acre) the 14K is most active.

Among their fifteen subbranches, two are plainly political and include several thousand ex-military Kuomintang agents. The biggest has 10,000 members and rallies anti-Communist feeling among some 500,000 poverty-stricken refugees. These Triads have discipline and ceremonials typical of such societies during many centuries. They are a form of group activity by which Chinese have traditionally sought to gain their own ends in preference to individual martyrdom: but of course they have become debased.

Every opium divan, every prostitute and pimp, drug peddler and dance-hall keeper in Hong Kong today pays some form of protection to the Triads and their associates. There are daylight choppings with the favorite choice of weapon, a cook-boy's hatchet. Men, women and children are beaten up in reprisal raids.

Tourists fly into Kowloon on the mainland side of the colony, rush deliriously from one crammed shop to the next and after dark roam safely under the neon lights from glittering night club to air-conditioned hotel. They would be horrified to discover they were among Triad gangs. The barefoot coolie hauling a two-wheeled rickshaw through fashionable Nathan Road is liable to be a 14K courier, thug or "fighter." His services are always available to his own subbranch, organized for concerted action whenever the moment arises. Such is the power of the 14K that Hong Kong police have great difficulty in finding witnesses to its many crimes.

All this is a corruption of original Triad aims, a corruption of its former ideals. The links with the past are found in the titles of the 14K officials: Tai Koh (Eldest Brother), Yee Koh (Second Eldest Brother), Pak Tse-sin (White Paper Fan), Cho Hai (Straw Sandals) and Hung Kwan (Red Pole).

These appear in the Triad history of the Five Ancestors who escaped the treachery of the second Ch'ing emperor. His armies recruited help to crush an invasion from Tibet during the 1650's. From Siu Lam Monastery came 128 militant monks. They were too militant for their own good. The emperor wisely considered the danger to his own supremacy of this band of battling bedesmen. He hired Ma Leng-yee to wipe them out.

Ma was Monk Number Seven, expelled for exhibiting his physical prowess among the ladies. In the century's second Gunpowder Plot, he blew up the priory, fellow friars and all.

Eighteen scrambled from the ruins through a jagged hole, nine points at the bottom and twelve splinters at the top. Thirteen died of their wounds and then there were five. They all crossed the Yangtse, having only one straw sandal among them.

The Five Ancestors were helped by a fruit seller and supported by one of the Imperial Censors known as White Paper Fan. They found a base at Muk Yeung in Fukien province where they established a society for the destruction of Ch'ing emperors. An early recruit was Chu Hung-yuk whose arms reached below his knees and whose ears hung down to his shoulders . . . or so it is said.

Young Yuk, with a good sense of timing, revealed he was grandson of the deposed Ming Emperor, whereupon all agreed this fortuitous circumstance made him their natural leader. Thus the first known Triad Society was called the Hung Clan. It appointed five generals and elevated them to Ng Fu-tseung, the Five Tiger Generals, with a council of Four Great Loyal Subjects. The Officer-in-Charge of Fortunetelling was wise enough to advise the Society to scatter and spread the gospel, rather than attempt to recapture the throne alone. They obediently crept away from their meeting place, the Red Flower Pavilion, on a day when the sky was inexplicably red. Chinese today sometimes point out this felicitous omen, for the name of their leader and of their Clan also signifies red.

On a warm Hong Kong evening in September 1952, a number of red paper banners bearing the symbols of the Five Ancestors, the Red Flower Pavilion and the God of War might have been perceived advancing upon a wooden hut from the direction of what the British, in one of their sudden descents from dignity to drollery, have named Gin Drinkers' Bay.

This was the start of a 14K initiation ceremony and its details have been authenticated by the Hong Kong Criminal Investigation Department. It occurred at Tsuen Wan, a cluster of eight very old Chinese villages on the Castle Peak Road west of Kowloon. The location, we shall see later, has a certain significance.

Guards surrounded the hut and lookouts were posted along all the approaches. The recruits were guided by Mai Goh (Fruit Seller) and there would be normally present the Five Tiger Generals and Eight Immortals. Before them on an altar was a huge wooden pot containing chicken feathers, charcoal and uncooked rice. On the wall were red paper "tablets" with Chinese ideographs recording the perfidy of Number Seven Monk Ma, the escape of the Five Ancestors, the secret title of the Clan and several coded characters.

Into the altar pot went the Ten Precious Articles. They included a red lamp to distinguish true from false; a red pole such as the Siu Lam monks used for punishments; a straw sandal, monks' robes and prayer beads. There was a white paper fan with which to strike down traitors; its outer supports represented the capitals of Peking and Nanking, and thirteen inner ribs signified the Ming Dynasty provinces. A sword made from peachwood was copied from the magic sword used by the Five Ancestors; when waved in front of an enemy, his head fell off. There were also a joss-stick pot and a mirror like that presented to the Goddess of Heaven to identify the virtuous and the vicious.

The Heung Chiu (Officer-in-Charge) added to this strange collection a further heap of mystic objects. There were scales to weigh loyalty, a ruler to measure conduct and an abacus to reckon the time it would take to destroy the Ch'ings. Scissors would rip open the dark clouds in the ill-fated Ming's sky. An umbrella symbolized the Ming emperors and there were three paper coins in imitation of the old metal coins used as badges of membership.

Subvert Ch'ing — Restore Ming declared the imperative ideographs on white banners before the altar. Red banners around the walls had nine serrations on the hypotenuse and twelve on the base.

Coolies crouched in dark corners of the earthen floor, tapping lightly on drums and gongs. The Vanguard Officer made each recruit bow before the altar while joss sticks were burned and a seven-branched oil lamp lit. Officials slipped into their monks' gowns, ruffling their hair and tying it with red cord.

Wine was poured before the tablets at the altar and each recruit received a slice of date. A paper cutout of three human figures was now held up and all present knelt to pray for the destruction of Ma the Traitor, Chan the Sorcerer's Apprentice and the wicked Ch'ing emperor. Then the head of each figure was removed with a knife taken from the altar.

Slowly the candles and the seven-branched lamp were extinguished. The joss sticks glowed in the darkness. With windows and door shut, the little hut with indistinguishable figures crammed inside became a sweatbox.

"Praise the Pot," chanted the ritual chiefs and all knelt in a circle to worship the sacred contents of the great wooden bowl. Officials around the assembly represented guardians of the hole through which the monks escaped.

Each recruit bowed before the altar, holding a lighted joss stick toward the floor. As an official touched each man on the neck with a chopper, he asked: "Which is harder, your neck or the sword?" The reply: "My neck," signified that each would prefer death to divulging Society secrets.

Then began the swearing of oaths. There were thirty-six, mostly designed to produce good citizens and emphasize obedience to parents and respect for the relatives of all 14K members. Some are worth recording:

Do not try to sell widows.
If rich do not scorn the poor. If strong do not insult the weak.
Subscribe to the coffin of a fellow member if he dies. Help the member in difficulties
Assist in any fight waged by the Society.

After the swearing-in, recruits threw down their joss sticks and asked that their own lives should be similarly extinguished if the oaths were broken. The methods of extinguishment laid down by 14K rules include: death from ten thousand knife cuts, death from clubbing, and being blasted by thunder from all directions.

If these punishments were imposed, 14K members might be

fairly good citizens, but as British police reports wryly observe, the death rate from thunderclaps is extremely low.

A complex series of maneuvers was now required from the young initiates. The ceremony simulated the escape of the monks and finished with them back at the altar, drinking water and each eating one red date.

Now began the vital part of this weird ritual, The Iron Dragon Tactics. The head of a live cock was sliced off and the blood mixed with sugar, wine and cinnabar in a bowl. Blood was taken from the middle finger of the left hand of each recruit, added to the concoction and then drunk by all.

With further rituals completed, the new member bowed before a tablet to the wife of the original Triad leader and were ceremoniously "washed clean" with a grubby towel. Thus each man was reborn into the family of the 14K.

There are passwords: "Why is your face so pale?" — "My face is pale but my heart is red," special codes and methods of visual identification which must be learned. The oaths are forgotten as quickly as repeated. But the recognition signals play an important part in criminal activity. The best known is reminiscent of Freemasonry (just as the ritual invites comparison with the Catholic Mass): on shaking hands, bend the middle finger to stroke lightly the other man's palm. Another, used in teahouses, is one of many techniques for signaling your presence at a crowded table: the pot is held in a certain way and three drops of tea poured into each cup first. There are several ways of offering, lighting or smoking cigarettes, and a greeting can become so infested with secret signals that it resembles a ritual in itself.

There is little doubt these ceremonies persist in one form or another in Red China. The elaborate code systems of the teahouse survive in country regions. They have intriguing names like Seven Fairy Sisters' Descent to Earth, and it is unlikely that a Triad member would be detected by security agents if he performed the movements involved.

But of course the high moral purpose of the old Triads has been mostly lost. The religious fervor which captures many young Chinese has been in recent years canalized through

Communist Party jargon. Mao Tse-tung had an intimate knowledge of peasant beliefs. He understood the unbearable punishment of making a man "lose face." Much of the Party's discipline today is not based on force or terror in the melodramatic sense of those words. It derives from simple but effective humiliations as well as a strict code.

"He who has been crowned with the tall paper hat loses face for ever," wrote Mao in 1927. His report was ignored by Party leaders of that time who failed to see how Communism could be adapted to Chinese traditions. Mao understood very well that a bullying landlord's spirit could be crushed by making him parade in a dunce's cap.

In Peking the Chinese find it difficult to understand why such "persuasion" cannot be substituted for brutality in Eastern Europe. But the subtle pressures to which a Chinese will respond are almost incomprehensible to a Westerner. These pressures are just as effective within the Party as within any earlier secret society. For instance the honesty you find everywhere in modern China is compounded of fear and respect for the new Party teachings. Two French colleagues discovered this for themselves in an odd way.

Like most visitors to modern China, they found it almost impossible to throw away old razor blades or to discard threadbare clothing. One of them was unable to divest himself of underwear long past its prime. He would deposit his torn clothing in wastebaskets at the hotels where he stayed during a prolonged tour, and when these rags were returned to him at the next destination, he would attempt to give them away to the floor boy, who invariably returned with them neatly washed and ironed. In the end it became a game. The Frenchman wrapped them up in old newspapers and concealed them under chairs, or tried leaving them surreptitiously in the backs of cars. Finally, on the night before he left Shanghai, he made them into a parcel which he gave to his French colleague with instructions to keep them until he had gone, and then to conceal them in the farthest dark corner of a linen cupboard over the wardrobe of his vacated room.

Three days later he arrived at the Hong Kong border and

was presented with his underwear by a smiling representative of the China Travel Service.

I got so much into the habit of leaving suitcases unlocked and money lying around hotels that once I was robbed within a few hours of leaving the mainland, simply because I failed to adjust my habits to our own free (and easy) society.

It would be too glib to say that fear alone has forced the Chinese to become honest and incorruptible. One official admitted sadly, "It could be so," when I asked if a man caught stealing from a foreigner might be shot. But it is fair to add that Party leaders see no virtue in killing every man with the initiative to steal or plan some elaborate swindle. They would prefer to retain such a man's ability and direct his energies into more useful channels. Some hot-gospelers in the service of Mao are reformed swindlers and their evangelical missions abroad are fervently executed.

The moral pressures exercised by the Party were effective, I discovered, among the new generation of students. In Peking there was an East European newspaperman who somehow acquired a mistress. His name was Jan and one day he called to see me.

"I got in trouble with the police," he said resentfully.

The illicit affair had never troubled his conscience but his girl was studying at Peking University and for some time had shown signs of uneasiness. She awoke early one morning and said: "My thoughts are bothering me. I have never before kept anything back from my comrades, and I feel I must make a confession."

Jan was alarmed. "But why? Your parents will never know."

She insisted. "It is not whether anybody knows or not. That is not important. I must search my own conscience, rectify my work style and resolutely uproot wrong tendencies. I cannot face my comrades with secret errors on my mind."

It became evident that she was undergoing one of the frequent campaigns of self-rectification. But Jan was totally unprepared for what followed. He braced himself for what he felt would be an inevitable interview with the girl's parents.

Instead he was visited by the police. The girl ignored her parents throughout the crisis. She made a full public confession at a special meeting of University students and staff.

Her ex-lover's face flushed with embarrassment as he unfolded this story. The incident was beyond his comprehension, beyond the experience of a European no matter how devout a Communist.

With the debasement of the old societies, the Cromwellian spirit of the Party has an undeniable appeal for young Chinese living abroad. The iron discipline is something they discover when they return; and then it is often too late. Today in Chinese schools in Singapore and Hong Kong, Malaya and Indonesia, the Maoist creed is largely self-generating. Like the Triads which sprang up everywhere without the benefit of a written history or a central organization, the Maoist societies would probably spread even if Chinese schools abroad were not using textbooks printed in Peking.

Mao Tse-tung, like any leader of a fanatical sect, cannot permit the existence of a strong rival. He shows particular sensitivity to societies like the Triads. This is reflected in the attitude of his acolytes. One of them, a Canton official, stopped me one day from boarding the train to the border. It was October 11, 1956.

"There are riots," he announced lugubriously. "Triad agents of the Kuomintang have occupied Kowloon. There are many dead. The Triads have attacked the British and are now crossing the harbor to take over Hong Kong."

What had happened was this. In the densely crowded districts of Kowloon and the industrial area around Tsuen Wan, quarrels arose over the display of Nationalist and Communist flags. Each year such disputes rumble among more than a million Chinese who have no stake in Hong Kong but have good reason to hate one or other of the two regimes. On October 1 the Communists celebrate. On October 10 (the "Double Tenth") the Nationalists celebrate.

On this occasion the red flags were more in evidence than ever before when the Communist anniversary came round. In Tsuen Wan, the scene of that earlier 14K initiation ceremony, there are seventy-five factories. Many workers live in dormi-

tories. Some are members of left-wing unions and some belong to Nationalist organizations. There were small squabbles
over rival displays of banners and flags, which erupted after
the "Double Tenth" into riots. Mobs led by men with large
Nationalist flags were directed to attack shops, factories and
houses where red sympathies had been publicly shown. Leaders used whistles and white wristbands for recognition. If a
factory hoisted the Nationalist flag or paid protection money,
the ransacking mob withdrew.

Rioters dragged workers from "left wing" factories and
brutally assaulted them. Textile workers suspected of Communist sympathies were hustled to one of two *pailaus* bamboo
Nationalist structures with pictures of Chiang Kai-shek and
K.M.T. decorations. Here the workers were mercilessly beaten,
often into unconsciousness, by rioters later identified as 14K
officials. Men and women were forced to kotow before the
image of the Generalissimo.

In northwest Kowloon riots had exploded out of three re-
settlement areas built for squatters and refugees. The biggest,
Shek Kip Mei, had been the battleground for the gang war
which left the 14K victorious. The Triad couriers quickly
spread word that a dispute over flags could be exploited. It
was. Four weaving factories, a toy and metal factory, a stone-
works, several other small factories, thirty shops, twenty private houses and flats, a number of schools and Government
buildings were looted or put to the torch.

At one time there were twenty-one British police riot squads
in action. They were supported by the 15th Medium Regiment Royal Artillery, the 74th Light Anti-Aircraft Regiment,
three infantry battalions (Green Howards, North Stafford-
shire and Northamptonshire Regiments), the 24th Field Engineer Regiment, scout cars of the 7th Hussars, the 27th R.A.
Light Battery, the 15th R.E. Field Park Squadron and Internal Security Troops. "A juggernaut," suggested a veteran of
the Indochina war, "to crush yeggs."

Two incidents will illustrate the savagery of the mobs and
both occurred at about the time the Canton authorities were
warning me, from eighty miles inside the Communist frontier,
to stay away.

On the Castle Peak Road a mob of one thousand advanced on Tsuen Wan police station. Threatened with Bren-gun fire, they swept round the small group of self-controlled defenders and attacked clinics and dispensaries of left-wing trade unions. Inmates of other left-wing premises had been already beaten and humiliated. Now the screaming mob was directed to its new targets by leaders who planted large Nationalist flags on bamboo poles outside the buildings to be assaulted. From two socialist welfare centers thirty-one struggling inmates were dragged away while the premises were set alight. Four women were hauled out of a clinic. All victims were lashed together in pairs with strips of cloth and four later died.

In Kowloon the rioting took another murderous turn. The wife of a Swiss vice-consul died from burns after her taxi was set alight. Within a few hours, fifty-nine people had been killed and some 400 were badly injured. Police arrested 6000 Chinese. Out of these, 740 were charged with murder, arson and looting, and most of them were either Triad members, suspected Triad thugs or had been encouraged by Triad associates.

The simple Western mind retires baffled before the tangled and contradictory evidence that follows such an eruption. Secret society influence runs like a thread through a Chinese community and the most ruthless counter-measures fail to break the contacts.

Mao Tse-tung was not alone in deciding that if he could not break the societies, he would join them.

Chiang Kai-shek's own Moscow-trained organizers had been at work among the Triads and particularly the 14K. The latter was infiltrated by men under the direction of Lieutenant General Siu Wong of the Nationalist army. The general himself went through the Triad rank of *White Paper Fan,* the preamble to which reads: ". . . [General Kot] assumes duty as No. 30 holding degree from Hung Shun Tong, Kan Lan Kwun, prince, administrator in charge of the two capitals and thirteen provinces."

When the general retired to Formosa in 1950, he directed operations from there among refugees and squatters. His task, according to official Hong Kong sources, was to provide intelli-

gence agents and prepare a large force in the colony to assist a
Nationalist invasion of the mainland. It is hardly surprising
therefore that Peking has watched the Triads and the course
of riots with some alarm. Premier Chou En-lai summoned the
British chargé d'affaires after the October disturbances and
warned him that "my Government reserves the right to make
further demands, since British authorities in Hong Kong had
failed to preserve Chinese property and lives, or to restore order."

Thus the groundwork was laid for further Communist pressure should Hong Kong ever become a serious embarrassment.
Some British residents considered that Chou protested for
good reason. Some Americans were convinced the Communists were behind the entire incident.

But perhaps the most significant aspect of these events
seemed to be soon forgotten. Thousands of Chinese had rioted
in response to group discipline. Men and women, who moved
humbly and diligently about their daily chores for the remaining
360 days in the year, erupted into a howling, frantic mob. Children who spent most of their lives submitting to every kind of
hardship were impelled to push slabs of concrete upon the heads
of Chinese constables, to kill and burn and loot. For seven years
the refugees and settlers had suffered in silence, their plight so
bad that I had seen Europeans openly cry when suddenly confronted with the teeming straw-roofed shacks.

For seven years there was no protest from these down-trod-
den regiments of the poor; no single voice raised in anger at
the intolerable differences between rich and poor. The ragged
figures shuffled along amid the glittering Cadillacs, finding
room in alleys beneath the air-conditioned apartments, glad
to scavenge among the refuse bins.

There were no martyrs among them who dared to defy the
colony's sweeping police powers; none willing to risk deportation by publicly protesting against their exploitation by rich
mill owners. But this was not a stupid, brute mass of dumb
clods. Each did the best he could within the existing system.

There was no such thing as politics but there were the secret
societies. The privilege of serving a European family, of sleeping in a large cupboard, and earning $19.60 a month for

working some 100 hours a week, was enjoyed only by members of a closed guild. To toil at the looms in slightly better conditions usually meant buying your way into another society.

You mounted no soapbox; you unfurled no lone banners. If you were Taoist you said with Lao Tzu: "Desire not to desire, and you will not value things difficult to obtain. Learn not to learn, and you will revert to a condition which man in general was lost. Leave all things to take their natural course and do not interfere."

If you were Maoist you might say with Mao Tse-tung: "There has been no love of mankind since the human race was divided into classes . . . True love of mankind is attainable when class distinctions have been eliminated throughout the world."

Or you might belong to a corrupted Triad society and believe in grab as grab can.

One thing was sure. There were great simplifications to which you could respond, as the people of other countries responded to political slogans. You might remain docile through hardship and submissive under foreign rule, waiting for the simple utterances that would stir your limbs. When you did act, when you were driven by the gusts of collective decision, the earth trembled.

Mao the Great Simplifier had worked out key phrases, austere ideographs and uncomplicated ideas, that became in his hands the most effective tools for molding a mass mind. He could talk thrillingly about the elimination of class distinctions and create the image of all mankind marching elbow to elbow in a single direction. But there were still a few men and women in China who were unwilling to believe in such simplicities; scholars and professionals whose knowledge of the outside world told them that as fast as you erased one class, another came in its place; who knew that it required a privileged class of bureaucrats to handle the estates of the landlords after their own class was abolished; who perceived other and hitherto unexpected class barriers arising on the ruins of the bureaucratic walls which Mao wished to have destroyed.

These were the last enemy. These were the men and women

of intelligence who understood how tyrants are made when
great leaders go too long uncontradicted; who saw another
Asian despotism growing out of the sacrificial love of Mao
for his people.

Mao had to destroy them. And yet he must keep their brains
for employment in the creation of a new China that would be
physically strong enough to spread the true gospel throughout
the underdeveloped areas of the world. Left alone, the intellectuals with their differing opinions and their quarrelsome
views were a disruptive element. They wasted time and delayed production. If Mao was to succeed in the use of brute
reason he must strike below the intellect. Therefore he must
reduce his intellectuals to the status of agreeable, tail-wagging
dogs with an ability to perform tricks.

His campaign began with a plea for greater intellectual
freedom and it was received in the West and by China's Asian
neighbors as proof of the Party's desire for more liberal policies. It ended with the denunciation of intellectuals in high
places; with the confessions of non-Communist Government
ministers; and with the exposure of secret societies, whose
members were drawn from the educated classes and who allegedly conspired to topple Mao from his place behind the
lectern above the Dragon Throne.

CHAPTER THIRTY-ONE

Resurrection of Comrade Confucius

◉ ◉

Nothing is clearer than what is concealed;
Nothing more manifest than what is minute.
FROM THE CONFUCIAN *Doctrine of Ways and Means*

THE EMPEROR WU came two thousand years before Chairman
Mao but he also wished to strengthen his pet ideology (which
happened to be Confucianism) by the encouragement of "free"
discussion. He made it impossible for young men to assume
official posts unless they were word-perfect in the dogma of his
times. He smelled out witches and wizards by the simple device of inviting them all to perform before his courts. Those
who proved good magicians to the point of heresy were strangled.

I was referred to the Emperor and that period of Chinese
history by no less than Comrade Chen Pai-ch'en, key Party
agent on a committee set up to guide the thoughts of two thousand writers. These poets, storytellers and playwrights had
been under pressure to produce "realistic" works, and they
lost heart until Chairman Mao uttered the magic words, "Let
all flowers bloom." If this was meant to stimulate creative
art, too many writers remembered the sudden fate of Hu Feng,
a renowned dramatist, who was arrested and charged with attempting to overthrow the regime by the use of his pen.
However, Comrade Chen's organization (called the China

Writers' Association) had persuaded Hu Feng's colleagues
there was nothing more to fear. My talk with Comrade
Chen took place at the end of 1956 when artistic flowers
were blooming all over the scene. He explained the campaign
quite briefly: "When this Chinese saying was popular, we had
the epoch of the Warring States, and this was a time when diverse schools were allowed to contend each other's thoughts.
The result was an era of academic development. But later
came the Han Dynasty when Confucianism and rigidity of
thinking were identical, with the consequence that China remained for many centuries shackled to ancient ideas."

On the face of it, Chen seemed to be saying: "We know it's
impossible for any nation to progress if its intellectuals are
forced to wear blinkers." But then I learned about the Emperor Wu.

He created a ruling class of scholar-gentry who knew all the
Confucian classics by heart, but next to nothing about irrigation. They were coached at an Imperial University established
by Wu to make all public officials capable of reciting chunks of
the fashionable doctrine. The result was that public services
were soon to suffer from an excess of learned young men who
parroted the Ten Duties of a Son to His Father, but who would
never cut canals, control rivers or expand communications.

The Emperor Wu faced up to this problem in a curious way.
He could have reduced the time wasted on the ancient dialectic,
but this would have meant rejecting many of the accumulated
wisdoms, without which there could never be a China so great
as this one whose celestial powers made all other nations appear as satellites. Wu had a mystical faith in the inviolability
of the majestic phrases; he found a kind of magic in the ideographs said to stem from Confucius' own brush made of rabbit's fur and his ink mixed from soot and cinnabar.

And so he undertook to mold the intelligentsia in such a
way that they would conduct their affairs in strict accordance
with Confucian tenets. Within this framework, they would
plan and build and glorify the nation. However, he found
that many artisans harbored secret dissensions. They mouthed
dogma in order to get work. He thereupon invited all skilled
men to collaborate with his government and he assured them

of his tolerance of non-Confucian ideas. In this way he extracted useful work from heretics, and at the same time persuaded them to express their thoughts so that he might have Confucian scholars grapple with them.

There were at this time magicians and sorcerers whose powers were said to be immense. The Emperor Wu wished to discover their secrets and also eliminate them as proponents of a rival doctrine. He sent forth messengers to call forward the necromancers and alchemists and he had these wizards make magic before the imperial court. From some he learned tricks. From others he acquired enough knowledge of their influence to desire their conversion or else their liquidation. Some he was able to incorporate into his own schemes and the others were strangled.

Soon news of Wu's deceit spread. He tried to reassure survivors, but the market in magicians grew thin. The Emperor proclaimed his sincerity in an appeal directed to the greatest wizard of them all, Luan Ta, who boasted of many talents: gold could be made, heavenly hosts invoked, rivers bent to the imperial will and great joy brought to all the land.

Luan was told he might speak freely and so he yielded to these blandishments. Facing the Emperor, he said: "Pardon our humble selves for dissembling a little. We magicians have been upset by the fate of our comrades. Our hands tremble. We cover our mouths."

"Nonsense!" roared the Emperor. "Your comrades died from eating too much horsemeat."

"Ai-ya," murmured Luan politely. "Then we were wrongly informed."

He proceeded to make very good magic. The Emperor Wu, who was really a kindly man and had only his people's interest at heart, considered that much of this man's wizardry could be put to practical use. He therefore made Luan a Master Magician of Heaven and Earth, Marshal of the Grand Communion with Heaven, and put him into several minor posts as well. Luan was greatly emboldened by this and he spoke freely on a number of important matters. He was outspokenly critical of the system which seemed to be enveloping all China, wherein officials talked a good deal of pious nonsense and did nothing.

Sadly, the Emperor Wu had him strangled. "He was a magician," he announced sternly. "He could not reform his outlook."

This may not be historically an exact story, but it illustrates
the state of affairs about the time that men were learning to
marvel at the Israelite exodus from Egypt. Times have changed
elsewhere but, during twenty centuries, China remained a sealed
empire where men covered their mouths if their views clashed
with official dogma.

Mao the Marxist mandarin took a modest bow as a classical
poet with the first issue of a poetry magazine in 1957. In a
diffident foreword he admonished young people: "Some
poems in the old forms may be written but they should not be
promoted because these forms restrict one's thinking."

Such a statement taken at face value is encouraging. It suggests that Mao understands the crippling effects of tradition
or slavish imitation. He added to this impression by submitting eighteen poems "not in any way distinguished, but since
you think them worth publishing I bow to your wishes."

The editor who failed to publish them would have been a
candidate for the psychiatrist's couch. One poem quoted
Confucius who at one time had been *passé* among Mao's intimates; it was written apparently to commemorate the Chairman's swimming of the Yangtse and it concluded: "There is so
much room to move around. The words of Confucius by the
river come to me: 'Time flies, like water running into the sea.'"

All this was calculated to deceive and confuse those remaining intellectuals who still "covered their mouths." One of
them, Lao Sheh, was famous as a novelist in the West for his
book *Rickshaw Boy*. Soon he was saying: "In recent years
there has been a disease of formalism, of indulging in stereo-
typed generalizations built round cut-and-dried formulas. It
is right and proper for writers to study hard and improve
themselves ideologically, but they are going about it the wrong
way if *either by design or accident* they pack their work with
didactic ideas, if their plots are nonexistent and their imagery
trite."*

Lao revealed the chief worry of his masters: that the heavy

* Peking, *People's China*, January 1, 1957 (*italics are mine* — W.S.)

indoctrination conducted among creative artists would lead to another version of the era which followed the Emperor Wu's reign.

Yet Maoism, or Communism, by its very nature insisted upon the destruction of all rival theories, and therefore put China back into the same quandary as before. The great number of Chinese writers, scientists and scholars had been educated in the pre-1949 period when there was free access to Western ideas. When Mao took power, he had widespread sympathy among scholars and academicians who remained: the actively anti-Communist intelligentsia had gone to Formosa with Chiang Kai-shek.

Mao began to convert these nonhostile citizens in 1951 with the Provisions for Suppression of Counterrevolutionaries. It was made clear that benevolent neutrality was not enough. Premier Chou En-lai made a five-hour speech to introduce the Thought Reform Movement. A phrase coined at the time became associated with anti-Communist propaganda: "to wash brains clean."

Suddenly professional Chinese, who often were remembered with kindly feelings by their Western associates, began to denounce their old tutors or publicly apologize for fraternizing with "imperialist agents." Their extraordinary utterances, puzzling to outside observers, were easily explained. The regime required no mere appearance of conformity, but utter surrender to the State will.

To achieve this, "study groups" were organized. Members must not only discuss abstract problems of ideology, but also search their own souls for evidence of past errors. Autobiographies were written and read aloud to the group, which then freely criticized their authors for sins of omission. The confessor found it necessary to recall every conceivable act or expression of opinion that might possibly make him appear to be "an enemy of the people." To fail in this was to invite intervention from the supervising official.

This technique of criticism and self-criticism, well known to Korean war prisoners, frightened many intellectuals into obedience. Other creative minds still pursued the comfortable theory that art was independent of politics, and therefore the individual could continue his activities in a different and non-political world secure from official annoyance. Chief spokesman of this view apparently was Hu Feng, who is said to have uttered certain immortal words upon hearing of the suspected sabotage of the *Kashmir Princess* with Chinese delegates on their way from Peking to the Bandung Conference.

"Now our propagandists have something to write about," Hu Feng is reported to have said. "What a windfall . . ."

Soon newspapers launched a drive throughout China to "Smash Hu Feng's Snake Den, Heighten Our Revolutionary Vigilance."

I asked Chen Pai-ch'en, the Party member on the China Writers' Secretariat, if the case of Hu Feng had not merely frightened everyone else into silence.

"There is that possibility," he said gravely.

I asked what Hu Feng's crimes were. "It became known to us that he was an agent of Chiang Kai-shek" was the reply.

"How did it become known?"

"Our security teams discovered he was writing in a satirical vein, *particularly in private letters.*"*

A few more questions made it painfully clear that Hu Feng was the victim of fanatics who read into his works all kinds of evil attacks upon their faith. The campaign against this writer and others suspected of similar wickedness began as a demand "from The People" (most of whom were illiterate and certainly had never heard of Hu). Passions were aroused and possibly the movement gained too much momentum, because in the middle of 1956 there came the famous "Let all flowers bloom" speech of Chairman Mao.

His purpose was clarified by the Minister of Culture, Kuo Mojo: "We are determined to destroy all harmful schools of thinking."

Peking Radio dotted the *i*'s.

> When the Chairman says, "Let diverse schools of thought contend," he means the ideological remolding of the intellectuals; that through contention a correct outlook may be formed enabling those who still hold idealistic views to see the truth.

* Italics mine — W.S.

The free-speech campaign reached a remarkable climax several months after events in Poland and Hungary during 1956 demonstrated the danger of suppressing students and scholars. At one time, Peking University was covered with slogans in which blunt criticisms were expressed. Youngsters stood on soapboxes in the quadrangles, shouting their denunciations of certain bad features in the Government. Tremendous excitement was created and in some universities remote from Peking, there were rebellions in which students attacked Party members and tore down Party symbols.

The poor wretches who were lured into the open by these artificially stimulated demonstrations were dealt with in a careful manner. They were divided into groups, some of which were "antagonistic" and some of which were not. Altogether, the so-called People's Courts handled in twelve months of free speech about one million cases, according to Tung Pi-wu, President of the Supreme People's Court. Of these, many were a direct result of outspoken criticism.

However, the bulk of critics were dealt with inside their own "study groups." They were wrestled with by Party members. It was clearly understood that secret doubts could not be stamped out: they must be uprooted by means of endless discussion. In the words of an instruction issued to officials during the campaign: "Free discussion will continue and all views may be expressed until there is unanimous agreement with the supervising official."

By the middle of June 1957 it was difficult to believe that newspapers in Peking were published on Communist authority. Three non-Communist Cabinet Ministers were reported to have called for a "political planning board" so that China's eight puppet parties would have status equal to or greater than Mao's party. The agricultural minister was attacked for "interfering in the duties of a newspaper photographer." Russia was criticized for escaping the cost of the Korean war. Professor Ko Pei-chi of Peking People's University wrote in Mao's official newspaper: "The people really want to overthrow the Communist Party and kill Communists."

Out of hiding crept the wicked magicians, the sorcerers and

necromancers of this twentieth century, beguiled into the same trust of Chairman Mao as had been displayed by their predecessors of two thousand years ago.

Then down dropped the guillotine. Into the People's Hall of Magnanimity stumped Premier Chou En-lai to face 1602 members of the National People's Congress. Chou, speaking unemotionally in his high-pitched, singsong voice set forth government policy: criticism was getting out of hand, there must come a halt. He warned the critics they were in danger of being identified as "enemies of The People if they persist in their anti-Socialist position." He threatened to expel non-Communist officials (who made up one quarter of Chinese officialdom). "The Communist Party," he said, "will allow no wavering . . . on the basic system of our party."

His eyes traveled slowly along the ranks of tunicked, hushed Congressmen. "Some Rightists are now attacking the basic system of the State on the pretext of helping the Party," he said. "They claim to improve the Party's working style. Their real aim is to sever the State power from the working class and its vanguard, the Communist Party. Their aim is to take the country from the course of Socialism to Capitalism. The People will not tolerate this."

While he spoke, the modern descendants of the Emperor Wu's victims went tumbling down. Poor old Chang Po-chun, the Minister of Communications, a leader of the allegedly independent Democratic League which was largest of the non-Communist parties, made his painful confession.

Timber Minister Dr. Lo Lung-chi, tainted too by early contact with Western education (he attended Columbia University), also recanted: "I am greatly ashamed . . ." This vice-chairman of the Defense Council, ex-warlord General Lung Yun, was forced to stand before his own Kuomintang Revolutionary Committee and, with tears streaming down his cheeks, to confess his error in "slandering" the Soviet Union. As for Professor Ko, he simply vanished.

Right through China swept the new purge. Students who voiced complaints were herded into discussion groups to continue their political studies while toiling on remote construction sites. New and hitherto unsuspected "sabotage rings" were exposed and found to be linked with prominent intellectuals. The atmosphere of fear and suspicion returned overnight, but by this time it did not need the reinforcements of terror and brute force. All over the country, the Persuasion Brigades began their garrulous new drives.

These shock troops of propaganda had been carefully briefed between March and June of 1957 in the correct interpretation of a key speech, made by Chairman Mao before a closed meeting of the Supreme State Conference. This speech, as we have seen already, appeared to be a direct result of uprisings in East Europe. It was Mao's first major attempt to present his doctrine before the world: and it caught the attention of Communists everywhere because it preached the new (yet paradoxically old) Chinese technique of persuasion.

Mao's classic utterance reveals a man feeding upon his own suspicions, convinced that he can correctly distinguish between good and evil, and determined to protect The People against wicked plots. He is the Emperor Wu all over again, proclaiming equality of opportunity for men of all classes, while in fact creating a scholar-gentry united into a powerful elite by their own Maoist language too complex for the masses to learn.

Mao admitted that differences could arise between the Party and The People. He defined what was meant by The People: "The term has different meanings . . . at different times. During the War of Resistance to Japanese Aggression, all those classes, strata and social groups which opposed Japanese aggression belonged to the category of The People. Chinese traitors and pro-Japanese elements belonged to the category of enemies of The People."

Mao made it clear the definition could be altered arbitrarily. It depended upon the expediencies of the moment. "At the present stage of building socialism, all classes, strata and social groups which approve, support and work for the cause of socialist construction belong to The People, while those social forces and groups which resist the socialist revolution and are hostile and try to wreck socialist construction are enemies of The People."

He divided into separate categories the differences among

The People: "Contradictions within the working class; within the peasantry; within the intelligentsia; between the working class and the peasantry; between the working class and the peasantry on one hand and the intelligentsia on the other; between the working class and other sections of the working people on one hand and the national bourgeoisie upon the other . . ."

If you remember, while reading this brief summary, that every word of Mao's speech had to be learned subsequently by every Chinese activist until he was word perfect and capable of applying its philosophy to others, you may agree that precious little time would be left for officials to get on with their practical labors. They were immobilized by the new Confucianism.

"Our People's Government truly represents the interests of The People yet certain contradictions do exist between the Government and the masses. These include contradictions between the interests of the State, collective interests and individual interests; between democracy and centralism; between those in positions of leadership and the led . . ." Mao explained how hostile differences could be transformed into friendly disputes "by a policy of uniting, criticizing and educating" a seemingly antagonistic group such as businessmen. These friendly disputes in time could be eliminated by patient persuasion. But if the businessmen refused to accept this policy, they would be classed as enemies of The People.

In other words, Mao's gentle tactics left no real alternative. They exploited the fact that most human beings can be enticed into a trap but seldom forced; that a willing slave is more economical than a man in chains.

Having made it clear that The People could change identity in accordance with shifting Party policy, Mao then blandly labeled China's Government "a democratic dictatorship exercised by The People." Its first function was not to build a better life, or undertake great adventures. It was "to suppress the reactionary classes . . . to solve contradictions between us and our enemies . . . to arrest, try and sentence certain counter-revolutionaries, and for a specified period deprive landlords and bureaucrat capitalists of their right to vote and freedom of speech . . . Secondly, to protect our country from subversive activities and possible aggression by the external enemy. Should that happen it is the task of this dictatorship to solve the external contradiction between ourselves and the enemy." What Mao obviously meant in that last sentence was that China must go to war if threatened. But in the course of seventeen thousand words, he never once plainly spoke his mind. The uninstructed Westerner might feel justified in thinking he had lost the capacity for clear reasoning and was already enveloped in his own mysteries.

For instance, the Hungarian rebellion evidently fed his blackest suspicions about the West, and he talked about China's political and democratic rights: "But this freedom is freedom with leadership and this democracy is democracy under centralized guidance, not anarchy."

His revised version of events in Hungary deserves to go on record as an example of self-delusion or, if you like, self-brain-washing.

> In Hungary a section of the masses, deceived by domestic and foreign counterrevolutionaries, made the mistake of resorting to acts of violence against the People's Government . . . There were other people in our country who took a wavering attitude toward the Hungarian events because they were ignorant of the actual world situation. They felt there was too little freedom under our People's democracy and that there was more freedom under Western parliamentary democracy . . . But the so-called two-party system is nothing but a means of maintaining the dictatorship of the bourgeoisie . . .
>
> Both democracy and freedom are relative, not absolute, and they come into being and develop under specific historical circumstances. Within the ranks of The People, democracy stands in relation to centralism, and freedom to discipline. They are two conflicting aspects of a single entity, contradictory as well as united. . . We cannot do without democracy nor without centralism; we cannot do without freedom nor without discipline. Our democratic centralism means the unity of democracy and centralism and the unity of freedom and discipline.

The People, according to Mao, wanted their Government to "issue suitable orders of an obligatory nature."

It is a pity that the speech is too long to reproduce here be-

cause it reveals how great is the gulf between Mao and the
Western language of ideas. His doctrine was reported by
the optimistic *Manchester Guardian* as evidence of relaxation. But Mao himself defined the phrases used: phrases which
to us mean one thing, to him another. He talked about uniting
with non-Communist groups and of uniting with non-Communist states. Then he explained that this enabled the Party
to "thrash out questions of right and wrong through criticism
or argument and so achieve a new unity on a new basis" in
which conflicting ideas would be vanquished.

He emphasized (evidently for the benefit of Russian and
other foreign listeners) that Chinese experience in this method
went back fifteen years. "Treat the illness in order to save the
patient," repeated Mao. "Use this subjective desire for unity
so the struggle does not get out of hand. Use unity-criticism-
unity today in our factories, co-operatives, business establish-
ments, schools, Government offices, public bodies, in a word
among all the 600 million of our people."

Mao took the physical conflict between Communism and its
enemies into the realm of peaceful, ideological struggle and
he carefully pointed out that this was not heresy but, in fact,
true Marxist philosophy. "I pointed out [in 1949] that to
settle questions we use democratic methods of persuasion, not
compulsion."

This concept is still not fully understood in the West. Mao
and his Party are anxious to avoid any bloodshed, but they
remain ideologically aggressive. They wish to carry the campaign to Communize the world into the field of ideas, feeling
quite confident that they will win. One of the recurring
themes in Mao's speech was his insistence that Chinese Communists had found the Truth.

"This is how things stand today," he explained. "Turbulent
class struggles . . . have in the main concluded but class struggle is not entirely over. While broad masses welcome the new
system they are not quite accustomed to it. Government workers are not sufficiently experienced and should continue to examine and explore ways of dealing with questions relating to
specific policies."

He spoke at length about the necessity for winning intellectual support. He talked about ideological remolding: "Who says the working class does not need it? . . . Members of the bourgeoisie are being transformed from exploiters into working people [but] between them and the working class is still a considerable gap in ideology . . . They still need ideological remolding for quite some time . . . After they have attended study groups for some weeks they speak more of a common language with the workers."

He emphasized China's dependence on intellectuals. "Many are studying Marxism diligently and some have become Communists. Their number, though small, is growing steadily . . . Many of our comrades are not good at getting along with them, lack respect for their work and interfere in scientific and cultural matters. [Our intellectuals] must continue to remold themselves and acquire a Communist world outlook . . .

"We hope they will not stop halfway or, what is worse, slip back; for if they do they will find themselves in a blind alley."

Mao defended his campaign of "free speech" and said: "In the light of specific conditions in China, in recognition of differences still existing in a socialist society, and because of the country's urgent need to speed up its economic and cultural development, the slogans were put forward: 'Let a hundred flowers blossom and a hundred schools of thought contend.'" He made it clear that the drive was designed to improve practical techniques and eliminate political misgivings. Certain weeds would be forthcoming, and wherever these were found they must be struggled with, because it was dangerous "to ignore the necessity of waging the struggle in the ideological field. Ideological struggle is not like other forms of struggle. Crude coercive methods should not be used but only methods of painstaking reason."

Mao left no doubt about the treatment to be given recalcitrants. "The matter is easy: we simply deprive them of their freedom of speech."

On the other hand, he warned against outright suppression of ideas. "You may ban the expression of wrong ideas but the ideas will still be there. Correct ideas will not win against wrong ones if pampered in hothouses without exposure to the elements. That is why it is only by employing methods of discussion, criticism and reasoning that we can really foster correct ideas, overcome wrong ideas and really settle issues."

This, then, was what was meant by the word "brainwashing" defined in Mao's own terms. He explained how to distinguish between good and bad ideas, between flowers and poisonous weeds. He described a fragrant flower as being any idea that helped unite China, assisted socialist transformation, tended to strengthen and not to cast off or weaken the leadership of the Communist Party, and helped maintain the solidarity of the Communist bloc.

To reassure foreign Communists, he added: "We do not think other countries must or need to follow our way." This appeared to be a sop for Soviet feelings because there was no evidence that Mao would compromise with Russian methods, but every indication that he felt his own Party had throughout the years followed the correct policies, despite the disapproval of Stalinists.

He was more explicit about relations with Russia (which he praised for her physical assistance): "There are two ways of learning from others. One is a doctrinaire way of transplanting everything, whether suited to conditions of our country or not. This is bad. Another way is to use our heads and learn those things which suit conditions in our country, *that is to absorb whatever experience is useful to us.* This is the attitude we should adopt."

He uttered these words, ominous in the mild context of his speech: "The First World War was followed by the birth of the Soviet Union with a population of 200 million. The Second World War was followed by the emergence of the socialist camp with a combined population of 900 million. If imperialists should insist on launching a Third World War, it is certain several hundred million more will turn to socialism; then there will be little room left in the world for imperialism."

He sounded like a man trapped in his own nightmares and dreams as he admonished the most populous nation on earth to "unite" with Russia, with Asian and African countries and with the people of imperialist nations "although under no circumstances should we harbor any unrealistic notions about those [imperialist] countries."

Mao the Great Simplifier had come a long way since those days when he brooded on the banks of the Yangtse and wrote:

> The eagles command the sky,
> The fish make naught of the depths,
> All creatures for freedom vie.
> Looking far into the horizon
> One question haunts me:
> Who may the ruler of the universe be?

He had arrived at his own answer. The People ruled and his Party was their slave. His own arguments, confusing to a Westerner, nevertheless led him to conclude that the slave must choose his master; the Party must decide upon the nature of The People. The simple solution required a complicated exposition, just as Confucius required his interpreters, and the Emperor Wu needed his dogmatists. China, in breaking the doctrinaire chains of the past, had forged new ones. Whether he knew it or not, Mao was creating his own universe where all men should open up their minds one to another, having no secrets and therefore, no inspirations.

His ideas cloaked in jargon remained nevertheless just as naïve as the day he penned a curious geographical proposal while contemplating a large mountain:

> Could I but lean on heaven and draw my sword
> To cut thee into three portions!
> One I'd send over to Europe,
> The second give to America,
> And keep the third here in China.
> Peace then will be on earth;
> The world will share the same cold and heat.

Though he might wish to amend this project in the light of subsequent events, Mao displayed little scientific knowledge of the modern world, nor did he waste many words on practical matters. As president of the largest enterprise in human history, he was preoccupied with the construction of an anthill rather than an industrial machine. Had he been chairman of the directors in any commercial undertaking, his report would surely have been rejected by hard-headed shareholders.

CHAPTER THIRTY-TWO

High Tides and Anthills

◉ ◉

These quicker learners are the primitive leaders of the colony, the "excitement centers," because although they determine what activities are carried out and when, they do not do so by sitting down and thinking about it and then giving directions to the other ants, but they excite the other ants into doing the different jobs by starting to do them themselves . . . The key to the ant world is their openness one to another, their tuning to the slightest tremor of response in others . . . An alarm spreads excitement through the colony. The workers rush about with ever-increasing speed until suddenly all together the ponderous soldiers come to life. They run with open jaws and snap at enemies supposed or real. Gone is their lethargy; gone their vagueness; full of purpose they rush to defend the colony. The alarm is over, the excitement dies, the movement slows and suddenly they are back in lethargy . . . The mystery of the ants is in their empathy, the bond of nervous tension which builds so quick a response one to another that it seems more akin to a response to a nerve-carried impulse within a single individual than one involving two quite separate and recognizable characters separated by space . . . Lastly, remember the multitude of the ants.

DEREK WRAGGE MORLEY, *The Ant World.**

IT IS FATALLY EASY to find an analogy for the Chinese State, under Mao, in the world of ants. Communist cadres behave like excitement centers and give purpose to an energized citi-

* Published by Penguin Books Ltd.

zenry. Vast schemes of water control are tackled by armies of organized labor. The countryside is being transformed by workers who scurry without guards or apparent guidance between the supply centers and the construction sites. Where there were deserts there are now foundations for heavy industry. Railways and highways replace the caravan trails. Bribery and corruption, beggars and prostitutes, dirt and color and individuality are wrapped away without discrimination.

Where ants have their "movements," the Chinese now have their High Tides of popular enlightenment. Instead of laws there are campaigns. The cities reek of businessmen whose individuality is crushed by argument and who are swept up by mass emotion. The countryside smells of sawdust and cement. Eccentrics submit and railways grow just as swiftly as Peking launches each campaign.

The bond of nervous tension is certainly there. Once in Manchuria I watched children at play. They sat in a circle and one child kept his eyes closed. Another was selected to lead the rest in a series of gestures, making them all shout, raise hands, or laugh and shake heads in unison.

The boy in the middle, his eyes now open, tried to identify child whose gestures set the rest in motion. I tried it and found the task impossible. The leader was almost in telepathic communication with the rest, and I was reminded of this demonstration in mass response when, later, I saw youths from the same school singing and shouting slogans, as they marched behind banners to volunteer for work on the new oil-fields of the northwest.

When Dr. Sun Yat-sen compared his people to a tray of loose sand, he sighed for winds of reason that would give all those particles a sense of direction. His successors have retained many of his innovations, and it is often said that they will absorb foreign political doctrine and continue as before. This might be true if they were merely a higher form of ant life. But the Chinese are not ants. They are human beings now driven to unseen destinations by winds of immense emotional power. What is their leaders' goal? A collective will, perhaps, which will elevate the complicated society of an anthill to the higher level of human endeavors; a kind of communal life in which the individual and his personal idiosyncrasies must be subordinated to The People's welfare.

What is this hidden emotional power? The more I inquired, the deeper grew the mystery. Maoism and China seemed to be meant for each other. If revolution was inevitable, so, too, was Mao. His people submitted to the intellectual tyranny of a written language that was centuries old and immutable. Their children were docile. Their theater had changed little since Marco Polo's arrival. Their art remained simple, beautiful and also stagnant.

Yet (such is one's perplexity day by day in modern China) these arrogant judgments were followed at once by feelings of generosity. If the graceful Chinese script was hard to master, at least it remained incorruptible and its slaves were willing ones. Children were docile if they wished to survive. Chinese opera preserved with marvelous exactitude the events of past centuries in more palatable form than history books. And many Western connoisseurs would argue that a pitch of artistic perfection was long ago reached on which the Chinese sensibly refused to try to improve.

Everything favored the molding of a collective will, however. Marx was the tenuous excuse with which Mao got to work. Marx could not admit that in Asia the ruling-class was a bureaucracy. Such an admission meant he must recognize a ruling class which did not own the means of production. Mao ignored the doctrinal conflict about the nature of Chinese society. Huge labor forces had always come under bureaucratic controls and Mao set them in motion again, inspired this time with lumpish but magic phrases adapted from Marx and Lenin. What nobody, and least of all Mao, would admit was that bureaucrats who dominated Asia in the past could continue to do so in Communist society. The clanking machinery used to transfer the means of production from private to State ownership was a gigantic irrelevancy, since it took China no closer to a classless utopia.

Instead, it gave the new rulers sweeping powers to organize the country for production. All through my China travels ran the same theme: "This is good for production, that is bad for production." The new society meant equality of opportunity to slave at some productive job. All men were equal; whether ex-Nationalist generals earning their redemption at the prison looms, or the leaders in the Sea Palaces whose working day would anger a trade union for dictators, if there were one.

Sometimes I thought, after many days alone among them, that the Chinese made perfect ants. They moved in a steady, uncomplaining stream up a steep hillside in Szechuan. Nobody flogged them. Nobody seemed to direct them. They jogged along with rasping breath, hauling great red chunks of rock. Their leaders bore the heaviest stones and cried only: "Wei-wei Ho! Wei-wei Ho!" When it was time to shift around the hillside a bit, the whole stream diverted without apparent effort. Then one perspiring coolie paused beside me, and said something in French!

The shock of discovering them to be human beings resulted in a welcome condition of great tolerance and sympathy. How the French-speaking coolie got into an unguarded labor gang I never discovered, but he was a salutary reminder that the Chinese were not yet robots. Later, however, you marveled at the spectacle of an entire family listening to crickets in cages and apparently enjoying the monotonous insect songs, although they sat in a train that not only rattled and roared but screeched a wild symphony of loudspeaker noises.

Sometimes you became the unwilling participant in a conversation like this one:

University professor: "Production is most important. Here we have a student from Tibet."

Tibetan: "I have come to Peking as a student. When I first agreed to come, I wanted the pocket money, the regular meals and the excitement of the capital."

Professor: "Yes, indeed, we had to persuade him to make an auto-critique."

Tibetan: "But when I had confessed my selfish thoughts I began to like learning. I began to like learning too much. I became *enthusiastic*" [dropping voice].

Professor: "Yes, his interest was selfish. His enthusiasm was for his own selfish progress. He was reading Marx, Lenin and Mao Tse-tung *for his own pleasure*."

Tibetan: "Finally, I reached the last and correct stage: I studied diligently but in a disinterested manner."

Professor: "He was studying on behalf of The People."

While professor and pupil retired like players into the wings, I visualized another kind of China paralyzed for centuries by the anti-worldly philosophies of Buddhism and Taoism. Was it only a coincidence that these millions of black-haired, black-eyed people shared only one hundred names? Would they inherit the earth, being meek? Was their antlike society to be humanity's fate?

There were many more questions than answers in my mind as I left Peking for what might be the last time. The Chinese were emerging from the deep-freeze, not singly but in a solid mass. Their leaders were expedient, flexible and quite able to justify their actions by some tortuous interpretation of Marxist-Leninism that should satisfy the Russians.

Was the "Red" in China what the Kremlin had in mind? There was, of course, a Chinese Red Army, red walls around Mao's workshop and the Forbidden City. Every village had its great red star and in "converted" Catholic churches there were red-star lanterns hoisted over the altar.

Red means to most Chinese, however, all that is great, joyful and dignified. The color represented those virtues long before the arrival of Marx. It is mandarin red, a mantle for emperors.

It also signifies danger, even in China. The fact that under the red camouflage there pulsates a new breed of Chinese who may feel superior to Soviet Russia does not mean (as many have assumed) that they are less dangerous. Mao and his comrades believe in their myth of inevitability and they have tuned millions to respond to the tremor of the "excitement centers." If his people learn to think creatively within the State framework, their brains washed clean of heresies but still ticking over, something quite new will have been added to human experience. A world fully alive to the dangers of the fission bomb may wake up too late to this fresh danger to its sanity.

It would be comforting to believe the Chinese were themselves aware of the danger. They are, to us, a curious people with whom we have been infatuated in past centuries. Inversion is the stuff of their lives. They read their books backward, drink their wines hot, save their soup until after the meal, and believe in verbal promises. They marry in scarlet, get buried in white, keep hats on in company, and consider it bad taste to point the spout of a teapot in the direction of guests. They even play bridge with the conventional symbols A.K.Q.J., retained for honor cards, but convert the units from Spades to "Black Peaches" and from Clubs to "Plum Flowers."

They are endlessly fascinating, and it would be a thousand pities if the Chinese were to be studied merely as human machinery while the lubrication of their wit and wisdom is forgotten. But how much wit or wisdom was there in this typical item appearing in the *Shanghai Daily News* when I last left Peking?

> According to the Soviet standard, an elephant should have room space for 100 square meters. Our elephant house even with three elephants in it would still have 130 meters of extra space. We have been corroded by bourgeois concepts. Designers of our elephant house have been infatuated with the grandeur of outward appearance . . . fancy windows, wrought iron railings, a fountain . . . The solution is to set aside some of the elephant space for a study of evolution.

I contemplated this brief sermon, feeling rather solemn, as George my pedicab boy came to haul me on the first stage of a journey home. First there was the ride through town long before dawn. This was a dignified bucketing in the rear seat, while George bent double over the handlebars.

A quilted figure in white mask loomed out of the dust, preceded by a paper lantern. The apparition uttered guttural cries. A whip cracked. An ungreased axle shrieked, and your first instinct was to press back in alarm.

The demon horseman was only a muleteer skirting the Forbidden City with a cart of broken stones. He had left the Ming Tombs at midnight and was making delivery to Dormitory Number Three of the Second State-Owned Cotton Mill. He was merely wrapped in the mystery of the Yellow Wind.

The wind blew off the Gobi, penetrating my blue Chinese jacket and forcing George to slide from his saddle, and push. I peered timidly out of the black hood enclosing the seat. A group of muffled figures was dimly perceived, waiting patiently for the first clamorous tram. Under matting sheds, the ditch-diggers clustered below dimmed lights to gulp a breakfast of ravioli afloat in soya bean gruel.

The wind howled down the Street of Eternal Peace, shrouding a thunderous column of motorcycle troops. They swung in a compact, disciplined group through the vermilion and gold gate to the pavilions, where Mao wrestled with the problems of China.

Sand was everywhere, driven headlong in the same direction by unseen forces. Each particle hurried to its destination; perhaps into a mangy fur that once graced the back of a wealthy Shanghai matron, but now drooped in the darkest corner of the People's Market among the unwanted statuettes, the ownerless silver tea sets and the bric-à-brac of the formerly privileged and now purged elite. Some particles stuck to the sweating backs of political prisoners feeding the hungry looms of the People's Jail; some tumbled down the necks of solemn comrades exercising under the window of Premier Chou En-lai, as loudspeakers in the darkened city cleared their throats and barked the first of the day's Physical Interludes.

The grit was getting under George's earflaps. He removed his fur cap and the pedicab swerved dangerously in front of a lumbering Army truck. A fat little traffic cop descended from his platform in the center of the road and shouted through his mask. George yelled angrily back. A second policeman jumped onto the black and white plinth, waving his white baton to get traffic moving again.

George groaned. Peking's police are excessively zealous. They do not levy fines. This would be too simple. Besides, a fine falls heavily on a poor man. So they talk. Citizens would rather run a mile than stand there, writhing and publicly losing face — while the officer lectures them.

"You understand, comrade, it would have been my fault if you had been killed?"

"I respectfully admire your sincerity," George meekly replied.

"It is my duty to the State and my responsibility to Chairman Mao to prevent deaths of comrades in the street."

"I promise to proclaim and reflect upon my error at the next self-criticism," mumbled George.

You closed your eyes, but the sand crept into your nostrils, tickled your throat and irritated the lungs. You could stuff a finger in each ear but you could not stop breathing. The Yellow Wind seemed inescapable.

Or was it?

George was making harsh noises in the back of his throat. There were a few preliminary gurgles and then a gruesome rasp which began in his boots and ended in a spit.

I remembered the many officials who had told me: "One day we shall persuade them *not* to spit upon the ground." And I recalled the millions of spittoons standing beside restaurant tables, outside hotel rooms, under window ledges or lined along the corridors of Government buildings. *Spitting is unhealthy, disgusting and wastes the productivity of the men who clean our streets!* declared the posters, but still it went on. Somewhere a factory that might have made double-wheel plows or municipal drains was still turning out spittoons only because the people of China would not be persuaded to blow their noses.

Was it the Yellow Wind that made them spit so? I paid George the few cents my ride had cost and turned to climb into the airport bus.

Behind me there was the cheerful sound of a man spitting loudly and long.

EPILOGUE

"A revolution," said Mao, "does not follow a straight line."

THE CHINESE REVOLUTION is possessed of enormous patience. What seems like a retreat is often a detour. No attack is pursued to the point of disaster. The pattern of the dance persists: two steps forward, one back. Even the Year of the Great Leap Forward ended in December 1958 with more than the usual series of strategic withdrawals. There seemed, for instance, to be a reversal of policy on birth control without any significant muffling of propaganda on this thorny issue. Mao declared that China had nothing to fear from nuclear war since she alone among the nations had enough people to survive. In practice, however, frequent intercourse was made difficult for the masses busily occupied all day and much of the night with community projects and the discipline of the People's Communes.

The communes outraged humanists everywhere. There was general surprise at the speed of their organization. When the pilot model Sputnik was launched in central China the average size of a commune was set at 5000 families. In six months of intensive work (accompanied by unifying threats of war over Formosa and punctuated by the thunder of Red Army guns around Quemoy) some 540,000,000 Chinese became units in 26,000 communes. In reality the framework of these communes had been laid down by the big agricultural co-operatives that preceded them. The collectives were concerned with food production alone. The communes seemed more like human poultry farms: they supervised all agricultural, economic, cultural, political, educational, military and social activity. The communes were to be the final step toward collective ownership. Personal possessions were no longer necessary. Everything must belong to everybody.

To make Confucius worse confounded, the communes were given the classic title of Grandfather Society. One party magazine reported: "At daybreak bells ring and whistles blow . . . the peasants line up. At the command of company and squad leaders, teams march to fields holding flags . . . one hears measured steps and marching songs . . . Frames that bound individual families for thousands of years have been completely smashed . . .

"Individualism has no market here."

Grandfather Society was to destroy family ties. Grandfather himself was now the infallible Party with Mao as the temporary focal point for public adulation. "Since the beginning of history," proclaimed the *Liberation Army News* in a typical effusion, "there has never been a man like Chairman Mao."

In hundreds of articles and speeches, the leaders admonished the people to transfer their traditional sense of family loyalty to the larger family of the commune. Cried the *Red Flags:* "Undermine the family built on the basis of class exploitation. (The new family) is the socialist and communist collective body, where all take up labor with joy."

Outsiders who glimpsed this gigantic experiment were often dismayed. Some called it the most formidable mass movement in human history. General V. P. Moskovski, chief of Russian Agitprop (domestic propaganda), after a visit to China was reported as saying the Chinese were headed in wrong and dangerous directions. A veteran diplomat said: "I feel someone has got into the national control cabin and is madly pulling all the levers."

An authoritative comment came, however, from the organizers themselves. A central committee resolution of ten thousand words, published in mid-December 1958, identified some gross errors and implied the existence of other injustices. It advocated slower development of the communes. There was to be no physical coercion in the organization of new communes in the cities were resistance was growing. Party officials who shortly before talked of establishing in China the first true communist society now spoke of slower progress.

The resolution made it clear that whatever foreign Communists might think, China still believed in the commune as a basic unit in utopia. At the same time, Mao was officially supported in his decision to avoid re-election as Chairman of the Republic. His withdrawal was interpreted in Formosa as a personal defeat. Chinese Nationalist agents had correctly forecast Mao's decision two days before it was publicly announced.

But Mao still held the keys of political and military power. "A revolution," he had once said, "wanders where it can, retreats before superior forces, advances where it has room." For thirty years he drummed such lessons into receptive ears and whatever his personal fortunes, his ideas now permeated the nation. Mao might give up his ceremonial office but he was now the Grandfather he had often asked to be, offering guidance in the traditional Chinese way to his sprawling family.

The revolution was dipping and diving again. Nobody rejected the idea of the commune. It was lavishly praised. Among those resurrected to give it strength was the old gentleman whose name appears at the very start of this book: Chang Po-chan. His return was meant to reassure those intellectuals whose fear of communal life had driven them into neglect of their essential duties. It did not mean the end of Chang's "single god."

Naturally the propagandists in Formosa wished to make it seem so. Mao was said to have tumbled from the Dragon Throne because of his vain bombardment of Quemoy and because of the monumental failure of the communes. His Grandfather Society released one hundred million housewives from their kitchen jails only to shackle them to the production machines. The resultant confusion was said to provoke the anger of the God in heaven whose mandate Mao previously enjoyed.

Mao's nimble withdrawal from an untenable position did preserve the façade of a united country. His views on heavenly mandates were explained that very summer. He told again the tale of the foolish old grandfather whose faith moved mountains.

His house was blocked by two mountains. His two sons

were ordered to begin digging them away. The rest of the
village laughed. To the jeers, the old man replied: "When
they die, there are their sons. When those sons die, there will
be more sons, and so on to infinity. As to the mountain, it
cannot grow higher."

Such faith, said Mao, would remove the mountainous burdens lying like a dead weight on China. "We must persevere
and work unceasingly so we may also touch the heart of God
in Heaven. This God is none other than the mass of Chinese
people."

This emotional thread runs through all the twists and turns
of Chinese revolution. It appeared again in the resolution on
the communes, in the form of a brief reminder that individualism deserved respect. A mild defense of human personality,
perhaps, but significant because it followed earlier attacks
against individualism: attacks launched by party zealots eager
to hasten the creation of communes.

So in looking back over the circuitous route taken by Mao
one sees how easily misled is the observer who briefly studies
a single zig or zag. Chastened by these honest miscalculations,
one hesitates to pass glib judgments. The winds that blow
through China may be harnessed by the leaders but they are
deflected by human obstacles and they still represent the very
breath of millions. This breath of a new life may create an
Asian robot but one need not regard this as inevitable.

There are individuals still in China, inspired by emotion
more than cold scientific fact. They fight their lonely battles.
If their goal is still the communal society, one hopes they can
retain the spiritual quality of the old grandfather whose faith
moved mountains.

Meanwhile there is the warning of China's experience so
far. Mass organization, brain-washing, the creation of a collective mind are all part of the experiment to get order out of
the chaos of overpopulation.

Similar solutions are favored in our own society. Science
dazzles us with spectacular benefits and blinds us to sins against
the human spirit committed by organizers of mass opinion.
Jets banish distance: machines banish toil: we live longer,

grow taller, and underneath us from womb to tomb spread the everlasting arms of the insurance companies and the state welfare agencies. For this we pay the price of submerged individualism. Happy-pills banish despair: mass information media banish thought: technical jargon banishes the obligation to comment upon and if necessary act against national policies. Diplomats, nuclear scientists and the space explorers can hide from public criticism behind barricades of words that mean nothing to the layman. Words are bullets in the armory of other human engineers than Mao. We, the targets, need to remember that we are fully entitled to dodge and duck.

China's revolution is far from ended. If the Grandfather Society wins impressive gains in production it will sustain the arguments of others who want to engineer the human race into a smoothly efficient anthill. The day may come when the blue boiler suits of China differ little from our obedient men in gray flannel suits.

Already one hears the faint foreboding whistle of new propaganda shells: "Russia produces fifty million nuclear scientists a day: East Europe manufactures a trillion lies weekly: China shoots 80 per cent more rockets at the moon. Therefore let us have more scientists, better lies and bigger rockets."

China's revolution however has to run beyond many more hairpin bends before it hits the valley of peace and plenty. Dare one hope that along the way it may pick up a few more foolish old men?

CHRONOLOGICAL TABLES

551–479 B.C.	Confucius
208 A.D.	Tsao Tsao unified Yellow River territories leading to establishment of The Three Kingdoms
1644–1911	Ching Dynasties
1835–1908	Empress Tz'u Hsi (Venerable Ancestor)
1866	Sun Yat-sen born
1893	Mao Tse-tung born
1895	First of Sun Yat-sen's insurrections
1900	Boxer uprising followed by privileges extended to Western diplomats to create legation quarter in Peking with own troops. This was regarded as reducing China to the position of a semi-colony of colonialist powers
1906	Pu Yi born
1908	Pu Yi appointed heir to Emperor Kuang Hsu by Venerable Ancestor
1911	October 10 revolution began at Wuchang
1915	First president of the republic Yuan Shih-kai accepted the Twenty-One Demands of Japan
1917	Sun Yat-sen became leader of Canton military junta
1918	Marxist study groups formed at Peking University under Professor Li Ta-chao
1919	May Fourth student revolt started in Peking, spread to other centers. Its major themes: anti-imperialism, literary and social reforms and a Chinese cultural renaissance
1920	Chou En-lai, Ch'en I and other students in France formed the Chinese Communist Youth Corps
1921	June 30: first congress of Chinese Communist Party held in Shanghai, where Mao Tse-tung

	was one of twelve delegates but was not elected to office.
	October 10: Mao Tse-tung became secretary of Hunan branch of CCP
1922	August: central committee of CCP decided to infiltrate Kuomintang
	November to December. Radek recommended alliance between Kuomintang and CCP at Fourth World Congress in Moscow of the Communist Internationale
1923	January: Sun Yat-sen and Russian envoy to China, Joffe, issued joint manifesto in Shanghai on Sino-Russian relations, Communism and the Kuomintang
	June: CCP third congress authorized cooperation between Communists and Kuomintang
1923	Chiang Kai-shek sent to Moscow by Sun Yat-sen
1924	January: first congress of Kuomintang adopted "three great policies" of alliance with Soviet Union, alliance with CCP and support for workers and peasantry
	May: Whampoa Military Academy opened with Chiang Kai-shek as President and Chou En-lai as head of political department
1925	March: Sun Yat-sen died
	May Thirtieth movement started when workers in Shanghai fired upon by Sikhs under British command. General strike followed with anti-British and anti-Japanese demonstrations. CCP membership soared from 900 to 20,000. Mao Tse-tung began organizing peasants in Hunan
1926	Northern expedition began against warlords
	December: M. N. Roy arrived from Russia at Wuhan to represent Communist Internationale
1927	January: Mao's peasant associations in Hunan increased membership to two million
	March: CCP led Shanghai uprisings to pave way for Chiang Kai-shek's Northern Expeditionary Forces

April: Chiang launched anti-Communist coup in
Shanghai and Nanking where thousands of
Communists and leftists executed. Professor
Li Ta-chao and other CCP leaders executed in
Peking

September: Autumn Harvest Uprising organized
by Mao in Hunan. Mao reprimanded by central committee CCP when uprising failed, but
he continued to organize along his own lines

1928   January: Chu Teh led South Hunan uprisings of
peasants, miners and soldiers

May: Mao and Chu Teh joined forces at Chiang-
kan-shan, Hunan, to form Fourth Red Army.
Mao continued to organize peasants against
Party recommendations

July-September: Sixth national congress of CCP
held in Moscow suburb upheld leadership of
proletariat and elected Chou En-lai head of
Organization Bureau

1929   August: Mao and Chu Teh set up soviets in
Kiangsi

December: Mao formulated basic principles of
guerrilla warfare

1930   December: first KMT offensive against Communist forces checked

1931   May-June: second KMT offensive

July-October: third KMT offensive

November: first All-China Soviet Congress con-
vened in Kiangsi.

Mao Tse-tung made Chairman

1933   April-October: fourth KMT offensive

November: fifth KMT offensive

1934   October: Long March began. First Front Red
Army evacuated Kiangsi

1935   August-November: Mao Tse-tung, Chou En-lai
and Communist forces reached northwest and
joined up with local guerrillas

1936   December: Chiang Kai-shek arrested but re-

	leased on Communist mediation. Truce followed between CCP and KMT. Mao made Yenan headquarters of CCP
1937	July: Japan invaded North China
	September: Ten-year-old civil war ended, united front created, and Red armies reorganized as Eighth Route Army
1938	Mao published *On A Prolonged War* and *The New Stage*
1939	Mao published *The Chinese Revolution and the Communist Party of China* explaining need of class coalition during anti-Japanese united front, but with Communism as final goal
1940	Mao published *The New Democracy* giving "new democracy" as transitional stage toward Communism
1941	Mao published *The Strategic Problems of China's Revolutionary Wars*
	December: Pearl Harbor
1942	February: Rectification campaign launched by Mao to purify minds of followers
1945	April: Seventh congress of CCP "resolved to follow Mao Tse-tung's thought, as well as Marxism . . ."
	August: Japan surrendered
1946	January: Nationalist and Communist negotiators, with General Marshall mediating, reached cease-fire
	December: Communists denounced Nationalists
1947	December: Mao reported that revolutionary war had gone over to offensive, and suggested Far East Cominform
1949	January: Peiping captured by Communists
	September: Mao elected Chairman of Central People's government
	October: Proclamation of People's Republic by Mao
	December: Mao visited Moscow

1950   February: Mao returned to Peking
        June: Korean war began
        October: China launched Red armies into Tibet
        November: Chinese Red armies counterattack
           across Yalu against UN forces in Korea. One
           day, Mao Tse-tung's eldest son killed in action:
           Mao An-ying, whose death was not revealed
           until eight years later (Mao Tse-tung, over-
           hearing generals debate how to break news,
           said: "Other sons are dying — why spare me?")

1951   May: Dalai Lama's government signed agree-
           ment for peaceful occupation of Tibet and pro-
           vided for return of rival Panchen Lama

1952   April: Panchen Lama returned to organize Ti-
           bet so-called Panchen Kanpo Lija Committee

1954   April–July: Geneva Conference on Far Eastern
           affairs prepared armistice in Indochina after
           7½ years of war. Communist Vietminh won
           77,000 square mi. and 13 million people in
           North Vietnam
        September: Nikita Khrushchev visited Peking

1955   April: first conference of 29 Afro-Asian coun-
           tries, attended by Premier Chou En-lai

1956   May: first effects visible of a new campaign of
           licensed criticism launched earlier in secret
           directive from Mao.

1956   October-November: Hungarian revolt crushed
           by Soviet Russia

1957   January: Peking upheld Russian intervention in
           Hungary. Premier Chou En-lai placated E.
           European satellites, interrupting SE Asia tour
        February: Mao took four hours to explain "Let-
           one-hundred-flowers-bloom" campaign of free
           criticism
        June: full text of Mao's classic released, with
           deletions and changes. Flood of criticism fol-
           lowed, overwhelming authors of campaign
        November: Mao flew to Moscow, ostensibly to

attend 40th anniversary of Bolshevik Revolution. He was credited with persuading Poles to sign 12-party declaration that recognized Soviet Russia's pre-eminent position and denounced "revisionism" as greatest threat to Communism

1958   Summer: Khrushchev flew to Peking. Communist guns began heavy bombardment of Quemoy and Matsu, two offshore islands held by Nationalists. People's Communes were established with bewildering speed.

December: sixth plenary session of eighth central committee of Chinese Communist Party approved proposal of Mao that he should not be nominated for Chairman of the Republic at next National People's Congress. Session then adopted resolution on faults of People's Communes which began: "A new social organization appeared, fresh as the morning sun, above the broad horizon of East Asia. This was the large-scale people's commune."

FORMOSA (TAIWAN)

605 A.D.   Chinese tried to force Taiwan natives of proto-Malay stock to recognize Chinese suzerainty

1600–1620   Japanese and Chinese established settlements

Dutch got footholds on Taiwan, captured Pescadores

1626   Spanish began settling Taiwan

1662   Koxinga, born of Japanese mother by Chinese Christian, established his own Taiwan dynasty and died

1683   Manchus captured Taiwan which became Fukien province prefecture

1696   First rebellions began

1895   Japanese annexed Taiwan

1949   Nationalists retreated to Taiwan

1950   Taiwan "neutralized" by United States after
            Korean war began
1955   Communist air-sea attack on Nationalist garri-
            sons of Tachen islands forced their evacuation
1958   Demands from Peking that U.S. stop interfering
            in civil war between Nationalists on Taiwan
            and Communists punctuated with bombard-
            ments of offshore islands

◉

Index

◉

INDEX

⊙ ⊙

407

408

Ba Swe, U, 49, 50–51, 52, 53
Bandung Conference, 241–244, 354
Bao Dai (Emperor), 151–152, 153–154, 173
"Before Liberation" (B. L.), 312
Bhakra-Nangal dam, 212
Bhamo, 56
Bhandary, Raj, 202
Binh Xuyen, 151
Birth control, 337–349
    in China, 337–349; reversal of policy on, 393; opposed by Madame Sun, 339; by Madame K'ang, 340–341
    in India, 349
    Russian views on, 338–339
Blind storyteller of Paoshan, 48
Boris (Russian innkeeper, Nepal), 199–201
Bound feet, 310
Brahmaputra (Tsangpo) River, 40
    earthquake changes course of, 190
Brainwashing, 7–8, 396
    Chou Yang on, 3–4
    definition of, 382
    experiment in, 3
    Mao's self-brainwashing, 379
    origin of term, 373
    protests against, 255–256
    in U.S.A., 396–397
    See also Indoctrination; "Persuasion"; Thought control
British in Far East, 56, 57, 59, 62, 74, 140–141, 148, 223, 242
    opium trade, 341–342
    recognition of Peking, 292
    in Tibet, 182
Buddhism, in Burma, 51
    in China, 388
    Communist attitude toward, 61–62, 65, 285
    in Nepal, 196, 198, 205
    in Tibet, 183

Bulganin, Marshal, in India, 241, 244–246
    in London, 260
Bull, Geoffrey T., 190
Bureaucracy, in China, 95–96, 112, 127, 138, 256, 311, 386; Mao's views on, 266, 269
    in Russia, 136, 256–257, 258–261
Burma, aboriginal tribes in, 60–61
    British policy in, 62
    Chinese relations with, 49, 50, 52; infiltration of, by Chinese, 149, 150, 194; Chinese troops in, 49, 50, 54–64
    Constitution of, 62
    See also Head-hunting
Burma Road, 41–53, 88
Bushell, Stephen Wootton, 254–255

Canada, "medical" exports to China, 355
    member of Indochina Truce Commission, 160, 179
Canadian Broadcasting Corporation, author's broadcast to, on Suez crisis, 270–271
Cannibalism, 70, 71, 72–73
    See also Head-hunting
Canton, 236–239
    fear of Triads in, 355
    foreign concessions in, 237
    Overseas Chinese in, 238–239
Catholics, and Communism, 211, 388
    in Indochina, 153, 157
C.C.P., see Chinese Communist Party
Champa Jilla (child lama), 206, 209, 210
Chang Ching-wu (General), 180
Chang Ju-hsin, 37
Chang Po-chun, 4–6, 376, 395
Chang Yueh-ying, Mrs., 313–317
Chater, Bob, 195, 196

Date Due